PUBLIC SPEAKING

PUBLIC
SPEAKING

SECOND EDITION

Michael Osborn

Memphis State University

Suzanne Osborn

Memphis State University

'91

HOUGHTON MIFFLIN COMPANY ◆ BOSTON

Dallas ◆ Geneva, Illinois ◆ Palo Alto ◆ Princeton, New Jersey

*To the memory of speakers and listeners who
died in recent years in quest of freedom.*

Cover design by Dick Hannus.

Text and photo credits begin on page 487.

Printed in the U.S.A.

Library of Congress Catalog Number: 90-83038

ISBN 0-395-43257-X

CONTENTS

v

PART **II**   **Preparation For Public Speaking**   **77**

4   **Audience Analysis and Adaptation**   **79**

5 Selecting and Researching Your Topic   107

6 The Use of Supporting Materials   137

7   Structuring Your Speech   161

8   Outlining Your Speech   187

PART **III**   Developing Presentation Skills   211

---

11   Presenting Your Speech   273

15   Ceremonial Speaking   391

APPENDIX A Group Communication 413

APPENDIX B Speeches for Analysis 425

PREFACE

In our preface to the first edition of *Public Speaking*, we recalled how anxious we were as we taught our first public speaking classes some thirty years ago. Now we know that writing a textbook evokes another kind of communication apprehension, because a book is also a public performance. In our case the response has been warm and receptive, for which we are grateful. We are also pleased that the reception has justified an encore — a new edition of *Public Speaking*, allowing us to make improvements and to incorporate new ideas.

Some things of course do not and should not change. We have profound respect both for the subject we teach and for the students who will read this book. We are proud of a study that ancient educators thought should be placed at the very center of the educational discipline. Where else, they reasoned, are students required to think clearly and correctly, to speak responsibly and ethically, to adapt to the needs of others with sensitivity, and to express themselves with power and conviction, all at the same time and under the direct scrutiny of critical listeners? An effective public speech is like a bridge that joins people who otherwise would be quite separate. And because the study of public speaking covers both the ethical and effective use of language, it also teaches people how to exercise responsibly their political rights in a free society.

For these reasons we insist that a college or university course in public speaking provide more than what communication critic and theorist I. A. Richards called "the usual postcard's worth of crude common sense." We would argue with Richards that practical advice for beginning students is necessary — and the more practical, the better! The student must also understand, however, why certain techniques work and don't work in certain situations under certain conditions. In short, we continue to offer both the *how* and the *why* of public speaking — *how* so that beginning speakers can achieve success as quickly as possible, *why* so that they may add flexibility, understanding, and a sense of responsibility to their new skill. It must serve both them and society well in a world of accelerating change.

Public Speaking continues to offer the student both practical instruction in how to speak effectively in public and an introduction to the basic principles underlying effective communication. In the second edition there are more examples and models of successful speeches that illustrate how to prepare and present a speech. We continue to stress the value of speech training in the development of the total person. We also emphasize that successful public speaking is leadership-in-action and that improving one's speaking skills is excellent preparation for leadership. In addition, a solid understanding of the basics of public communication makes students more resistant to unethical speakers and more intelligently critical of daily communication. Our goal is to help students become both better speakers and better consumers of public communication.

FEATURES OF THE TEXT

In pursuit of these educational objectives, we have developed a number of special features.

Step-by-Step Presentation

Our presentation of topics helps students build knowledge and skills step-by-step to achieve positive results. Because it is important for beginning speakers to have a successful first experience, Chapter 2 offers an overview of these skills so that students can develop good speeches introducing themselves or others. This overview enables students to turn introductory speeches into engaging portraits that build a sense of classroom community and trust. In the chapters that follow, students learn how to listen critically, to analyze their audiences, to select, refine, and research speech topics, to develop supporting materials, to arrange these materials in appropriate structures, to organize their thinking in disciplined patterns, and to create effective visual aids. They next learn how to manage the power of words to achieve communication, and how to present their messages. They then learn about the major forms of public speaking, the nature of information and how to disclose it, the process of persuasion and how to accomplish it, and the importance of ceremonial forms of speaking. Appendix A, "Group Communication," offers concise practical advice on how to participate effectively in small groups. Although instructors may rearrange this pattern to suit different syllabuses and course strategies, the text's cohesiveness promotes learning.

The How and the Why

Consistent with our "how and why" philosophy, we base our practical advice on underlying principles of human communication. The book begins with a concept of public speaking as a dynamic circle that links speakers, listeners, language, the time and place of the speech, and the overall communication environment. As we offer advice on structuring speeches, we show how various structural designs can be explained by simple, basic concepts of Gestalt psychology, especially the concept of "good form." When we tell students how to manage the power of words, we discuss the basic communicative functions words can perform. We ground our advice on informative speaking in basic principles of learning theory, and our advice on persuasive speaking in a model adapted from social psychology. We show further how evidence, proof, and argument can function together as an integrated system that makes persuasion work. As we consider ceremonial speaking, we show how two basic principles, one derived from classical and the other from contemporary theory, provide essential techniques for successful ceremonial speaking. We draw from the past and present, from the social sciences and the humanities, in our effort to provide the most useful coverage of the elements of public speaking for the beginning speaker.

Focus on Planning and Structuring Speeches

We give special attention to selecting topics and to preparing and structuring speeches. Chapter 5 introduces a systematic method of topic selection in light of personal and audience interests and the requirements of the assignment. The chapter leads the student step-by-step through the process of analyzing and refining the selected topic. Chapter 6 explains four major forms of supporting material and their strengths and limitations. Chapter 7 shows how to combine these materials into an effective structure by determining, arranging, and developing the main points of a speech. The concept of good form helps us explain why some speeches succeed while others fail. Because outlining is such an important part of planning a speech, Chapter 8 guides students through its processes, including preparation, formal, and key-word outlines.

Emphasis on Ethics

Public Speaking introduces students to the ethical nature of communication and the social responsibilities of the speaker. Chapter 1 discusses the problem of plagiarism and challenges each class to develop a code of ethical conduct to be observed during the term. Chapter 5 introduces the concept of *responsible knowledge* as an ethical and practical requirement for all public speakers. Throughout the text, we warn against abuses of supporting materials, evidence, proofs, arguments, and certain potent stylistic forms. In addition, the book encourages thorough deliberation of critical public issues.

Learning Tools

The book provides models to guide students in their classroom speaking experiences. Sample annotated speeches and outlines illustrate the techniques appropriate to particular assignments; for example, the student speech at the end of Chapter 12 illustrates both informative speaking methods and the use of visual aids. In addition, the book abounds with contemporary examples that illustrate specific techniques — for instance, the controversies over abortion and the legalization of drugs demonstrate various forms of argument and counterargument (Chapter 14).

Each chapter is carefully designed to enhance the student's knowledge. Learning objectives cue the student to the content, and Speaker's Notes such as "Developing a Formal Outline" and "Evaluating Examples" reinforce learning as the chapter develops. Chapter summaries and Terms to Know remind the student of important points, and discussion and application exercises help put the knowledge to work. The twelve additional speeches for analysis in Appendix B represent an interesting variety of speech topics, contexts, and speakers, and illustrate the major forms of self-introductory, informative, persuasive, and ceremonial speeches.

CHANGES IN THE SECOND EDITION

This new edition has given us the chance to introduce some additional ideas and to refine and improve various pedagogical features.

Reorganization and Revision

We have made several changes in the structure of the second edition to make our book more cohesive and to enhance its value as a teaching tool. The chapter on "Audience Analysis and Adaptation" now precedes "Selecting and Researching Your Topic." This rearrangement reinforces the point that speakers must keep the audience constantly in mind as they select and refine topics. We have moved "The Use of Supporting Materials" so that students will understand more clearly that these materials are common to all forms of speaking. The new placement (now Chapter 6) ties these vital building blocks of public speaking to research on the one side and to structuring the speech on the other.

Other major revisions of the book include

- adding a section to Chapter 1 on how to avoid plagiarism.

- expanding Chapter 3, "Critical Listening and Speech Evaluation," to include critical thinking skills.

- providing abundant new examples to make the discussion clear and readable, such as the true story of how Anna Aley's student speech on unsafe housing conditions helped bring about reform in Manhattan, Kansas.

- emphasizing responsible knowledge as a realistic research requirement for public speakers.

- adding computer graphics to our chapter on visual aids.

- incorporating three fundamental principles underlying the best-known tools of language. Following our own advice on using language, we have made Chapter 10, "The Speaker's Language," simpler and clearer.

- clarifying and simplifying our presentation of the persuasive process.

- developing a concept of evidence, proof, and argument as an integrated system of ethical and effective persuasion.

New Learning Tools

We decided that it would be useful to provide learning objectives at the beginning of each chapter to show students what to expect. We also found that the vignettes and quotations at the beginning of most chapters help to place chapter materials in dramatic frames, and so we improved and replaced some of these introductions with this objective in mind. We have also added a glossary at the end of the book that defines all the Terms to Know. Speaker's Notes proved to be a successful way to reinforce learning, and so we have more than doubled their number. We have also increased the number of model speeches in the text.

Four-Color Design

Public Speaking is an exciting course of study, and the four-color design of this edition makes the book itself more colorful and appealing. The new color design highlights figures and charts, Speaker's Notes, the sample speeches, and the carefully selected photographs.

PLAN OF THE BOOK

The plan of the book is both logical and flexible. We have found that the present sequence of topics works well in the classroom, beginning with an overview of the communication process and gradually building toward more complex skills and deeper understanding. Teachers who prefer a different sequence, however, will find it easy to use our book because each chapter covers a discrete topic thoroughly and completely.

Part I, "The Foundations of Public Speaking," provides basic information that students need for their first speaking and listening experiences. Chapter 1 highlights the personal and social benefits of speaking effectively and explains the ethical responsibilities speakers must always bear in mind. We use a model to emphasize the dynamic interaction of speakers, listeners, language, the occasion and situation, and the overall communication environment in public speeches. The chapter concludes with criteria for determining a good public speech.

Chapter 2 offers students procedures for planning, outlining, practicing, and presenting their first speeches. The chapter helps them develop credibility for later speeches and cope with communication apprehension. It describes a speech assignment for introducing the self or others that can help break the ice and establish a constructive atmosphere in the class. An annotated student speech of self-introduction completes the chapter. Chapter 3, on critical listening, critical thinking, and speech evaluation, stresses the active role of the audience in public communication. The chapter identifies common listening problems and explains ways to overcome these problems. This chapter concludes by developing the criteria introduced in Chapter 1 into a useful listener's guide for evaluating speeches.

Part II, "Preparation for Public Speaking," provides in-depth coverage of the basic skills needed to prepare an effective speech: audience analysis, topic selection, research techniques, the development of supporting materials, and structuring and outlining. Chapter 4 emphasizes the importance of the audience one anticipates when preparing and developing a speech. We explain how to adapt to the speech occasion, to audience characteristics (including demographic information), and to audience dynamics. Chapter 5 provides systematic ways to select and refine topics so that the speech purpose is clearly framed. We also identify the library resources most useful for public speeches and offer suggestions for interviewing. Chapter 6 covers the types of supporting materials speakers must gather as they research their topics. The chapter discusses facts and figures, examples, and testimony. Responding to recent research, it introduces the narrative as another basic form of supporting material.

Chapter 7 ties the structuring of a speech into basic principles of Gestalt psychology. The chapter shows students how to determine the main points in the body of the speech and how to prepare effective introductions and conclusions. Extended examples guide students through the outlining process in Chapter 8, from developing an initial preparation outline to completing a formal outline and a key-word outline for use during presentation.

Part III, "Developing Presentation Skills," covers the use of visual aids, language, voice, and body for an effective presentation. Chapter 9 explains the development and appropriate use of visual aids to augment the message of a speech; examples illustrate the strengths and weaknesses of each type of aid. This chapter's discussion of computer graphics and of the role of color in the visual communication of ideas is distinctive. Chapter 10 provides a comprehensive understanding of the powerful role language plays in communication and offers many practical suggestions for using language effectively. Chapter 11 helps students develop presentation skills, offering useful exercises to develop both voice and body language. The aim of this chapter is to help students build an extemporaneous style that is adaptable to most public speaking situations.

Part IV, "Types of Public Speaking," discusses informative, persuasive, and major ceremonial types of public speaking. Chapter 12 covers the principles and practices of speeches designed to share information and increase understanding. The chapter explains the functions of informative speaking and presents designs suitable for structuring such speeches. We go beyond the mechanics to show how informative speaking serves listeners' basic desire to learn, and conclude the chapter with an annotated student speech.

Chapter 13 describes the principles underlying the persuasive process and the skills needed for persuasion. The chapter focuses on the types and challenges of persuasive speaking, covers designs that are appropriate to persuasive speeches, and offers an annotated student speech for analysis. This chapter demonstrates how persuasion operates in our daily lives. In Chapter 14 we explain the uses of evidence, proof, and argument and how to combine them in effective persuasion. The object is to show students how to form powerful arguments for or against policies or proposals. The chapter concludes by identifying the major forms of fallacy that can infest and discredit persuasion, so that students can avoid such errors in their own speeches and detect them in the messages of others.

Chapter 15 discusses speaking on ceremonial occasions, which we take very seriously. The chapter shows the relationship of such speaking to cultural values and emphasizes the important techniques of identification and magnification. We consider many types of ceremonial speeches, such as speeches of introduction, tribute, acceptance, inspiration, and celebration, including the after-dinner speech. A special section shows the uses and possible dangers of humor in such speaking. The chapter includes annotated speech excerpts and an annotated after-dinner speech to illustrate the major techniques.

Appendix A, "Group Communication," introduces students to the problem-solving process and the responsibilities of group participants. This appendix also provides guidelines for managing informal and formal meetings, and introduces students to the basic concepts of parliamentary procedure. Appendix B contains twelve additional speeches for study and analysis. Five are by prominent public figures: Elie Wiesel, recipient of the 1986 Nobel Peace Prize; Bill Cosby; presidents Ronald Reagan and George Bush; and Vaclav Havel, dramatist and political dissident who in 1989 became president of the republic of Czechoslovakia. The remaining seven speeches were developed by students on topics ranging from date rape to racial prejudice.

SUPPLEMENTARY MATERIALS

The following are available to users of *Public Speaking:*

- The *Instructor's Resource Manual with Test Items* was written by Suzanne Osborn with test questions supplied by Madeline Keaveney of California State University, Chico. In Part I, the manual includes sections on the purpose and philosophy of the course, preparing a syllabus, various sample syllabuses, an assortment of speech assignment options, a discussion of evaluating and grading speeches, a troubleshooting guide and teaching strategies for new instructors, and an extensive bibliography of resource readings. Part II of the manual offers a chapter-by-chapter guide to teaching *Public Speaking,* including learning objectives, suggestions for teaching, lecture/discussion outline, guidelines for using end-of-chapter items, additional activities, ancillary materials, transparency masters and handouts, and a bibliography of readings for enrichment. Part III offers test items for all chapters, and Part IV provides annotations for the speeches in Appendix B. The manual is the most comprehensive of its kind available, and can be used as a text for training teaching assistants.

- Speech outlining software, a computer program designed especially for this book, offers students a self-directed, step-by-step electronic tour through the discipline of outlining their speeches. It includes formats for each major speech design discussed in the text. This unique feature should improve the structure of student speeches, and should also result in better knowledge of speech design options.

- Transparencies may be used to enhance lectures and class discussions on such topics as the Dynamic Circle of Communication and the Step-by-Step Guide to Preparing a Self-Introductory Speech.

- Test generating software is available.

In addition, an extensive array of videotapes, ranging from student speeches introduced and critiqued by the authors to major public addresses on vital contemporary issues, is available to adopters of a minimum number of books. Users should contact Houghton Mifflin representatives for details.

ACKNOWLEDGMENTS

Many people deserve credit and thanks for helping us complete this revision of *Public Speaking.* The editorial staff at Houghton Mifflin Company has continued to offer dedicated, imaginative, and expert support during this revision. Sales representatives of Houghton Mifflin have become good friends: many have shared their excitement with us, and have offered encouragement. We are also grateful to the following teachers for their thoughtful and helpful critical readings of the manuscript of the first and second editions:

Phillip Anderson, Kansas State University

James R. Andrews, Indiana University

John Bee, University of Akron

Cecile S. Blanche, Villanova University

Don M. Boileau, George Mason University

Barry Brummett, University of Wisconsin–Milwaukee

Carl Burgchardt, Colorado State University

Francis E. Cheslik, Seton Hall University

Patrick J. Collins, John Jay College of Criminal Justice

Jo Ellen Cox, Northwest Mississippi Community College

James Darsey, Ohio State University

Jimmy T. Davis, Belmont College

Michael DeSousa, University of California–Davis

L. Patrick Devlin, University of Rhode Island

Robert J. Doolittle, University of Tulsa

Clyde Faries, Western Illinois University

Elizabeth Faries, Western Illinois University

Susan Fiechtner, Texas A & M University

Patricia Friel, University of Cincinnati–Clermont College

Darla Germeroth, University of Scranton

James Gibson, University of Missouri, Columbia

Ethel Glenn, University of North Carolina at Greensboro

Keith Griffin, BelSouth Services Incorporated

Clair O. Haugen, Concordia College

Susan A. Hellweg, San Diego State University

Judith S. Hoeffler, Ohio State University

Richard J. Jensen, University of New Mexico

Madeline M. Keaveney, California State University, Chico

Harold J. Kinzer, Utah State University

Robert S. Littlefield, North Dakota State University

Suzanne McCorkle, Boise State University

Patricia Palm McGillen, Mankato State University

Michael McGuire, University of Nevada–Las Vegas

Andrea Mitnick, Pennsylvania State University, Delaware Campus

Virginia Myers, West Texas State University

Donovan Ochs, University of Iowa

Mary F. O'Sullivan, Western Wisconsin Technical Institute

Charles J. Pecor, Macon Junior College

James W. Pence, Jr., University of North Carolina at Chapel Hill

James Phipps, Cedarville College

Ralph S. Pomeroy, University of California–Davis

Meredith Rouseau, Pennsylvania State University, York Campus

Thomas Seibert, College of Mount Saint Joseph

Aileen Sundstrom, Henry Ford Community College

Charles O. Tucker, Northern Illinois University

Beth M. Waggenspack, Virginia Polytechnic Institute and State University

Donald H. Wulff, University of Washington

Special appreciation goes to the following: Madeline Keaveney, who supplied material for the test bank; Phillip Anderson at Kansas State University, who brought Anna Aley's superb speech to our attention; Anna Aley, who travelled from Los Angeles to Memphis so that we could videotape her speech; Valerie Banes, our colleague at Memphis State, who has made her considerable expertise available to us in preparing videotapes; Pamela Palmer, Memphis State University librarian, who offered invaluable advice concerning resources of the reference room; Frances Goins Wilhoit, director of the Ernie Pyle Journalism Library at Indiana University; Chris DeSain, reference librarian, Indiana University Library; Marshall Swanson, assistant director of Information Services, University of South Carolina, who helped us contact Bill Cosby; and Hal Phillips, film writer and novelist from Corinth, Mississippi, who went out of his way to help us. Thanks also to Janis F. Andersen of San Diego State University, Patricia Andrews of Indiana University, and Jody D. Nyquist of the University of Washington. In addition, we want to acknowledge the generous support and encouragement of colleagues at Memphis State University, especially John Bakke and Richard Ranta, who have been our friends for many years.

We wish also to acknowledge an unexpected dividend from the first edition: all those new friends we made around the country who used the book, told us about their experiences, and occasionally sent us material for use in this revision. Finally, we would like to thank our old friends at Sugar Tree, Tennessee, who understood when we couldn't always go along on river excursions because we had to work on "Mike and Susie's book."

M.O.
S.O.

LIST OF SPEECHES

*Annotated

PUBLIC SPEAKING

I

THE FOUNDATIONS

— OF —

PUBLIC SPEAKING

> *The most important thing I learned in school was how to communicate.*
>
> — *LEE IACOCCA*

1

PUBLIC SPEAKING

— AS —

COMMUNICATION

This Chapter Will Help You

◆ develop a greater appreciation for the personal and social benefits of public speaking.

◆ become aware of the ethical responsibilities of public speakers.

◆ understand how the communication process works.

◆ appreciate what makes a public speech effective.

Professor Parrish, your mechanical engineering instructor, has just informed you that the research project assigned in his course must be presented orally. This oral presentation will count as 20 percent of the grade on your project.

You just had a telephone call from Ms. Foster, the personnel recruiter who interviewed you last week on campus for a marketing position with Dynamic Products, Inc. You have been invited to fly to Atlanta for an on-site interview. As Ms. Foster closed the conversation, she added, "By the way, be prepared to make a short presentation to our managers on that marketing project you told me about. Our director of promotions thinks it sounds terrific and wants to hear more about it. Let me know what audio-visual equipment you'll need."

You may find yourself in a position like that of Anna Aley, an undergraduate student at Kansas State University. Anna was living in substandard off-campus housing, and she wondered what she, as an individual student, could do about it. She heard that the Department of Speech was sponsoring a public forum of outstanding student speeches on local problems and hoped that she could win a place on the program and call attention to the issue.

Still wonder why you are in this public speaking course? Learning about public speaking can prepare you for some important moments in your life — times when a grade may be decided, when your chance for the job you really want hangs in the balance, or when a public problem that affects you directly needs action. Even speeches given in classes can result in changes that benefit the public good. Anna Aley's speech (the text of which follows Chapter 13), first heard in her public speaking class, was selected by her classmates to be presented in the public forum. Her speech made such an impression that the local newspaper, the *Manhattan Mercury,* reprinted it and began an investigation of the off-campus housing problem. The newspaper then followed up with a strongly worded editorial, and the mayor responded by calling for implementation of a rental inspection program.

The skills you build in this class can help you in whatever career you may undertake. A recent Office of Academic Affairs study in Wisconsin identified oral communication skills as a basic factor considered by employers when they assess job candidates. The study also found that such skills correlate highly with success in employment. Similarly, 250 companies surveyed by the Center for Public Resources rated speaking and listening problems, along with mathematical and science deficiencies, as the most critical areas in need of improvement among high school graduates and dropouts coming into the work force. An American Council on Education report, *Employment Prospects for College Graduates,* advises readers that "good oral and written skills can be your most prized asset" in getting and holding a desirable position.[1]

Finally, the abilities you acquire here can help you later in life as well. Picture the following scenarios:

The local school board has just announced that it will eliminate "frills" in order to balance next year's budget. Art and music classes must go! Your child is talented in drawing and painting, and you want to see her artistic training continue.

Moreover, you believe that education in the arts is important for all children. A public hearing on next year's budget has been scheduled for the school board meeting next Thursday evening. Someone must speak out in favor of keeping art and music in the public school curriculum. Because you feel so strongly about the issue, you must be that spokesperson.

A real estate developer is planning to build a shopping center and office complex on fifteen acres of undeveloped land near your home. You believe that such a development will not only devalue your property but also destroy the beauty and serenity of your neighborhood. The Land Use Control Board has scheduled a public hearing for next Tuesday afternoon. To protect your pocketbook as well as your style of living, you need to speak at that hearing.

At such vital moments family, spiritual, and material values may depend on your ability to speak effectively in public.

PERSONAL BENEFITS OF PUBLIC SPEAKING

Beyond such practical applications, education in public speaking can help develop your sensitivity and creativity. Public speaking requires you to explore your own interests and positions on issues and become more sensitive to the needs and interests of others. What issues concern you most? What makes them important to you? How might others react when you speak about them? What personal experiences can you draw upon to make these issues engaging to your listeners? What information is available to sharpen your understanding of them? Preparing an effective speech involves self-discovery and creative self-expression as you bring together new combinations of ideas and information.

One thing you will learn is the power of speech itself. There is a magic to the art of speaking well that has been acknowledged since civilization began. From the time of Homer, poets have marveled over the mysterious force that can move a speaker to eloquence. The Oglala Sioux, for example, thought that such speaking must have divine origins. They believed that "the ability to make a good speech is a great gift to the people from their Maker, Owner of all things."[2] As you speak before a group, you become aware of people responding to you. These responses can make your thoughts and feelings come to life in a way you have never experienced before.

In addition to sensitizing and broadening you as a person and teaching you the technical arts of preparing and presenting speeches, education in public speaking can help you listen better and critically evaluate what you hear. Becoming a sophisticated consumer of messages is increasingly important in our society. The daily barrage of media messages directed at us makes the ability to sort out honest from dishonest public communication a basic survival skill. People who cannot make such distinctions are open to exploitation.

A final bonus of your public speaking class is that you are an active participant in the learning process. *You* put communication to work. The speeches you give illustrate the strategies, the possibilities, and the problems of human communication. As you join in the discussions that follow these speeches, you learn to identify elements that can promote or block communication. Your public speaking class may develop its own vital sense of community. It is no accident that the words *communication* and *community* have a close relationship. They both derive from the Latin word for *common,* meaning "belonging to many" or "shared equally."

SOCIAL BENEFITS OF PUBLIC SPEAKING

The benefits you derive from your study of public speaking go beyond developing your personal skills. Public communication is a social act that takes place in a social setting. All societies governed by freely elected representatives depend heavily on public communication for their effectiveness. Free societies work only when citizens can make responsible decisions. Richard Sennett in *The Fall of Public Man* presents eloquent reasons for ordinary people to develop public speaking skills. He argues that civilization, serving the best interests of the people, cannot survive without the active participation of citizens. Sennett further notes that "the first recorded uses of the word 'public' in English identify the 'public' with the common good in society."[3]

Our American political system is built on faith in communication. Without open and responsible communication there can be no freedom of choice, no informed decisions, and no representative lawmaking by elected legislators. Thus, the founders of our nation realized the crucial importance of freedom of speech when they wrote the First Amendment to the Constitution to protect it:

> Congress shall make no law respecting an establishment of religion, or prohibiting the free exercise thereof; or abridging the freedom of speech, or of the press; or the right of the people peaceably to assemble, and to petition the government for a redress of grievances.

Such freedom is not without its risks, as noted by Supreme Court Justice William Brennan:

> Rulers always have and always will find it dangerous to their security to permit people to think, believe, talk, write, assemble and particularly to criticize the government as they please. But the language of the First Amendment indicates that the founders weighed the risks involved in such freedoms and deliberately chose to stake this Government's security and life upon preserving the liberty to discuss public affairs intact and untouchable by the government.[1]

To be able to speak without fear of retaliation, to have the opportunity to hear all sides of an issue, and to be free to make informed judgments that affect our lives are rights basic to our political system. Acquiring the presentation and

The Constitution and the Bill of Rights protect your right to peacefully assemble and speak out on issues that are important to you. Democracy flourishes when those on all sides of an issue feel they can express their thoughts without fear of retaliation. Speaking in public is a skill vital to the survival of a free society.

evaluation skills you need to keep this freedom alive is a central value of this course.

THE ETHICS OF PUBLIC SPEAKING

The personal and social consequences of public speaking impose special obligations. Speakers must assume the primary responsibility for the results of what they say. Listeners must make an active effort to assure that all sides of an issue have a fair hearing.

Because ethical responsibility is an imperative of public communication, it is important to understand what constitutes an ethical speech. *An ethical speech is based on (1) respect for the audience, (2) responsible knowledge of the topic, (3) accurate and objective reporting of information, and (4) concern for the consequences of the speech.*

Respect for the Audience

Respect for the audience begins with an appreciation for the diversity of views people may hold on a subject. Because people have different backgrounds, experiences, and interests, their opinions will often vary widely. Ethical speakers are sensitive to such differences and accept the possibility that bright and well-meaning listeners may disagree with their arguments. Consider two speakers: One comes before an audience with the attitude, "I have the truth. Those of you who disagree are either stupid or ignorant." The other approaches listeners with the attitude, "You are intelligent people. I have some information and ideas to share with you. I trust your judgment upon them." As we consider the probable consequences of these two approaches, we see that the more ethical speaker can also be the more effective.

Respect for the audience also means that speakers do not conceal their motives or their reasoning. Ethical speakers acknowledge all the options, even as they advocate their own position. Such practice is not only ethical but practical. Research has shown that these multisided presentations achieve a more stable and enduring attitude change with educated audiences than messages that reveal only the side of the issue favored by the speaker.[5]

Responsible Knowledge

Responsible knowledge of the topic requires that the speaker expend the time and effort necessary to be able to speak authoritatively. Assertions and conclusions are based on good evidence and sound judgment because the speaker has examined all sides of the issue. An ethical speaker avoids absolute claims like "We must not support South Africa" and provides instead qualified claims that fit the situation, for example: "*As long as these conditions do not change,* we must not support the government of South Africa."

Responsible knowledge also means that a speaker should assess the accuracy and objectivity of sources of information and be aware of the possibility of **bias.** A biased source of information has such strong self-interest in an issue that it cannot be expected to give a report or opinion that is entirely objective. For example, the American Cancer Society might be an excellent source of information on the relationship between cancer and smoking. However, on the question of government funding for medical research, the same organization might be biased because of self-interest.

Not only must speakers examine sources of information for bias, but they must be aware of their own personal prejudices as well. Ethical speakers try to be accurate and objective in the presentation of information, recognizing that there are some subjects on which they simply cannot speak without strong bias. For example, a speaker's opinion that mandatory drug testing for athletes is unfair may be based on a vivid and unforgettable personal incident that makes objectivity impossible. Ethical speakers need not avoid such subjects, but they do have a special obligation to reveal their biases so that these can be taken into consideration by listeners. Rather than making the speech ineffective, candor often creates respect for the speaker's integrity. Examples growing out of personal experience can also help a speech seem compelling and authentic.

Finally, ethical speakers avoid oversimplification and exaggeration and use language to clarify rather than to obscure ideas. Ethical speakers do not withhold information that seems to work against their position. Nothing can discredit a speaker more than being proven ignorant of vital information or guilty of trying to hide it. Rather than avoiding such information, ethical speakers must show how it can be interpreted so that it supports the position they favor.

Accurate and Objective Reporting of Information

The goal of accuracy and objectivity in a speech also means a speaker must draw careful distinctions among facts, opinions, and inferences. It is unethical to present an opinion or assertion as a fact. For instance, the statement that "drug testing is widespread" is a fact. The contention that "drug testing is unfair" is an opinion. The assertion that "drug testing is intended to protect the reputations of institutions more than the health of athletes" is an inference that must be supported by evidence. An ethical speaker will report the sources of factual data, present the qualifications of those who offer opinions, and show that inferences can be justified.

It is very important to specify the sources of information that you use in your speeches. Not doing so — presenting the ideas and words of others as if they were your own, and without acknowledging their origin — is called **plagiarism.** Colleges and universities consider plagiarism a major infraction of the student code and impose penalties ranging from grade reduction to suspension. Perhaps the worst result of plagiarism is its damage to your credibility

---

SPEAKER'S NOTES   *How to Avoid Plagiarism*

1. Never summarize a single article for a speech. You should not simply parrot other people's language and ideas.

2. Get information and ideas from a variety of sources; then combine and interpret these to create an original approach to your topic.

3. Introduce your sources as lead-ins to direct quotations: "Studs Terkel has said that a book about work 'is, by its very nature, about violence — to the spirit as well as the body.'"

4. Identify your sources of information: "According to *The 1990 Information Please Almanac,* tin cans were first used as a means of preserving food in 1811" or "The latest issue of *Time* notes that. . . ."

5. Credit the originators of ideas that you use: "John Sheets, director of secondary curriculum and instruction at Duke University, suggests that there are three criteria we should apply in evaluating our high school."

once it is discovered. During the 1988 presidential primaries, Senator Joseph R. Biden, Jr., who was campaigning for the Democratic Party nomination, was accused of "lifting the words of others" and using them in speeches as his own. Further investigation revealed that he had been disciplined for plagiarism while in college. The negative publicity surrounding these incidents forced him to withdraw from the campaign.[6]

Concern for Consequences

Having concern for the consequences of speaking means recognizing that the very words we use can influence the reputations and fate of others. During times of war, for example, speakers often characterize the enemy as more animal than human. But once we start thinking of people as animals, it becomes easier to hunt them down and kill them without our usual regard for the taking of human life. We may even feel justified in the "extermination" of large populations. Speakers who use such language must realize how powerful words can be. The greater the possible consequences to others, the more careful speakers must be to assess the potential effects of their language and to substantiate statements with solid evidence and sound reasoning.

Responsibilities of Listeners

Listeners also have ethical responsibilities. Ethical listeners should not prejudge a speech. It is irresponsible to say or think, "My mind is made up on that issue. Don't try to persuade me." John Milton, in his *Areopagitica*, observed that listening to those who disagree with us can be enlightening. We may learn that they know more than we do and thus gain a new and better view. Or, as we question and argue with them, we may learn *why* we believe as we do. Like our muscles, our ideas and beliefs become flabby if they are not used; they grow in substance and power when they are exercised. To protect ourselves from hostile ideas is to deprive ourselves of the chance to develop our own convictions.

An ethical listener is an active listener. Ethical listening means paying attention to information and arguments, noting strengths and weaknesses. As you respond to other speakers in the classroom, try to provide constructive reactions to their speeches. All sides benefit when speakers and listeners take their ethical roles seriously.

THE COMMUNICATION PROCESS

The communication process is that unique sharing of thoughts and feelings that defines us as humans. As an important form of that process, public speaking offers a message that should be carefully designed so that it merits serious attention from an audience.

The communication process in public speaking can be visualized as a *dynamic circle* because of the constantly changing relationships among its various parts (see Figure 1.1). Let us take as an example the speech by Anna Aley mentioned earlier in this chapter. As the model shows, communication begins with a **source,** in this case, Anna Aley. The source has an **idea** that justifies both speaking and listening, in this instance the idea that something needs to be done about substandard student housing. This idea is transmitted as a **message** that includes the words, voice, and gestures used to present the idea. The message is carried through a **medium,** or channel, usually the air through which the sounds and sights travel. The medium connects the source with a **receiver,** the audience that processes the message to consider the idea. In the case of Anna Aley's speech, the audience was extended through the publication of the text in the local paper. The message produces a **response** that can be both immediate and delayed. The immediate audience response, or **feedback,** of approval, disapproval, or confusion can be monitored by the speaker and used to adapt the message during presentation. The delayed

Figure 1.1
Communication as a Dynamic Circle

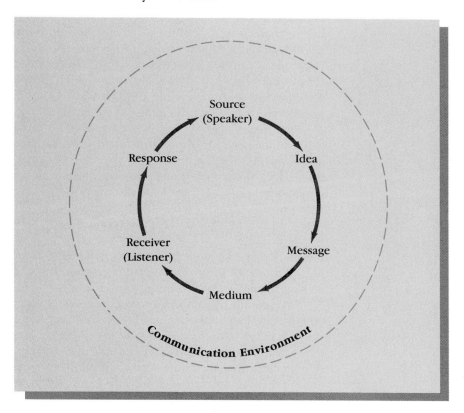

response is what happens as a result of the speech. The delayed response to Anna Aley's speech was the involvement of the mayor and the subsequent change in rental housing policy.

This process occurs within a **communication environment,** which can help or impede it. For example, a recent airline disaster might create a favorable environment for a speech on improving our air traffic control system because the audience is acutely aware of the problem. In contrast, a speech scheduled the day before spring break may suffer because the audience is distracted.

The communication environment was quite receptive to Anna Aley's speech. Previous speeches presented in the campus forum had brought about changes in the campus community. The local press was aware of the quality of work demonstrated in previous forums, and so they felt it important to provide press coverage, thus extending the influence of the speeches.

The Speaker as Source

Over two thousand years ago Aristotle suggested that speakers are more effective when listeners form favorable impressions of their competence, integrity, and personality. We are more likely to listen to and be influenced by people who appear to know what they are talking about, who strike us as honest and dependable, and who seem attractive and likable. Aristotle called these perceived characteristics **ethos.**[7] Contemporary terms often used to refer to different aspects of ethos are *credibility* and *charisma.* Modern research has confirmed Aristotle's observations and has uncovered one additional characteristic: *perceived power.*[8] We tend to respond to people who have strong personalities or who possess the power to affect our lives. People who have positive ethos are likely to emerge as our leaders.

Public speaking links two major needs in any group, the need for *leadership* and the need for *communication.* By listening to a speaker, an audience acknowledges that the person may have some special knowledge to offer or advice to give, or may be able to recall values and memories important to group identity. In short, the audience treats the speaker as a leader.

Idea

For successful communication, you must develop a meaningful idea — a complex of thoughts, feelings, information, and recommendations. What makes an idea meaningful in public speaking?

First, the idea is important to you. It is something you want to share with others. Substandard housing conditions were important to Anna Aley because she was living in them. Second, the idea must be useful and valuable to listeners. If Anna's speech proved to be effective, the results would benefit many students in substandard off-campus housing. Next, you should be qualified to present the idea through your previous knowledge or experience. And, finally, you must have done research that makes you an informed, authoritative speaker. Anna enhanced her personal experience with responsible research about her problem.

Generating meaningful ideas for speaking is essential. We deal with this problem in Chapter 2, "Your First Speech," and Chapter 5, "Selecting and Researching Your Topic."

Message

The message is the fabric of words, illustrations, voice, and body language that conveys the idea of the speech. Shaping the message is basic to the art of speaking. It is also a complex intellectual challenge that involves finding and organizing information and thoughts, selecting supporting materials, and determining which words to use.

The speaker prepares the message by developing ideas in a logical and effective way. The art of speech organization is covered in Chapter 7, "Structuring Your Speech." Within this overall structure, supporting materials — facts, examples, testimony, and narratives — make a message convincing. The use of supporting materials is addressed in Chapter 6, "The Use of Supporting Materials." To strengthen and clarify a message, the speaker may use visual aids, such as maps, models, or charts to add energy and variety to a speech. Visual aids are discussed in Chapter 9, "Visual Aids."

The wording of a message is very important. Words can be hard to manage. Their meanings are often tricky — sometimes highly technical, sometimes very confusing. The use of the wrong word before a certain audience can destroy your ethos and the effect of your speech. For instance, the speaker who talked about "fraud" when he meant "Freud" left the audience puzzled over his meaning, caused them to question his competence, and diminished the effectiveness of his message. But the right words can work just as powerfully for you. We discuss the effective use of language in Chapter 10, "The Speaker's Language."

Finally, as speakers actually present their speeches, they convey their message by the way they use their voices, facial expressions, and gestures. We cover these topics in Chapter 11, "Presenting Your Speech." Becoming a master of the message is a complicated process, but it is a goal you can achieve through practice and constructive advice from your teacher and classmates.

Medium

Your message travels to the audience through a medium. Because public speaking is typically a direct, face-to-face encounter between a speaker and an audience, this medium is usually the air that surrounds the participants. If a speech is to be presented outside or in a large auditorium, a microphone and amplifiers may be part of the medium. We tend to take the medium for granted — until we discover something wrong with it, like poor acoustics. When such problems arise, the speaker must make immediate adjustments, such as speaking more distinctly and slowly.

When they have the opportunity to speak on radio or television, speakers quickly learn that the change to an electronic medium can have profound effects on the entire communication process. Television brings a speaker up close and *very* personal, and so physical appearance becomes more important in affecting ethos. Radio, of course, emphasizes the attractiveness, clarity, and expressiveness of the speaker's voice. When speakers hope for coverage on television or radio news, they must be able to compress their ideas into fifteen- or twenty-second segments, so that they will fit the time constraints of electronic journalism. The language used must be instantly clear and colorful, so that casual listeners will be able to remember the message. For speakers accustomed to audience eye contact, the impersonal microphone of radio and the cold eye of the television camera may be disconcerting. To be effective, speakers must be able to imagine an ideal listener beyond the microphone and the camera, and speak to that person.

A change in medium can thus complicate the job of the speaker. But serious speakers also know that the electronic media present a rare opportunity to extend their message to mass audiences.

The Listener as Receiver

The audience is the receiver in the communication process. Wise communicators never forget the audience. Indeed, intelligent speech preparation begins by considering listeners. What kinds of subjects might interest them? What special experiences have they had? What biases might warp their reception of certain subjects? These questions may be critical to the selection of your topic and the way you frame your message. For example, it would be a waste of time and energy to tell people about something they already know or to attempt to persuade them to a position they already espouse. We consider the audience further in Chapter 4, "Audience Analysis and Adaptation."

Response

Effective speakers are alert to audience response and use it to modify their presentation. Feedback from the audience often occurs as facial expressions indicating excitement or bewilderment, or through body language showing interest or boredom. If the audience is craning forward or cupping their ears in an attempt to hear you, you should realize that you need to speak louder. You can also tell if you need to add an example or explain something more fully by monitoring audience feedback. We discuss feedback more in Chapter 11.

The Communication Environment

Public communication takes place within an environment that can encourage or discourage its effectiveness. Immediate events can change this environment almost overnight. Your carefully planned presentation attacking "oppressive campus security" could be jeopardized if there is a major crime on campus shortly before your speech. On the other hand, a campus incident illustrating overreaction by security forces could be a real bonanza. An effective speaker learns to cope with such events and make ethical use of them.

Audience expectations are another important part of the communication environment. If your listeners are anticipating an interesting self-introductory speech and instead receive a tirade against tax reform, the communication environment may become a bit chilly. In another time, another place, perhaps, your speech might work — but not in that particular circumstance.

Another key aspect of the communication environment is interference that can disturb speech effectiveness. Interference can be any physical noise that impedes the hearing of a speech, such as a plane flying over the building. Interference can also be psychological "noise" within listeners that can cause them to be inattentive, such as worries about an upcoming test. We discuss these elements of the communication environment further in Chapters 4 and 11.

Although the environment of a speech affects how it is processed and received, we must not forget that we are describing a *dynamic* circle. Speaking is shaped by events, but good speaking also shapes events. More than any other creatures, humans can control and create their own environment, and they do so largely through words.

WHAT MAKES A GOOD PUBLIC SPEECH?

What determines if a speech will be dynamic, if it will shape people and events? What standards should we use to judge the quality of a speech? These are important questions for anyone preparing to speak in public. The following nine criteria are often used to evaluate the quality and effectiveness of a speech: (1) speaker commitment, (2) a well-chosen topic, (3) a clear sense of purpose, (4) audience involvement, (5) substance, (6) appropriate structure, (7) skillful language use, (8) effective presentation, and (9) ethical consequences.

Speaker Commitment

Commitment is the dedication that listeners can sense in you and your speech. Commitment is caring; you must let your listeners know that the subject means a lot to you and that you want others to share your feelings. Commitment means allowing enough preparation time. A good speech generally cannot be prepared at ten-thirty the night before you are scheduled to speak. You need time to select and analyze your topic, do an adequate amount of research, organize your thinking, and practice your presentation.

Anna Aley's speech on off-campus housing problems, mentioned earlier in this chapter, is a good example of commitment. The topic was important to her personally and to the welfare of other students. It took her more than two

Public speaking links two major needs in any group, the need for *leadership* and the need for *communication.* Participation in campus activities often calls for public speaking skills. Others will listen more attentively and be more receptive to your ideas if you present a well-organized, substantive message.

weeks to research her topic and prepare her speech for classroom presentation. Then she revised and polished it some more for the public forum on campus. Her commitment was rewarded when her speech was successful.

Commitment also suggests that you respect your listeners, that you see them as people who can be helped by your speech and who can help the cause it may represent. Such commitment provides the personal motivation that makes a speech effective. Motivated speakers communicate enthusiastically, and enthusiasm is contagious. Commitment is the spark in the speaker that can touch off fire in the audience.

Well-Chosen Topic

A well-chosen topic is one that interests you and should interest your audience, once you bring it to life with facts, examples, and stories that show listeners how it affects their lives. Generally you should already know something about the topic you select. This knowledge serves as the foundation for further research that will enable you to speak responsibly and authoritatively.

A well-chosen topic is also one that can be handled within the time limits for your speech. Time passes quickly when you are talking about something that is important to you. You may have to narrow your topic and time your speech as you practice. You won't be able to tell listeners all they need to know about your subject in a short time, but you can acquaint them with an important part of it.

Finally, a well-chosen topic is appropriate to the time and place of the speech and to your assignment. If your community is suffering from a crime wave, a good choice might be "What You Can Do to Prevent Crime." If your assignment is to inform your audience, you might discuss "The Causes of Crime"; if you are to persuade, you could advocate tough new laws with a speech titled: "Let's Crack Down on Criminals."

Clear Sense of Purpose

The kind of speech you present will depend on your general purpose. **Persuasive speeches** are intended to influence the attitudes or actions of listeners. **Informative speeches** aim at extending understanding. **Ceremonial speeches** emphasize the importance of common values. The major differences among these types of speeches are summarized in Figure 1.2. Beyond these general purposes, speeches should also have a specific purpose. For example, an informative speech may have the specific purpose of increasing listeners' knowledge of what they should do if an earthquake hits.

A speech that lacks a clear sense of purpose will seem to drift and wander as though it were a boat without a rudder, blown this way and that by whatever

Figure 1.2

Types of Public Speeches

Type	Functions	Examples
Informative	Share ideas and knowledge, extend understanding, shape perceptions, clarify options	Speeches of description, explanation, or demonstration
Persuasive	Influence attitudes or behavior, urge commitment, encourage change	Speeches addressing attitudes, urging action, or contending with others
Ceremonial	Celebrate events and occasions, recognize heroes, renew values, revitalize group commitment	Speeches of tribute, acceptance, introduction, inspiration, or celebration

thought occurs to the speaker. Developing a clear purpose begins with thinking about your audience. Deciding precisely what you want to accomplish with listeners helps give direction to your preparation.

Audience Involvement

Effective speakers are listener-centered. This means that during preparation you should weigh each possible technique, each potential piece of data or evidence in terms of audience reaction. Will this example interest your listeners? Is this information important for them to know? How can you get them involved? The audience should always be at the center of your thinking as you plan and prepare.

One way to involve the audience is to ask questions at the beginning of the speech: "Have you ever thought about what it would be like not to have electricity?" Also, using the pronoun *we* throughout a speech seems to draw the audience, speaker, and subject closer together. The close involvement of subject, speaker, and listener is called **identification.** It is vital for effective speaking.

Being listener-centered brings another advantage as you present the speech. If you concentrate on sharing your message with your audience, you will be less aware of your own natural nervousness about speaking before a group. Focusing on the audience can help relieve communication apprehension.

Substance

A good speech has **substance.** This means the speech has an important message, a carefully thought-out plan of development, and enough facts, examples, and testimony to support its claims. Your personal experiences can be a valid source of information and can make your speech seem more meaningful and real. Library research or interviews of other people can provide additional substance. A substantive speech shows that you care about your subject and your listeners, that you have invested your time and energy in an effort to do justice to the one and to reward the other.

Examples, which may either be based on actual experiences or developed out of your imagination, can help the audience better understand what you are talking about. *Facts and figures* add authority to a speech and provide needed backing for conclusions. Skillful speakers often combine statistical data with an example to make the information come to life. For instance, you can say, "The base of the Great Pyramid at Giza measures 756 feet on each side." This information will be more meaningful and more interesting for many audiences if you add, "More than eleven football fields could fit in its base."

Testimony adds what someone else has said to the substance of your speech. In many cases you will use the words of experts on your topic. At other times you may express the "voice of the people," using testimony from ordinary people with whom listeners might identify.

Appropriate Structure

A good speech follows a planned design so that each part seems to belong exactly where it is placed and contributes to the overall effect. Without such structure a speech may seem to consist of random parts that move in no purposeful direction. A well-structured speech will be organized in a manner that is appropriate to the subject, assignment, audience, speaker, and occasion. Consider this introduction to a self-introductory speech:

> I note with some interest and sorrow that our instructor has made me the first speaker of the day. Let me tell you about another time I went first — first down Devil's Canyon in our new campus white-water canoeing club!

This introduction suggests that the speech will be a personal narrative. As most of us enjoy listening to good stories, the design should produce an interesting speech. Moreover, since it pokes fun at the speaker's coming first, it relieves some of the tension.

Every speech needs an *introduction,* which should arouse interest and draw listeners into the topic. A second essential part is the *body* of the speech, which presents your main points and the material needed to develop and support them. The final necessary design element is a *conclusion,* which summarizes the main points of the speech, reflects upon the meaning of the message, and ties the speech into a satisfying whole.

The introduction may begin with an example, a quotation, or a question that draws the audience into the topic, such as "How many of you would like to raise your grade point average this semester?" Once you have gained their attention, you will usually prepare listeners for what is to come in the body of your speech by disclosing your purpose. More suggestions for developing introductions can be found in Chapter 7.

The organization of the body of your speech will vary according to your material and purpose. If your speech tells your audience how to do something — for instance, how to mat and frame a picture — your main points should follow the order, or *sequence* in which it is done. If the subject breaks naturally into parts, such as your three favorite authors, you can use *categories* to discuss them in an order that seems most appropriate and effective. Chapters 12 and 13 discuss these and other designs for speeches.

A variety of concluding techniques can be used to tie the speech up nicely. If you have covered several points in the body, you may want to summarize them into a final statement that will remain with your listeners. Another effective concluding technique is to connect the end of the speech with its beginning. This provides a strong sense of closure for the audience. Note how the following conclusion echoes the introduction:

> So, first down Devil's Canyon, first to speak today. You're not as tough as white water, but I can tell you that both trips were exciting!

Additional information on developing conclusions is provided in Chapter 7.

Effective speeches also contain *transitions* that link the various parts of the speech. They signal the audience that something different is coming and help the speech flow better. Transitions should be used between the introduction and body of a speech, between the body and conclusion, and between the main points within the body. Transitions can be a single word, such as *next* or *finally,* or they can be whole sentences, such as "Having shown why we need a change, now I want to describe that change." Transitions bridge ideas and aid understanding. You will learn more about them in Chapter 7.

Skillful Language Use

Communication does not take place unless meaning is shared with listeners through language. In oral communication listeners don't have an instant-replay button they can push if they don't understand. Your sentence structure should be simple and direct. Avoid long sentences with complex chains of dependent clauses. Compare the following examples:

> Working for a temporary employment service is a good way to put yourself through school because there are always jobs to be found and the places you get to work are interesting — besides, the people you work for treat you well, and you don't have to do the same thing day after day — plus, you can tailor the hours to fit your free time.

> Working for a temporary employment service is a good way to put yourself through school. Jobs are readily available. You can schedule your work to fit in with your classes. You don't stay at any one place long enough to get bored. And you meet a lot of interesting people who are glad to have your services.

Which is easier to follow? The first example is rambling; the information is presented in no particular order, and the speaker pauses only to catch a breath. In the second example the sentences are short, and the meaning is clear.

Concrete words are generally preferable to abstract ones because they create vivid pictures for your audience and enhance understanding of your meaning. Consider the following levels of abstraction:

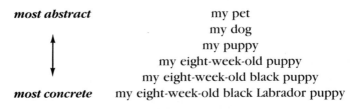

most abstract   my pet
                           my dog
                          my puppy
                    my eight-week-old puppy
                 my eight-week-old black puppy
most concrete   my eight-week-old black Labrador puppy

As the language goes from abstract to concrete, the audience is better able to visualize what is being talked about, and there is less chance of misunderstanding. Other language factors that help improve communication are discussed in Chapter 10.

Effective Presentation

A good speech is one that is presented effectively. Effective presentation sounds natural and enthusiastic. It draws attention to the speaker's ideas rather than to the speaker and avoids distracting mannerisms.

To achieve these qualities, most class assignments call for an **extemporaneous presentation.** In this style of speaking, the speech is carefully prepared and practiced but *not* written out or memorized. You speak from an outline. Extemporaneous speaking allows you to speak spontaneously and to adapt to your audience during the presentation of your speech. If listeners seem confused, you can rephrase what you have said or provide another example. This kind of speaking requires practice, however; extemporaneous does *not* mean "off the top of your head." In addition to doing research, organizing materials, and outlining what you want to say, you must practice speaking from your outline.

Practice may not make perfect, but it certainly improves your chances of doing a good job. Some techniques that may look good on paper may not sound good at all. It helps if you can tape-record your speech, leave it alone overnight, then play it back to yourself. Get your roommate or friends to listen to the speech. See if they can identify your purpose and your main points.

SPEAKER'S NOTES   *How to Create a Good Public Speech*

1. Choose a subject that is important to you.

2. Choose a topic that interests you, that you know something about, and that you can bring to life for your audience.

3. Decide on a clear purpose. What would you like your audience to do as a result of your speech?

4. Involve your listeners by asking for their response and relating your topic directly to them.

5. Use testimony, facts, examples, and stories to add substance to your speech.

6. Organize your ideas into a logical design.

7. Use clear, colorful, concrete language.

8. Practice your speech until you can present it smoothly.

9. Show respect for your audience.

Imagine your audience in front of you as you practice. If possible, find a time when your classroom is not being used so that you can try out your speech where you will actually be giving it. The more you practice your presentation under these conditions, the better it should flow when you stand before your audience in class.

When you actually present your speech, speak loudly enough to be heard in the back of the room. It is hard to hold the attention of an audience if you speak too softly. Body language is also an important part of effective presentation. Your posture should be relaxed. Keep your hands out of your pockets; it is difficult to gesture when they are stuck there. Keep your movements natural. Speakers who point to their heads every time they say "think" or who spread their arms out wide every time they say "big" are not gesturing naturally. Gestures should complement what you have to say, not compete with it. Additional suggestions for effective presentation can be found in Chapter 11.

Ethical Consequences

The final measure of a speech is whether it is good or bad for listeners. If there is a Golden Rule for speaking, it might be: *Do unto listeners as you would have speakers do unto you.* An ethical speech shows respect for listeners and grows out of responsible knowledge of the topic. Such a speech makes clear any self-interest the speaker may have and does not hide evidence that might contradict the speaker's position. An ethical speech avoids oversimplifying the character and motives of others in order to attack them. Above all, an ethical speech is one that listeners are the better for having heard.

IN SUMMARY

Personal and Social Benefits of Public Speaking. Your study of public speaking should help you develop practical skills and your personal potential. It should also make you a more effective member of society. Self-government cannot work without responsible and effective public communication, and public speaking is the basic form of such communication.

The Ethics of Public Speaking. Public speaking places special ethical demands on both speakers and listeners. Speakers must understand the potential consequences of their messages and be willing to accept responsibility for them. An ethical speaker shows respect for the audience, has responsible knowledge of the subject, reports information accurately and fully, and understands the power of speech to influence the lives of listeners. Listeners should strive to be open-minded and offer a fair hearing even to speakers and points of view that may at first seem wrong or obnoxious.

The Communication Process. The communication process may be described as a dynamic circle that begins with the *source,* or speaker. Audience impressions of the speaker's competence, character, personality, and power can affect the fate of the speech. At the heart of every significant speech is an *idea,* a complex of thoughts and feelings concerning a subject. The idea is contained in a *message,* which is projected through words, illustrations, voice, and body language. The message travels through a *medium* that connects the source with the *receiver,* the audience that processes the message. This processing produces a *response* in the form of *feedback.* The communication process occurs within an overall *environment* that can promote or impede the speech.

What Makes a Good Public Speech? The quality of a speech can be measured by nine basic criteria: (1) speaker commitment, (2) appropriate topic selection, (3) clear sense of purpose, (4) audience involvement, (5) substance, (6) clear structure and design, (7) clear, concrete language, (8) effective presentation, and (9) ethical consequences.

TERMS TO KNOW

bias	communication environment
plagiarism	ethos
source	persuasive speeches
idea	informative speeches
message	ceremonial speeches
medium	identification
receiver	substance
response	extemporaneous presentation
feedback	

DISCUSSION

1. Discuss how the ethics of communication might be applied to advertising. Bring to class an example of an advertisement that you think is unethical and explain why.

2. During the revolutionary takeover of a country, the means of public communication is usually one of the first things to be controlled by the new government. Why is this so?

3. What personal and social benefits are lost in societies that do not encourage the free and open exchange of ideas?

APPLICATION

1. The Speech Communication Association has adopted the following code of ethics concerning free expression:

Credo for Free and Responsible Communication in a Democratic Society

Recognizing the essential place of free and responsible communication in a democratic society, and recognizing the distinction between the freedoms our legal system should respect and the responsibilities our educational system should cultivate, we the members of the Speech Communication Association endorse the following statement of principles:

We believe that freedom of speech and assembly must hold a central position among American constitutional principles, and we express our determined support for the right of peaceful expression by any communicative means available.

We support the proposition that a free society can absorb with equanimity speech which exceeds the boundaries of generally accepted beliefs and mores; that much good and little harm can ensue if we err on the side of freedom, whereas much harm and little good may follow if we err on the side of suppression.

We criticize as misguided those who believe that the justice of their cause confers license to interfere physically and coercively with the speech of others, and we condemn intimidation, whether by powerful majorities or strident minorities, which attempts to restrict free expression.

We accept the responsibility of cultivating by precept and example, in our classrooms and in our communities, enlightened uses of communication; of developing in our students a respect for precision and accuracy in communication, and for reasoning based upon evidence and a judicious discrimination among values.

We encourage our students to accept the role of well-informed and articulate citizens, to defend the communication rights of those with whom they may disagree, and to expose abuses of the communication process.

We dedicate ourselves fully to these principles, confident in the belief that reason will ultimately prevail in a free marketplace of ideas.

Working in small groups, discuss how you would adapt this credo into a code of ethics for use in your public speaking class. Each group should present the code it proposes to the class, and through discussion the class should determine a code of ethics to be used during the term.

2. Attend a public speech and analyze it using the communication process model described in this chapter. How did the source rate in terms of ethos? Were the ideas clear? Was the message well structured? Did the medium pose any problems? How did listeners respond? Did the communication environment have an effect on the speech? Report your analysis to the class.

3. Begin keeping a speech analysis notebook in which you record comments on effective and ineffective speeches you hear both in and out of class. Use the nine criteria for evaluating speeches discussed in this chapter.

4. Among the speakers represented in Appendix B, Elie Wiesel makes his commitment to human rights compelling and Bill Cosby uses humor to involve his audience. Study their speeches to determine how these qualities are established.

NOTES

1. From "Statements Supporting Speech Communication," ed. Kathleen Peterson (Annandale, Va.: Speech Communication Association, 1986).
2. "The Lakota Family," *Bulletin of Oglala Sioux Community College, 1980–81* (Pine Ridge, S. Dak.), p. 2.
3. Richard Sennett, *The Fall of Public Man* (New York: Knopf, 1977), p. 16.
4. William Brennan, "Commencement Address," Brandeis University, 1986; cited in *Time,* 9 June 1986, p. 63.
5. Carl Hovland, Arthur A. Lumsdaine, and Fred D. Sheffield, "The Effects of Presenting 'One Side' versus 'Both Sides' in Changing Opinions on a Controversial Subject," in *Experiments on Mass Communication* (Princeton, N.J.: Princeton University Press, 1949), pp. 201–27; William J. McGuire, "Inducing Resistance to Persuasion," in *Advances in Experimental Social Psychology,* ed. L. Berkowitz, vol. 1 (New York: Academic Press, 1964), pp. 191–229.
6. *Commercial Appeal,* 17 Sept. 1987, p. A-1.
7. Book 2.1 of the *Rhetoric,* trans. Lane Cooper (New York: Appleton-Century-Crofts, 1932), p. 92.
8. Gary Cronkhite and Jo Liska, "A Critique of Factor Analytic Approaches to the Study of Credibility," *Communication Monographs* 43 (1976): 91–107.

Without speech there would be
no community. . . .
Language, taken as a whole, becomes
the gateway to a new world.

— *ERNST CASSIRER*

2

YOUR FIRST SPEECH

This Chapter Will Help You

- ◆ manage the impressions you make on others as a speaker.

- ◆ select the best approach for a speech introducing yourself or another.

- ◆ develop an effective introduction, body, and conclusion for your first speech.

- ◆ compose preparation and key-word outlines for your first speech.

- ◆ acquire effective presentation skills, including focusing on ideas, speaking conversationally, and controlling communication apprehension.

Jimmy Green worried about his introductory speech assignment. How could he give a speech about himself when nothing exciting had ever happened to him? Jimmy opened his speech on his life in Tipton County by referring to a popular song, "A Country Boy Can Survive." Then he held the interest of his urban audience with delightful descriptions of jug fishing for catfish and night-long barbecues where "more than the pig got sauced." Jimmy was surprised that the class found his speech not only interesting but fascinating.

In the discussion following her introductory speech, Sandra Baltz told her classmates that she was taking the course on a pass-fail option. She had dreaded the class and had put it off as long as possible because she felt she wasn't good at talking to groups and was afraid she would do poorly. Her successful speech of self-introduction appears at the end of this chapter.

Mary Gilbert, an engineering student, was assigned to introduce Spider Lockridge, defensive halfback on the football team. She told the class that although Spider was best known for his fierce tackles in the open field, he also had another side. Spider's hobby was writing poetry. Mary read several of his poems to the class, which revealed him as a sensitive and witty person. Later, Mary said she was amazed her audience was not more aware of how nervous she felt.

Many of us do not appreciate the value of our experiences or realize that others can find us quite interesting. Most of us underestimate our speaking ability. Even though we go around talking each day, the idea of "public speaking" may seem intimidating. We are certain that everyone will know how anxious we are. We may be amazed when we discover that our listeners are so caught up with our message they do not even notice our anxiety. *All the students just described surprised themselves by giving excellent speeches.*

The first speeches in a class can begin to build a communication environment that nurtures both effective speaking and effective listening. No matter what the exact nature of your assignment is, your first challenge is to present yourself as a credible source of ideas. In this chapter we show you how to begin building credibility as a speaker as you introduce yourself or others. We discuss how to find the best topic for such speeches and how to develop and present them convincingly.

Before the first speeches are delivered, you and your classmates are usually strangers. Introductory speeches serve as an icebreaker, giving members of the class a chance to know one another better. You will likely find that your classmates are diverse and interesting, and you will be able to develop an appreciation for each person as an individual. What you learn about other class members will prove helpful in preparing later speeches. It will give you insights into the knowledge, interests, attitudes, and motivations of your listeners that will help you to select your topics and adapt your messages. Because it is easier to communicate effectively with people you know, you should also feel more comfortable about speaking before the class. Most important, your introductory speech can be helpful in establishing your credentials for later messages. As we noted in Chapter 1, people are more likely to respond favorably to those they respect and like.

Gaining skill in introducing yourself will also serve you well later in life. Making a good impression in your first appearance at a business conference, social club, or PTA meeting can have important consequences for your career and your personal life. Public speaking skills can also help develop your leadership potential.

MANAGING THE IMPRESSIONS YOU MAKE

When you stand before others to offer information, ideas, and guidance, you are performing a natural leadership role for that group. Indeed, the functions of public speaking and leading are closely connected. You may have never thought of yourself as a leader, but as you develop speaking ability, you will also be growing in leadership potential. Then, as you learn the critical listening skills discussed in Chapter 3, you will also develop the corresponding ability to become a more effective follower.

Both able leading and communicating begin with listeners forming favorable impressions of speakers based on perceived qualities of competence, integrity, attractiveness, and power. How can you as a beginning public speaker convey these desirable qualities of ethos?

Competence

It is easy to project competence if you know what you are talking about. Competence is based on your knowledge of the topic, the relevance of your education or training, and your personal experience. People listen more readily to competent speakers. You can build this impression by selecting topics that you already know something about and by doing sufficient research to qualify yourself to speak responsibly.

As discussed in Chapter 1, your expertise can also be enhanced by citing authoritative sources. For example, if you are speaking on the link between nutrition and heart disease, information from the American Heart Association or a quotation from a prominent medical specialist will lend credence to your claims. When you cite authoritative sources, you are in effect "borrowing" their ethos to enhance your own as you strengthen the points you make in the speech. Personal experience related as stories or examples can also help a speech seem authentic, bring it to life, and make you seem more competent. Your competence will be further enhanced if your speech is well organized, if you use language ably and correctly, and if you have practiced your presentation. See the sample speech of self-introduction by Sandra Baltz for a good example of the use of personal experience to convey competence and authenticity.

Integrity

A speaker who conveys integrity appears honest and dependable. An audience is more receptive to messages when its members perceive the speaker as straightforward, responsible, and motivated by good intentions. Integrity is enhanced when you present all sides of an issue and explain why you have chosen your position. In addition, you should show that you are willing to follow your own advice. A persuasive speech asks listeners to make commitments to an attitude or course of action — it should be clear to listeners that you are not asking more of them than you would ask of yourself. The greater the risk to the audience, the more important the speaker's integrity becomes.

Let us look at how integrity can be conveyed in a speech.

> Mona Goldberg was preparing a speech on welfare reform. The more she learned about the subject, the more convinced she became that budget cuts for welfare programs were unwise. In her speech Mona showed that she took her assignment seriously by citing many authorities and statistics. She reviewed arguments both for and against cutting the budget, and then showed the audience why she was against reducing aid to such social programs.
>
> Finally, Mona revealed that her own family had had to live on unemployment benefits at one time. Her candor showed that Mona was willing to trust her listeners to react fairly to this sensitive information. Her audience responded in kind by trusting her and what she had to say on the subject. She had built an impression of herself as a person of integrity.

Mona's experience shows how competence and integrity are often closely linked in judgments of speaker credibility. Speakers who rank high in one quality often rank high in the other.

Attractiveness

Attractive speakers are likable. Audiences are more inclined to accept ideas and suggestions from speakers they see as warm and friendly. A smile and direct eye contact can signal listeners that you want to communicate. As your speech develops, you can demonstrate other appealing human qualities. Attractive speakers share their feelings as well as their thoughts. Their humanity emerges in their speeches. They enjoy laughter at appropriate moments, especially laughter at themselves. Being able to talk openly and engagingly about mistakes or worries can make you seem more human and appealing.

The more likable speakers seem, the more audiences want to identify with them.[1] *Identification* — the feeling of sharing or closeness that speakers and audiences can enjoy — can be achieved in many ways. On one level, audiences

The character and personality of a speaker can influence how well a message is received. Speakers who know what they're talking about and who seem trustworthy, warm, friendly, and self-confident are most likely to be effective.

may identify with speakers who talk or dress the way they do. Audiences respond well to speakers who use gestures, language, and facial expressions that are drawn from ordinary conversation. When talking to an audience, you should speak a little more formally than you do in everyday conversation, but not much more. Similarly, you should dress well for your speech, but not extravagantly, just simply and nicely. Although superficial, these identification factors can be important. You do not want to create distance between yourself and listeners by language or dress that is too formal.

On a deeper level, speakers can invite identification by sharing stories and experiences that help listeners achieve fresh insights into old values and beliefs. Jimmy Green's stories of his outdoor life helped his audience to understand both him and his background. By educating them and engaging their interest, he bridged the gap between his rural background and their urban experiences. Here is how another speaker, Kim Sung, handled the problem of creating a feeling of closeness with her audience despite a different cultural background:

> Even though she still had some difficulty with spoken English, Kim Sung was able to establish identification with her class. She enchanted her American audience with fairy tales from her native Korea, which both explained her unfamiliar cultural background and revealed basic similarities in feelings and values between herself and listeners. She was an appealing, attractive speaker.

Speaker attractiveness, an important element of effective leadership, is under your control and can be developed in your class.

Power

As a student you may not have much formal or **conferred power**, but you can have a great deal of informal or **natural power**. Conferred power comes from assigned responsibility and status, but people earn natural power from their manner of dealing with others. Natural power can arise from the other qualities we have discussed. If you are perceived as likable, trustworthy, and competent, you will command respect and enjoy the power to influence your listeners' attitudes and actions.

Natural power also arises from your manner. Jimmy Green, who gave the speech on the joys of country living described at the beginning of this chapter, later confessed to us that before his speech he lacked confidence, was not sure how his speech would be received, and worried that he might make a mistake. But when Jimmy walked to the front of his class to begin, he appeared confident, decisive, and enthusiastic. Whatever he might have secretly felt, his audience responded only to what they saw, and gave him high marks for his sense of command. Learning from Jimmy's example, you too can gain power if you appear confident, decisive, and enthusiastic.

At first you may not feel at all confident about public speaking, but it is important for you to *appear* so. If you strive to appear self-assured, listeners may respond to you as if you are, and you may find yourself *becoming* what you appear to be. In other words, you can trick yourself into developing a very desirable characteristic! When you appear assured, you also help put your listeners at ease. They feel freer to relax and enjoy your message. This feeling comes back to you as positive feedback and further reinforces your confidence.

To achieve natural power, you must also appear decisive. In persuasive speeches, you should cover all the important options available to your audience, but there should be no doubt by the end of the speech where you stand and why. Your commitment to your position must be strong.

Finally, you can demonstrate enthusiasm in your presentation by focusing on what your speech can do for your listeners. Your face, voice, and gestures should indicate that you care about your subject and about the audience. Your enthusiastic manner endorses your message. We discuss specific ways of developing confidence, decisiveness, and enthusiasm in your speech presentations at the end of this chapter and in Chapter 11.

Just as integrity often blends with competence, power often combines with attractiveness. The hard work you do to improve any of these qualities tends to have a favorable influence on the others — and all of these factors together contribute to your ability to present credible, effective speeches and to take, if you wish, a leadership role.

INTRODUCING YOURSELF AND OTHERS

A speech of introduction is often the first assignment in a public speaking class because it provides an opportunity to develop credibility. There is, of course, no way to tell your entire life history or another person's history in a short speech. At best, such an effort relates a few superficial facts, such as where you went to high school or what your major is. These reveal very little about the person involved.

Fortunately, there are better ways to give a speech of introduction. One good approach is to isolate the one thing that best defines and identifies you or your classmate. *What is it that describes you or your subject as a unique person?* You should focus on that theme in such a way that the person introduced gains favorable credentials for later speeches. Jimmy Green established himself as a person with strong outdoor interests, and later he gave interesting, effective speeches on environmental problems. Sandra Baltz developed fascinating speeches about Middle Eastern ideas and customs. Mary Gilbert not only established Spider Lockridge as a multidimensional person, but she also established herself as an individual who enjoyed both sports and literature.

There are a number of questions you can ask to help you isolate essential traits about yourself or the person you will be introducing. As you ask these questions, you will be conducting a **self-awareness inventory** of yourself or your subject.

1. *Is the most important thing about you the* **environment** *in which you grew up?* Were you shaped more by your cultural background than by anything else? How is this so? What stories or examples demonstrate this influence? How do you feel about its effect on your life? Are you pleased by it, or do you feel that it limited you? If the latter, what new horizons would you like to explore?

2. *Was there some particular* **person** — *a friend, relative, or childhood hero* — *who had a major impact on your life?* Why do you think this person had such influence? Often you will find that some particular person was a great inspiration to you. Here is a chance to share that inspiration and to honor that person. As you honor others, you will be telling much about yourself.

Renee Myers told how the members of her high school basketball team became "closer than family" when her brother was in a coma after an automobile accident. They brought food to the home, drove her family back and forth to the hospital, and came in and did the laundry and housework — all without being asked. For Renee these people defined the meaning of friendship: "Being a friend means doing something for someone without being asked." Through her speech the audience gained an impression of Renee as a sincere, trustworthy person.

3. *Have you been marked by some unusual **experience**?* Why was it important? How did it affect you? What does this tell us about you as a person?

The experiences that shape people's lives are often dramatic. If you have had such an experience, it could provide the theme for a very effective speech.

George Stacey, a student in an evening class, related an incident that happened while he was working as a security guard at a bank. A customer had a heart attack in the bank, and George wasn't trained to handle such a crisis. The customer died before emergency services arrived. As a result of that experience, George enrolled in first aid and cardiopulmonary resuscitation training courses and now works as a volunteer with the county emergency services. He concluded his speech by telling about a person whose life he had saved, using his new skills. This speech gave the audience a glimpse of George's humanity and also established his credentials for presenting a later successful informative speech on CPR.

Experiences need not be this dramatic to be meaningful. Rod Nishikawa related how an encounter with prejudice at an early age changed his life and helped him develop personal inner strength. His self-introductory speech is reprinted in Appendix B. Sharing such experiences can help establish an atmosphere of trust in the classroom.

As you plan your self-introductory speech, consider experiences and activities that have helped shape you into the unique individual that you are. Exploring what these have meant to you can deepen your own understanding of yourself.

4. *Are you best characterized by some* **activity** *that brings pleasure and meaning to your life?* Remember, what is important is not the activity itself but *how* and *why* it affects you. The person being introduced must remain the focus of the speech. Talk about the specific elements in the activity that are related to your personality, needs, or dreams. When you finish, the audience should have an interesting picture of you.

David Smart told his audience how golf had helped shape him as a person and prepare him for college. He presented a two-point speech that discussed how he coped with frustration and developed determination. His use of narrative and humorous example helped even those who did not play golf to identify with him and to share his feelings. After the speech, his classmates felt they knew David well. His speech is reprinted in Appendix B.

5. *Is the* **work** *you do the determining factor in making you who you are?* If you select this approach, focus on how your job has shaped you rather than simply describing what you do. What have you learned from your work that has changed you or made you feel differently about others?

In introducing Mike Peterson, Mary Solomon told how his work as a bartender had influenced him. She explained that his job involved more than just mixing drinks — that it had taught him how to get along with many different, and sometimes difficult, people. She used vivid examples of unusual customers he had met to enliven her introduction. After her speech the audience saw both Mike and his work in a new light. Mary's introduction helped him earn the respect of the audience.

6. *Are you best characterized by your* **goals** *or* **purpose in life?** A sense of commitment to some deep purpose will usually fascinate listeners. If you choose to describe some personal goal, again be sure to emphasize *why* you have this goal and *how* it affects you.

Tom McDonald had returned to school after dropping out for eleven years. In his self-introductory speech he described his goal of finishing college. Tom originally started college right after high school but "blew it" because he was interested only in athletics, girls, and partying. Even though he now holds a responsible job, Tom feels bad because he lacks a degree. His wife's diploma hangs on their den wall, but he is represented "only by a stuffed duck." As he spoke, many of the younger students began to identify with Tom; they saw a similarity between what caused him to drop out of school and their own feelings at times. Although he wasn't "preachy," Tom's description of the rigors of working forty hours a week and carrying nine hours a semester in night school carried its own clear message.

7. *Are you best described by some* **value** *that you hold dear?* How did this value come to have such meaning for you? Why does it continue to be

SPEAKER'S NOTES   *Questions to Help You Focus*
                                   Your Introductory Speech

1. Were you influenced by your childhood *environment?*

2. Did some *person* have a great impact on your life?

3. Were you shaped by some unusual *experience?*

4. Is there some *activity* that reflects your personality?

5. Can you be characterized by the *work* that you do?

6. Do you have some special *goal* or *purpose in life?*

7. Does some *value* have great meaning for you?

important? Often such speeches also describe environmental or family factors, because many of our principles grow out of early life experiences. Values are abstract, so you must rely on concrete examples to bring them to life.

Dan Johnson introduced Velma Black by describing how hard work, education, and family ties had become important to her as one of thirteen children growing up on a small farm in Missouri. Through the stories he told of Velma's early life, he was able to reveal her values and why they meant so much to her.

As you explore your own background or that of a classmate, we suggest that you ask *all* these questions. Don't be satisfied with the first idea that occurs to you. As you explore your subject thoroughly, you will get to know yourself or a classmate better. The self-awareness inventory may even lead you to a different approach than those we have identified. Beth Riley worked through the questions and came up with a unique idea. She described herself as she talked about certain qualities of her favorite color, red.

DEVELOPING THE INTRODUCTORY SPEECH

Once you have found the right approach, you can begin developing your speech. The introductory speech is usually short, so you must keep its design simple. The speech must move quickly to its purpose and develop it concisely. Plan carefully so that every word counts.

Designing Your Speech

Think of your speech as an organic whole in which the introduction, body, and conclusion are closely related. The entire speech should flow out of one controlling idea. How can you identify the organizational pattern or design you should use? Usually it is suggested by the topic you select, your purpose, and the main points you wish to make. Different topics or purposes will suggest different choices from the designs we discuss in Chapters 12 and 13. Let us look at how a design develops in an introductory speech that focuses on environment.

If you decide that the major factor in your life was your childhood neighborhood, then you might select a *categorical* design. You could begin with the setting, a description of a street scene in which you capture the sights, sounds, and smells of the locale: "I can always tell a Swedish neighborhood by the smell of *lutefisk* on Friday afternoons." Next you might narrow the focus and describe a certain neighbor who influenced you — perhaps the neighborhood grocer, who loved America with a patriotic passion, helped those in need, and always voted stubbornly for the Socialist party. Finally, you might widen the scope again and talk about the street games you played as a child and what they taught you about people and yourself. This "setting-people-games" categorical design structures your speech in an orderly manner.

The example also suggests how the introduction, body, and conclusion of your speech can be related. Your introduction could be the opening street scene that sets the stage for the rest of your speech. In the body of the speech you could describe the people, using the grocer as an extended example, then go on to describe the childhood games that reinforced the lessons of sharing. Your conclusion should make clear the point of the speech:

I hope you have enjoyed this "tour" of my neighborhood, this "tour" of my past. If you drove down this street tomorrow, you might think it was just another crowded, gray, uninteresting urban neighborhood. But to me it is filled with colorful people who care for each other and who dream great dreams of a better tomorrow. That street runs right down the center of my life.

Other topics and purposes might suggest other designs. If you select an experience that influenced you, such as "An Unforgettable Adventure," your speech might follow a *sequential* pattern as you tell the story of what happened. Again, you could use the introduction to set the scene and the conclusion to summarize the effect this experience had on you. Should you decide to tell about a condition that has had a great impact on you, a *cause-effect* design might be most appropriate. Maria One Feather, a Native American student, used such a design in her speech "Growing Up Red — and Feeling Blue — in White America." In this instance she treated the condition as the cause and its impact upon her as the effect.

The steppingstones to success in your first speech (and all subsequent ones) are to select your topic, decide on your purpose, focus what you want to say, and determine the design best suited to develop the speech. The design you choose will suggest how you should open the speech, develop its body, and bring it to a satisfactory conclusion.

Let us consider some specific examples that illustrate how this procedure may work in introductory speeches. Although we discuss the introduction, body, and conclusion of the speech as separate units, keep in mind that they are part of a larger organic whole. To be effective, these parts must fit and work well together in the finished product.

Introduction

The basic purposes of an **introduction** are to arouse the interest of your audience and to prepare them for the rest of the speech. Randy Block captured the attention of his listeners when he opened his introductory speech with this statement:

> I want to tell you about a love affair of mine that won't upset my wife, even if she finds out about it!

This opening *startled* his audience into listening and produced considerable curiosity about what would follow. Randy next revealed his main idea: his "love affair" was with a bicycle. This declaration of the main idea of the speech is called the **thematic statement.** Using a categorical design, Randy then proceeded to develop a speech that explained the main reasons he was fond of his bicycle. Fortunately, Randy's speech was colorful and interesting, for any speaker who creates such intense curiosity must justify that interest. An introduction should never upstage the message of a speech.

Eric Whittington engaged his listeners by reciting a list of place names, pausing after each name:

> California . . . Virginia . . . Florida . . . Hawaii . . . Washington . . . South Carolina . . . Guam . . . Michigan . . . Tennessee. I'm twenty years old. I've lived in eight different states and one trust territory. I've moved eighteen times in my life and attended schools in nine different school systems. You might think that moving so much wouldn't be good for a child, but it provided me with the opportunity to get to know and appreciate many different lifestyles.

This introduction prepared the audience for the speech's *spatial* design; Eric moved from area to area describing each one's various customs and activities and their effects on his life.

Suzette Carson opened her introductory speech using a sequential design by referring to an earlier speech given in the class.

Last Monday Elizabeth told us how she enjoyed being an "obedient wife." I admire her honesty and her courage for saying that. I too was an obedient wife and daughter most of my life. But the result was that it took a long time for me to learn who I was and how I could be independent. I'd like to tell you about my quest for myself, in hopes that it may help some of you who have the same problem.

Body

Each of these students used a different technique to arouse the interest of the audience and lead into the body of the speech. The **body** of your speech is where you develop your main points. In a short presentation it is difficult to cover many main points adequately. Limit their number and develop these few in depth. For a three- to five-minute assignment, you should restrict yourself to two or three main points.

For example, Randy developed two main points explaining why he loved his bike: (1) biking gave him a sense of freedom, and (2) biking provided him with an opportunity for adventure. Eric explained his love of diverse activities by focusing on three main points, his enjoyment of (1) sail surfing in Hawaii, (2) rock climbing in Washington State, and (3) scuba diving in Florida. Eric's use of *examples* as he developed these points provided interesting, specific detail that illustrated and enlivened his theme. Suzette described three main phases in her quest for self: (1) her life in an overprotective home, (2) her life with a domineering husband, and (3) finally finding herself on her own. Her speech used *narratives,* or extended stories, to illustrate her main points.

Narratives can be especially useful in the introductory speech, where they can help develop a feeling of closeness between the audience and the speaker. They hold the interest of the audience while revealing some important truth about the speaker or the topic. Narratives should be short and to the point, moving in natural sequence from the beginning of the story to the end. The language of narration should be colorful, concrete, and active; the presentation, lively and interesting. Randy used a narrative effectively to show how his bicycle provided him with an opportunity for adventure. He told about the time he traveled 130 miles in fourteen hours of continuous biking, and what happened when he crawled under a bridge to escape the blazing midafternoon sun. As Randy told the story, his voice and face came alive, and he began to gesture spontaneously.

Narratives and examples are among the basic forms of *supporting materials* used to provide content and substance, especially in the body of a speech (see Chapter 6 for further information). *Facts and figures,* another basic form, help augment the impression that the speaker possesses *responsible knowledge.* For example, Randy might have introduced the number of bicycles sold in the United States last year to suggest that others shared his passion for biking. These figures would not only add an interesting bit of information: they would also enhance his perceived competency.

SPEAKER'S NOTES   *Preparing Your Introductory Speech*

1. Select a design appropriate to your topic and purpose.

2. Develop an introduction that arouses attention and interest as it leads into your topic.

3. Limit yourself to two or three main points.

4. Develop each main point with narratives, examples, facts and figures, and/or testimony.

5. Prepare a conclusion that ties your speech together and reflects on your meaning.

A fourth form of supporting material is *testimony.* Had Randy been able to cite quotations from prominent psychologists about the desirable connection between biking and freedom and adventure, he would have provided even more in-depth knowledge about his subject and himself. In citing figures or quoting testimony, be sure to identify the sources of your information and the credentials of those experts you are quoting, including the positions they hold, when and where they spoke, and the honors they may have received. Thus, you might say: "Norman F. Ramsey, professor at Harvard University and winner of the Nobel Prize in physics, said last month in New York that. . . ."

By concentrating on two or three main points in the body of your speech and developing them with examples, narratives, facts and figures, and testimony, you can provide your audience with more useful and appealing listening experiences.

Conclusion

Finally, these students all concluded by showing how the experiences they related had affected their lives. The **conclusion** often includes a **summary statement**, which reinterprets the main idea, and **concluding remarks**, which reflect on the meaning of the speech. Randy used these techniques to end his speech.

Now you know why I have this "love affair" with my bike. I love the sense of freedom and the opportunity for adventure that it gives me. Perhaps you would also enjoy this kind of affair. Give it a fling!

Eric concluded his speech by explaining that moving so much had allowed him to develop diverse interests and a deep appreciation for nature. Suzette explained that although she now considers herself liberated and independent, she does not think of herself as a stereotype. She is not so much a feminist as an individual. "I'm not Gloria Steinem," she said in her conclusion. "*My* name is Suzette Carter."

OUTLINING THE INTRODUCTORY SPEECH

It is easier to put together an effective speech if you compose a full-sentence *preparation outline* to help you organize your ideas. The outline displays your introduction, thematic statement, main ideas (along with examples, narratives, or other forms of supporting materials), and your conclusion so that you can see if all these elements work together. You can use a shortened form of this outline, called the *key-word outline,* as you practice and present the speech.

In the following preparation outline for a self-introductory speech, several critical parts of the speech — the introduction, thematic statement, and conclusion — are written out word for word. They anchor the meaning of the speech and determine whether your entrance into and exit from the speech will be smooth and effective. Thus, it is important that they be planned exactly. Note, however, that the entire speech is not written out, leaving room for spontaneity in the actual presentation.

CONTROLLING MY ANOREXIA

Introduction

I. *Attention-arousing and orienting material:* When most of you look at me, you see a tall, slender girl with dark hair and eyes who looks fairly healthy. You're right, I am. But I'm one of the lucky ones. You see, five years ago I weighed sixty-four pounds and was diagnosed as anorexic.

   A. Anorexia is an eating disorder characterized by an irrational desire to be thin.

   B. Anorexics see themselves as fat, no matter how much or how little they weigh.

   C. Anorexics literally starve themselves to meet their ideal of thinness.

II. *Thematic Statement:* Today I want to share with you what having been anorexic has meant in my life, how it has taught me to recognize and cope with irrational fears.

Body [three main points using narrative to develop a sequential design]

    I. My anorexia was related to my being a dancer.

        A. Dancers need to be thin.

        B. Losing weight is seen as the key to professional success.

        C. Dieting can become an obsession.

   II. After obsessive dieting I experienced a crisis period.

        A. I lost 50 percent of my body weight.

        B. My parents were shocked by my appearance during a dance recital.

        C. I was hospitalized for treatment.
           1. I was given physical treatment with intravenous feeding.
           2. I underwent psychotherapy to find the cause of my problem.

  III. I finally was shocked into resolving my problem.

        A. I overheard the doctor telling my parents to "expect the worst."

        B. I decided to prove him wrong by beating the odds.

        C. Many difficulties lay ahead for me.
           1. I had to develop the same kind of will power to eat that I had used for dieting.
           2. I had to stop thinking of food as my "enemy."

Conclusion

    I. *Summary Statement:* My desire to be a thin dancer became an obsession that almost killed me.

   II. *Concluding Remarks:* Like alcoholism, anorexia is never cured; it is simply controlled.

        A. For the rest of my life a piece of chocolate cake will always represent FAT in big, ugly capital letters.

        B. But I have learned to recognize the irrationality of such fears, and this realization, I am determined, will continue to keep my anorexia an arm's length away.

PRESENTING THE INTRODUCTORY SPEECH

Once you have analyzed, designed, developed, and outlined your introductory speech, you are ready to prepare for presentation. An effective presentation spotlights the ideas, not the speaker, and is neither read nor memorized but delivered in a natural, extemporaneous manner. It is normal, even desirable, to feel nervous before giving a speech. In an effective presentation, the speaker uses communication apprehension to energize the message and the idea.

Spotlight the Ideas

The presentation of a speech is the climax of planning and preparation — the speaker's time to stand in the spotlight. Though presentation is important, it should never overshadow the speech. Have you ever been party to this kind of exchange?

> "She's a wonderful speaker — what a beautiful voice, what eloquent diction, what a smooth delivery!"
> "What did she say?"
> "I don't remember what she said, but she sure sounded good!"

Sometimes the skills of presentation can be used to cover up a lack of substance or even disguise unethical speaking. When this happens the audience loses sight of the basic purpose of public speaking: *the exchange of ideas in messages that have been carefully designed and prepared so that they deserve the attention they receive from an audience.* All of the arts of speaking should be focused on the *idea.*

As you practice speaking from your outline and when you present your speech, concentrate on the ideas you have to offer. *You should have a vivid realization of these thoughts during the moments of actual presentation.*[2] In other words, the ideas should come alive as you speak, joining you and the audience.

Sound Natural

An effective presentation preserves the best qualities of conversation. It sounds natural and spontaneous, yet has a depth, coherence, and quality that are not normally found in social conversation. The best way to approach this ideal of *improved conversation* is to present your speech extemporaneously. An *extemporaneous presentation* is carefully prepared and practiced but not written out or memorized. If you write out your speech, you will be tempted either to memorize it word for word or to read it to your audience. Reading or memorizing usually results in a stilted presentation. *Do not read your speech!* That defeats the purpose of public communication because it robs the audience of its chance to participate in the creation of ideas. *Exact wording is not as important as audience contact.* The only parts of a speech that should be memorized are the introduction, the conclusion, and other critical phrases or sentences such as the punch lines for humorous narratives.

Key-Word Outline

To sound conversational and spontaneous, talk with your audience from an outline of ideas imprinted on your mind. Practicing your speech from a key-word outline, condensed from your preparation outline, will help you remember the order of ideas. (The following key-word outline is based on the preparation outline presented earlier.)

ANOREXIA

Introduction

    I. Look healthy, had anorexia

    II. Disease's meaning in my life

Body

    I. Relation to dancing ambition

       A. Thinness key to professional success

       B. Dieting as an obsession

    II. My crisis

       A. Lost 50% body weight

       B. Parents notice

       C. Hospitalized for IV feeding and psychotherapy

    III. Resolution

       A. Doctor: expect the worst

       B. Prove him wrong

       C. Challenges
          1. Will power to eat
          2. Food not "enemy"

Conclusion

    I. Almost killed me

    II. Never cured, just controlled

       A. Chocolate cake = FAT

       B. Recognize irrationality

Practicing Your Speech

You may use the key-word outline to prompt your thinking as you practice and present your speech. If you are using a lectern, place the outline high on the lectern so that you do not have to lower your eyes when you look at it. If you are not using a lectern, print your outline on notecards that you can hold in your hand. Try to limit yourself to three notecards: one for the introduction, one for the body of the speech, and one for the conclusion. Don't try to hide the outline and don't feel guilty or embarrassed if you need to refer to it. Your audience probably won't even notice it unless you make a big issue of needing to use it. Remember, your listeners are far more interested in what you have to say than in any awkwardness you may experience. You should be idea-conscious rather than self-conscious. Idea-consciousness comes from preparation, practice, and a commitment to put your message across.

As you practice your speech, imagine your audience in front of you. Maintain eye contact with your imaginary listeners, just as you will during the actual presentation. Look around the room so that everyone feels included in your message. Try to be enthusiastic about what you are saying. Let your voice suggest that you are confident. Strive for variety and color in your voice: avoid speaking in a monotone, which never changes pace or pitch. Pause to let important ideas sink in. Let your face and body respond to your ideas as you speak them.

Make Nervousness Work for You

As you give your first speech, it is only natural for you to have some **communication apprehension.** In fact, there would be something wrong with you if you didn't have such feelings. The absence of any nervousness could suggest that you do not care about the audience or your subject. Almost everyone who faces a public audience experiences some kind of concern. We once attended a banquet where an award was presented to the "Communicator of the Year." Before sitting down to eat, the recipient of this award confessed to us, "I really dread having to make this acceptance speech!" We were not at all surprised when he made a very effective speech.

There are many reasons why public speaking is somewhat frightening. The important thing is not to be too anxious about your apprehension. Accept it as natural and remind yourself that you can convert these feelings into positive energy. One of the biggest myths about public speaking classes is that they can or should rid you of any natural fears. Instead, they should teach you how to harness the energy generated by apprehension so that your speaking is more dynamic. No anxiety often means a flat, dull presentation. Transformed anxiety can make your speech come to life.

How can you put this energy to work for you? Begin by understanding how it can become a problem. Some people develop a negative dialogue with themselves and actually talk themselves into being less effective. For example, they might say to themselves, "Everybody will think I'm stupid," or "Nobody wants to listen to me." If you find yourself engaging in self-defeating behavior, consciously replace such statements with positive messages that focus on your ideas and your audience. For example, "I've done my research, so I know what I'm talking about" could substitute for "I'm going to sound stupid." This approach to controlling communication anxiety, called **cognitive restructuring,**[3] is a habit you can acquire by deliberately replacing negative thoughts with positive, constructive statements.

There are other things you can do to control communication apprehension. First, select a topic that interests and excites you, so that you get so involved with it that there is little room in your mind for worry about yourself. Second, choose a topic that you already know something about so that you will be more confident. Then build on the foundation of your knowledge to learn more. Visit the library and interview experts. The better prepared you are, the more confident you can be that you have something worthwhile to say. Third, practice, practice, and then practice some more. The more you are a master of your message, the more comfortable you will be. Fourth, develop a positive attitude toward your listeners. Don't think of them as "the enemy." Expect them to be helpful and attentive. Fifth, picture yourself succeeding as a speaker, then practice with the image in mind.

Finally as we stated earlier, *act* confident, even if you don't *feel* that way. Never discuss your anxiety with classmates before you speak. When it is your turn, walk briskly to the front of the room, look at your audience and establish eye contact. If appropriate to your subject, smile at the audience, then begin your presentation. Whatever happens during your speech, remember that listeners cannot see and hear inside you. They know only what you decide to show them. Show them a controlled speaker communicating well-researched and carefully prepared ideas. *Never place on your listeners the additional burden of sympathy* — their job is to listen to what you are saying. Don't say anything like "Gee, am I scared!" Such self-indulgent behavior may make the audience uncomfortable as well. If you put your listeners at ease by acting confident yourself, they can relax and provide the positive feedback that will make you a more assured and better speaker.

When you reach your conclusion, pause, and then present your summary statement and concluding remarks with special emphasis. Maintain eye contact

---

SPEAKER'S NOTES

Controlling Communication Apprehension

1. Replace self-defeating statements with positive statements.

2. Select a topic that interests and excites you.

3. Select a topic you know something about and research it thoroughly.

4. Practice, practice, practice!

5. Expect your audience to be helpful and attentive.

6. Picture yourself being successful.

7. Act confident, even if you don't feel that way.

for a moment before you move confidently back to your seat. This final impression is very important. *You should keep the focus on your message, not on yourself.* Even though you may feel relieved that the speech is over, don't say "Whew!" or "I made it!" and never shake your head to show disappointment in your presentation. Even if you did not live up to your aspirations, you probably did better than you thought.

Thus far, we have discussed controlling communication apprehension in terms of what the speaker can do, but the audience also can help by creating a positive communication environment. As an audience member, you should listen attentively and look for something in the speech that interests you. Even if you are not excited about the topic, you might pick up some techniques that will be useful when it is your turn to speak. When you discuss or evaluate the speeches of others, be constructive and helpful. Listen to others the way you would have them listen to you.

IN SUMMARY

Many of us tend to underrate our potential for public speaking. Starting with your first speech, you can work to build a positive communication environment for yourself and others. You can also develop your ethos as a speaker.

Managing the Impressions You Make.   Listeners acquire positive impressions of you based on your ability to convey competence, integrity, attractiveness, and power. You can build your perceived competence by citing examples from your own experiences, by quoting authorities, and by organizing and presenting your message effectively. You can earn an image of integrity by being accurate and complete in your presentation of information. You can promote attractiveness by being a warm and open person with whom your listeners can easily identify. *Natural power* comes as a result of your competence, integrity, and attractiveness and from listeners' perceptions of you as a confident, enthusiastic, and decisive speaker.

Introducing Yourself and Others.   The speech of introduction helps establish you or your classmate as a unique person. It may focus on environmental influences, a person who inspired you, an experience that affected you, an activity that reveals your character, the work you do, your purpose in life, or some value you cherish.

Developing the Introductory Speech.   In developing your introductory speech, determine the appropriate design to organize your thoughts. Organizational strategies include categories, sequences of events, cause-effect relationships, and spatial patterns. Your speech should begin with an *introduction* that gains attention as it leads into the body of your message. Your introduction will also include your *thematic statement,* which expresses the main idea of your speech. The design you select suggests how the *body* of your speech will be structured and developed. Narratives and examples are especially useful in developing speeches of introduction. Other forms of supporting material useful in developing the body are facts and figures and testimony. Finally, your speech should come to a satisfying *conclusion.* Your conclusion should include a *summary statement* and *concluding remarks* that highlight the meaning.

Outlining the Introductory Speech.   You can improve your chances for presenting a well-developed and well-structured speech by building a preparation outline. As you practice and present the speech, you may find it helpful to use a key-word outline, a shortened version of the preparation outline.

Presenting the Introductory Speech.   When presenting your first speech, keep the spotlight on the message, strive for a conversational presentation, and use your natural anxiety as a source of energy. Never let presentation skills overshadow your ideas. Cope with *communication apprehension* by practicing *cognitive restructuring,* which replaces negative messages to yourself with positive ones. In addition, you should select a topic that interests you and that you already know something about so that you can build on this foundation. You should practice until you feel confident, imagining your audience in positive terms and picturing yourself as being successful. During actual presentation you should act confident and avoid expressions of personal discomfort.

TERMS TO KNOW

conferred power	conclusion
natural power	summary statement
self-awareness inventory	concluding remarks
introduction	communication apprehension
thematic statement	cognitive restructuring
body	

DISCUSSION

1. Although we have defined ethos in terms of public speakers, other communicators also seek to create favorable impressions of competence, integrity, attractiveness, and power. Advertisers always try to create favorable ethos for their products. Bring to class print advertisements to demonstrate each of the four dimensions of ethos we have discussed. Explain how each ad uses ethos.

2. Select a prominent public speaker for ethos analysis. On which dimensions is this speaker especially strong or weak? How does this affect the person's leadership ability? Present your analysis for class discussion.

3. Political ads often do the work of introducing candidates to the public and disparaging their opponents. Study the television ads in connection with a recent political campaign. Bring to class answers to the following questions:

   a. What kinds of positive and negative identities do the ads establish?

   b. Which of these ads are most and least effective in creating the desired ethos? Why?

   c. Which of the self-inventory questions discussed in this chapter might explain how the candidates are introduced?

4. Identify any negative messages you might send yourself concerning public speaking. How might you change these messages, using the principles of cognitive restructuring? Share the original self-defeating messages and their positive counterparts with your classmates.

APPLICATION

1. As the introductory speeches are presented in your class, build a collection of portraits of your classmates as revealed by their speeches. At the end of the assignment, analyze this group of portraits to see what you have learned about the class as a whole. What kind of topics might they prefer? Did you detect any strong political or social attitudes to which you might have to adjust? Submit one copy of your analysis to your instructor and keep another for your own use in preparing later speeches.

2. At the end of the introductory speeches in your class, use the criteria suggested in Chapter 1 for speech evaluation and decide which was the best speech presented. Write a brief paper defending your choice.

3. Build preparation and key-word outlines of your self-introductory speech. On a separate sheet of paper, identify the organizational design you are using and discuss why this design is most appropriate. Turn in a copy of your outlines and your rationale to your instructor.

4. Outline the student speech that follows. Do the ideas flow smoothly? Might the structure have been improved? Is supporting material used effectively?

NOTES

1. The concept of identification was introduced by Kenneth Burke in *A Rhetoric of Motives* (Berkeley: University of California Press, 1969), pp. 20–23.
2. Donald C. Bryant and Karl R. Wallace, *Fundamentals of Public Speaking,* 4th ed. (New York: Appleton-Century-Crofts, 1969), p. 233.
3. William J. Fremouw and Michael D. Scott, "Cognitive Restructuring: An Alternative Method for the Treatment of Communication Apprehension," *Communication Education* 28 (May 1979): 129–133.

SAMPLE SPEECH OF SELF-INTRODUCTION

My Three Cultures

— Sandra Baltz —

Sandra's introduction identifies the three cultures that have influenced her life. Her opening example stirred up interest and curiosity. Her awareness of public affairs and fluency in Spanish suggested that she was a competent, complex, and interesting individual.

Several years ago I read a newspaper article in the *Commercial Appeal* in which an American journalist described some of his experiences in the Middle East. He was there a couple of months and had been the guest of several different Arab families. He reported having been very well treated and very well received by everyone that he met there. But it was only later, when he returned home, that he became aware of the intense resentment his hosts held for Americans and our unwelcome involvement in their Middle Eastern affairs. The journalist wrote of feeling somewhat bewildered, if not deceived, by the large discrepancy between his treatment while in the Middle East and the hostile attitude that he learned about later. He labeled this behavior hypocritical. When I reached the end of the article, I was reminded of a phrase spoken often by my mother. "Sandra," she says to me, *"respeta tu casa y a todos los que entran en ella, trata a tus enemigos asi como a tus amigos."*

This transition into the body of the speech establishes Sandra's integrity while foreshadowing the idea that serious problems may arise from cross-cultural misunderstandings. Sandra's thematic statement helps to overcome negative perceptions of the Arabic influence on her life.

This is an Arabic proverb, spoken in Spanish, and roughly it translates into "Respect your home and all who enter it, treating even an enemy as a friend." This is a philosophy that I have heard often in my home. With this in mind, it seemed to me that the treatment the American journalist received while in the Middle East was not hypocritical behavior on the part of his hosts. Rather, it was an act of respect for their guest, for themselves, and for their home — indeed, a behavior very typical of the Arabic culture.

Since having read that article several years ago I have become much more aware of how my life is different because of having a mother who is of Palestinian origin but was born and raised in the Central American country of El Salvador.

By comparing and contrasting the advantages and disadvantages of growing up bilingual, Sandra continues to build her ethos. We learn that she has traveled widely and is a premed student (competence). We find that she wants to serve people (integrity). As Sandra talks about her dialect problems and family reunions, the light humor increases her attractiveness. Her statement that "there really is no language

One of the most obvious differences is that I was raised bilingually — speaking both Spanish and English. In fact, my first words were in Spanish. Growing up speaking two languages has been both an advantage and a disadvantage for me. One clear advantage is that I received straight A's in my Spanish class at Immaculate Conception High School. Certainly, traveling has been made much easier. During visits to Spain, Mexico, and some of the Central American countries, it has been my experience that people are much more open and much more receptive if you can speak their language. In addition, the subtleties of a culture are easier to grasp and much easier to appreciate.

I hope that knowing a second language will continue to be an asset for me in the future. I am currently pursuing a career in medicine. Perhaps by knowing Spanish I can broaden the area in which I can work and increase the number of people that I might reach.

Now one of the disadvantages of growing up bilingually is that I picked up my mother's accent as well as her language. I must have been about four years old before I realized that our feathered friends in the trees are called "birds" not "beers" and that, in fact, we had a "birdbath" in our back yard, not a "beerbath."

Family reunions also tend to be confusing around my home. Most of my relatives speak either Spanish, English, or Arabic, but rarely any combination of the three. So, as a result, deep and involved conversations are almost impossible. But with a little nodding and smiling, I have found that there really is no language barrier among family and friends.

In all, I must say that being exposed to three very different cultures — Latin, Arabic, and American — has been rewarding for me and has made a difference even in the music I enjoy and the food I eat. It is not unusual in my house to sit down to a meal made up of stuffed grape leaves and refried beans and all topped off with apple pie for dessert.

I am fortunate in having had the opportunity to view more closely what makes Arabic and Latin cultures unique. By understanding and appreciating them I have been able to better understand and appreciate my own American culture. In closing just let me add some words you often hear spoken in my home — *adios* and *allak konn ma'eck* — goodbye, and may God go with you.

I think the one lesson I have learned is that there is no substitute for paying attention.

— DIANE SAWYER

3

CRITICAL LISTENING

—— *AND* ——

SPEECH EVALUATION

This Chapter Will Help You

- ◆ develop an appreciation for critical listening skills.

- ◆ identify and work on overcoming your listening problems.

- ◆ build critical thinking skills to analyze what you hear.

- ◆ establish criteria for evaluating speeches.

Carrie Bolden, the city's first female candidate for mayor, was scheduled to speak at the campus political forum. Mary Beth Jackson was excited about the upcoming speech. She considered herself a feminist and could hardly wait to hear the candidate in person. Mary Beth just knew that she would agree with everything Ms. Bolden had to say. She relished the opportunity to meet the candidate and planned to volunteer to work in her campaign.

On the other hand, Sara Thomas didn't care much for politics or politicians. She would attend the forum only because she was required to write a report on the speech for her class. Sara also was annoyed because she would miss her favorite television show.

Neither of the two students described above will be a critical listener at the political forum. Although Mary Beth will be enthusiastic, it's doubtful she will critically evaluate what she hears. Her initial attitudes will predispose her to agree with almost anything the candidate has to say. Sara's listening ability also will be affected by her attitudes. Indifference toward the subject and a negative attitude toward the speaker can reduce listening effectiveness.

Although these two students represent extremes, it is true that a good listener can be hard to find. And without effective listeners, the dynamic circle of communication is broken. When audiences don't listen well, they can't provide useful feedback for speakers. Without such feedback, speakers can't adapt their messages so that their listeners will better understand them. Communication is most effective when audiences practice critical listening skills.

Critical listening involves paying attention, hearing, interpreting and comprehending, analyzing and evaluating, remembering, and responding. First, you must focus on the sounds that constitute the message, and block out other noises, visual distractions, thoughts, or feelings that may compete for your attention. Second, you must be able to hear a message in order to listen, even though you don't necessarily listen to everything you hear. *Hearing* is an automatic process in which sound waves stimulate nerve impulses to the brain. *Listening* is a voluntary process that goes beyond simply reacting to sounds. For listening to take place, you need to interpret and comprehend what you hear. You must understand the language and point of view of the speaker. Comprehension is followed by analysis and evaluation, in which you examine the message rather than accepting it at face value. Remembering is the next step, as you mentally store what you have learned for further use. In short, critical listening allows you to extract the potential value from messages to which you are exposed.

Although we have listed responding as the final step in critical listening, providing feedback is one of the most important aspects of critical listening behavior and can actually occur at any point in the process. As mentioned in Chapter 1, *feedback* is the ongoing response behavior of listeners that lets speakers know how their messages are being received. It is vital because of the interactive nature of communication. For example, if the speaker is not clear or is speaking too softly or too loudly, listeners may frown with uncertainty, or strain forward to hear, or push backwards to escape the irritating loudness. Alert speakers will recognize these behaviors as feedback messages and will attempt to clarify the point or to increase or reduce their volume. Good speakers constantly monitor audience feedback for signs of successful or flawed communication. Good listeners provide honest feedback so that speakers can make their messages more effective. Listeners who smile and nod encouragingly even though they don't understand a thing the speaker is saying must share the blame for failed communication.

Listening is the most pervasive communication activity in our lives. It is also the least developed. Adults spend approximately half of their communication time listening; the remainder is divided among speaking, reading, and writing.[1] In school we learn to read, write, and speak, yet we are seldom taught listening skills. Is it any wonder, then, that we typically retain less than a quarter of what we hear?[2] This chapter will consider the benefits of critical listening, listening problems, and ways to improve listening skills. You can reach the goal of critical listening once you have minimized listening problems and learned how to combine the skills of effective listening and critical thinking. Finally, you will learn to relate critical listening to the evaluation of classroom speeches.

BENEFITS OF CRITICAL LISTENING

Listening may be an underappreciated skill in our society because we often associate it more with following than with leading. We frequently focus on speaking and leading without realizing that critical listening is a vital part of any communication interaction. Because of the feedback they provide, critical listeners can help speakers become better, more sensitive, and more responsive leaders.

Listeners who understand, analyze, and respond critically to messages can help protect themselves from unscrupulous leaders. Some who seek power are interested mainly in personal gain. Such speakers frequently cover up a lack of information or faulty reasoning with a glib presentation or emotional appeals. The best defense against such charlatans is the ability to listen critically to their messages. The Hitlers of the world are created more by uncritical listening than by proficient speaking. Critical listeners learn not to accept anyone or anything at face value, but to analyze and evaluate messages for themselves.

Critical listening skills also are important because much of the mass communication to which we are exposed is highly sophisticated. Each day we are inundated with a barrage of advertising, much of which relies on irrelevant or misleading appeals. Such ads make you think that their products will satisfy all your basic needs, even when the products have no direct relationship to such needs. How many times have you seen television ads that use attractive,

The body language and facial expressions of effective listeners provide feedback to speakers. Without effective listeners the dynamic circle of communication is broken. Can you identify the more involved listeners in this audience?

scantily clad women to sell everything from soft drinks to automatic transmission repair services? Similarly, these ads may ask you to buy what "doctors" recommend without telling you anything about the expertise of these "doctors." These are obvious examples, but less transparent abuses may be more difficult to detect. Critical listening skills will make you more aware of such deceptions.

You also can enhance your performance as a student by developing critical listening skills. College students spend close to 60 percent of their communication time listening.[3] Research indicates that students who listen effectively earn better grades and achieve beyond what their intelligence levels might have predicted.[4] A good listener learns to concentrate on what is being said, to identify the main points and the most important information, and to evaluate supporting materials. Responsible listeners read assigned materials before a lecture. The information they gain from reading provides a foundation for understanding what they hear. Critical listeners also question the ideas that they hear. Through questioning they gain greater understanding.

At work, improved listening skills may mean the difference between success and failure, both for individuals and companies. A survey of Fortune 500 organizations found that poor listening is "one of the most important problems" and that "ineffective listening leads to ineffective performance. . . ."[5] If you listen effectively on the job, you will make fewer mistakes. You will improve your opportunities for advancement. Companies that encourage the development of critical listening skills enjoy many dividends. They suffer less from costly misunderstandings. Employees contribute ideas more enthusiastically because they sense that management is listening. Morale improves, and the work environment becomes more pleasant and productive. As a result, the company becomes more dynamic and creative. The all-important "bottom line" — improved profits — looks a lot better! For these reasons many prominent companies, such as the Sperry Corporation, have invested substantially in listening training for their employees.[6]

OVERCOMING LISTENING PROBLEMS

The road to critical listening starts with acknowledging our listening problems. To become more effective listeners, we first need to become aware of what causes our poor listening behavior. Listening problems are often a function of our personal reactions, our attitudes, and bad habits we have acquired. At best these problems pose a challenge to the careful listener; at worst they defeat communication. Once we understand what our listening problems are, we can begin to correct them. Figure 3.1 should help you identify some of your listening problems. Read through the list and make a check mark next to the problems you need to work on.

Personal Reactions

One of the most common listening problems is simply not paying attention. How many times have you found yourself daydreaming, even when you know you should be listening to what is said? This problem stems from the fact that the human mind can process information much faster than most people speak. Typically we speak in public at about 125 words per minute, but we process information at about 500 words per minute.[7] This time gap gives listeners an opportunity to drift away to more delightful or difficult personal concerns. When this happens, listeners might just as well hang "out to lunch" signs around their necks, and speakers might just as well address blank walls! Both personal reactions to words and distractions can trigger such behavior.

Reactions to Words.   As you listen to a message, you react to more than just the **denotative meanings,** or dictionary definitions, of words. You also respond to the **connotative meanings,** the emotional or attitudinal reactions that certain words arouse in you. You may react adversely, for example, to the use of the word *girls* in reference to adult females. The term *girls* acts as a **trigger word** that sets off a negative emotional response. Suppose a speaker is describing opportunities for advancement in the Crypton Corporation and makes reference to "one of the girls in the typing pool" who moved up into a personnel management position. His use of *girls* suggests to you that this is a

Figure 3.1
Listening Problems Check List

_____ 1. I have always thought of listening as an automatic process, not a learned behavior that I could improve.

_____ 2. When I find a topic uninteresting, I stop listening and begin thinking about something else.

_____ 3. I feel so strongly about some issues that it is hard for me to listen to speeches about them.

_____ 4. Certain words trigger extreme responses in me.

_____ 5. I am easily distracted by noises when someone is speaking.

_____ 6. I don't like to listen to speakers unless they are experts.

_____ 7. Some people are so objectionable that I don't want to listen to them.

_____ 8. I get sleepy when someone talks in a monotone.

_____ 9. I can be so dazzled by an impressive presentation that I don't really listen to what the speaker says.

_____ 10. I don't like to listen to speeches that violate my values.

_____ 11. When I disagree with a speaker, I spend my time thinking up counterarguments rather than really listening.

_____ 12. I know so much about some topics that I can't learn anything else from a speaker.

_____ 13. I believe the speaker is solely responsible for the effectiveness of communication.

_____ 14. I often have so much on my mind that I find it hard to listen to others.

_____ 15. I sometimes stop listening when the subject is difficult.

_____ 16. I can look as though I'm listening even when I'm not.

_____ 17. I listen only for the facts and ignore the rest of a message.

_____ 18. I try to write down everything a lecturer says.

_____ 19. I let a speaker's appearance determine how well I listen.

_____ 20. I often jump to conclusions and put words in a speaker's mouth.

sexist organization. As you sit there stewing over his semantic insensitivity, you miss his later statement that over the past three years two-thirds of all promotions into management have gone to women.

Attention also can be disrupted by chance associations you make with some words. The speaker may mention the word _desk,_ which reminds you that you need to fix a better place to study in your room, which reminds you that you have to buy a new lamp, which starts you thinking about where you should shop for the lamp. By the time your attention drifts back to the speaker, you have lost the gist of what is being said. Feeling hopelessly lost, you may just give up listening altogether.

Distractions. Both internal and external distractions can disrupt attention. If you are tired, hungry, angry, worried, or pressed for time, you may find it difficult to concentrate. Your personal situation will usually take precedence over listening to a speaker. Physical noises can divert attention if they drown out the speaker's voice or are unusual or unexpected. A room that is uncomfortably hot or cold may make it hard for people to concentrate. Visual aids left out during a speech can steal attention from the message. Materials distributed before a speech can also compete for attention.

Controlling Reactions and Distractions. We all have problems from time to time with attention. To improve your ability to concentrate, you need to become aware of those situations that cause you to "drift away" from a speaker. One way you can do this is to keep a **listening log** in your lecture classes. As you take notes, put a minus mark (−) in the margin each time you notice your attention wandering. By each mark, jot down a word or two pinpointing the cause, perhaps a distraction or a trigger word. After class, note the number of times your mind drifted and reconstruct in more detail the causes. Is there a pattern to your behavior? How might you control your daydreaming? This exercise will help you identify the conditions that lead to inattention and will also make you more consciously aware of your tendency to daydream. Once you realize how often and why you are mentally drifting, you can more easily redirect your attention to the message.

If you find yourself reacting emotionally to trigger words, ask yourself: *What is this reaction doing to my listening ability? Is the speaker unaware of the power of these words, or are they being used for a purpose? What effect is the speaker seeking?* By concentrating on such questions, you can defuse much of the power of such words and psychologically distance yourself from your own emotional reactions. Then it will be easier to refocus your attention on the message.

You can also control inattention that is related to internal distractions. Come to your classes well rested, well fed, and ready to listen. Remind yourself that you can't really do your homework for another class when someone is talking. Leave your troubles at the door even if it means scheduling a time to worry later in the day. Clear your mind and your desk of everything except paper on which to take notes. Sit erect, establish eye contact with the speaker, and start to listen.

Do what you can to control external distractions as well. Try to sit near the front of the room for psychological as well as physical reasons. You will be able to hear better, and you will also be indicating a commitment to listen. Your teacher and the other speakers will appreciate this positive signal that you want to help make communication successful. Moreover, you are less likely to daydream if you are sitting front and center. If outside noises distract you, unobtrusively get up and close a door or window. Do not try to read charts or handouts unless and until the speaker refers to them. Constantly remind yourself that you are there to listen.

Attitudes

You may have strong positive or negative attitudes toward the speaker, the topic, or even the act of communication itself that can diminish your listening ability. All of us have biases, or prejudices, of one kind or another. Listening problems arise when our biases prevent us from receiving messages accurately. Some of the ways that bias can distort messages are through filtering, assimilation, and contrast effects.[8]

Filtering means that you simply don't process all of the information to which you are exposed. You screen the speaker's words so that only some of them reach your brain. In other words, you hear what you want to hear. Listeners who filter will hear only one side of "good news, bad news" speeches — the side that confirms their prejudices. When you engage in **assimilation,** you interpret positions that are similar to your own as being closer to it than they actually are. Assimilation most often occurs when you have a strong positive attitude toward a speaker or topic. For example, if you believe that President Bush can do no wrong, you may be tempted to assimilate everything he says so that it seems consistent with all your beliefs.

A **contrast effect** occurs when you see positions that are dissimilar to your own as being even more distant. It is most often a problem when you have strong negative attitudes toward a speaker or topic. If you are a staunch Democrat, for example, you may think anything Republicans say is far removed from what you believe, even if that may not always be the case. Bias can also make you put words in a speaker's mouth, or take them away. Should you hear something that does not fit your expectations, you may rationalize it away with an excuse.

Attitudes Toward Speakers.

If you have had previous contact with speakers or have heard about them from others, you may have developed attitudes that can cause listening problems. The more competent, interesting, and attractive you expect speakers to be, the more attentive you will probably be and the more likely you will be to accept what they have to say. If your positive feelings are extremely strong, like those of the first listener in our chapter opening example, you may accept anything you hear without considering its merits. But if you anticipate incompetent, uninteresting, or unattractive speakers, you may be less attentive and less likely to accept their information or advice. You may dislike speakers because of positions they have previously defended or groups with which they are associated. You may even develop strong positive or negative feelings about speakers based on such extraneous factors as hair style, dress, delivery, accent, or mannerisms.[9] These attitudes can affect your critical listening ability.

Attitudes Toward the Topic.   Your attitudes toward certain topics also can affect how well you listen. If you believe that a topic is relevant to your life, you may listen more carefully than if you are indifferent. Speeches about retirement planning usually fall on deaf ears with young audiences. You may listen more attentively, although less critically, to speeches that support positions you already hold. If you feel strongly about a subject and oppose the speaker's position, you may find yourself developing counterarguments instead of listening. For example, if you have strong feelings against gun control, you may find yourself silently reciting the Second Amendment to the U.S. Constitution instead of listening to a speaker's arguments in favor of gun control. When you engage in such behaviors, you may miss much of what the speaker actually has to say and deprive yourself of a learning experience. Finally, you may think that you already know enough about a topic. In such cases, you are not likely to listen effectively and may miss out on new, interesting information.

Attitudes Toward Communication.   You also may have attitudes about communication that can affect how well you listen. You may mistakenly equate listening with hearing. Recall that hearing is automatic and involves no effort on the part of the receiver. Listening is voluntary and requires energy and effort for it to be effective. If you confuse hearing and listening, you may become a mere passive recipient of messages.

If you believe that the speaker is solely responsible for communication effectiveness, you are likely to neglect your role as a listener and break the dynamic circle of communication. A good listener is an active participant in the communication process. Looking at the speaker and responding with nods, smiles, or other appropriate facial cues can help improve the quality of communication and keep the dynamic circle intact.

Controlling Your Attitudes.   Biases are not easy to control. The first step in overcoming their influence is to be aware that you may have them. Strive for objectivity by delaying judgments and reactions until you have given a message a full and careful hearing. Being objective does not mean that you must agree with a message. It simply means you recognize that others may hold different positions and that you can learn something from listening to them. Try not to prejudge a speaker, but go into communication situations with an open mind. Exposure to opposing points of view may cause you to reevaluate your position, but you may also find yourself strengthening what you already believe. Don't let yourself be distracted by extraneous characteristics such as the speaker's appearance or mannerisms. Tell yourself it's all right if Kate wears blue nail polish or John has long hair — this doesn't mean they have nothing worthwhile to say.

Motivate yourself to listen. Even if you have little or no interest in a topic, look for something in the speech that will benefit you personally. You may surprise yourself by acquiring new knowledge, developing new interests, or

SPEAKER'S NOTES   *Guides for Effective Listening*

1. *Be conscious of your listening behavior.* Identify your listening problems and work to solve them.

2. *Motivate yourself to listen.* Be opportunistic. Get all you can out of the messages you hear.

3. *Prepare yourself to listen.* Put problems and biases aside so that you can be more attentive and open to new learning experiences.

4. *Control your reactions.* Learn to recognize situations that cause daydreaming and strive to control them. Identify your trigger words so that they become less powerful. Resist distractions. Postpone evaluations and judgments until you have heard all the speaker has to say.

5. *Work at listening.* Develop a plan to extend your attention span. Seek out new and varied listening experiences that exercise your mind.

6. *Listen for ideas.* Do not try to write down everything you hear. Focus on identifying the main points the speaker is making.

7. *Concentrate on the message.* Don't allow extraneous factors to interfere with listening effectiveness.

learning things that will prove useful at some later time. Even poor speeches can provide valuable learning experiences through negative examples of what not to do when you are presenting a speech. Remember that good listeners are rewarded in both work and school.

If you are prone to developing counterarguments when you should be paying attention, practice the Golden Rule of listening: *Listen to others as you would have them listen to you.* Keep in mind that listening is an opportunity for learning. Reserve judgment until you have heard all of a message. Always remember that you, as a listener, are an integral part of the communication process. Without your participation there can be no effective communication.

Bad Habits

Many listening problems stem from bad habits. Since we do so much listening and very few of us have been trained in listening skills, we may have acquired many bad habits. We may feign attention or avoid listening to difficult materials. Our attention spans may have been shortened from too much television viewing. Unless a message is entertaining, we may try to "change the channel" even when the message is not on television. Our experiences as students may have conditioned us to listen just for facts or to try to write down everything we hear. Such habits can interfere with effective listening.

Feigning Attention.

All of us have learned how to look attentive to stay out of trouble. We know how to sit erect, focus our eyes on the speaker, even nod or smile from time to time (although not always at the most appropriate times), and not listen to one word that is being said! As an adult, you may fall back on such behavior when a message covers a difficult, technical, or abstract topic. If the speaker asks, "Do you understand?" you may nod brightly, sending false feedback just to be polite.

Avoiding Difficult Material.

It is not uncommon to want to avoid listening to difficult material. This tendency may be related to a fear of failure. Rather than exerting the effort needed to understand unfamiliar material, we may lapse into inattention. If we are asked questions later, we can always say, "I wasn't really listening," instead of, "I didn't understand." Additionally, our desire to have things simplified so that we can understand them without much effort makes us susceptible to "snake oil" pitches, those oversimplified remedies for everything from fallen arches to failing government policies.[10]

Listening Only for Facts.

Your experiences as a student may contribute to another bad listening habit: listening only for facts and trying to write down everything that is said. If you do this, you may miss the forest because you are so busy counting the leaves on the trees. Placing too much emphasis on fact and detail and too little emphasis on understanding ideas can make you a poor consumer of messages. Listening just for facts also keeps you from attending to the nonverbal aspects of a message. Effective listening includes integrating what you hear and what you see. Gestures, facial expressions, and tone of voice can communicate nuances that are vital to the meaning of a speech.

Television-trained Listener Habits.

Many of our poor listening habits may stem from a habit of heavy television viewing. Ninety-eight percent of American homes have at least one television set, and it is on for over seven hours a day.[11] Heavy television viewing can result in a shortened attention span and a strong desire to be entertained by everything we see or hear. Television messages are characterized by fast action and the presentation of short bits of information at a time. Habitual television viewing may lead us to expect all messages to follow this format. William F. Buckley has commented that "the television audience...is not trained to listen...to 15 uninterrupted minutes."[12] Our television-watching experiences may also lead us into what James Floyd refers to as "the entertainment syndrome," in which we demand that speakers be lively, interesting, funny, and charismatic to hold our attention.[13] Unfortunately, not all subjects lend themselves to such treatment, and we can miss much if we attend only to those who put on a "dog and pony show."

Coping with Bad Habits. Overcoming bad habits requires effort. When you find yourself feigning attention, ask yourself, "Why am I doing this?" and "What is this doing to my listening ability?" Keep in mind that honest feedback helps speakers but that inappropriate responding deceives them.

When you know you will be listening to difficult or complicated material, do some advance preparation so that you will be familiar with the ideas and vocabulary you will encounter. Don't try to remember everything or write down all that you hear. Instead, concentrate on absorbing the important information. Listen for the thematic statement and the overall idea of the speech and identify the main points. Use the difference between speaking- and mental-processing speeds to paraphrase what you hear so that it makes sense to you. Consider the choice of examples and the way they are related to the main points. Also look for nonverbal cues. Does the speaker's tone of voice change the meaning of the message? Are gestures and facial expressions consistent with words?

Figure 3.2
Differences between Good and Poor Listeners

Poor Listeners	Good Listeners
1. allow their minds to wander.	1. focus attention on the message.
2. respond emotionally to "trigger words."	2. control reactions to "trigger words."
3. let personal problems keep them from listening effectively.	3. leave their worries at the door.
4. succumb to distractions.	4. take action to reduce distractions.
5. are unaware that their biases may distort messages.	5. guard against letting personal biases distort messages.
6. react strongly to a speaker's style or reputation.	6. don't let the speaker's style or reputation impair listening.
7. "tune out" dry topics.	7. listen for what they can use.
8. hold the speaker responsible for effective communication.	8. recognize the important role of the listener in communication.
9. listen passively.	9. listen actively.
10. mentally rehearse counterarguments during a speech.	10. reserve judgment until a speaker is finished.
11. feign attention, giving false feedback to the speaker.	11. provide honest feedback to a speaker.
12. avoid difficult material.	12. become familiar with topic and vocabulary ahead of time.
13. listen only for facts.	13. listen for main ideas.
14. seek out entertaining messages.	14. exercise their minds by listening to other types of communication.

Practice extending your attention span. If your original listening log shows that you drifted away from a lecturer twenty times in one class session, see if you can reduce this to fifteen, then to ten, then to five. To become a more effective listener, you need to keep in mind the differences between good and poor listeners. These differences are summarized in Figure 3.2.

CRITICAL THINKING AND LISTENING

Once you have become a more effective listener, you can work toward being a critical listener. Critical listening goes beyond effective listening by applying critical thinking skills to the analysis of messages. **Critical thinking** is an integrated way of examining information, ideas, and proposals. It involves

- using your intelligence and knowledge to question, explore, and deal effectively with yourself, others, and life's problems;

- developing your own view of the world by examining ideas and arriving at your own conclusions;

- being receptive to new ideas and willing to analyze issues from different perspectives to develop greater understanding;

- supporting your personal views with reasons and evidence and understanding the reasons and evidence that support alternative viewpoints;

- discussing your ideas with others to test and enrich your thinking.[14]

The Importance of Critical Thinking and Listening

Perhaps the best way to appreciate the importance of critical listening is to consider a case in which it was totally absent. Such a situation occurred in 1978 in a small Central American country, when 912 followers of Jim Jones, a religious cult leader, accepted his order to drink punch laced with cyanide and commit mass suicide. As horrible as this tragedy was, it teaches us a vivid lesson about listening behavior. The people at Jonestown refused to rely on their own intelligence, accepted Jim Jones's sick view of the world without question, refused to consider other ideas, and were oblivious to evidence and reasoning. Fortunately, such extreme audience behavior is the exception rather than the rule, but even lesser flaws in critical listening behavior can cause serious difficulties.

Throughout this course the skills and knowledge you acquire as you learn to prepare speeches will be useful also for analyzing and evaluating messages you receive. You will learn how to use and evaluate supporting materials and

Critical listeners never accept anything at face value. They question speakers and request support for assertions. Good speakers welcome such an exchange as a sign of interest and as an opportunity to clarify ideas.

different language resources in speeches. As you learn to prepare responsible arguments, you will also be learning how to evaluate the arguments of others. Although these topics will be covered in more depth in later chapters, we will preview some questions that should start you on the path to critical listening skills.

Questions for Critical Thinking and Analysis

Does the speaker simply make assertions and claims? Responsible communicators back up assertions and claims with supporting materials such as facts and figures, examples, testimony, and narratives. The "supporting materials" for Jim Jones's speeches were probably shaky at best. Messages without supporting materials should alert you to the possibility that something is amiss. Don't be hesitant about asking questions. Before they drank the cyanide, Jim Jones's followers first swallowed his unsupported assertions and claims.

Is the supporting material relevant, representative, recent, and reliable? Supporting materials should relate directly to the issue in question. They should be representative of the situation as it exists rather than exceptions to the rule. Facts and figures should be timely, a particularly important consideration when knowledge about a topic is changing rapidly. Supporting materials should come from reliable sources, ones that are trustworthy and competent in the subject area. Controversial material should be verified by more than one source. Because they were isolated in Central America, followers of Jim Jones had no way of knowing whether his claims were relevant, accurate, or reliable. He was their sole source of information.

Are credible sources cited? Responsible speakers present the credentials of their sources so that listeners can make independent judgments. When the sources' credentials are left out or described in vague terms, their testimony may be questionable. We recently found an advertisement for a health food product that contained "statements by doctors." A quick check of the current directory of the American Medical Association revealed that only one of the six doctors cited was a member of AMA and that his credentials were misrepresented. Always ask yourself, "Where does this information come from?" and "Are these sources qualified to speak on the topic?"

Is there a clear distinction among facts, inferences, and opinions? Recall that facts are verifiable units of information that can be confirmed by independent observation. Inferences make projections based on facts. Opinions add interpretations or judgments to facts: they tell us what someone thinks about a subject. For example, "Mary was late for class today" is a fact. "Mary will probably be late for class again tomorrow" is an inference. "Mary is an irresponsible student" is an opinion. It may sound easy to make these distinctions among facts, inferences, and opinions, but you must be constantly alert as a listener to detect accidental or intentional confusions of them in messages.

Is the language concrete and understandable or purposely vague? When speakers have something to hide, they often use vague or incomprehensible language. Introducing people who are not physicians as "doctors" in order to enhance their testimony on health subjects is just one form of such deception. Another trick is to use pseudoscientific jargon such as, "This supplement contains a gonadotropic hormone similar to pituitary extract in terms of its complex B vitamin–methionine ratio." If it sounds impressive but you don't know what it means, be careful.

Am I being asked to ignore reason? Although it is not unethical to use emotional appeals in a speech, reason should support the feeling. Examples that stress the emotional aspects of a situation may be used to humanize a topic, but information and logic should also justify the claims of a message.

The situation that triggered the mass suicide in Central America was a visit from California congressman Leo Ryan, who had heard that several of his constituents were being held there against their will. Jones ordered the murder of Ryan and the reporters who had accompanied him. In his speech advocating mass suicide, Jones said: "We can't go back, and they won't leave us alone. They're now going back to tell more lies, which means more congressmen. And there's no way, no way, we can survive."[15] In this speech the facts were fabricated, the logic crazed. Reason was not just ignored, but perverted.

Is the reasoning plausible? Plausible reasoning looks and sounds sensible. When reasoning is plausible, conclusions appear to follow from the points and supporting material that precede them. The basic assumptions that support arguments are those on which most rational people agree. Cause and effect are not confused with coincidence. Whenever reasoning doesn't seem plausible,

SPEAKER'S NOTES

Guides for Critical Thinking and Listening

1. *Require that statements and claims be supported* with facts and figures, testimony, examples, or narratives; insist that these be relevant, representative, recent, and reliable.

2. *Do not accept what anyone says at face value.* Examine the credentials of sources, particularly in terms of their competence and trustworthiness.

3. *Differentiate among facts, inferences, and opinions.*

4. *Be wary of language that seems purposely vague or incomprehensible.*

5. *Be on guard against claims that promise too much.*

6. *Look for plausible reasoning,* especially when messages arouse emotion.

7. *Be receptive to new ideas and perspectives* but scrutinize them carefully.

8. *Ask questions.* Responsible advocates welcome serious questions; others fear them and usually become defensive.

ask yourself why, and then question the speaker or consult with independent authorities before you make decisions or commit yourself.

Is the message believable, or does it promise too much? If an offer sounds too good to be true, it probably is. The health-food advertisement described previously contained the following claims: "The healing, rejuvenating and disease-fighting effects of this total nutrient are hard to believe, yet are fully documented. Aging, digestive upsets, prostrate [*sic*] diseases, sore throats, acne, fatigue, sexual problems, allergies, and a host of other problems have been successfully treated. . . . [It] is the only super perfect food on this earth. This statement has been proven so many times in the laboratories around the world by a chemical analyst that it is not subject to debate nor challenge." Maybe the product is also useful as a paint remover and gasoline additive.

How does this message fit with what I already know or believe? A good test of any message is whether it fits our previous knowledge or beliefs. Of course, we should be open to the possibility of new knowledge and realize that we have been wrong before. But when a message contradicts what we know and believe, we should be ready to apply critical thinking skills. Ask questions of the speaker and use the library to check information in the speech.

EVALUATING SPEECHES

You can use your critical listening skills to evaluate the speeches you hear in your class. During discussion following a speech, you may ask questions, comment on effective techniques, or offer suggestions for improvement. Your feedback always should be aimed at helping the speaker improve.

There is a difference between criticizing a speaker and giving a **critique**, or evaluation of a speech. Criticism often suggests an emphasis on what someone did wrong. This approach can create a negative, competitive communication environment. When you give a critique, your manner should be helpful and supportive. Give credit where credit is due. Point out strengths as well as

Figure 3.3
Guidelines for Evaluating Speeches

Commitment

Did the speaker seem committed to the topic?

Had the speaker done enough research?

Topic

Was the topic worthwhile?

Did the topic fit the assignment and the time limit?

Was the topic handled imaginatively?

Purpose

Was the purpose of the speech clear?

Audience involvement

Was the topic adapted to the audience?

Were you able to identify with the speaker and the topic?

Substance

Were the main points supported by evidence?

Were the examples clear and interesting?

Was the reasoning clear and correct?

Language

Was the language clear, simple, and direct?

Were grammar and pronunciations correct?

Was the language concrete and colorful?

Structure

Did the introduction spark your interest?

Was the speech easy to follow?

Was important information emphasized?

Were transitions used to tie the speech together?

Did the conclusion help you remember the message?

Presentation

Was the speaker enthusiastic?

Was the speech presented extemporaneously?

Did gestures and body language complement ideas?

Was the speaker's voice expressive?

Did the speaker maintain good eye contact?

Were notes used unobtrusively?

Were the rate and loudness appropriate to the material?

Ethics

Did this speech reveal its actual purpose?

Did the speaker discuss all options?

Would the consequences of this speech be desirable?

weaknesses. Whenever you point out a weakness or problem, you should also point out possible remedies or solutions. This type of interaction creates a classroom environment that stresses the willingness of students to help each other.

To participate in the evaluation of speeches, you need a set of criteria or standards to guide you. Your instructor may have a special set of criteria for grading your presentations, and the criteria may be weighted differently from assignment to assignment. For example, your instructor may assess your informative speeches primarily in terms of their structure and the adequacy of information and examples, but may evaluate your persuasive speeches more for your use of evidence and reasoning.

Regardless of what special criteria are involved, there are some general guidelines you can use to evaluate speeches. In Chapter 1 we discussed the factors that make a speech effective. You may wish to review that discussion at this time. These same factors may also be used to assess classroom speeches. Figure 3.3 presents these standard criteria.

IN SUMMARY

Listening is as vital to effective communication as speaking. *Critical listening* is more than just hearing. It is a learned skill that involves attending, hearing, comprehending, analyzing, remembering, and responding to a message. To become critical listeners, we must first overcome our listening problems. Then we must combine the skills of effective listening and critical thinking.

Benefits of Critical Listening.   Critical listening skills are important in school and work situations. They also make us less vulnerable to unethical advertising or to dishonest political communication. The critical listener is especially on guard against irrelevant or misleading appeals. There is a strong correlation between critical listening and success in life.

Overcoming Listening Problems.   Listening problems may arise from personal reactions, attitudes, or bad listening habits. Personal reactions to *trigger words* that set off strong negative or positive emotions can block effective listening. Both internal and external distractions can also interfere with listening, as can biased attitudes toward the speaker or topic. Bad habits, such as pretending we are listening when we are not or listening only for facts, can also impair our listening behavior.

Effective listening skills can be developed. The first step is to identify your listening problems. Next you should cultivate a "what's in it for me" attitude. Concentrate on the main ideas and the overall pattern of meaning in the speech. Strive for objectivity, withholding value judgments until you are certain you understand the message.

Critical Thinking and Listening. *Critical thinking* skills help you analyze and evaluate messages more effectively. Critical listeners question what they hear, require support for assertions and claims, and evaluate the credentials of sources. Critical listeners differentiate among facts, inferences, and opinions. They become wary when language seems incomprehensible or overly vague, when reason and rationality are absent in a message, or when a message promises too much. When what they hear does not fit with what they know, critical listeners pause, consider the message very carefully, and ask questions.

Evaluating Speeches. Speech evaluation takes the form of a *critique,* a positive and constructive effort to help the speaker improve. Criteria for speech evaluation include speaker commitment, choice of topic, clarity of purpose, audience involvement, substance, structure, language, presentation, and ethics.

TERMS TO KNOW

critical listening	filtering
denotative meaning	assimilation
connotative meaning	contrast effect
trigger words	critical thinking
listening log	critique

DISCUSSION

1. Complete the listening problems check list on page 60 of this chapter. Working in small groups, discuss your listening problems with the other members of the group. Develop a listening improvement plan for the three most common listening problems in your group. Report this plan to the rest of the class.

2. List three positive and three negative trigger words that provoke a strong emotional reaction when you hear them. One person should serve as recorder to write these words on the chalkboard. Try to group the words into categories, such as sexist or ethnic slurs, political terms, ideals, etc. Discuss why these words have such a strong impact on you. Do you feel your reactions to them are justified?

3. Think of a person (public speaker, teacher, etc.) to whom you like to listen. List all the adjectives you can that describe this person. Think of another person to whom you do not like to listen. List the adjectives that describe this person. Compare the two lists and share your conclusions with the class.

APPLICATION

1. Review the notes you have taken in one of your lecture courses. Are you able to identify the main points, or have you been trying to write down everything that was said? Compare your note taking before and after studying listening behavior. Can you see any difference?

2. Read the following paragraph carefully:

   Dirty Dick has been killed. The police have rounded up six suspects, all of whom are known criminals. All of them were near the scene of the crime at the approximate time that the murder took place. All had good motives for wanting Dirty Dick killed. However, Larcenous Lenny has been completely cleared of guilt.

   Now determine whether each of the following statements is true (T), false (F), or is an inference (?).

   T F ?   1. Larcenous Lenny is known to have been near the scene of the killing of Dirty Dick.
   T F ?   2. All six of the rounded-up gangsters were known to have been near the scene of the murder.
   T F ?   3. Only Larcenous Lenny has been cleared of guilt.
   T F ?   4. The police do not know who killed Dirty Dick.
   T F ?   5. Dirty Dick's murderer did not confess of his own free will.
   T F ?   6. It is known that the six suspects were in the vicinity of the cold-blooded assassination.
   T F ?   7. Larcenous Lenny did not kill Dirty Dick.
   T F ?   8. Dirty Dick is dead.

   The answers are found following the Notes at the end of the chapter. Were you able to distinguish between inferences and facts?

3. Prepare a critique of a speech by a prominent political or religious leader. What advice would you offer this person?

4. Evaluate a contemporary speaker on ethical grounds. Be sure to distinguish between ethical uses of speech techniques and the moral consequences of messages. Be prepared to present and defend your judgments in class.

NOTES

1. James J. Floyd, *Listening: A Practical Approach* (Glenview, Ill.: Scott, Foresman, 1985), p. 2.
2. Larry L. Barker, *Listening Behavior* (Englewood Cliffs, N.J.: Prentice-Hall, 1971), pp. 3–9.

3. Walter Pauk, *How to Study in College* (Boston: Houghton Mifflin, 1989), pp. 121–33.

4. W. B. Legge, "Listening, Intelligence, and School Achievement," in *Listening: Readings,* ed. S. Duker (Metuchen, N.J.: Scarecrow Press, 1971), pp. 121–33.

5. Gary T. Hunt and Louis P. Cusella, "A Field Study of Listening Needs in Organizations," *Communication Education* 32 (Oct. 1983): 399.

6. Andrew D. Wolvin and Carolyn Gwynn Coakley, *Listening,* 2nd ed. (Dubuque, Iowa: William C. Brown, 1985), p. 22.

7. Wolvin and Coakley, p. 177.

8. J. J. Makay and W. R. Brown, *The Rhetorical Dialogue: Contemporary Concepts and Cases* (Dubuque, Iowa: William C. Brown, 1972), pp. 125–45.

9. Jill Scott, "What Did you Say? I Was Listening to Your Tie," *English Journal* 73 (1984): 88.

10. Waldo Braden, "The Available Means of Persuasion: What Shall We Do About the Demand for Snake Oil?" in *The Rhetoric of Our Times,* ed. J. Jeffry Auer (New York: Appleton-Century-Crofts, 1969), pp. 178–84.

11. Kathleen Hall Jamieson and Karlyn Kohrs Campbell, *The Interplay of Influence: Mass Media and the Publics in News, Advertising, Politics,* 2nd ed. (Belmont, Calif.: Wadsworth, 1988), p. 4; and Anthony M. Casale and Phillip Lerman, *USA Today: Tracking Tomorrow's Trends* (Kansas City, Kans.: Andrews, McMeel & Parker, 1986), p. 19.

12. William F. Buckley, "Has TV Killed Off Great Oratory?" *TV Guide,* 12 February 1983, p. 38.

13. Floyd, pp. 23–25.

14. John Chaffee, *Thinking Critically,* 2nd ed. (Boston: Houghton Mifflin, 1988), p. 59.

15. Cited in James Reston, Jr., *Our Father Who Art in Hell* (New York: Times Books, 1981), p. 324.

Answers to Application item #2:   1. ?; 2. T; 3. ?; 4. ?; 5. ?; 6. ?; 7. ?; 8. T.

PREPARATION
— FOR —
PUBLIC SPEAKING

> *Oratory is the art of enchanting the soul, and therefore one who would be an orator has to learn the differences of human souls.*
>
> — *PLATO*

4

AUDIENCE ANALYSIS

— *AND* —

ADAPTATION

This Chapter Will Help You

◆ adapt your speech to environmental factors such as time, place, context, occasion, and audience size.

◆ adjust your message to audience demographics such as age, gender, education, group affiliations, and sociocultural background.

◆ plan for audience dynamics such as motivations, beliefs, values, and attitudes that influence the reception of your message.

Imagine that you are a company manager who must talk about the same project to different audiences. You are directing a study of employee promotion procedures and will make your first presentation to the board of directors. This group wants to know what the company will gain from your work. Next you must address the company's managers, who may feel that the new procedures will take away their power to reward good performance. Later you have to speak to representatives of the company's union. They will want to know how the new procedures will affect the seniority system and job security. The topic in each case is the same, but to be effective you must tailor your speech to the different interests of each audience.

Clearly, the needs of your listeners can have a profound effect on how you develop your speech and what you decide to say. Moreover, the setting for your speech can make a big difference in how you present it: your manner of presentation, as well as the language you choose, may vary from the executive board room to the union hall.

In this chapter we consider the audience for your speech and the setting in which you will speak. Considerations of audience and surroundings should affect every step of your preparation and presentation. As you research, you should look for examples the audience can relate to and experts whose advice or testimony they will accept. You need to develop a special sensitivity to your audience, so that your adaptation is intelligent and effective.

Who constitutes the actual audience for your speech? Your real audience is not just a collection of people who may gather to hear you talk. Rather, certain members of your audience are your intended listeners, the ones you want to hear you. Those who have gathered to listen will be different in many ways. They may differ in sex, age, education levels, interests, motivations, and attitudes. The more diverse the group, the more difficult it becomes to reach everyone present. Consequently, effective speakers will target their messages and appeals for maximum impact. The **target audience** for a speech is *that person or persons who are capable of making the speaker's words effective.* For example, in an antidrug speech you may be addressing both users and susceptible nonusers who might be tempted to start — these people are the target audience for your message, those you hope to influence or change. As you speak you may also reinforce the beliefs and attitudes of adamant nonusers, but they are not the target for your persuasive efforts.

Clearly, speakers must analyze the audiences they anticipate as carefully as the topics they select. *Indeed, careful consideration of the audience, who they are and what they need, will often influence the selection of topic.* As you analyze anticipated listeners during speech preparation, ask yourself the following questions:

- Who makes up my target audience?
- How important is my topic to these listeners? Do they already care about it? If they don't, how can I make them care?

- What particular aspects of the topic will be most relevant for them? How can I best gain and hold their interest and attention?

- What will listeners already know about my topic? What will they want to know? What do they need to know?

- How will my audience feel about the topic? Are they likely to be positive, neutral, or negative? How open will they be to new ideas?

- What do I share with my listeners? Are our needs, interests, beliefs, attitudes, or values similar? How can I build on this common ground to increase identification?

As you prepare and present your speech, you can make either *long-range* or *immediate* adjustments to the communication environment or audience. You make long-range adjustments as you prepare your speech. For example, you may believe your classmates have become so accustomed to emotional antidrug appeals that they no longer pay attention to them. Instead, you decide to give a speech that will focus on facts, careful inferences, and well-developed arguments to make your point. You believe this approach will make your speech different and interesting to listeners and allow it to make a contribution to the antidrug movement. However, on the day of your speech, you discover that you need to make some immediate adjustments. The room is hot and stuffy. The speech before yours was tedious, and the audience is drowsy. You realize you must speak more dramatically than you had planned, wake listeners up with your introduction, and cut some of the factual material you planned to use in your speech.

In this chapter we discuss (1) *external factors* in the communication environment, many of which may require immediate adjustments; (2) *demographic factors*, which are objective, observable traits of audience members; and (3) *audience dynamics*, or internal factors that influence listeners from within. The demographic and dynamics factors typically affect the long-range planning of the speech. We will consider these factors both in relation to your classroom audience and to other types of audiences you may encounter. Our aim is to prepare you to speak in the classroom and in the world beyond.

ADJUSTING TO THE COMMUNICATION ENVIRONMENT

The time, place, context, nature, and purpose of the occasion, and probable size of audience are all important considerations as you design and present your message. It is relatively easy to get information on these external factors, so we consider them here before moving on to the more complex aspects of audience analysis.

Time

The time of day you present your speech can be important.[1] If you have an early morning class or are speaking at a breakfast meeting, many of your listeners may be half asleep, and you will need some lively or startling examples to awaken them. If your speech is scheduled on a Monday, when people may not yet have readjusted to being back at work or school, you may need a light, bright touch to hold their attention. On a Friday you may need to be more direct and to the point to keep listeners' minds from drifting to the weekend ahead.

Even the time of year can influence audience response. Gloomy winter days and the balmy days of spring can put people in different frames of mind. As you consider such factors, think of the changes you can make to compensate for potential problems. For example, a bit more humor or a more forceful presentation might enliven an audience on a dreary day.

Place

You must also consider where you will give your speech. Will you be indoors or outside? If you are speaking outside, you may have to cope with weather problems or other distractions, such as animals, passing traffic, or even the beauty of the scenery. Your speech needs to be especially interesting or dramatic to hold your audience's attention in such surroundings.

Is the environment quiet or noisy? Even in a classroom speakers must learn to adjust to distracting noises — construction may be taking place on campus, or another class may have been released early and be making a lot of racket outside the room. In an office building you can often hear phones ringing or typewriters clattering. How can you cope with such distractions? If the problem is temporary, such as a helicopter passing overhead, you might pause until the noise abates. With constant noise the obvious solution is to speak louder. But if the competing sound is so loud you have to shout to be heard, you should pause and close the window or door. The important consideration is to take such problems in stride and not let them distract you from your purpose of communicating with your listeners.

Will the audience be seated or standing? If the seats are hard or people must stand throughout your speech, your message must be short and lively, or you may lose your audience. If listeners are wriggling in their seats or beginning to wander away, you will need to make some immediate adjustments in your speech to sustain attention.

The size of the room can also affect the audience's ability to hear you. Will you have access to a microphone? Will there be a lectern and a place to display any visual aids you might wish to use? If you need electronic equipment, will it be available? Always try to survey ahead of time the place where you will be giving your speech. Then you can make adjustments in advance.

Context

Anything that has happened in the immediate past becomes part of the context of your speech, and central to its communication environment. Recent speeches as well as recent events make up this context, which can influence how the audience responds to you.

The Context of Recent Speeches.   In the classroom the speeches that precede yours create an atmosphere in which you must work. This atmosphere can have a **preliminary tuning effect,** which may establish in your audience a predisposition to respond positively or negatively to your speech.[2] For speeches presented outside the classroom, the preliminary tuning is often carefully planned. At political rallies patriotic music and "spontaneous" demonstrations often tune the audience for the appearance of the featured speaker. The same effect may be observed at evangelical meetings, where music and prayer tune the audience, or at rock concerts, where warm-up groups prepare listeners for the star. Such planned preliminary tuning creates a mood and a sense of anticipation that favors the featured speaker or artist.

In the classroom preliminary tuning is more difficult to control. Sometimes instructors encourage an effective speaker to lead off, knowing that a good speech can create a positive atmosphere for those that follow and stimulate

Elie Wiesel, recipient of the 1986 Nobel Peace Prize, had to overcome many distractions when speaking at this Holocaust memorial service. But a compelling message, a sincere commitment, and a forceful presentation can help speakers cope with such problems as traffic noise and inclement weather.

others to do their best. This type of positive momentum also helps listeners become more receptive audiences. However, less successful speeches, especially if they come one after another, can set off a downward spiral that both speakers and listeners must work hard to reverse.

At times preliminary tuning may affect the mood of a classroom audience. If the speech immediately preceding yours was on a sensitive topic such as abortion, it may have aroused strong emotions. In this case you may need to ease the tension before you can expect the audience to turn their minds to your message. One way of handling such a problem is to acknowledge the reactions and use them as a springboard into your own speech:

> Well, it is obvious that many of us feel strongly about abortion. It's a subject that is very important to most of us. What I'm going to talk about is also very important — but it is something I think we can all agree on — the challenge of finding ways to stop the AIDS epidemic now sweeping across our country.

With lighter topics, you may want to use a humorous story to defuse tension and overcome negative preliminary tuning. You will have to use your judgment about whether it is appropriate to use humor. People who are angry or upset may not be in the mood for a joke.

In contrast, if the speech that preceded yours was light and humorous, whereas yours covers a more serious topic, you may also have to modify your introduction to get the audience in the proper frame of mind:

> Darren's descriptions of the hazards of break dancing were delightful, but I'd like to talk with you about something that isn't a laughing matter. In fact, it's become a matter of life or death on many college campuses: the problem of fraternity hazing that has gotten out of control.

In addition to dealing with the mood created by earlier speeches, you may also need to adapt your message to their content. Suppose you have spent the past four days preparing to discuss the advantages of air-bag safety restraints in automobiles. You are scheduled to speak third that day, and the first speaker gives a convincing presentation on the *disadvantages* of air-bag safety restraints. What can you do? Try to use such apparently negative preliminary tuning to your advantage. Again, the answer lies in adjusting your introduction. Point out that the earlier speech has established the importance of the topic but that — as good as that effort was — it did not give the total picture: "Now, you will hear the *other* side of the story."

The Context of Recent Events.   As listeners enter the room the day of your speech, they bring with them information about recent local, national, and international events. This knowledge forms a context that they will use to evaluate and react to what you say. Not being up-to-date on recent events relevant to your topic can have serious consequences. A student in one of our classes once presented a very interesting and well-researched speech comparing public housing in Germany with that in the United States. She was able to add firsthand knowledge to her research since she had lived in Germany for several years. Unfortunately, she was unaware of a current scandal involving local public housing. For three days before her presentation, the story had made front-page headlines in the local paper and was the lead-off story in area newscasts. Everyone in the class seemed to know about it but her, and everyone expected her to mention it. Her failure to incorporate this important local material weakened her credibility.

In contrast, Rod Nishikawa used a recent tragedy to lead into his persuasive speech urging greater controls on the sale and ownership of automatic weapons. Shortly before his speech, a crazed gunman using such a weapon had killed or injured a number of children in a school yard in Stockton, California. Rod presented a very effective speech urging his classmates at the University of California–Davis to contact their local representatives in support of pending gun-control legislation. Because Stockton is near Davis, his references to the nearby massacre evoked vivid images. The message is clear: as a speaker you should stay abreast of news relevant to your subject.

At times the context to which you must adjust your speech may be problematic. The answer is to try to turn problems into advantages — make the context work *for* you rather than *against* you. During the 1985 graduation at Loyola Marymount University, the institution's president fell off the platform immediately before the commencement address. The speaker, Peter Ueberroth, organizer of the 1984 summer Olympic Games, recaptured the audience's attention and brought down the house by awarding the president a 4.5 in gymnastics.[3]

SPEAKER'S NOTES

Questions to Ask about the Speech Occasion

1. Will the time of the speech pose any problems?

2. Are the room arrangements adequate? Will I have all the equipment I may need?

3. Is there any late-breaking news on my topic?

4. What does the audience expect on this occasion?

5. Will there be other speakers or activities preceding my presentation?

6. How large will the audience be?

Nature and Purpose of the Occasion

In preparing your speech you must also consider why listeners have gathered and what they expect. People have rather definite ideas about what is and is not appropriate for specific speech occasions. If the speaker does not deliver what the audience anticipates, the speech is likely to be judged inappropriate. At best listeners will be puzzled by the speaker's behavior: at worst they will be seriously put off. For example, if an audience has been led to expect an informative lecture and hears instead a sales pitch, some listeners may become annoyed.

Size of Audience

The larger your audience, the more diverse it is apt to be and the more you may need to target specific subgroups to achieve maximum effectiveness. The size of the audience will likely call for modifications in your manner of presentation. With small audiences (under fifteen people) you get more feedback and can interact more effectively. It is easier to make and maintain eye contact with nearly everyone present. Small audiences are typically more receptive to an informal style of presentation. You can even ask questions and solicit audience response, modifying your presentation on the spot if necessary. Standing at a lectern and never deviating from your formally prepared presentation may seem inappropriate, creating a barrier to effective communication.

On the other hand, the larger your audience, the more formal your presentation will need to be. With a larger audience casualness may be interpreted as lack of preparation or of serious purpose. Speak more slowly and loudly, enunciating your words more carefully, when you are addressing a large group. Because you cannot make or sustain eye contact with everyone, select representative listeners in various sections of the audience and change your visual focus from time to time. Establishing eye contact with listeners in all sections of the room helps more people feel included. With a larger group your gestures must be more emphatic so that everyone can see them, and any visual aids you use must be large enough that those in the back of the audience can understand them without strain.

ADJUSTING TO AUDIENCE DEMOGRAPHICS

The demographic make-up of your audience includes such objective characteristics as their age range, gender, education level, group affiliations, and sociocultural background. Knowing these factors can help you plan and prepare your speech. If you are familiar with the group you are addressing, you can plot their demographics rather easily. If not, ask the person who invited you to describe the group. You might also talk with group members or contact others who have addressed them.

Gathering information systematically about such characteristics is called **demographic audience analysis.** During political campaigns demographic analyses are often conducted so that a candidate can tailor speeches to fit particular audiences. In the college classroom situation such information can help you estimate audience interest in your topic, how much listeners may already know about it, how they may feel about it, and how you might best motivate them to listen. Figure 4.1 is a sample of a questionnaire that might be useful in demographic audience analysis. Your instructor may choose to conduct such an analysis early in the term and distribute the results to the class. If introductory speeches were presented in your class, they should also have provided useful demographic data. All such information, combined with timely insights from public opinion and consumer surveys, can help you adjust your message more precisely to your anticipated audience.[4] The demographic information you gather may be useful in helping you focus your topic, but the different factors may vary in relevance from topic to topic. For example, if you were speaking on "Government Services — Yours for the Taking," age might be an important consideration but sex or religious preference might be irrelevant.

Age

Age has been used to predict audience reactions from the time of Aristotle, who suggested that young listeners are optimistic, trusting, idealistic, and easily persuaded. The elderly, he said, are more set in their ways, more skeptical, cynical, and concerned with maintaining a comfortable existence. Those in the prime of life, Aristotle suggested, present a balance between youth and age, being confident yet cautious, judging cases by the facts, and taking all things in moderation.[5]

Contemporary communication research demonstrates the relationship between age and persuasibility that Aristotle predicted. Maximum susceptibility to persuasion occurs during childhood and declines as people grow older.[6] Psychological research also suggests that younger people are more flexible and open to new ideas, while older people tend to be more conservative and less receptive to change.[7]

What expectations might you have about your classroom audience? To begin with, the average college student is getting older. In 1987, 16 percent of college students were over 35; by 1997 this figure is expected to rise to 22 percent.[8] If your audience contains both younger and older students, you may need to consider your topic selections and speech strategies with this fact in mind. As an example, if your audience consists mainly of eighteen year olds,

Figure 4.1
Audience Analysis Questionnaire

Sex: M F Age _____ Academic Year: FR SO JR SR GPA _____ Race _____

Marital status _____ Religious preference _____

Major _____ State lived in longest _____

Current job (full- or part-time) _____ Hours per week _____

Career aspirations _____

Persons I admire most (male) _____ (female) _____

Political preferences (liberal, conservative, moderate) (Democrat, Republican, other)
                            (*circle one*)   (*circle one*)

Group memberships (occupational, political, religious, or social) _____

_____

Father's occupation _____ Mother's occupation _____

Place of birth _____ Places lived _____

Travel _____

Hobbies _____

Positive "trigger words" _____

Negative "trigger words" _____

The most important thing in my life right now is _____

Topics on which I would like to hear an informative speech (name three) _____

_____

Topics on which I would like to hear a persuasive speech (name three) _____

_____

they may be interested in a speech on campus social activities. But if your audience is composed more of older students, this topic could seem trivial or uninteresting.

What else does contemporary research tell us about college students? They are optimistic about the future.[9] They want good jobs that pay well. And although political conservatism is alive and well on campus, students are fairly liberal when it comes to sexual freedom, sexual equality, and racial issues. Family ties are important: 85 percent of those surveyed expect to marry, and 88 percent want children. Information like this can be helpful as you plan a speech, but keep in mind that these impressions are based on national survey data. Your listeners may be different. Find out as much as you can about *them* so that you can tailor your messages effectively.

Gender

In our rapidly changing society, gender is a less effective predictor of audience behavior than it was in the past. Traditional attitudes about "appropriate" roles and interests are changing rapidly. For instance, automobiles have traditionally been considered a "male domain," yet women now buy 40 percent of all new cars and help decide on the purchase of another 40 percent.[10] Similarly, 57 percent of all first-time New York Stock Exchange investors are women.[11] Politics are also changing: a higher percentage of women than men now vote, and more and more women are seeking and being elected to public office.[12] Formerly "male" professions are now attracting women at a rapid rate; the number of women working as engineers or computer programmers is increasing dramatically.[13] Such rapid changes in our culture suggest that you should be careful about making assumptions based on the gender of your listeners.

One assumption you can make, however, is that most women and many men in your audience will find sexual stereotyping and sexist language objectionable. **Sexual stereotyping** occurs when broad generalizations are made about men and women based on outmoded assumptions, such as "women don't understand investments," or "men don't know how to take care of babies." Although men and women are different, sexual stereotyping implies that these differences justify discrimination. You should be especially careful not to portray gender roles in ways suggesting superiority and inferiority.

Sexist language involves the use of masculine nouns or pronouns in situations where the gender is unknown or irrelevant — a case in point would be referring to "man's advances in science" or using *he* when the intended reference is to both sexes. You can correct this tendency simply by saying "she or he" or by converting the subject into the plural "they." As noted in Chapter 3, sexist language may also involve using emotional trigger words, such as calling adult females "girls." If your listeners find your use of such language offensive, they may reject both you and your message. The lesson is clear: avoid sexual stereotyping and sexist language in your speeches.

Educational Level

Educational level may better indicate listeners' knowledge and interests than age and gender. The more education audience members have, the more you can assume they know about general topics and current affairs. According to the research in this area, they are likely to be more concerned with social, consumer, and environmental issues and more active in politics. Similarly, the higher the educational level of your listeners, the broader their range of interests is likely to be. They will probably enjoy active sports such as golf, tennis, backpacking, and jogging, and spend less time watching television than their less well-educated counterparts. Finally, better-educated audiences are usually more open-minded. They are apt to be more accepting of social and technological changes and more liberal in their attitudes toward women's rights.[14]

These educational differences also suggest that certain strategies may be more effective than others in speeches. Better-educated audiences will be more critical listeners than those with less education. If there is more than one position on an issue or more than one option available, you should assume that they will be aware of these possibilities. Because your classroom audience will fall within the better-educated range, it is best to acknowledge alternatives and then explain carefully why you have selected your position.[15] Research your topic responsibly and supply evidence and examples that can stand up under close scrutiny. If you are not well prepared, your perceived competence or trustworthiness may suffer.

Group Affiliations

The groups we belong to tell a lot about us. Therefore, memberships in occupational, political, religious, and social groups are often good predictors of audience interests and knowledge. Group membership implies shared interests, attitudes, and values.

Occupational Groups.   Occupational groups have special interests that unite their members. For example, members of the Speech Communication Association are concerned with matters related to their profession such as educational policies and practices, ethics in communication, freedom of speech, and opportunities for research. In industrial organizations union members are typically concerned with matters of seniority, salary, fringe benefits, and working conditions.

The similarity of interests of occupational groups, however, goes beyond job-related concerns. People within occupational groups also frequently share leisure activities, civic concerns, and even reading and television-viewing habits.[16] Knowing your listeners' occupational affiliations, or in the case of your classmates their occupational aspirations, can suggest the type of examples that should work best in your speeches or the authorities your audience will accept. If many of your classmates are business majors, for instance, you could decide to use testimony from Lee Iacocca.

Occupational group membership can also provide insight into how much your audience knows about a topic and which aspects of it should be more interesting to them. It can even suggest the wording of your speech. For example, a speech on tax-saving techniques given to professional writers and then to certified public accountants should not have the same focus for both groups. With the writers you might want to stress record keeping and business deductions and avoid technical jargon. With the CPAs you might concentrate on factors that lead to audits by the IRS, and you would not have to be so concerned about translating technical terms into lay language.

Unless you are attending a highly specialized school, your classroom audience will probably contain students majoring in everything from accounting to zoology. It will be helpful for you to know the occupational aspirations of your classmates and what type of jobs they hold while attending college. Let this information help you select topics, choose examples, find authorities your listeners should respect, and suggest the kind of language you use.

Political Groups. Membership in political organizations or political party preference can also be useful sources of information.[17] Members of organized political groups are typically interested in policies and problems of public life. Although inferences about individuals can miss the mark, Democrats tend to show greater interest in social and domestic programs than Republicans, who are often more concerned with business interests and individual initiative.

People with strong political ties usually make their feelings known. Some of your classmates may be members of the Young Democrats or Young Republicans on campus. Your college may conduct mock elections or take straw votes on issues of political interest, reporting the results in the campus newspaper. Be alert for information that might be helpful in preparing your speeches.

Religious Groups. Religious group membership can be important because religious training is one of the primary means of instilling values. These values form the foundations of many social attitudes. Members of fundamentalist religious groups are likely to have conservative religious, social, and political attitudes. Baptists tend to be more conservative than Episcopalians, who in turn are often more conservative than Unitarians. In addition, a denomination may advocate specific beliefs that most of its members accept as a part of their religious heritage. You might expect audiences that are primarily Roman Catholic to have more negative attitudes toward abortion and birth control because these are part of the church's teachings.

Americans consider their religious preferences to be personal rather than public issues. Consequently, audiences may be quite sensitive on topics that touch their religious convictions. As a speaker you should be aware of this sensitivity and attuned to the religious make-up of your anticipated audience. Appealing to "Christian" values before an audience that includes members of other religious groups is one way to insult listeners unnecessarily and perhaps create a boomerang effect.

Even in church-sponsored colleges you cannot always rely on uniformity of religious belief or on the influence of religion on social attitudes. A *USA Today* survey of college students indicated no differences in alcohol or drug use between students attending religious and those attending nonreligious institutions, although those enrolled in church-affiliated colleges were twice as likely to have a "great deal of faith in organized religion" and only half as likely to have a live-in romantic relationship.[18] However, since religious affiliation may be a strong indicator of values, it is wise not to ignore its potential importance as a demographic factor.

Social Groups. Membership in social groups can be as important to people as any other kind of affiliation. Typically, we are born into a religious group, raised in a certain political environment, and end up in an occupation as much by chance as by design. But we choose our social groups on the basis of our interests. Photographers join the Film Club, business people become involved with the Chamber of Commerce, outdoor enthusiasts may be members of the Sierra Club, feminists may join the National Organization for Women.

SPEAKER'S NOTES

Questions to Ask about Audience Demographics

1. What is the average age of audience members? Is this relevant to my subject?

2. What is the gender make-up of the audience? Should this be an important consideration?

3. How well educated are listeners?

4. What occupational groups are represented in the audience?

5. What social-group memberships are important to the audience?

6. What sociocultural factors should I take into account?

Knowing which social groups are represented in your audience and what they stand for is important for effective audience adaptation. A speech favoring pollution-control measures might take a different focus depending on whether it is presented to the Chamber of Commerce or to the Audubon Society. With the Chamber of Commerce you might stress the importance of a clean environment in inducing businesses to relocate in your community; with the Audubon Society you might emphasize the effects of pollution on wildlife. People tend to make their important group memberships known to others around them. Be alert to such information from your classmates and consider it in planning and preparing your speeches.

Sociocultural Background

The sociocultural background of an audience includes everything from the section of the country in which the audience lives to its racial composition. People from different sociocultural backgrounds have different experiences, interests, and ways of looking at things. If your audience is composed primarily of urbanites, it may be difficult for you to create much interest in farm-support programs. Similarly, a rural audience might find it hard to identify with the problems of rush-hour commuting. A basically white, middle-class audience could have difficulty understanding what it means to grow up in a minority ghetto. Midwesterners and southerners may have misconceptions about each other.

If your topic involves interests and issues that are alien to your audience, you will need to establish common ground among issues, listeners, and yourself as speaker by using supporting materials that highlight similarities of experience. Interesting personal stories or humorous anecdotes that audiences can enjoy together often create a sense of identification. It will also help if you demonstrate to audience members that they share a common stake in problems that may at first seem distant. Those who want to arouse concern in America for the anti-apartheid movement in South Africa must overcome barriers of race, culture, and physical distance to create identification. Examples that reveal the humanity of the black South Africans victimized by apartheid can help to bridge that sociocultural gap.

Most college classes represent a diversity of backgrounds that presents a special challenge to speakers. You must seek out a common denominator that will help you reach the majority without offending the minority. Your appeals and examples may have to be more general, calling on those experiences, feelings, and motivations that people hold in common. It may be helpful to envision smaller audiences within the larger group. You may even want to direct specific remarks to these smaller groups. You might say, for example, "Let me tell you liberal arts majors what computer skills you'll need to survive the '90s," or "Let me warn you business majors that large corporations are looking for people with breadth of perspective." Such direct references to specific subgroups within the audience can keep your speech from seeming too general.

If your classmates gave introductory speeches, you may have a good idea of the diversity of their backgrounds and interests. When you accept invitations to speak outside the classroom, ask questions about the age, gender, education level, group affiliations, and sociocultural background of your anticipated audience. The more information you have about listeners, the better you should be able to adapt your message and the better it should be received.

ADAPTING TO AUDIENCE DYNAMICS

Although demographic factors are an important part of any audience analysis, you should also consider the forces shaping audiences that arise within the listeners themselves. These powerful internal sources of influence mean that you must understand **audience dynamics:** the motivations, attitudes, beliefs, and values that influence the behavior of listeners.

Motivation

Our needs, wants, and wishes constitute **motivation,** the force that impels us to action and directs our behavior toward specific goals. When we think of motivation in public speaking, we may think first of its use in persuasive messages. Making people aware of a need, and then showing them a way to satisfy it, is a major persuasive strategy. But motivational appeals are also vital in informative speeches. *People will listen, learn, and retain your message only if you can relate it to their needs, wants, or wishes.* You must understand these aspects of human behavior so that you can adapt your speeches to accommodate them.

All people share certain motivations, but these can vary in importance according to particular personal and social situations.[19] If you have recently entered a new school or moved to a new town, your desire to make friends may be very important and may lead you to seek out places where you can meet others. At such times you may be unusually susceptible to advertising that links products to friendship. Similarly, if you find yourself living on a minimum-subsistence budget, as many college students do, you may be more receptive to information on money-saving menus and other suggestions on how to "make it through the crunch." When your financial status changes, these motivations will become less important. The importance of specific motivations can also change across time with shifts in social or political conditions. One group of psychologists reported that between 1957 and 1976 women developed increasing needs for achievement and autonomy.[20] These changes are consistent with the increasing feminist consciousness in our culture. The sensitive speaker will be aware of such changes.

Not only can personal and social situations affect your need or desire for certain things, but your interest in them can also be aroused either purposefully or accidentally. Suppose you have just eaten a very satisfying meal and are not the least bit hungry. When someone enters the room with a tray of freshly baked chocolate chip cookies, the sight and smell of these goodies can be enough to make you want some, even though you don't need more nourishment. Astute speakers use motivational appeals to make their ideas and proposals enticing, even for listeners not originally interested.

In an extensive, classic study of human motivation, Henry A. Murray and his associates at the Harvard Psychological Clinic catalogued more than twenty-five different human motives.[21] You can appeal to many of them in your speeches. The motives listed below may be helpful in understanding audience dynamics.

Comfort.   The need for comfort involves such things as having enough to eat and drink, keeping warm when it's cold and cool when it's hot, and being free from pain. Advertisements often appeal to these needs. Storm window manufacturers contrast a warm interior scene complete with a fireplace and children playing on the floor with the cold, snowy weather outside. Over-the-counter-drug advertisements stress the way to spell *relief!* If you can show listeners that your topic could increase their comfort, you'll have most of them sitting up and listening. Such speech topics could include "Meals in Your Room: The Alternative to Cafeteria Food" or "No Pain, No Gain? How to Stay Fit without Hurting."

Safety.   All of us need to feel free from threats to our well-being. Rising crime rates, environmental pollution, natural disasters, and accidents are major sources of concern. Such needs are often the focus of advertising. Dead-bolt lock ads arouse fears over safety: "Can your door be opened with a credit card? Johnson's Safety Locks are jimmy-proof!" Water-filtering-device ads stress security from contamination. Antilock automobile brakes are touted as reducing injuries from accidents. Such appeals rely on awakening the audience's sense of fear, but you should be cautious when using them. If you arouse too much anxiety in listeners, they may resent it, particularly if your message does not provide clear instructions on how the danger can be averted or overcome. Examples of speech topics that appeal to safety needs are "What to Do When the Sirens Go Off: Some Practical Advice for Coping with Tornadoes" and "Protecting Yourself from Rape."

Friendship. People need other people to give and receive affection and companionship. This need explains our desire to join with others in groups and take pride in our affiliations. It may also underlie our longing for romantic relationships. Probably the most prevalent appeal in American advertising is to our need for association with others.[22] We want to "join the Pepsi generation" so that we won't be left out of the fun. Some speech topics based on the need for friendship include "New Interests, New Friends: Finding Your Place on Campus," "Love Makes the World Go 'Round: A Look at Computer Dating Services," and "Overcoming Loneliness: Volunteers Help Others While Helping Themselves."

Recognition. Most people like to be treated as valuable and important; they like others to acknowledge their existence and accomplishments. They often place great value on trophies or awards as signs of earned respect. Advertisements that associate their products with elegant homes, expensive cars, or luxury boats appeal to this need. By buying the product, we too — the ads suggest — will be worthy of recognition. We are told that using MasterCard will give us "clout," and an American Express card tells others that we are important people (even if they don't recognize our face). Recognition appeals in speeches may stimulate pride in either individual or group accomplishments. Speakers touch this need when they find clever ways to compliment the audience — an advisable tactic when the speaker is not well known or uncertain of acceptance.

Variety. Too much of anything — even a good thing — can be dull. If you had steak to eat every night, you might find yourself longing for a hot dog. Our

---

SPEAKER'S NOTES   *Questions to Ask about*
                                        Audience Dynamics

1. What needs, wants, or wishes are important to this audience?

2. What do my listeners believe about my subject? Are their beliefs based on information or misinformation?

3. What attitudes toward the subject are represented in the audience? Are listeners positively disposed, negatively disposed, or neutral?

4. What values are important to my audience? What values do I share with my listeners, especially with the target audience?

need for variety may manifest itself in a longing for adventure, a desire to do something different and exciting, a yen to travel to exotic places or to meet new and interesting people. A 1986 Roper poll suggested that the most prevalent topic of people's daydreams was traveling abroad.[23] Advertisers recognize our need for variety. Exotic locales lure us into purchasing a special perfume. Sailors consume instant Maxwell House coffee on solo trips around the world. We may not be able to share directly in these adventures, but we can at least enjoy a sense of participation by buying the products associated with them. Offering your audience an opportunity to satisfy its desire for variety can help you attract and hold their attention. Speech topics that appeal to this need include "Break Away over Spring Break: Try Skiing for a Change!" or "Around the World at the Dinner Table!"

Control.   No one likes to feel buffeted by forces beyond his or her control. All of us like to feel we have some say over our destiny. Data from a *USA Today* survey suggest that gaining control over our lives may be one of the major motivations of the 1990s.[24] The strong desire to achieve control may place us in competition with others. Razor-blade manufacturers promise that their product will give you "that winning edge." Speeches that show listeners how they can gain control typically have a strong appeal. Examples of such speech topics are "Five Steps to Leadership" or "Managing Your Time Better: Taking Control of Your Life."

Independence.   Although we need other people, we also want to feel that we can stand on our own — that we do not have to rely on others to help us. The idea that we can improve ourselves by hard work is so deeply engrained in our society that we find it hard to resist in advertising or speeches. Virginia Slims ads trace women's climb from subservience into independence — and connect that somehow in a positive way with smoking! Speeches that show the audience "how to do it yourself" often appeal to this need.

Curiosity.   We want to understand the world and the people around us, so we look for the causes of events and try to figure out why people act as they do.[25] According to a group of prominent psychologists, we are likely to seek the causes of highly unusual or unpleasant events or anything that creates doubt about the future.[26] We may be drawn to watching television coverage of catastrophes, not because we enjoy watching people suffer, but because we are curious about such events (especially if we live in an area subject to storms or earthquakes). Speech topics that are unusual, that explain the causes of events or behaviors, or that discuss fears about the future may satisfy this need.

Tradition.   Most people value things that give them a sense of roots. Though we may seek novelty or variety in some areas of our lives, there are certain things we don't want to change. Thanksgiving dinner is supposed to be turkey and dressing, cranberries, and pumpkin pie. Even couples who have lived together for a long period of time may want a traditional wedding ceremony to signal the totality of their commitment. Advertisements often draw on such traditions or call on cultural heroes or myths. Kool-aid tells us "You loved it as a kid, you trust it as a mother." The Marlboro Man still rides his horse on the American frontier. Showing your audience that you share its traditions, that you value many of the same things it values, can be important to creating identification in speeches.

Success. The need for achievement and accomplishment is one of the most thoroughly studied human motives.[27] Although winning may not be everything, most of us feel that losing doesn't have much to recommend it. Thus, self-improvement books glut the market. We can share success vicariously with our sports heroes if we rent Hertz cars like O. J. Simpson or drink Coke like "Mean Joe" Greene. Speeches that show your audience how they can improve themselves and enhance their chances in life touch on this important motivator. Some sample topics include "Making It in the '90s: The Jobs for the Future" or "Six Quick Tips for Better Studying: How to Improve Your Grades."

Nurturance. It makes people feel good to be able to care for, protect, and comfort the helpless or the less fortunate. Did you ever notice how many ads have babies, small children, or animals in them? Although many of these appeals are directed especially to women, not all are. In his essay on advertising appeals, Fowles points out that "all over America [there] are businessmen who don't know why they dial Qantas Airlines when they have to take a trans-Pacific trip; the koala bear knows."[28] Speech topics that depend on our desire to nurture might include "Help Yourself and Others by Donating Blood" and "Wanted for Worthy Cause: Student Volunteers!"

Enjoyment. People do need to have fun occasionally, especially college students who may find themselves inundated with assignments, tests, and papers, not to mention full- or part-time work. Advertisers appeal to this need when they urge us to "grab all the Gusto we can" because we'll "only go around once," and we surely "deserve a break today." If you can show listeners how to bring pleasure into their lives, you can be sure of sustaining their attention. Here are some sample topics: "Fifteen-Minute Time-outs: Life's Short Pleasures" and "Weekend Break-aways: The Alternative to Long, Expensive Vacations."

Incorporating any of these motivational appeals into your speeches can help arouse attention, sustain interest in your message, and influence or persuade listeners. The use of such appeals is basic to the persuasive speech design known as the *motivated sequence,* which we discuss in detail in Chapter 13, "The Nature and Kinds of Persuasive Speaking."

Attitudes, Beliefs, and Values

When we use the word *attitude,* we are typically referring to our feelings about something — whether we like or dislike, approve or disapprove of people, places, events, or ideas. Actually, an attitude is more than just a feeling.[29] **Attitudes** also include our **beliefs** — what we know or think we know about a subject — and the way we are predisposed to act towards it. For example, you may have an attitude that favors affirmative action for minorities. This could lead you to welcome any speech supporting that policy without considering the merits of the ideas offered. Similarly, a negative attitude toward a particular ethnic group could predispose you to avoid interacting with its members. Such an attitude might also make it difficult for you to accept positive information about individual members of that group.

Our important social attitudes are anchored by our **values,** how we think we should behave or what we regard as an ideal state of being.[30] These ideals guide much of our thinking and behavior. Because they underlie our most important beliefs and attitudes, values are frequently invoked in political speeches.[31] In his speech accepting the nomination as Republican presidential

A partisan audience usually responds enthusiastically to speakers who reaffirm its sentiments. References to shared values can increase listener/speaker identification. Information about the attitudes, beliefs, and values of your target audience can help you adapt your message for maximum effectiveness.

candidate in 1980, Ronald Reagan emphasized the following American values: the work ethic, family, freedom, peace, and a strong America. Values combine with love of traditions to form a powerful source of *proofs* for persuasive speeches, discussed in Chapter 14, "Evidence, Proof, and Argument."

Information about your audience's values, beliefs, and attitudes can be very useful in planning your speeches. References to shared values can increase identification between the speaker and the audience and can enhance the persuasive impact of a speech.[32] Knowledge of your audience's beliefs can reveal what new information you need to supply or what misinformation you should correct. Understanding your listeners' attitudes toward your topic can suggest strategies to get a fair hearing for your message. For example, suppose you are preparing a speech opposing capital punishment, and you know that most members of your audience strongly favor this practice. Audiences that have negative attitudes toward your position may distort your message, discredit you as a communicator, or even refuse to listen to you. Audience attitudes can affect the way listeners receive informative as well as persuasive messages. Understanding these facts, how can you maintain your position and still reach listeners? One technique for dealing with a negative audience stresses establishing identification between speaker and audience, avoiding the use of threats, relying mainly on rational appeals, limiting what you hope to accomplish, and acknowledging opposing positions.[33] This and other strategies for handling reluctant audiences are discussed in detail in Chapter 13.

How can you find out about your audience's values, beliefs, and attitudes? In the classroom it is not very difficult because people can hardly open their mouths without revealing this kind of information. Classroom discussions following earlier speeches should provide valuable cues. Outside the classroom such information may be harder to obtain. However, as you question the person who invites you to speak concerning audience demographics, insights about audience beliefs should also emerge. You can ask specific questions about audience beliefs, values, and attitudes related to your topic.

IN SUMMARY

The audience and the communication environment for your speech can affect what you present and how you present it. Consideration of these factors can cause you to make long-range, in-depth adjustments to your message. The situation you actually encounter at the time of your speech may also necessitate immediate, on-the-spot adjustments of the message you present.

Adjusting to the Communication Environment.   Environmental factors you should consider include the time and place of your speech. Previous speeches and current events form a context that influences the interpretation and reception of your message. Additionally, audiences often have specific expectations about what types of speeches are appropriate for certain occasions. If you violate these expectations, you may have problems. Finally, the size of your audience may affect how you present your speech.

Adjusting to Audience Demographics. Your *target audience* includes those listeners whose responses can make your words effective. As you consider this audience, analyze its interest in, knowledge of, and attitudes toward your topic. Knowing the demographic composition of your audience provides insights into its interests, knowledge, and attitudes. Important factors that you should consider in *demographic audience analysis* include age, gender, educational level, group membership, and sociocultural factors such as race and social class.

Adapting to Audience Dynamics. An understanding of human *motivation* can also enhance your ability to adapt your message to your audience. Tying your topic to the needs, wants, and wishes of your listeners can help you gain their attention and maintain their interest, as well as move them toward action. Some motivational appeals you may want to use in speeches are comfort, safety, friendship, recognition, variety, control, independence, curiosity, tradition, success, nurturance, and enjoyment.

Your audience's *attitudes, beliefs,* and *values* can affect the way your message is received and interpreted. If your audience is very negative toward your topic, you may have to adjust your message to receive a fair hearing.

TERMS TO KNOW

target audience
preliminary tuning effect
demographic audience analysis
sexual stereotyping
sexist language
audience dynamics
motivation
attitudes
beliefs
values

DISCUSSION

1. How might the following situations affect a speech you are about to give, and how would you adapt to them?

   a. You are the last speaker during the last class period before the Thanksgiving holiday.

    b. A lost student walks into the class right in the middle of your speech, looks around, says, "Excuse me," and walks out.

    c. The speaker right before you gives an incredibly successful speech, which brings spontaneous applause from the class and high praise from the instructor.

    d. The speaker right before you bombs badly. The speech is poorly prepared, the speaker is very nervous and simply stops in the middle and sits down, visibly upset.

    e. (It rarely happens, but . . .) The speaker right before you gives a speech on the same topic, taking the same general approach.

2. Bring to class an example of an advertisement that exemplifies sexual stereotyping or the use of sexist language. Discuss why such techniques might be used and who the target audience might be. In your opinion what is the effect of such language? Do you think the ad is successful?

3. Rank the twelve human needs discussed in this chapter in terms of their power as motivators for you. Discuss how the three needs you ranked highest might make you susceptible to certain speech topics and approaches.

4. Construct a hypothetical person who represents the average student at your school in age, gender, educational background, group affiliations, and sociocultural background. What speech topics would this hypothetical person find most interesting? What motives, values, and attitudes might this person bring to these topics?

APPLICATION

1. Explain how you would tailor a speech on the general topic of food for an audience of

    a. high school sophomores
    b. senior citizens
    c. student dieticians
    d. football players

2. If you were to speak on the general topic of food, what kinds of examples might you develop to appeal to the following audience needs?

    a. safety
    b. friendship
    c. variety
    d. tradition

3. You have been invited to speak before the Futures Club of your city. Using the following information about your audience, what will be your topic and purpose and what major strategies will you follow in your speech?

a. *Speech occasion:* The occasion will be a weekly meeting of the Futures Club, a group of business people interested in forecasting trends and encouraging those that seem most beneficial to the community. The meeting consists of a luncheon, an officer's report, and your speech, in that order. You should plan for a fifteen-minute presentation. There will be a time for questions and discussion following your speech. The luncheon will be held in a large dining room of a downtown hotel. A speaker's lectern will be provided, and distractions should be minimal. There will be fifty to sixty people present. At the meeting before your speech, the Futures Club heard an advocate of "gray rights" urge reforms that will help older Americans. Before that, they heard a state senator present an agenda for major legislation in the next decade. They should be interested in your view as a student of what should be conserved and what should be changed in the future. However, you are free to select your own topic and frame your own purpose.

b. *Demographics:* The typical Futures Club member is thirty-five-years old, a highly successful, rapidly rising executive in a local firm. Membership is 60 percent male, 40 percent female. The typical member is a college graduate. Many graduated with honors, and a few have advanced degrees. The members are "joiners" — many are boating, golf, and tennis enthusiasts and belong to various clubs promoting these interests. Republicans outnumber Democrats two to one. Religious commitments are not particularly intense: if there is any preferred faith, it is Episcopalian. Most of the members come from white, upper-middle-class families that expected them to succeed. A few have rebelled against this background and are tolerated in the club as a kind of maverick element. The club has five or six black members. Three years ago members realized (with some embarrassment) that there were no Asian or Hispanic members. These ethnic groups are now represented.

c. *Dynamics:* Economically, the club members are well off, although their marriages are often unstable. They have intense needs for friendship, recognition, and success. The Futures Club itself helps to satisfy these needs. The members do not fear change, and they have powerful impulses toward control and independence. Their attitudes and values are flexible and somewhat pragmatic: they value programs that produce measurable results. They share a desire to see qualitative improvements in the life of the community, and they want to be part of a positive movement toward such change.

NOTES

1. James W. Gibson and Michael S. Hanna, *Audience Analysis: A Programmed Approach to Receiver Behavior* (Englewood Cliffs, N.J.: Prentice-Hall, 1976), pp. 25–26.

2. For more about preliminary tuning, see Theodore Clevenger, Jr., *Audience Analysis* (Indianapolis: Bobbs-Merrill, 1966), pp. 11–12.

3. Reported in *Time,* 17 June 1985, p. 68.

4. James Atlas, "Beyond Demographics," *The Atlantic Monthly* (Oct. 1984): 49–58.

5. *The Rhetoric of Aristotle,* trans. Lane Cooper (New York: Appleton-Century-Crofts, 1960), pp. 131–37.

6. William J. McGuire, "Attitudes and Attitude Change," in *The Handbook of Social Psychology,* vol. 2, ed. Gardner Lindzey and Elliot Aronson (New York: Random House, 1985), pp. 287–88.

7. Milton Rokeach, *The Open and Closed Mind* (New York: Basic Books, 1960).

8. Anita Manning, "Adults Are Giving the Old College Try," *USA Today,* 12 September 1989, pp. D1–2. The publication *American Demographics* is an excellent source of recent survey information.

9. Anthony M. Casale and Philip Lerman, *USA Today: Tracking Tomorrow's Trends* (Kansas City, Mo.: Andrews, McMeel & Parker, 1986), pp. 150–83.

10. Casale and Lerman, p. 47.

11. Ibid.

12. Ibid., p. 10.

13. Ibid., p. 56.

14. P. Schonback, *Education and Intergroup Attitudes* (London: Academic Press, 1981); Rokeach, *The Open and Closed Mind;* Arnold Mitchell, *The Nine American Lifestyles: Who We Are and Where We're Going* (New York: Macmillan, 1983); and Atlas, "Beyond Demographics."

15. McGuire, pp. 271–72.

16. Vernon G. Zunker, *Career Counseling: Applied Concepts of Life Planning* (Monterey, Calif.: Brooks Cole, 1981), pp. 120–23.

17. For a detailed analysis of this topic, see Donald R. Kinder and David O. Sears, "Public Opinion and Political Action," in *The Handbook of Social Psychology,* vol. 2, pp. 659–741.

18. Casale and Lerman, pp. 172–83.

19. The material in this section is based on the work of John P. Houston et al., *Invitation to Psychology,* 3rd ed. (San Diego: Harcourt Brace Jovanovich, 1989); Abraham H. Maslow, *Motivation and Personality,* 2nd ed. (New York: Harper & Row, 1970); and Janusz Reykowski, "Social Motivation," *Annual Review of Psychology,* 33 (1982).

20. J. Veroff et al., "Comparison of American Motives: 1957 versus 1976," *Journal of Personality and Social Psychology* 39 (1980): 1249–62.

21. Henry A. Murray, *Explorations in Personality* (New York: Oxford University Press, 1938).

22. Jib Fowles, "Advertising's Fifteen Basic Appeals," *Et cetera* 39, no. 3 (Fall 1982); reprinted in Robert Atwan, Barry Orton, and William Vesterman, *American Mass Media: Industries and Issues,* 3rd ed. (New York: Random House, 1986), pp. 43–54.

23. Tom Biracree and Nancy Biracree, *Almanac of the American People* (New York: Facts on File, 1988), p. 35.

24. Casale and Lerman, pp. 34–35.

25. B. Weiner, "A Cognitive (Attribution)-Emotion-Action Model of Motivated Behavior," *Journal of Personality and Social Psychology* 39 (1980): 186–200.

26. Houston et al., p. 366.

27. J. W. Atkinson, *Personality, Motivation, and Action* (New York: Praeger, 1983).

28. Fowles, p. 48.

29. McGuire, pp. 235–53.

30. Milton Rokeach, *Beliefs, Attitudes, and Values: A Theory of Organization and Change* (San Francisco: Jossey-Bass, 1970), pp. 109–32; and *The Nature of Human Values* (New York: Free Press, 1973), pp. 26–52.

31. See, for example, Henry E. McGuckin, Jr., "A Value Analysis of Richard Nixon's 1952 Campaign Fund Speech," *Southern Speech Communication Journal* 33 (1968): 259–69; and Wayne N. Thompson, "Barbara Jordan's Keynote Address: The Juxtaposition of Contradictory Values," *Southern Speech Communication Journal* 44 (1979): 223–32.

32. Henry Z. Scheele, "Ronald Reagan's 1980 Acceptance Address: A Focus on American Values," *Western Speech Communication Journal* 48 (1984): 51–61.

33. Herbert W. Simons, *Persuasion: Understanding, Practice, and Analysis,* 2nd ed. (Reading, Mass.: Addison-Wesley, 1986), pp. 121–39.

> *Learn, compare, collect the facts! . . .*
> *Always have the courage to say*
> *to yourself — I am ignorant.*
>
> — *IVAR PETROVICH PAVLOV*

5

SELECTING

—— _AND_ ——

RESEARCHING YOUR TOPIC

This Chapter Will Help You

- ◆ select a topic that is meaningful and that suits the audience and occasion.

- ◆ focus on the general purpose, specific purpose, and thematic statement for your speech.

- ◆ find sources of responsible knowledge to add substance to your speech.

"I have to speak for *five whole minutes?* What can I talk about for that long? What do I know enough about to sound reasonably intelligent?" Your instructor has just given you your assignment. You are to prepare an informative speech on a subject of your choice. Your stomach starts to tighten as you worry. "Speech about what? How do I *begin?*"

Don't succumb to panic and head for the "drop" office or the High Sierras! There are systematic ways to find a good topic, develop your speech purpose, and expand your knowledge so you can make an informed and responsible presentation. This chapter will introduce you to these techniques.

In order to find the right approach, you must first understand the nature of a good speech topic. Your topic must be meaningful and substantive — one that is important both in its own right and important to you personally. The topic must also be appropriately adapted to its audience. Finally, the topic must be one on which you can acquire *responsible knowledge.*

A good speech topic is meaningful. Your topic need not concern an earth-shaking issue to be worthwhile, but it should affect your audience or community, or be an issue on which you believe the audience should be informed. Trivial topics, such as "How to Make Popcorn in a Microwave," waste the time of both speakers and listeners. Additionally, the topic should be important to you personally. In preparing your speech, you will invest many hours thinking, researching, organizing, and practicing. To make such an investment requires a real commitment on your part. If your topic is not important to you, you will find it hard to make this investment. Personal commitment also helps the presentation of your speech. People who speak on topics to which they are committed seem more sincere and enthusiastic. Their enthusiasm is contagious. It carries over to listeners and gets them involved in the message.

A good speech topic is adapted to its audience. Analysis of your audience should go hand-in-hand with topic selection. As you put together your information on audience demographics and dynamics, ask yourself such questions as, "What are their interests and concerns? What is happening that they should know about?"

If you combine what you have learned from your audience analysis with information from earlier speeches and class discussions, you should have a good idea of your listeners' interests. Perhaps one of your classmates gave a speech honoring his family doctor's sense of caring. The speech sparked a lively discussion and started you thinking about your own less pleasant experiences with doctors. There could be a potential speech topic lurking in these related ideas. You could develop an informative speech on the relationship between personal physician care and patient recovery or a persuasive speech advocating training in interpersonal skills for physicians. If you have a topic in mind but are not sure your audience will share your enthusiasm, then you must try to generate interest. You may need to show your listeners how this topic affects them personally and what they stand to gain from your message.

A good speech topic also fits the time, place, and purpose of the speech. It should meet the audience's expectations about what is appropriate for the occasion. A celebration in honor of a friend is *not* the time to deliver a political tirade.

A good speech topic is one that you can learn enough about to speak on responsibly. When you select a complex subject, you must focus on some *manageable aspect* of it for your presentation. Instead of trying to cover all the problems involved in the disposal of nuclear waste, it would be better to limit yourself to discussing your state's role in nuclear waste disposal. That topic would be more manageable and also more meaningful for your audience.

SELECTING A GOOD TOPIC

The goal of a topic search is to identify an idea that justifies your speaking and others' listening. To find the right topic, you may need to work through several stages of the discovery process, including

1. charting your own interests and the interests of your listeners;

2. analyzing potential topics to refine and focus them;

3. selecting one topic on the basis of its meaningfulness, its audience appropriateness, and your ability to acquire responsible knowledge of it.

Charting Interests

The best way to begin your search is to develop lists of your own interests and those of your listeners as revealed in class discussions and the first speeches. You can employ the same kind of questions you used to generate ideas for introductory speeches.

1. Are you interested in *places?*

2. Are you interested in *people?*

3. What *activities* do you enjoy?

4. What *events* are foremost in your mind?

5. What *work* do you do or hope to do?

6. What are your long- and short-range *goals?*

7. What *values* are important to you?

8. What *problems* concern you most?

A chart of your interests might look like that in Figure 5.1.

Figure 5.1
Interest Chart

Places	People	Activities	Events
Grand Tetons	Uncle Benny	camping	U.S.-Soviet summit
Dinosaur Monument	Jesse Jackson	writing poetry	earthquakes
Wounded Knee	Manuel Noriega	collecting comics	rock concerts
Santa Fe	Judy Garland	boating	Earth Day
Washington, D.C.	Barbara Bush	traveling	trip on Green River
	Dan Quayle	movies	fall of Berlin wall

Work	Goals	Values	Problems
fast-food service	complete college	peace in world	air + water pollution
selling boats	own boat business	close family ties	endangered species
political campaigning	have a family	equality	sex discrimination
campus radio announcing	visit Mexico over spring break	kindness	cigarette smoking
			drug addiction
			global warming

Getting Ideas from the Popular Media

Another way to develop a potential list of speech topics is to use newspapers, magazines, or television to stimulate your thinking. Go through the Sunday newspaper, scan *Time* or *Newsweek,* or watch the evening news on television. Study the headlines, titles, advertisements, and pictures. What catches your attention? What might be adapted to the interests or needs of your audience?

One student developed an idea for a speech after seeing an advertisement for bank services. The ad stirred some unpleasant memories of writing a check that bounced. This experience suggested a speech on keeping better personal records. His problem was getting listeners to see the importance of this topic to their lives. His solution was to develop an introduction that startled the audience into attention.

Last month I committed a crime! I wrote a bad check, and it bounced. The check was for $4.67 to a local grocery store where I bought the ingredients for a spaghetti supper. The bank charged me $15.00 for the overdraft, and the store charged me $10.00 to retrieve my bad check. That was the most expensive spaghetti dinner I've ever eaten!

The headline "Travel Money Tips Offered" might inspire a speech entitled "Champagne Travel on a Beer Budget." The personals section in the classifieds might prompt a speech on the dangers of computer-dating services.

You must be careful not to misuse media sources for generating topics. The media can direct you to ideas for speeches, but they do not provide the speeches for you. You can't simply read an interesting article, then summarize it for presentation. Use the article as a starting point. Search out more information. *Your* speech must be designed to appeal to *your* specific audience. You should always bring something new to your subject — a fresh insight or an application to the lives of your listeners.

Matching Your Interests to Your Audience

After you have charted your own interests, make a similar chart of apparent audience interests as revealed by class discussion and your demographic analysis. What places, people, events, activities, work, goals, values, and problems concern them? Now study the two charts together, looking for possible points of convergence in order to pinpoint your best topic possibilities. To do this systematically, make a three-column *topic inventory chart*. In the first column (personal interests), list those topics from your personal interest list and media search that you find most appealing. In the second column (audience interests), list those topics suggested by demographic analysis and class discussion. In the third column (possible topics), match columns one and two to produce speech possibilities. Figure 5.2 shows a sample topic inventory chart.

In this example your interests in travel and camping are matched with the audience's interest in unusual places and developed into a possible speech topic: "Camping in the Rockies — Getting Off the Beaten Path." Similarly, your concerns for good health and smoking are paired with the audience's interests in physical fitness and deceptive advertising to generate another possibility: "'You've Come a Long Way, Baby!': The Effects of Cigarette Smoking on Women." Your interest in movies could combine with audience interests in leisure and investments to lead to the topic "Movies Are Big Business." Not all of your interests or those of your audience will result in possible topics. It is the *matching* of these interests that concerns you.

Analyzing Your Topic

Once you have identified possible topic areas, you must determine your specific speech topic. Going from a general to a specific topic involves focusing on those aspects that would be most interesting or appropriate for your audience. One systematic way to approach *topic analysis* is to ask yourself the questions news reporters use to assure that they investigate a story thoroughly. The writer Rudyard Kipling described the questions in this poem:

Figure 5.2
Topic Inventory Chart

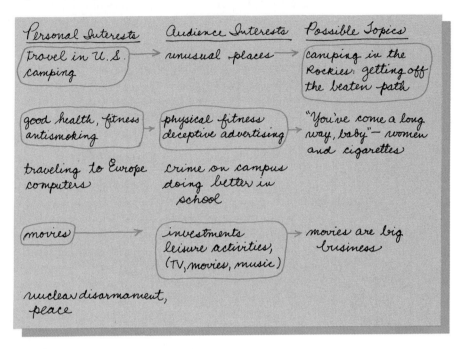

I keep six honest serving-men
(They taught me all I knew);
Their names are What and Why and When
And How and Where and Who.[1]

Formulating these questions in connection with a topic area can help you better identify specific speech topics. The questions may also suggest specific directions for your research. Not all the questions will apply equally well to every topic, but by working through the list systematically, you should be able to develop several specific possibilities. Let's take "movies" as a topic area and see where these "six honest serving-men" might lead us:

Who invented movies? Who produces movies? Who writes scripts? Who directs movies? Who acts in movies? Who attends movies? Who watches movies on television? Who makes the most money from movies? Who edits the film? Who runs the camera? Who designs the sets? Who designs the costumes? Who chooses a location for filming?

What are movies? Are they a form of entertainment, a means of education, or an instrument of persuasion? What is the difference between movies made for television and movies made for theaters? What are the differences between "art" movies and popular movies? What do people like best in movies? What happened to movies when television became popular? What has happened to the old-time movie houses?

When and *where* are movies made? When were movies invented? When did talking movies start? When did Technicolor become popular? When did Hollywood develop as the movie capital? Where are the new centers of movie making? Where are movies premiered? When are movies released to television?

Why are movies made? Are they for entertainment only? Is the motivation usually to make money? Why do people go to movies? Why do people watch the same movie more than once? Why do scholars study movies?

How are movies made? How are special effects created? How do people train for movie careers? How do movies influence us? How is money raised to produce movies? How much does it cost to produce a movie? How long does it take to make a movie? How are actors selected? How are women portrayed in movies? How are minorities portrayed in movies?

As you cover the six prompts, write down as many questions about your topic as you can. Do not be satisfied too quickly — these questions may lead to additional topic possibilities. For example, "What Has Happened to the Old-time Movie Houses?" could lead you to "Has One Been Restored or Renovated in Our City?" This question might then emerge as the speech topic "The Rebirth of the Orpheum: A Grand Old Theater Gets a Second Chance."

As you look through your questions, you may notice that some of them form clusters. For example, questions about how money is raised to produce movies, how much money it costs to produce them, and who makes the most money in the process could reinforce the selection of "Movies Are Big Business."

Our example describes a search for an informative speech topic. The same types of questions can be used to analyze topics for persuasive speeches. Because persuasion often addresses problems, you can simply change the focus of the questions and add some areas that are specific to persuasive situations:

Who is involved in this problem?

What issues characterize the situation?

Why did the problem arise?

Where is this problem happening?

When did the problem begin?

How is this problem affecting people?

How is this problem like or unlike previous problems?

How extensive is the problem?

What options are available for dealing with the problem?

Selecting Your Topic

After you have completed your interest charts and analyzed your subject, two or three specific topics should emerge as important and appealing possibilities. Now you should ask:

- Does this topic fit the nature of the assignment?
- Can I give this speech in the time available?
- Can I learn enough about this topic to give a responsible speech?
- Why do I want to give a speech on this topic?

The final question on this list is especially important because it tests whether you have a clear idea of your own motives in developing a certain speech and helps you determine your purpose.

Determining Your Purpose

"Why do I want to give a speech on this topic?" Your answers to this question suggest the **purpose** of your speech. You will be able to develop a successful speech only when your purpose is clear.

To gain a clear understanding of your purpose, you must focus on your topic as though your mind were a microscope. You look through one lens and see the topic and your purpose in a broad, hazy outline. Replace that lens with another, and now you can see this topic-purpose interaction in sharper detail. Replace the second lens with a third, and now you can see to the heart of your message.

General Purpose

The broad and hazy outline seen through the first lens is the **general purpose** of your speech. The general purpose is often assigned for your classroom speeches. For example, you may be asked to prepare a speech *to inform* or *to persuade.* If you are to inform, your general purpose is to share knowledge with your audience. If you are to persuade, your general purpose is to influence the thinking or behavior of listeners.

The general purpose of a speech is usually stated as an infinitive: *to* inform, *to* persuade. This reflects the nature of public speaking as an activity that has consequences for listeners. It calls attention to the audience because there must be someone *to* inform or *to* persuade. This active way of stating the general purpose symbolizes the importance of the audience as you plan a speech.

When speaking outside the classroom, the general purpose may be left for you to decide. You may be asked to address a group because you are a specialist on a subject, because you are a respected member of the community, or simply because you have a good reputation as a speaker. When this happens, you will have to determine your own general purpose, taking into account the audience and the occasion. For example, if your audience knows very little about your topic, you might decide that your general purpose should be to inform these listeners. If the topic demands a change in public policy, your general purpose could be to persuade them to action. Good sense will usually point you to the right general purpose.

Specific Purpose

The second lens of your microscope focuses on your **specific purpose.** Your specific purpose indicates what kind of response you want from your audience, what you want to accomplish. It identifies what you want listeners to understand, believe, or do. Having your specific purpose clearly in mind helps direct your research toward relevant information so that you don't waste time searching for materials that will not be useful.

You should be able to state your specific purpose clearly and succinctly as a single idea. For instance, a speech on movies might have one of the following specific purposes:

to inform my listeners why war movies remain popular

or

to persuade my audience to resist censorship of movies
in our community

How can you tell if you have selected a good specific purpose? Your specific purpose should focus on those aspects of your topic that are most relevant or interesting to your audience. It should also enrich the audience by offering new information and ideas or new advice. You waste time and energy when you try to inform listeners about things they already know or convince them of things they already believe. A good specific purpose will be ambitious. Audiences appreciate speakers who take risks — who avoid trivial or stale topics. Just as Olympic divers receive higher scores for executing more difficult dives, classroom speeches that take chances usually earn more respect from the audience (and often higher grades!).

Finally, your specific purpose should be manageable in the time allotted to you. In a five-minute speech you have only about seven hundred words to get your message across. *If you can't cover the material in the time allowed,*

SPEAKER'S NOTES

Questions for Finding a Specific Purpose

1. Is this specific purpose *important* enough to deserve attention?

2. Does this specific purpose offer my listeners *new* information or advice?

3. Is the specific purpose *ambitious,* or is it trivial and stale?

4. Is the specific purpose *manageable* in the time allotted?

then your purpose may not be specific enough. You will need to narrow your focus to some aspect you can handle.

Let's look at some examples of poor specific-purpose statements and see how they might be improved:

poor	To inform my audience of the influence of television on our lives.
improved	To inform my audience of the impact of television on women's desire to achieve.
poor	To persuade my audience that driving while drinking is dangerous.
improved	To persuade my audience to accept the idea of *responsible* drinking and driving.

In our first example, the specific purpose "the influence of television on our lives" is *poor* because it is too general for a short classroom speech. It does not narrow the topic enough. Entire books have been written on the influence of television; you could not possibly cover the topic in a short presentation. Moreover, it does not specify what aspect of television's influence you will discuss. With this *nonspecific* purpose you could prepare a speech on the impact of cartoons on children's aggressiveness, on the relationship between television viewing and academic achievement, on the "couch potato syndrome," or on a multitude of other topics. The *improved* specific purpose limits the topic so that it can be handled within the time permitted. This helps you concentrate your research efforts on those materials most useful to your speech.

The second *poor* specific purpose is also too general. Furthermore, it would not enrich the audience. It would be hard to find anyone who would argue that driving while drinking is not dangerous. Even more, the subject may be overworked. Unless the speaker can offer a fresh perspective, there may be problems maintaining attention or motivating the audience. The *improved* specific purpose is more limited in scope and offers something new to the audience: the concept of *responsible* drinking and driving. (See Betty Nichols's speech in Appendix B.)

Thematic Statement

The third lens in your mental microscope focuses your **thematic statement.** The thematic statement should bring the heart of your message into sharp detail. *It should specify precisely what you want your audience to learn or accept, and it should identify the main point or points you will develop in your speech.* You should be able to condense these ideas without strain into a single declarative sentence. Often the thematic statement is worked into the beginning of your speech as a preview of what will follow. At times speakers may leave the thematic statement unstated, to be constructed by listeners from cues within the speech. Note, for example, how Cecile Larson left the thematic statement implicit in her speech, "The 'Monument' at Wounded Knee," which appears in Appendix B. Speakers may leave the thematic statement unstated in order to create a special dramatic or ironic effect. Long ago Aristotle observed that the satisfaction listeners experience from discovering a meaning for themselves can lead them to accept the message. The danger of leaving the thematic statement implicit is that some listeners may misunderstand the speaker's intention. Regardless of how and whether it appears directly in the speech, unless you have a clear thematic statement in mind your speech is apt to wander and never accomplish its goal.

The following examples show how thematic statements go a step beyond specific purposes in focusing the central ideas of speeches.

> *Specific purpose:* To inform my audience of the impact of television on women's desire to achieve.
> *Thematic statement:* The lack of heroines in prime-time television shows leaves young women without appropriate role models for achievement.

> *Specific purpose:* To persuade my audience to accept the idea of *responsible* drinking and driving.
> *Thematic statement:* You should practice responsible drinking and driving by knowing your tolerance for alcohol, having a designated driver, and not letting friends drive while intoxicated.

Let us now look at the process of moving from general topic area to thematic statement to see how these evolve in speech preparation:

Topic area: Vacations in the United States

Topic: Camping in the Rockies

General purpose: To inform

Specific purpose: To inform my audience that there are beautiful, uncrowded places to camp in the Rockies.

Thematic statement: Three beautiful, uncrowded camping areas in the Rockies are Bridger-Teton National Forest in Wyoming, St. Charles Canyon in Idaho, and Dinosaur National Monument in Utah.

With the purposes and major ideas clearly specified, a speech titled "Camping in the Rockies: Getting off the Beaten Path" might take the following form:

Introductory Material	(Horror story about crowded camping at Jenny Lake in the Grand Tetons.)
Transition and Thematic Statement	Not every place is like this. Let me tell you about some places I found on a camping trip last summer. Three of the most interesting, beautiful, and uncrowded were Bridger-Teton National Forest in Wyoming, St. Charles Canyon in Idaho, and the Dinosaur National Monument in Utah.
Main Points	1. Bridger-Teton National Forest at Slide Lake has a magnificent view of the Tetons.
	2. St. Charles Canyon on a white-water stream offers the ultimate in seclusion.
	3. At Dinosaur National Monument you can watch the excavation of gigantic skeletons that are millions of years old.
Transition and Conclusion	There are interesting, beautiful, and uncrowded places to camp if you know where to look. Try the National Forest Service campgrounds or national monuments rather than the overcrowded national parks. (Relate account of a peaceful camping experience to balance the horror story in the introduction.)

Although the thematic statement appears in the foregoing example, you will note that the speaker *does not* begin with "My thematic statement is. . . ." Rather, it is artfully worked into the introduction, where it indicates the main points the speech will develop. It also suggests that this speech may give us interesting facts, illustrated by vivid examples and perhaps by action stories. Moreover, it tells us what kind of informative speech we will hear (descriptive) and implies the overall design or pattern the speech will follow (categorical).

With such a clearly drawn thematic statement, the speaker can now engage in focused research to acquire responsible knowledge of the topic. In this case the speaker might use pamphlets, brochures, or books purchased at the sites mentioned; national-recreation-area attendance figures from almanacs; and materials available in the government documents section of the library.

ACQUIRING RESPONSIBLE KNOWLEDGE

Your research for a speech may begin long before you frame your thematic statement. Indeed, in order to determine your specific purpose and the major points you should address, you may have to find out more about your topic. Once you have your specific purpose and thematic statement clearly in mind, you can begin that concentrated phase of research that will provide **responsible knowledge** for your speech. Responsible knowledge of a topic includes information on or about

- its main issues or points of interest;
- what the most respected authorities say;
- the latest major developments;
- local concerns or applications of special interest to *your* audience.

Although you cannot become an authority on most topics with ten hours or even ten days of research, you can learn enough to speak responsibly. Your research should result in your knowing more than the rest of the class about your topic. The sources of information available to you are your own knowledge and experiences, library resources, and interviews. Each of these sources can supply facts, testimony, examples, or narratives to use as supporting materials in your speech.

Personal Experience

You should begin your research by taking stock of what you already know about your topic. Personal experience and firsthand knowledge add credibility, authenticity, and freshness to a speech. As valuable as personal knowledge is, however, you should not depend on it as your *sole* source of information because it may be limited or unreliable. Your experiences may not be truly representative. As you read or hear what others have to say on your topic, you should be willing to correct your previous impressions if they prove to be narrow or distorted.

You can actively seek out personal experience that will add credibility to your speech. Suppose you want to deliver a speech on how television news shows are put together. You could arrange to visit a nearby station that produces a live newscast. Take in the noise, the action, and the excitement that occur before and during a show — this atmosphere can enrich your speech.

You must take the initiative to arrange such experiences. For example, if you want to give a speech on the boredom of assembly-line work, you might phone a local union for help in gaining firsthand exposure. To test this recommendation, we phoned the local Labor Council headquarters and talked with a union leader, who said the problem of worker boredom was acute in many local industries. We then asked if his office would help student speakers who wanted to arrange interviews with workers or make visits to plants. He responded enthusiastically, "Just tell the students to give us a call." Such willingness to cooperate is understandable. Any large organization likes favorable publicity. As a speaker, you control part of that publicity. You will never be more aware of the power of public speaking than when someone "rolls out the red carpet" to make the kind of favorable impression they hope will surface in your speech.

Although personal experience is often a good starting point for your research, it is rarely enough to support an entire speech. To fill in the gaps and verify your knowledge and information, you next should turn to library resources.

Library Research

Although knowledge obtained from the library may lack the excitement and immediacy that personal experience provides, it has definite advantages. Library research can give you a broad perspective and a sound basis for speaking responsibly. It can extend, correct, and enrich your experience by acquainting you with others' experience and knowledge.

Most college and large municipal libraries have the following major research resources to help you:

1. *Catalog* of books and major publications alphabetized by author, title, and subject, either on cards or on computer terminals.

2. *Reference room* containing timely information and bound or computerized indexes to magazines, newspapers, and journals.

3. *Government documents area* containing federal, state, and local government publications.

4. *Nonprint media archives* of films, videotapes, recordings, and microfilms.

5. *Special collections areas* with materials that can help you adapt your topic to local needs and interests.

Reading the best books on your topic can give you a deeper understanding and make your speech more authoritative. Library research is the key to acquiring responsible knowledge.

6. *Computerized search services* to provide bibliographic assistance.

7. *Holding areas,* or stacks, where books and bound volumes of periodicals are shelved.

With such a multitude of resources available, it can be difficult to know where to begin your research. The most valuable resource in any library is the professional librarian, who can steer you to the most appropriate sources of information in *your* library for *your* topic. The following review of library resources focuses on the special needs of student speakers, who must spend their limited research time to best advantage.

Reference Room.   The first stop in your quest for responsible knowledge should be the reference room, which has convenient guides to timely and concentrated sources of information. The reference librarian may be able to steer you to the most useful sources of information for your research. Some of the materials you will find useful are described below.

Encyclopedias.   Encyclopedias can either be general or about a specific subject. They are most helpful in providing background information or historical perspectives on your topic. Encyclopedias are less useful on current issues and are not the best sources of testimony or examples. Among the prominent general encyclopedias are

Encyclopaedia Britannica
World Book Encyclopedia
Great Soviet Encyclopedia (compare its perspective on social or political issues with the others)

Subject-specific encyclopedias include

Encyclopedia of Religion and Ethics
International Encyclopedia of the Social Sciences
Encyclopedia of World Art
Encyclopedia of Education

Sources of Current Facts.   Up-to-date information is important to many topics. You must be aware of recent events related to your topic, or you may damage your credibility with the audience. For the most recent information, start with a newspaper index such as the *New York Times Index.* The reference librarian can steer you to the best indexing services available in your library. These indexes identify articles published during a given period of time. Who won this year's Nobel Peace Prize? How are *glasnost* and *perestroika* affecting world trade? The index will tell you where articles related to such questions can be found in the newspaper and may also provide a summary of the article. For even more up-to-date information, look through current issues of *Time, Newsweek,* or other relevant weekly or monthly publications. An easy-to-use source of recent information is *Facts on File,* which reports weekly on current events by topical categories.

Other Indexes and Abstracts.   Periodical indexes direct you to magazine and journal articles on your topic. These articles may not always be current, but they provide depth of information. They often reduce situations, issues, and arguments to the essentials. In addition, the books and authors mentioned in the articles can lead you to other sources of information. *Abstracts* provide a summary of the articles that may help you determine their relevance to your purpose.

Indexes and abstracts range from the highly specialized to the very general. Your reference librarian can direct you to the source most suitable to your topic. The following indexes and abstracts are frequently used:

Reader's Guide to Periodical Literature contains author and subject references to articles in over 175 popular periodicals. This source is especially useful for speakers because these articles are written for a general readership that is probably similar to the type of audience you will have in class. The magazines indexed attract reputable writers and experts and will add credibility to your speech when cited. Where is acid rain a problem and what is being done about it? How is increased attendance affecting the environment in our national parks? *Reader's Guide* can direct you to articles that might contain the answers to these questions.

Business Periodicals Index covers a wide range of business and economic magazines and journals and is helpful for speeches on topics like career choices, sales techniques, or advertising appeals.

Public Affairs Information Service (PAIS) publishes an index that covers periodicals, pamphlets, and other documents reporting on civic and governmental issues that range from land use policy to tax reform.

Social Sciences Index covers articles you may find useful on topics involving social problems.

Index to Journals in Communication Studies includes references to topics particularly interesting to communication students. What made Abraham Lincoln an effective speaker? What are the major arguments used to promote nuclear disarmament? What can be done about communication apprehension? Articles addressing these and similar questions are indexed here.

Atlases. If your topic calls for geographical information or comparisons among regions and areas, you may wish to consult an atlas like *The Times Atlas of the World.* Such atlases contain more than just maps; they often include information on issues such as religious preference by states, population density of countries, or the agricultural or industrial production of a given area. Such an atlas may also suggest designs for effective visual aids.

Biographical Information. You can find out about noteworthy people by consulting one of the many biographical resources found in most libraries. The *Who's Who* series provides brief information on important living people; the *Dictionary of American Biography* covers famous Americans of the past. *Current Biography* contains longer essays on people who are prominent in the news.

Books of Quotations. Quotations are especially useful in speeches. Quotations from famous sources are indexed by topic and author in such books as *Bartlett's Familiar Quotations, The Oxford Dictionary of Quotations,* and *Simpson's Contemporary Quotations.*

Almanacs, Yearbooks, and Directories. Almanacs provide compilations of facts and figures on a wide range of topics. What movies were the biggest hits in the 1940s? What was the strongest earthquake ever to rock the United

States? Who is the director of the Boston Pops? You can find this kind of information in an almanac like *The Information Please Almanac, The World Almanac,* or the *Book of Facts.* Yearbooks such as the *Statistical Abstract of the United States* provide data on everything from the annual catch of abalone to the yearly production of zinc. Directories like the *Encyclopedia of Associations* tell you about the members, leaders, and functions of organizations.

Vertical File.   Many libraries maintain a clipping and filing service on topics of local interest, usually referred to as the "vertical file." The vertical file might contain pamphlets, newspaper clippings, or magazine stories on prominent people and important happenings in your area. Also check to see if your local or campus newspaper has such a service (often called the "morgue" of the newspaper).

Government Documents.   Most government documents are housed in their own section of the library. These documents provide more in-depth information than that found in most almanacs. Such material includes reports on congressional hearings, legislation, and proceedings; the proclamations, orders, and other formal statements of the president; and opinions and decisions of the Supreme Court. Some of the major government publications include

> *Congressional Record,* which contains a daily account of the proceedings of Congress.
>
> *Federal Register* of proclamations and orders of the president and regulations of various departments of government.
>
> *United States Reports,* which records opinions and decisions of the Supreme Court.
>
> *Monthly Catalog of United States Government Publications,* the master list of government documents.
>
> *Selected Rand Abstracts,* a guide to unclassified reports, papers, and books of the Rand Corporation, which conducts government-sponsored studies.
>
> *American Statistics Index,* a master guide to government statistical publications.
>
> *Undex (United Nations Document Index),* which covers publications issued by the United Nations.

Computerized Search Services.   Many libraries now have a computerized card catalog that allows you to conduct research from one convenient place. Some libraries have a computerized newspaper index such as *The Na-*

tional Newspaper Index or a periodical index such as *Infotrac,* which covers both general publications and government documents. To conduct a search, you simply type in your subject and push the computer key labeled "search." The references to articles on your subject then appear on the screen. Some of the references contain abstracts as well as bibliographic information. A printer attached to the computer allows you to print out your references. Many of the articles are available on microfilm cassettes that are part of these programs. The articles are available for immediate viewing and copying. Using such a service you can find your references, record the bibliographic information, read the article, and make a copy — all in the same place! Figure 5.3 is an example of an Infotrac entry with an abstract.

If your subject is complex, spanning several disciplines and interests, a more detailed computer search conducted through the Information Retrieval Service can help you establish a working bibliography. Such a search will generate a list of citations on your topic and may also print out abstracts of the

Figure 5.3
Sample Infotrac Entry

```
                                        General Periodicals Index-P

COLLEGE STUDENTS
-Attitudes


   From ban the bomb to Benetton. (changing attitudes among college students) by Joe
Schwartz  v9  American Demographics  Sept '87  p58(2)  33T3589
   An American Council on Education (ACE) report on 20-year trends among university
freshmen indicates that obtaining financial wealth is an important goal for 70 percent
of today's students. A high priority for 75 percent of college freshmen in 1970 was to
develop a meaningful philosophy of life. Increased materialism does not seem to have
eroded traditionally liberal student attitudes: 78 percent want stricter government
control of pollution, 66 percent believe that not enough government attention is paid
to disarmament, and 73 percent feel that the government spends too much on defense. The
ACE study also reveals that women have become the majority of college freshmen,
representing 53 percent of that population, up from 45 percent in 1970. Young women are
leaving traditionally female professions such as nursing and teaching in favor of law
and medicine, and both women and men are abandoning the liberal arts in favor of studies
with more earning potential, such as business.
```

articles listed. For example, suppose you wish to find information on companies involved in medical product development using biotechnology. You instruct the computer to search for articles on biotechnology *and* companies *and* health. The *and* is very important because the computer will cross-check these references against each other and give you a list of articles that link all three topics. On this particular subject, a computer actually identified 93 articles on biotechnology, 31,841 articles on companies, 7,512 articles on health, and 8 articles on biotechnology *and* companies *and* health.[2] These last eight articles are the ones that should prove most useful. There is typically a charge for this more detailed search service.

Card Catalog.   Students are often told to start their research with the subject listings in the card catalog. This advice may not always be best for speakers because on popular subjects you might find fifty or even five hundred books listed, and you have no way to determine which are most relevant or most helpful. However, in the articles you read on your topic, you may encounter references to books that sound particularly interesting. Reading the best books on your topic can give you a deeper understanding that will make your speech more authoritative and impressive.

Interviewing for Information

Interviewing experts can give you credibility similar to what you acquire through personal experience. If you can say, "The personnel director of Nupak Automotive Parts told me . . . ," listeners will sit up and take notice. Like personal experience, however, interviewing has its limitations. Finding the right person to interview can be a problem. You may have a tendency to accept the word of your expert without further investigation. If you know little about the subject, it will be difficult for you to evaluate what you hear.

To minimize these problems, check your library's vertical file or the local newspaper morgue to help identify people whose knowledge can enhance your speech. The news clippings and your other research may also help you think of questions to ask during an interview. Prepare for the interview by learning about the topic in advance.

Establishing Contact.   If time permits, write to the person you wish to interview. In your letter state the purpose of the interview and demonstrate your seriousness. Follow up with a telephone call to set a time and place for the interview. Figure 5.4 is a sample interview-request letter.

Such a letter helps establish your credibility. It also establishes an agenda for the interview and gives your expert some idea of what you wish to discuss. It suggests that you are serious enough to have done research on the topic. If you do not have time to establish contact by letter, phone the person to ask for an interview. Don't be shy. A request for an interview is a compliment.

Figure 5.4
Sample Interview-Request Letter

Room 225, Adams Hall
Biltmore College
Detroit, MI 72641
November 7, 19—

Ms. Carol Johnson, Director of Personnel
Nupak Automotive Parts
1427 Beltway Drive
Detroit, MI 72678

Dear Ms. Johnson:

I am a student at Biltmore College enrolled in a public speaking class. I am preparing an informative speech on company- and union-sponsored programs aimed at overcoming boredom on the job. Marcia Thomas, an old family friend, suggested that I could learn a great deal from the quality circles program you have developed at Nupak. I would appreciate very much the opportunity to interview you about the program.

I am especially interested in your ideas and opinions on the following questions:

1. Have the quality circles generated workable programs to counteract boredom?
2. Does job enrichment work in the auto parts industry?
3. Might job restructuring be a possible alternative?
4. Have there been any changes in absenteeism or job turnover since starting this program?

I am scheduled to speak at the end of next week, and I will call your office Thursday morning to see if we can arrange an interview. My dormitory phone number is 834-4922. I will be very grateful for your help and look forward to meeting you.

Sincerely,

Richard Mardsen

Designing the Interview.   Either in your letter or at the beginning of the interview, establish why you are there and what you hope to learn. Plan questions that invite your expert to discuss the meaning of events. Avoid questions that invite yes or no answers, such as "Do you think quality circles are worthwhile?" Never supply the answer you want in your question, as in "Don't you think that quality circles work because they make employees feel important?" Design your questions in a sequence so that the answers form a coherent line of thought.

"When did you adopt the quality circles idea?"

"Why did you go with the quality circles approach?"

"How did you implement the concept?"

"What have been the results?"

"How would you evaluate the program?"

Allow the person you are interviewing to complete the answer to one question before you ask another. Don't interrupt and don't jump in with another question every time your expert pauses. Your expert may go from one point to another and may even answer a question before you ask it. You should be flexible enough to adapt to a spontaneous flow of information.

Design your questions so that your expert is not made defensive by the way they are worded. Questions such as "When are managers going to stop exploiting workers?" are not only argumentative but ill-mannered. Save any controversial questions for late in the interview after you have established rapport. Ask such questions honestly but tactfully: "Some union leaders have said that quality circles are just 'the latest ploy to exploit workers.' How do you feel about such criticism?" If asked with sincerity rather than hostility, this kind of question may produce the most interesting part of your interview.

Should you plan to tape-record your interview? A tape recorder can free you from note taking and help you get the exact wording of answers. But setting up and running a tape recorder can be a nuisance that interferes with establishing rapport. Also, many people dislike being tape-recorded. Never attempt to record interviews without obtaining prior consent.

Conducting the Interview.   Arrive for the interview on time. Dress nicely to show that you take the interview seriously and as a sign of respect for the person you are interviewing. When you meet your expert, take time to get to know the person on an informal basis before you get into your prepared questions. Try to establish common ground. On one occasion, as we were interviewing the late Supreme Court Justice Hugo Black, the justice discovered during small talk before the interview that our people had come from the hill country of north Georgia. Since these were also his family roots, he felt instant rapport with us. This reduced the tension, and we went on to enjoy a productive interview.

When you interview an expert, get to know her on an informal basis before you ask prepared questions. The information you acquire from such interviews can make your speech more credible and impressive.

Let the expert do most of the talking while you do the listening. Be alert for opportunities to follow up on responses by using probes, mirror questions, verifiers, or reinforcers.[3] **Probes** are questions that ask the expert to elaborate on a response: "Could you tell me more about how you got the quality circles program started?" **Mirror questions** reflect back part of a response to encourage further discussion. The sequence might go as follows:

> "So I told Melvin, 'If we want to change the workers' attitudes toward us, we're going to have to change our attitudes toward them.'"

> "You said management would have to change first?"

A **verifier** confirms the meaning of something that has been said, such as "If I understand you correctly, you're saying. . . ." Finally, a **reinforcer** encourages the person to communicate further. A smile, a nod, or a comment such as "I see" are reinforcers that can keep the interview moving.

If you feel the interview beginning to drift off course, you can often steer it back with a transition. As your expert pauses, you can say, "I believe I understand how the quality circles work. Now let me ask you about the results of the program."

Do not overstay your welcome. As the interview draws to a close, summarize the main points you have learned and how you think they may be useful in your speech. A summary allows you to verify what you have heard and reassures the expert that you intend to use the information fairly and accurately. Show your gratitude for the interview as you conclude, then follow up with a thank-you letter in which you report the successful results of your speech.

After the interview is concluded, find a quiet place, go over the notes you have taken, and get down the wording of important answers while they are still fresh in your mind. Nothing is more frustrating than to recall that your expert made a striking statement that would be perfect for the conclusion of your speech, but you can't remember what it was.

RECORDING INFORMATION

As you conduct your research, you will come across facts and figures, ideas for examples and narratives, or quotations that might be useful in your speech. It is impossible to remember all of these items, or even to remember where you saw them, unless you keep notes. Many researchers use index cards to record the information they discover. These cards are easy to handle and sort by categories. The note cards you prepare during your research should show what the information is and where it was obtained. You will be preparing two major kinds of research note cards: information cards and source cards.

Information Card

The **information card** records ideas and information from an article or book, usually one item to a card. For any single article or book you may have several cards. While you are doing your research, you will not always know whether something will be useful in your speech. When in doubt, write it down. The more information you have to select from, the better your speech should be. Avoid getting into situations in which you remember that you read something important but can't remember what it was, and — worse still — you can't remember where you read it.

Each card should contain a *heading* describing the information contained on the card, the *source* where the information was obtained, and the *information* itself, which may be either a direct quotation or a paraphrase of what the author said. Figure 5.5 shows an information card.

Source Card

You should also prepare a **source card** for each article or book you use. The source card contains the author, title, place and date of publication, and page references. This information permits you to document precisely your sources of data when you introduce them in your speech. Establishing who said some-

Figure 5.5
Information Card

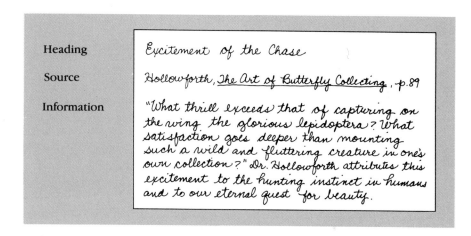

Heading   *Excitement of the Chase*

Source   *Hollowforth, The Art of Butterfly Collecting, p.89*

Information   *"What thrill exceeds that of capturing on the wing the glorious lepidoptera? What satisfaction goes deeper than mounting such a wild and fluttering creature in one's own collection?" Dr. Hollowforth attributes this excitement to the hunting instinct in humans and to our eternal quest for beauty.*

thing, where it was reported, and when it was said is important to the credibility of your information.

The source card for a book typically takes the following form: author, title, place of publication, publisher, and date of publication (see Figure 5.6). A source card for an article lists the author, article title, name of the periodical, volume number, date, and pages. The source card may also be used to list important information about the author, book, or periodical that might be

Figure 5.6
Source Card

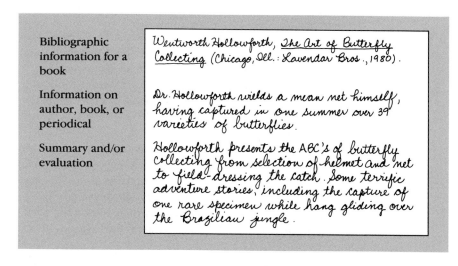

Bibliographic information for a book   *Wentworth Hollowforth, The Art of Butterfly Collecting (Chicago, Ill.: Lavender Bros., 1980).*

Information on author, book, or periodical   *Dr. Hollowforth wields a mean net himself, having captured in one summer over 39 varieties of butterflies.*

Summary and/or evaluation   *Hollowforth presents the ABC's of butterfly collecting from selection of helmet and net to field-dressing the catch. Some terrific adventure stories, including the capture of one rare specimen while hang gliding over the Brazilian jungle.*

helpful. This information can be useful as you introduce sources in support of points you make during your speech. You may also use your source card to write down a *brief* summary of the material, including some comments on its quality and significance.

Testing Information

Researching a speech is sometimes like mining for gold. First, you have to find what you think might be valuable. Then you must test it to be sure it is authentic. Your research should help you find facts and figures, testimony, examples, and narratives that will add substance to your message. Before you use these materials, you should evaluate them carefully. Guidelines for evaluating supporting materials are covered in detail in Chapter 6. Regardless of the type of supporting material your research uncovers, you should check its reliability, thoroughness, recentness, and precision.

Reliability refers to the trustworthiness of information and is critical to the credibility of a speech. Reliable information comes from sources that are qualified by education or experience and that are free from self-interests that might result in bias. **Thoroughness** of information is also an important consideration. You must try to discover all the important information you need to make a responsible presentation. **Recentness** is essential when knowledge is changing rapidly on a subject. **Precision** is important if you are speaking on a topic that varies widely from place to place, such as unemployment rates or the incidence of AIDS. You must be certain that your information applies in the specific situation you are talking about in your speech. Applying these tests of research to the different types of supporting materials is covered in detail in the next chapter.

IN SUMMARY

To give a successful speech, you must find a good topic, determine your general and specific purposes, decide on a thematic statement, and expand your base of knowledge so that you can speak responsibly. A good topic is meaningful to both you and your audience. A good topic will be limited so that you can research it adequately and develop a speech that will fit within the allotted time.

Selecting a Good Topic.   One way to discover promising topic areas is to chart your interests. You can also scan television news, magazines, and newspapers for ideas. Next, chart audience interests as disclosed in previous speeches and match them with your interests. To develop topic possibilities, use a topic analysis method based on six key questions: who, what, when, where, why, and how. When applied to a topic area, these questions can guide you to specific topics. As you move toward your selection, consider whether a given topic fits the assignment, whether you can develop a responsible speech on it within the time limit, and what your *purpose* is for speaking upon it.

Determining Your Purpose. Your *general purpose* describes the overall function of the speech. Your *specific purpose* identifies the kind of response you would like to evoke, what you want to accomplish. Your *thematic statement* expresses the central ideas of your speech in a single sentence. A clearly defined thematic statement gives direction to your speech.

Acquiring Responsible Knowledge. In order to speak responsibly on your topic, you should gather as much relevant information as time allows. You can obtain useful knowledge from personal experience, library resources, and interviews. Personal experience can make your speech seem highly credible and authentic, but you should not rely on it as your only source of information. Library research can add objective, authoritative information to your speech. The aim of such research is to acquire *responsible knowledge,* which means knowing the major features, issues, experts, latest developments, and local applications relevant to your topic. Interviewing puts you in direct contact with experts. The knowledge you obtain through interviewing can add freshness, vitality, and local relevance to your speech.

Recording Information. As you conduct research, record what you learn on index cards so that you can sort your material easily. Use *information cards,* which separate the ideas and information you find into useful categories, and *source cards* for each article, book, or interview. The source card identifies the author and place of publication fully. It may be used to record background information about the source and an overall summary and evaluation of the material. As you collect research for your speech, you should ask four basic questions: does this material satisfy the tests of *reliability, thoroughness, recentness,* and *precision* so that I can use it responsibly in my speech?

TERMS TO KNOW

purpose	**reinforcer**
general purpose	**information card**
specific purpose	**source card**
thematic statement	**reliability**
responsible knowledge	**thoroughness**
probe	**recentness**
mirror question	**precision**
verifier	

DISCUSSION

1. Working in small groups, exchange a chart of your interests with your classmates. Discuss the most promising areas for speech topics among your interests. Report these to the class.

2. Using the topic analysis method, analyze the most promising topic areas identified in Item 1. As you consider these topic possibilities, discuss what general purposes they might serve.

3. As a follow-up to Items 1 and 2, develop specific purposes and thematic statements for the three topics that interest you most. Evaluate them in class, using the criteria for selecting good topics and determining specific purposes described in this chapter.

4. In what ways might personal experience limit and distort your knowledge as well as enrich it? Discuss in class, drawing on examples from your own experience.

APPLICATION

1. Working in small groups, scan a variety of resources to generate topic areas for speeches. Each group should be responsible for checking one of the following materials:

   a. the local Sunday newspaper
   b. a television news program over a week's time
   c. a recent issue of a weekly news magazine
   d. a recent issue of a general-interest magazine such as *The Saturday Evening Post*

   In the first part of a class period, meet as groups to generate a list of topic ideas. Each group should select five topic ideas. In the second part of the class period, a representative should present each group's recommendations to the class and explain how and why the topics were chosen. Which kind of media resource produces the best speech topics? What are the strengths and limitations of each?

2. Choose one of the topics you selected from Application 1 and identify the most likely sources of information you could use to develop it.

3. Take a walking tour of your library and locate the various resources described in this chapter. While you are there, try to find the answers for the following questions. Do not ask the librarian for assistance. Record the source of each answer.

   a. Who is the United States's wealthiest person and how wealthy is he or she?

b. What television shows did Norman Lear produce?

c. Who is the curator of New York's Museum of Modern Art?

d. What ABC program was interrupted on October 17, 1989, and by what event?

e. What horse holds the record in the Belmont Stakes?

f. Which movie won the Academy Award for best picture in 1960?

g. Who said, "The only thing we have to fear is fear itself"?

h. What is the life expectancy for infants born this year in the United States, and how does this compare with fifty years ago?

i. How many grizzly bears are there in the United States?

4. Discuss the following thematic statements in terms of their effectiveness:

a. You ought to protect yourself from date rape.

b. The role of superstitions in our lives.

c. Young children should not be admitted to horror movies.

d. Weekend trips are preferable to long vacations.

e. Nutritious meals you can cook in your dorm room.

Improve those that do not meet the criteria for effective thematic statements.

NOTES

1. Rudyard Kipling, *Just So Stories* (Garden City, N.Y.: Doubleday, 1921), p. 85.

2. From a brochure of Dialog Information Services, Inc.

3. Lois J. Einhorn, Patricia Hayes Bradley, and John E. Baird, Jr., *Effective Employment Interviewing: Unlocking Human Potential* (Glenview, Ill.: Scott, Foresman, 1982), pp. 135–39.

> *The universe is made of stories, not of atoms.*
>
> — MURIEL RUKEYSER

6

THE USE

— OF —

SUPPORTING MATERIALS

This Chapter Will Help You

- ◆ use facts and figures in ethical and effective ways.

- ◆ use expert, prestige, and lay forms of testimony when each is most appropriate.

- ◆ use examples to enliven your speech and to emphasize important points.

- ◆ use narratives to involve your listeners and to illustrate abstract ideas.

It's the day of our birth. It's been a really tough passage for us to get through the birth canal, and we're sleeping deeply, encased in a blue blanket in the nursery. Three friends of our mothers come in. They come over, give us a cursory glance. "Oh, yes, that *is* a baby." Far more important to them is, "But how is the mother?"

Second high point in life's passage. It's the day of our marriage. It's a high gala event. Front and center in all her radiant glitter is the bride! As the groom, at best we are a fringe figure, way in the background.

Finally, the last somber chapter in life's passage. We are laid out. We are in the viewing room. Friends of our wives come in. They give us a perfunctory glance. "Yes, he *does* look natural." But the question that they must have answered before they leave the funeral home, which will provide meaningful conversation for the next two weeks, is "Just how much did he leave her?"[1]

N arratives are stories with a purpose. Professor Charles Hampton's purpose, as he began his speech to the Rotary Club in St. Joseph, Michigan, was to engage his listeners' interest in the topic "Men Are an Endangered Species." Because his speech went against the current of thinking that assumes that only women need liberating, his choice of a narrative opening both aroused attention and focused listeners in a new direction.

Narratives, along with facts and figures, testimony, and examples, provide the speaker with **supporting materials,** the building blocks of speeches. Supporting materials provide the substance, reliability, and appeal a speech must have before listeners will place their faith in it. As you research your topic, you should ask yourself: Does an article contain relevant and useful information? Does it cite experts who support your position? Are there any interesting examples that could help your speech? Can you find stories that illustrate your ideas? Your quest for responsible knowledge should focus on finding supporting materials that will add substance and interest to your speech.

Supporting materials do more than fill up time so you can make it through your five-, seven-, or ten-minute presentation. Supporting materials perform three important functions. First, *they demonstrate the meaning of topics* and emphasize their importance. Second, *they show the relevance of topics* to listeners' lives, often through examples or narratives such as that used in our opening vignette. Third, *they verify controversial statements and claims.* Although this third function would seem to relate mainly to persuasive speeches, informative speeches can also make surprising claims that require support from facts, figures, and expert testimony. If you assert, "American cars are inferior to foreign-made cars," your audience might very well ask, "Says who?" "Says me!" would not be a satisfactory answer. You must be able to show where you got your information and confirm that these sources are reliable. In persuasive speeches this burden usually does become heavier. If you are asking people to change their beliefs or modify their behavior, you must be able to verify your claims with powerful supporting material.

The conclusion seems inescapable that a statement without support will not bear the weight of examination that most audiences will place upon it. The forms of support we discuss in this chapter will be essential to you as you prepare successful speeches. As we examine each of the major kinds of supporting materials, we will discuss its nature and significance, how to evaluate it, and how to put it to work for improved speech effectiveness.

FACTS AND FIGURES

When we think of supporting material for speeches, often the first thing that comes to mind is information. Such information takes two basic forms: general facts and statistics.

Facts

In our "no-nonsense" society, facts are an especially powerful form of supporting material. Richard Weaver, a prominent critic of communication practices, once observed that Americans honor facts as the highest form of knowledge. Facts constitute our *truth*. When facts are confirmed by scientists, he noted, they carry even more weight in supporting claims and are less likely to be questioned. The contemporary American audience respects scientific facts and numbers in the way that other societies respect the word of God.[2]

What this means for you as a speaker is that you must master the facts surrounding your topic if you want to be credible. But what exactly are facts? **Facts** are verifiable units of information, which means that independent observers see and report them consistently. The following statements may be considered facts because they can be verified as either true or false:

AIDS is a communicable disease.

Most Metro Tech students work to put themselves through college.

Most State College students have never used cocaine.

When they are verified as correct, factual statements can stand by themselves, but speakers rarely use them without interpreting what they mean. Although interpretation aids understanding, it can also be a source of distortion. As soon as you start handling facts so that they serve your purpose in a speech, you create the possibility of distorting them. Biased interpretations can creep into otherwise factual statements with just a few additional words, turning them into opinions:

Facts, figures, and expert testimony are powerful and often necessary forms of support for speeches. Listeners feel reassured when they know your ideas and interpretations are based on sound information. Here Joseph L. Goldstein, recipient of the 1985 Nobel Prize in medicine, explains the factual basis of his research.

AIDS is a *shameful* communicable disease.

Most Metro Tech students *have to* work to put themselves through college.

Most *intelligent* students have never used cocaine.

We often are tempted to read into facts what we want to find in them. Speakers may even ignore information that contradicts the way they want to see things, rejecting it as atypical or irrelevant. These observations suggest that we should not put blind faith in what *appear* to be factual statements. In your communication roles as speaker and listener, you should examine all factual statements carefully.

Because we usually cannot directly verify the accuracy of factual statements, they are often combined with expert testimony, which we cover in detail later in this chapter. All information comes from somewhere, so you must consider how your audience might react to your sources of information. Periodicals have certain reputations that make them more or less acceptable to different audiences. For instance, William F. Buckley's *National Review* is known as a conservative magazine, and *The New Republic* is considered a more liberal periodical.[3]

Statistics

When you use numbers to describe the magnitude of events or to predict future patterns, you are using **statistics.** There are two basic types of statistics: **descriptive statistics,** which explain something in terms of its size or distribution, and **inferential statistics,** which make predictions, show trends, and demonstrate relationships.

Descriptive statistics may describe a topic by its size or average occurrence. The following excerpt shows the use of statistics and contrast to establish the size of a problem:

> Although more than 1,500 of the students on our campus have experimented with cocaine, most of us — nearly 12,000 as reported in a recent University Health Services survey — still get our kicks from that less spectacular drug, alcohol. The average student has not even tried cocaine and has no particular desire to do so. But, that same student has not only tried alcohol — he or she continues to use it each week.

Descriptive statistics also may be used to describe the way something is distributed or spread out:

> Most of us work to help pay our way. Information from the Registrar's Office indicates that 18 percent of us don't need to work — we are fully supported by parents or spouses. Twenty-one percent of us work full time — at least forty hours a week — and attend school on a part-time basis. The rest of us — the vast majority, 61 percent of us — work part time while carrying a full-time course load.

When the numbers you are presenting are large or unfamiliar, it helps if you can tie them to something the audience can relate to more easily. Note how a prominent physician helped his listeners understand the enormity of his statistical information on health care:

> Last year the health-care industry had total expenditures of $384 billion. That is three times the revenue of the American auto industry. Think of it, $1 billion in the last twenty-four hours. When I worked in Washington, I heard Everett McKinley Dirksen, the late Minority Leader of the United States Senate, [say], "A billion here, a billion there, pretty soon it adds up to real money!" One billion per day equals $42 million per hour, and that is real money! Looked at another way, we spent more than $1,600 for every man, woman, and child in the nation last year. For a family of four that's $6,400, the price of a compact automobile. Seldom do we think of the trade-off of a new car each year for health care.[4]

Inferential statistics, which make predictions or claim causal relationships, are based on probability, not on absolute certainty. Therefore, you should be especially cautious as you use and interpret them. Inferential statistics often focus on *correlations,* which show the relationships between two factors, and *trends,* which describe and predict changes over time. John McGervey, a physicist from Case Western Reserve University, has described in detail the probability of common occurrences. For example, in looking at the disasters people commonly worry about, McGervey points out the following correlation: a trip in a commercial jet airplane carries a one-in-a-million risk of death, but 120 miles of driving in a car (with a seat belt) or 60 miles (unbelted) carries the same level of risk. Therefore, driving 12,000 miles a year is 100 times riskier than a commercial airline flight.[5] Had McGervey gone on to report significant changes in this correlation over the past decade, he would have been describing a trend.

Evaluating Facts and Figures

Before you incorporate information into your speech, you should use your critical thinking skills to evaluate it. As you research your speech, you may discover much interesting information about your topic that does not *directly* relate to your specific purpose. No matter how fascinating it may be, if the information does not help develop your thematic statement, don't use it. A speech that is cluttered with interesting digressions is difficult for listeners to follow. You may lose them on one of the side paths!

In evaluating facts and figures, you should also consider how current your information is, especially when your topic area is one in which information is changing rapidly. Save yourself the possible embarrassment of a listener's pointing out that your information is obsolete.

SPEAKER'S NOTES   *Evaluating Facts and Figures*

1. Are the facts and figures relevant?

2. Is the information recent?

3. Is the information reliable? Do other authorities confirm it?

4. Are the sources credible? Are they competent, trustworthy, and unbiased?

5. Is the information complete? Has anything important been omitted or withheld?

6. Is this factual information, or is it opinion masquerading as fact?

It is also important to avoid relying too much on any one source. Information that is confirmed by more than one authority is apt to be more reliable. The more controversial the topic, the more critical the reliability of your information and the credibility of your sources will become. Examine even "factual" material for potential bias, distortions, or omissions. Compare what different expert sources have to say and look for areas of agreement. Be certain that what you have are facts and not opinions.

Finally, consider whether your information will be impressive enough to stand on its own, or whether you must use comparisons, contrasts, or perhaps a vivid example to bring out its meaning. The recitation of numbers in a speech may impress some listeners, but for statistics to work well as supporting material you must often combine them with examples so that they are clearer and more memorable. Recent research suggests that good examples may be better than statistics alone at gaining and holding attention and are easier for listeners to comprehend.[6] On the other hand, reliable statistical information provides the firm base of knowledge needed to make the use of examples responsible.

Using Facts and Figures

Once you have found and evaluated your information, you must next determine how to use it. You should have an abundance of information pertinent to each main point of your speech, so that you can *select the best* as supporting material. Identify your sources of information. Bring statistics to life by using examples or concrete comparisons. Be careful not to distort factual and statistical statements by the way you word them. Remember that statistical information is probable, but not certain.

TESTIMONY

Testimony involves citing other people, institutions, or publications in your speech, either by quoting them directly or by paraphrasing what they have to say. Three types of testimony are useful as supporting material. **Expert testimony** comes from sources who are authorities on the topic. **Prestige testimony** comes from someone who is highly regarded but not necessarily an expert on the topic. **Lay testimony** involves citing ordinary citizens who have firsthand experience.

Expert Testimony

As you research your topic, you will probably run across statements by experts offering important opinions, information, and interesting quotations. Use this type of testimony to establish the validity of your facts and interpretations.

When you use expert testimony, you are calling on witnesses to support your case in absentia — you allow their words to speak for them in their absence. In a sense, using expert testimony allows you to borrow ethos from those who have earned it through their distinguished and widely recognized work in a field. Expert testimony is especially important when your topic is innovative, unfamiliar, highly technical, or controversial.

When using expert testimony, do not overlook the power of titles such as *scientist* or *doctor*. Also remember that certain publications and institutions carry more weight than others. Financial information from the *Wall Street Journal* may be better received than the same type of information from your local newspaper. Medical studies conducted at the National Institutes of Health may be more respected than similar studies done in smaller, less well-known institutions.

Because most beginning speakers are not really authorities on their topics, expert testimony is a very important source of support in student speeches. But even speakers who are highly qualified by education or experience often call on other experts to substantiate their messages. In a speech entitled "Changing Relationships between Men and Women," Dr. Bernice Cohen Sachs relied on university-conducted surveys and opinions from psychiatrists, sociologists, and other specialists to support her interpretations. Dr. Sachs, herself a noted physician, was always careful to make certain that the audience was aware of the credentials of her sources. She introduced a discussion of the effects of outside employment on women in the following way:

> Mary Howell, M.D., Ph.D., mother of six and coordinator for evaluation and education at the Geriatric Clinical Center at the Bedford, Massachusetts, Veterans' Administration Medical Center, said that employment outside the home....[7]

Be sure to introduce the experts you quote in the same careful way. You may wish to emphasize their expert background, the nature of their research project, or where and when they made the statement you are citing, depending on the circumstances of your speech.

Prestige Testimony

Prestige testimony can enhance the general credibility of both you and your speech. When you use prestige testimony, you associate yourself with the source's good name and positive reputation. Often the source of prestige testimony is a well-known and respected writer or public figure. Quite frequently, it is the insight provided by the source or the eloquent use of language that makes prestige testimony effective. Geraldine Ferraro used prestige testimony in the introduction to her acceptance speech at the 1984 Democratic National Convention:

As I stand before the American people and think of the honor this great convention has bestowed upon me, I recall the words of Dr. Martin Luther King, Jr., who made America stronger by making America more free.

He said: "Occasionally in life there are moments which cannot be completely explained by words. Their meaning can only be articulated by the inaudible language of the heart."

Tonight is such a moment for me.

My heart is filled with pride.

My fellow citizens, I proudly accept your nomination for the vice president of the United States.[8]

In her acceptance speech, Ms. Ferraro quoted her source **verbatim;** that is, she used the exact words of the source. Providing a verbatim quotation is preferable to paraphrasing when the citation is short, when the exact wording is important, or when the source has said something with such clarity, grace, and force that you know you cannot improve on it.

If the testimony is taken from a long passage or excerpted from a series of passages, you might find it more advantageous to paraphrase or restate it in your own words. Consider the following example from a student speech:

In an article on teen-age pregnancy published in the *Ladies' Home Journal,* Eunice Kennedy Shriver pointed out that over 600,000 teen-aged girls will become mothers this year and that nearly 40,000 of this number will not have turned fifteen when they become pregnant.

Whether quoted verbatim or paraphrased, prestige testimony does *not* establish the factual validity of a statement. Citing Eunice Kennedy Shriver as a source of information concerning teen-age pregnancy could demonstrate a misuse of prestige testimony. What might the audience know about Eunice Kennedy Shriver? That she is the sister of former president John F. Kennedy or the wife of Sargent Shriver, the first director of the Peace Corps? So how, one might ask, does this qualify her to serve as an expert on teen-age pregnancy? What the speaker failed to do in this example was to present Ms. Shriver's credentials as professional social worker with experience at the House of the Good Shepherd in Chicago and the Federal Penitentiary for Women in West Virginia. Once this background information has been supplied, her testimony carries more authority and is not improperly used. Indeed, her testimony then becomes *both* prestigious and expert, a powerful blend.

Lay Testimony

Speakers often use lay testimony to add authenticity and a sense of humanity to a speech. Lay testimony can be particularly important in speeches presented in the United States, where ordinary people enjoy special status as the source of political power. Therefore, speakers often give high regard to "the voice of the people," so much so, in fact, that *USA Today* features their testimony along with that of experts on its editorial page.[9] If you were preparing a speech on assembly-line boredom, you might quote factory workers to add a real-life dimension to your message. Similarly, for a speech on campus security you might find it useful to cite other students and faculty members.

Lay testimony also can be used to increase identification — the sense of close relationship — between your listeners and your speech. If listeners can identify with the sources you use because they are "just like us," then they may be more willing to accept the point you are making. Ronald Reagan made effective use of lay testimony in his first inaugural address, as he quoted the diary of Martin Treptow, a young soldier who died on the Western front during World War I.

On the flyleaf under the heading, "My Pledge," he had written these words: 'America must win this war. Therefore I will work, I will save, I will sacrifice, I will endure, I will fight cheerfully and do my utmost, as if the issue of the whole struggle depended on me alone.'[10]

Treptow's pledge represented the kind of dedication President Reagan wished to inspire in American citizens.

Evaluating Testimony

Like facts and figures, testimony must be evaluated in terms of how relevant, how recent, and how accurate it is. You must be particularly careful that a quotation you select reflects the overall meaning and intent of its author. Never twist the meaning of testimony to make it fit your purposes. Such unethical practice is called "quoting out of context." Advertising that often accompanies movies or plays is notorious for quoting out of context, especially when citing reviews. A review may slam a play as boring and dull but praise the costuming as the "one brilliant grace in an otherwise disastrous production." The advertisement then appears, "'Brilliant,' says the *New York Times!*" Be certain you are not guilty of such an ethical misdemeanor in your speeches.

Some sources may also have a vested interest in what they advocate. For example, a doctor who promotes vitamin therapy may be the part-owner of a company that sells vitamins. If you rely on such a source in your speech, it could damage your credibility.

In addition to these basic tests, you must also consider whether the type of testimony is appropriate for your purpose. Lay testimony can be used to humanize a speech and to provide a basis for identification. Prestige testimony can be used to enhance the general credibility of both speech and speaker, but only expert testimony should be used to demonstrate that a statement is factually true. If you are using expert testimony, be sure your source is an authority in the topic area. Expertise is specific to a topic. The entire field of

SPEAKER'S NOTES   *Evaluating Testimony*

1. Is the testimony relevant and recent?

2. Is the testimony truly representative of the source's position?

3. Is the source objective, unbiased, and an authority on the topic?

4. Has the proper kind of testimony — expert, prestige, or lay — been used?

medicine is beyond the grasp of any one doctor, and no professor can lay claim to the entire range of human knowledge. Be certain that your source of testimony is qualified to speak on your topic.

Using Testimony

Testimony is an important type of supporting material, but you must use it ethically. Be careful to quote or paraphrase your sources accurately. Have direct quotations written out on cards so that you can read them, rather than relying on memory. Use testimony from more than one source, especially when your topic is controversial or there is a possibility of bias. Find the most up-to-date testimony available and emphasize its recentness. As you introduce testimony into your speech, point out the qualifications of your sources so that you establish their credibility. A transition, such as "According to . . ." or "In the latest issue of . . . ," leads gracefully into such material. You can find much useful information about your sources in the biographical resources mentioned in Chapter 5.

EXAMPLES

Examples bring a speech to life. Just as pictures serve as graphic illustrations for a printed text, **examples** serve as verbal illustrations for an oral message. In fact, some scholars prefer to use the term *illustration* rather than example. The word *illustration* derives from the Latin *illustrare,* which means "to shed light" or "to make bright." Good examples illuminate the message of your speech, making it clearer and more vivid for your audience.

Examples serve many important functions in speeches. They may be used to arouse attention, sustain interest, and clarify ideas by providing simple concrete applications. Speakers acknowledge these functions when they say, "Let me give you an example." Similarly, examples may be used to personalize your topic and humanize your speech. Examples about other people give the audience someone with whom they can identify, thus involving them in the speech. Personalized examples help the audience to experience the meaning of your ideas, not simply to understand them.

Examples may also be used for emphasis. When you make a statement and follow it with an example, you are pointing out that what you have just said is IMPORTANT. Examples amplify your ideas. They say to the audience, "This bears repeating." They are especially helpful when you introduce new, complex, or abstract material. Not only can an example make such information clearer, it also provides the audience with time to digest and understand what you have said before you move on to your next point. Finally, examples help demonstrate the validity of your message by showing that what you have said either has happened or could happen.

Examples are often used in the introductions and conclusions of speeches. In introductions examples help the speaker gain attention. In conclusions they can help give the speech lasting effectiveness because they are easily remembered. Dianne Feinstein, former mayor of San Francisco, opened a speech with the following example to illustrate an outdated perspective of the role of women in politics:

> About thirty years ago, Senator Margaret Chase Smith was asked by *Time* magazine what she would do if one day she woke up in the White House. She replied that she would apologize to Bess Truman and leave immediately.[11]

By using this example Mayor Feinstein did more than just arouse interest. She also lightened the mood of the audience and suggested that for women things had indeed changed for the better. Examples often carry more meaning than their simplicity would suggest. They can be equally as effective as support for the main points in your speech. Use them to emphasize a point or to increase understanding.

Types of Examples

Examples take different forms, and these forms have different functions. An example may be brief or extended and may either be based on an actual event or on something that might have happened.

Brief Examples.   A **brief example** mentions a specific instance to demonstrate a more general statement. Brief examples are concise and to the point. Often a speaker will use several of them together, either for the sake of contrast or to reinforce the point. A student speech on teen-age pregnancy made effective use of brief examples:

> Teen-age pregnancy occurs among the rich and the poor. Take Mary Thompson. Mary's father was one of the town's leading doctors, and she lived in a five-bedroom home in Steir Park. She had a child at fifteen. In another case, Janet Reese delivered when she was sixteen. Her father was a sanitation worker, and she grew up in a two-room shack next to the stockyards. Youthful pregnancy does not respect status. There is no group in our society that is not cursed by it. Indeed, we can safely say that teen-age pregnancy is an equal opportunity disaster.

Brief examples provide support by extending the meaning of an idea. As a rule they refer to something that is more concrete and familiar to the audience than the statement they demonstrate.

Extended Examples. An **extended example** contains more detail and allows you to dwell more fully on a single instance. Our student speaker could have described a teen-age mother with an extended example like the one that follows:

> Alicia Thomas is fifteen years and ten months old. She lives with her mother, father, and younger brother in suburban Bellaire. Alicia is a sophomore at Clearwater Preparatory School. Like many other fifteen-year-olds girls, Alicia wears braces. Like many other fifteen-year-old girls, Alicia loves rock music and MTV. Like many other fifteen-year-old girls, Alicia spends a lot of time on the phone. But while most girls her age are looking forward to getting their driver's licenses, Alicia is looking forward to something else. You see, Alicia is six months pregnant. She is looking forward to being out of school for a year and to the heartbreak of giving her baby up for adoption.

This extended example gives us enough detail so that we feel we know Alicia. It allows the speaker to make two indirect points: first, teen-age pregnancies are not confined to the poor, uneducated segments of our society; and second, teen-age pregnancies are deeply disruptive to the lives of young girls. Also, the extended example permits the speaker to convey a feeling about a topic that might be lost if the speech relied solely on brief examples.

Factual Examples. As the name implies, a **factual example** is based on a real event or person. In the preceding extended example, Alicia could be the cousin of the speaker, a friend or neighbor, or even someone the speaker read about in a newspaper or magazine article. The important consideration is that Alicia is an actual person (whose name may have been changed to protect her identity). Factual examples provide strong support for any assertion because they ground the point you are making in reality. If the speaker's association with topics is direct — when you actually know the persons involved as opposed simply to having read about them — the factual examples are even stronger.

President Reagan was a master at using factual examples. In a speech delivered at Pointe du Hoc, Normandy, as a D-Day memorial to the Allied forces who fought there during World War II, the president introduced the audience to Bill Millin:

> Do you remember the story of Bill Millin of the 51st Highlanders? Forty years ago today, British troops were pinned down near a bridge, waiting desperately for help. Suddenly, they heard the sound of bagpipes, and some thought they were dreaming. Well, they weren't. They looked up and saw Bill Millin with his bagpipes, leading the reinforcements and ignoring the smack of the bullets into the ground around him.[12]

Although the president may not have known Bill Millin personally, he knew about him, and he knew that the veterans in his audience either knew him or had heard of him. In this particular case, the example of Bill Millin is used to exemplify the courage shown by the soldiers at Normandy, many of whom were in the audience for the memorial. The factual example that relates directly to the experience of the audience is exceptionally potent.

Hypothetical Examples.   Examples need not be real to be effective. **Hypothetical examples** made up to represent reality can also be useful, especially when factual examples are hard to find. A hypothetical example is usually a synthesis of actual people, situations, or events. Although not real itself, it must be credible as representing reality. It is a fiction that may open the door to truth even better than a factual example. Velva White used such a hypothetical example to illustrate the concept of poverty:

> Let me tell you about Mary Jones. Mary lives in a shack in Tunica, Mississippi. Her home, if you can call it that, backs up to what the newspaper calls "Sugar Ditch." But that's not what the residents call it. Because none of the houses in the area have inside plumbing, raw sewage is often dumped into the ditch. That's where it gets the name residents use. Mary, her sister Jasmine, Mary's four children, and Jasmine's two children all live in this three-room shack. The outside

SPEAKER'S NOTES

Evaluating Examples

1. Are the examples relevant and representative?

2. Do the examples seem plausible and authentic?

3. Are the examples fresh and interesting?

4. Are the examples tactful and tasteful?

walls are covered with tarpaper. Inside, wadded-up newspapers are jammed into cracks to keep out the cold winter winds. An old pot-bellied stove provides heat and a way for Mary to cook. Does Mary Jones exist? Yes and no. There is not *a* Mary Jones, but there are *many* Mary Joneses in Tunica and in other towns and cities in our nation. We all pay the price for the way they must live.

Hypothetical examples must have an appearance of truth. They must represent the realities of the situation and conform to what is generally known and believed if they are to be accepted.

Evaluating Examples

Just as information and testimony must be relevant and representative, so must examples. You should not have to strain to make them fit. If you feel you have to explain their relevance, then the examples are probably not very useful. Examples must also be representative. They should reflect what is typical, or they will not seem plausible to your audience. Listeners will not accept them as authentic if they don't conform to what the audience already knows and believes. The more incredible your examples, the more you must buttress them with factual information or expert testimony.

You should also consider whether examples will be interesting and memorable. They should meet acceptable standards of tact and taste and fit the mood and spirit of the occasion. You should risk offending listeners only when you have no other choice — only when listeners must be shocked before they can be informed or persuaded.

Using Examples

Examples can frequently make a difference between a speech that is humdrum and one that is quite successful. Use examples in your speeches to clarify the meaning of technical or abstract ideas. Make your examples seem authentic by being as specific as possible. Provide the names of people, places, and institutions. It is much easier for a listener to relate to Matt Dunn of the local General Motors plant than to some anonymous worker in an unnamed company. Use transitions to move smoothly from statement to example and example to statement. Phrases such as "For instance . . ." or "Case in point . . ." work very nicely. Finally, you should use examples selectively to emphasize and clarify statements of major importance.

NARRATIVES

The **narrative** goes beyond the example by *telling a story* within the speech. Narratives may be used to illustrate some important truth about the speaker's topic. Because people love stories and get caught up in the action, narratives

— perhaps more than any other technique — can capture and hold attention and demonstrate the meaning of what the speaker is trying to communicate. A narrative may be remembered long after the rest of the speech is forgotten.

Narration has a considerable history in public discourse. Aesop's fables have long warned children of the dangers of pride and deception. Jesus used parables to illustrate moral lessons: the parable of the Good Samaritan exemplifies compassion. Narratives usually invite audiences to discover the "truth" for themselves. With narratives the audience becomes involved in the creation of the message — it becomes *their* discovery, *their* truth. Such involvement enhances the impact of the message. Personal narratives are especially powerful because they increase identification between speaker and audience.[13]

A well-told story creates anticipation and suspense and brings a sense of concreteness to abstract concepts or principles. In public speeches narratives function like a speech within a speech. They begin with an attention-arousing introduction, continue with a body in which the story develops, and end with a conclusion that reinforces the point in question.

Narratives are frequently used as the introduction to a longer speech because they actively involve the audience with the topic. Father Peter Sartain of St. Anne's Parish in Memphis used the following narrative to open a wedding sermon:

Narratives involve listeners and teach them the meaning of abstract concepts through stories that are often long remembered. New York governor Mario Cuomo concluded his keynote speech at the 1984 Democratic National Convention with a moving narrative of how his parents taught him about faith, hard work, and democratic values.

> There was once a sculptor working in his studio with hammer and chisel on a large block of marble. A little boy who was watching him saw nothing except large and small pieces of stone falling to the right and left. He didn't know what was happening. When the little boy returned a few weeks later, he saw to his great surprise a large and powerful lion sitting in the place where the stone had stood. In amazement he turned to the sculptor and asked, "How did you know there was a lion in there?"[14]

This narrative introduced the topic of the sermon, "how to know when there is love in a relationship." It set the stage for the message that followed and created a mood appropriate to the occasion.

Narratives are also used within the body of the speech, especially when the speaker wishes to illustrate an abstract concept that is difficult to define in any other way. President Reagan used narration to define the essence of courage in his D-Day memorial speech:

> At dawn, on the morning of the 6th of June, 1944, 225 Rangers jumped off the British landing craft and ran to the bottom of these cliffs. Their mission was one of the most difficult and daring of the invasion: to climb these sheer and desolate cliffs and take out the enemy guns. The Allies had been told that some of the mightiest of these guns were here and they would be trained on the beaches to stop the Allied advance.
>
> The Rangers looked up and saw the enemy soldiers [at] the edge of the cliffs shooting down at them with machine guns and throwing grenades. And the American Rangers began to climb. They shot rope ladders over the face of these cliffs and began to pull themselves up. When one Ranger fell, another would take his place. When one rope was cut, a Ranger would grab another and begin his climb again. They climbed, shot back, and held their footing. Soon, one by one, the Rangers pulled themselves over the top, and in seizing the firm land at the top of these cliffs, they began to seize back the continent of Europe.
>
> Two hundred and twenty-five came here. After two days of fighting, only 90 could still bear arms.[15]

When a narrative is used in the conclusion of the speech, it leaves the audience with something to remember and establishes a mood that can endure long after the last words have been spoken. In his keynote address to the Democratic National Convention in 1984, Mario Cuomo, governor of New York, used the following narrative as part of his conclusion:

> It's a story I didn't read in a book, or learn in a classroom. I saw it and lived it. Like many of you.
>
> I watched a small man with thick calluses on both hands work 15 and 16 hours a day. I saw him once literally bleed from the bottoms of his feet, a man who came here uneducated, alone, unable to speak the language, who taught me all I needed to know about faith and hard work by the simple eloquence of his example. I learned about our kind of democracy from my father. I learned about our obligation to each other from him and from my mother. They asked only for a chance to work and to make the world better for their children and to be protected in those moments when they would not be able to protect themselves. This nation and its government did that for them.

And that they were able to build a family and live in dignity and see one of their children go from behind their little grocery store on the other side of the tracks in south Jamaica where he was born, to occupy the highest seat in the greatest state of the greatest nation in the only world we know, is an ineffably beautiful tribute to the democratic process.[16]

Some narratives directly involve the audience in the story by making them part of the action. In the chapter-opening vignette, Professor Hampton used this technique: "It's the day of *our* birth. It's been a really tough passage for *us* to get through the birth canal, and *we're* sleeping deeply..." (italics added). Speakers can create the same kind of effect by beginning with, "Picture yourself in the following situation..." or "Imagine that you are...." The direct assignment of a role within a narrative tends to increase audience involvement with the topic.

In a narrative, **dialogue** is almost always preferable to **paraphrase.** When speakers use dialogue, they reproduce conversation directly. When they paraphrase, they summarize what was said. Paraphrasing can save some time, but it can also rob a narrative of power and authenticity. Paraphrase sparingly and let people speak for themselves in your narratives. Sam Ervin, the late senator from North Carolina, was a master storyteller. Note how he used dialogue in the following narrative, which opened a speech on the Constitution and our judicial system:

Jim's administrator was suing the railroad for his wrongful death. The first witness he called to the stand testified as follows: "I saw Jim walking up the track. A fast train passed, going up the track. After it passed, I didn't see Jim. I walked up the track a little way and discovered Jim's severed head lying on one side of the track, and the rest of his body on the other." The witness was asked how he reacted to his gruesome discovery. He responded: "I said to myself, 'Something serious must have happened to Jim.'"

Something serious has been happening to constitutional government in America. I want to talk to you about it.[17]

Had "Mr. Sam" paraphrased this story, "The witness reported that he knew instantly that the victim had had a serious accident," he would have destroyed its effect. Dialogue makes a narrative come alive by bringing listeners close to the action. Paraphrase distances the audience.

Evaluating Narratives

You evaluate narratives in much the same way that you test examples. First you should question whether the narrative is relevant to your purpose. Speakers sometimes "borrow" a narrative from anthologies of stories or jokes, and then have to strain to establish a connection between it and the topic. Narratives should never be used simply for the sake of telling a story or amusing your audience. An irrelevant narrative distracts your audience and may even overpower your actual message.

You should also consider whether the narrative fairly represents the point you wish to make. Is the story typical, or have you selected one that is an exception to the rule? Ethical considerations require that your narratives be representative. In addition, they must seem plausible to the audience. The characters should be believable and the dialogue realistic.

You must also be concerned about whether the narrative will seem appropriate. It should establish a mood consistent with the topic and meet acceptable standards of taste. Finally, ask yourself whether the narrative will be interesting. If the audience has heard your story before, it may be hard to hold their attention. If in doubt, throw it out!

Using Narratives

There is an art to telling a story well. Narratives are usually set off from the rest of a speech by oral or physical punctuation marks. For example, you might pause before beginning a narrative or even move physically closer to the audience. Voice and dialect changes may signal listeners that a "character" is speaking, not the narrator. Gestures and a change of pace may help convey the action and excitement of the story. Strive for an intimate style of presentation that creates a sense of closeness and good will between you and the audience. Good storytellers seem to be sharing a secret or an inside joke with listeners. This impression helps build ethos and establish identification.

The language you use should be colorful, concrete, and vivid. Some verbs convey a sense of action and character better than others. There is a considerable difference, for instance, between someone who "struts" down a street and one who simply "walks." Use active verbs. When the late baseball player and sports announcer Dizzy Dean said, "Bartkowski stole home!" he was using an active verb. Had he said, "Home was stolen by Bartkowski," the passive form

SPEAKER'S NOTES   *Using Narratives*

1. Set the narrative off from the rest of your speech with oral or physical punctuation marks.

2. Strive for an intimate style of presentation.

3. Use colorful, concrete, active language and emphasize dialogue.

4. Avoid digressions and be economical.

5. Save narratives for special moments. Don't let your speech become a string of loosely connected stories.

would have robbed the sentence of its punch. Remember that in most cases using dialogue is better than paraphrasing.

Finally, be economical. Include only those details necessary to convey the proper mood and get your point across. Develop a linear, progressive form of storytelling. Begin with an introduction that excites curiosity; then develop the narrative in an orderly manner. Avoid digressions such as, "That reminds me . . ." or "Speaking of. . . ." Deliver your punch line with a punch! Don't let your conclusion simply dwindle away.

A well-told narrative can add much to a speech, but its use should be reserved for special occasions. Too many narratives can turn a speech into a rambling string of stories without focus. Use narratives to arouse or sustain attention, to convey a special mood for your message, or to demonstrate some important but abstract truth.

IN SUMMARY

Facts and figures, testimony, examples, and narratives are the supporting materials of successful speeches. They demonstrate the meaning and relevance of topics and help verify controversial statements and claims.

Facts and Figures.   Information in the form of facts and figures is a powerful type of support, particularly in American society. *Facts* are verifiable units of information, but they can be distorted when speakers interpret them. It is always important to consider the source of your information in terms of its competence, trustworthiness, and acceptability to listeners. *Statistics* are numerical facts. *Descriptive statistics* may be used to describe the size and distribution of an object or occurrence. *Inferential statistics* are used for demonstrating relationships and predicting trends. They are based on probability estimates.

Evaluate information in terms of its relevance, recentness, reliability, and completeness. Ask yourself whether the facts and figures can stand alone, or whether you must supplement them with other supporting materials, such as testimony and example, to make them more effective. Have more facts and figures than you need so that you can be selective, and remember that facts and figures put probability — not certainty — on your side.

Testimony.   When you use *testimony,* you cite the ideas or words of others in support of your points. Testimony may employ either *verbatim* quotations or a *paraphrase* of what has been said. You can use *expert testimony* from recognized authorities to support the validity of ideas. *Prestige testimony* from well-known public figures can enhance the overall credibility of your speech. *Lay testimony* from peers can help humanize a topic and enhance identification.

Be sure that the sources you cite are objective and unbiased and that the type of testimony you use is appropriate to your purpose. Check to be certain that the experts you cite are speaking within the area of their competence. Be sure to state the qualifications of your sources, especially if these are not well known to listeners.

Examples.   *Examples* serve as verbal illustrations for an oral message. They may be used to create and sustain interest, to clarify ideas, to aid in the retention of information, to personalize a topic, to provide emphasis, and to demonstrate the truth of your message. *Brief examples* extend the meaning of an idea by citing specific instances in support of a statement. *Extended examples* contain more detail about a single instance and give the speaker more room to build impressions. *Factual examples* are based on something that actually happened or that really exists. *Hypothetical examples* are a synthesis of what might have happened, of probable persons and events. Use specific names to personalize examples and transitions to integrate examples into the orderly flow of ideas.

Narratives.   *Narratives* are stories that illustrate some important truth about the topic and are an effective technique for involving the audience. Like good speeches, good narratives have a clear-cut beginning, body, and conclusion. They help establish a mood for a speech. Narratives should be told in language that is colorful and concrete. Active sentence structure and *dialogue* help a narrative come to life. An easy and familiar style of presentation can enhance narration.

TERMS TO KNOW

supporting materials	verbatim
facts	example
statistics	brief example
descriptive statistics	extended example
inferential statistics	factual example
testimony	hypothetical example
expert testimony	narrative
prestige testimony	dialogue
lay testimony	paraphrase

DISCUSSION

1. Evaluate the use of testimony in two of the student speeches in Appendix B. What types of testimony are used? Are they appropriate to the purpose? Do the speakers introduce source qualifications?

2. President Reagan was known as a speaker who used narrative very effectively. Find examples of his speeches in the *Weekly Compilation of Presidential Documents* and study his use of narrative as supporting material.

What vital functions did narrative perform for him? Did he rely too heavily on it? If so, how did this over-reliance weaken his speeches?

3. Select a speech from a recent issue of *Vital Speeches of the Day* that uses statistical information for support. What kind of statistics are used? Are they used effectively? Did the speaker supplement the statistical information with examples? Share your analysis with your classmates.

4. Look in newspapers or magazines for recent statements by public officials that purport to be factual but that may actually contain distortion. What tips you off to the distortion? Would most people be likely to detect this bias?

APPLICATION

1. Develop a hypothetical example or narrative to illustrate one of the following abstract concepts:

   love
   compassion
   charity
   welfare
   justice

2. Note how television advertisements often give facts and figures, testimony, examples, or narratives in combination with visual aids. Using the criteria provided in this chapter, analyze and evaluate a current TV ad with respect to these techniques.

3. Determine which types of testimony might best support the following statements:

   a. Recent NCAA rulings are unfair to minority athletes.
   b. Campus security measures are inadequate.
   c. Teen-age pregnancy is a national disaster.
   d. Soviet-American relations have taken a turn for the better.
   e. The proper diet can help prevent cancer.
   f. Asian immigrant children are outperforming their American-born counterparts in public schools.
   g. Religious training is an important part of a child's development.
   h. Sororities perform an important function on our campus.

   Defend your choices in class.

NOTES

1. Charles F. Hampton, "So You Think It's a Man's World: Men — An Endangered Species," presented to the Rotary Club, St. Joseph, Michigan, 24 Oct. 1983, in *Vital Speeches of the Day* 50 (15 Mar. 1984): 335.

2. Richard Weaver, "Ultimate Terms in Contemporary Rhetoric," in *The Ethics of Rhetoric* (Chicago: Henry Regnery, 1953), pp. 211–32.

3. For similar commentary on other periodicals, see Howard Kahane, *Logic and Contemporary Rhetoric: The Use of Reason in Everyday Life* (Belmont, Calif.: Wadsworth, 1984), pp. 312–13.

4. William L. Kissick, "Health Care in the '80s: Changes, Consequences and Choices," presented to the Greater Philadelphia Committee for Medical Pharmaceutical Sciences of the Philadelphia College of Physicians, Philadelphia, 26 Sept. 1985, in *Vital Speeches of the Day* 52 (15 Jan. 1986): 213.

5. Reported in Al Sicherman, "Playing the Odds: McGervey Estimates the Risks," *Commercial Appeal,* 30 Oct. 1989, p. C-1.

6. S. E. Taylor and S. C. Thompson, "Stalking the Elusive 'Vividness' Effect," *Psychological Review* 89 (1982): 155–81.

7. Bernice Cohen Sachs, M.D., "Changing Relationships between Men and Women," presented to Medical Women's International Congress, Vancouver, B.C., 29 July-4 Aug. 1984, in *Vital Speeches of the Day* 50 (1 Oct. 1984): 757–62.

8. Geraldine Ferraro, "Acceptance Speech," presented at the Democratic National Convention, San Francisco, 19 July 1984, in *Vital Speeches of the Day* 50 (15 Aug. 1984): 644.

9. For a detailed analysis of the power of lay testimony, see Michael Calvin McGee, "In Search of the People: A Rhetorical Alternative," *Quarterly Journal of Speech* 61 (1975): 235–49.

10. Ronald Reagan, "Inaugural Address: Putting America Back to Work," presented in Washington, D.C., 20 Jan. 1981, in *Vital Speeches of the Day* 47 (15 Feb. 1981): 258–60.

11. Dianne Feinstein, "Women in Politics: Time for a Change," presented at Impact '84: A Leadership Conference for Democratic Women, Washington, D.C., 28 Sept. 1983.

12. Ronald Reagan, "Remarks to Veterans at Pointe du Hoc," Normandy, France, 6 June 1984, in *Weekly Compilation of Presidential Documents* 4 (11 June 1984): 841.

13. For a detailed discussion of personal narratives, see Kristin M. Langellier, "Personal Narratives: Perspectives on Theory and Research," *Text and Performance Quarterly* 9 (Oct. 1989): 243–76; and Robert Coles, *The Call of Stories* (Boston: Houghton Mifflin, 1989).

14. Presented 7 June 1986, St. Michael's Church, Memphis.

15. Ronald Reagan, "Remarks to Veterans at Pointe du Hoc," 840–41.

16. Mario Cuomo, "Keynote Address," presented at the Democratic National Convention, San Francisco, 17 July 1984, in *Vital Speeches of the Day* 50 (15 Aug. 1984): 649.

17. Sam J. Ervin, Jr., "Judicial Verbicide: An Affront to the Constitution," presented at Herbert Law Center, Louisiana State University, Baton Rouge, 22 Oct. 1980, in *Representative American Speeches 1980–1981,* ed. Owen Peterson (New York: H. W. Wilson Company, 1981), p. 62.

Every discourse ought to be a living creature; having a body of its own and head and feet; there should be a middle, beginning, and end, adapted to one another and to the whole.

— *PLATO*

7

STRUCTURING

YOUR SPEECH

This Chapter Will Help You

- ◆ appreciate the importance of simplicity, symmetry, and orderliness in speech designs.

- ◆ determine your main points and arrange them effectively.

- ◆ develop introductions that capture attention, establish credibility, and preview your topic.

- ◆ prepare conclusions that summarize your speech, provide a sense of closure, and make a lasting impression on the audience.

- ◆ use transitions to make your speech flow smoothly.

BLUMENFELD, THERESA   Professor Blumenfeld's lectures are easy to understand and follow. She covers the most important material point by point, supplementing what is in the textbook with interesting examples from her own experiences as a practicing clinical psychologist. You don't have to waste time trying to reorganize your lecture notes to make sense out of them. They are very helpful in preparing for the departmental examinations given in the course.

KATZ, RUBIN   Professor Katz has a marvelous repertoire of funny stories. Unfortunately, these don't seem to tie in well with topics covered in the course. When test time comes, you're on your own. Don't rely on his lectures to help you understand the book or pass the exams. When he does cover the material, it's hard to follow him. He is so disorganized that you have problems figuring out where he's coming from and where he's going.

You plan to take Psychology 1101 this term. At registration the Students for Better Education distributed the above evaluations, which demonstrate the vital role of structure in communication. When a topic is important, most of us will choose the speaker who is well organized and easy to follow over the entertainer. Communication research has confirmed that not only are disorganized messages more difficult to understand, they also negatively affect the way we perceive the speaker.[1] A well-structured message helps convey the message of the speech *and* build the ethos of the speaker.

In this chapter we look at the principles that explain why people prefer well-organized messages. We then use these principles to examine the structure of the body of the speech. Next, we discuss how to prepare effective introductions and conclusions. Finally, we consider how to use transitions to connect the parts of a speech into a smoothly flowing finished product.

PRINCIPLES OF GOOD FORM

The structure of a speech should follow the way people naturally see and arrange things in their minds. According to the Gestalt psychologists, all experience is organized in accordance with certain perceptual principles.[2] The primary principle of structure is the idea of **good form,** which is based on simplicity, symmetry, and orderliness. You can build good form into your speeches by presenting your material as clearly and simply as possible, developing a well-balanced presentation, and arranging your main points so that they seem to lead naturally from one to another.

Simplicity

Simple designs are preferable to elaborate designs in public speaking. Public speaking is based on the sharing of ideas, information, or advice. The more complex your message, the harder it will be for you to communicate it effectively. **Simplicity** of structure can be achieved by limiting the number of main points in your speech and by keeping them short and direct.

The Number of Main Points.   In general, the fewer main points you have, the better. Short classroom speeches (no longer than ten minutes) usually should not have more than three main points. Even longer speeches outside the classroom, those that may last up to an hour, should not normally attempt more than five main points. Consider what happens when a speech becomes overburdened with main points:

Thematic statement: Government welfare programs aren't working.

Main points:

1. There are too many programs.
2. The programs often duplicate coverage.
3. Some people who really need help are left out.
4. They are underfunded.
5. They waste money.
6. Recipients have no input into what is really needed.
7. The programs create dependence and stifle initiative.
8. They rob the poor of self-respect.

Each of these points may be important, but presented in this way, they could be overwhelming. The audience would have problems remembering them because there are too many ideas and they are not organized into a meaningful pattern. Let's see how these ideas can be concentrated into a simpler structural pattern:

Thematic statement: Our approach to welfare in America is inadequate, inefficient, and insensitive.

Main point
Subpoints
	1. Our approach is inadequate.
	    A. We don't fund it sufficiently.
	    B. Some people who need help get left out.

Main point
Subpoints
	2. Our approach is inefficient.
	    A. There are too many programs.
	    B. There is duplicate coverage in some areas.
	    C. Money is wasted.

Main point
Subpoints
	3. Our approach is insensitive.
	    A. It creates dependence and stifles initiative.
	    B. It robs the poor of self-respect.

This simpler structure will make the speech easier to follow. The ideas have been grouped together into three main points. Overlapping points have been combined and unnecessary ideas omitted. The audience will find it easier to follow the speech and remember the thrust of the message.

The Phrasing of Main Points. You should word main points as simply as possible. In the preceding example not only has the number of main points been reduced, but the wording of these points has become clear and direct. Parallel phrasing has been used for emphasis. This strategic repetition helps listeners remember the message. It also allows the speaker to refer to the "Three *I*'s" (Inadequate, Inefficient, and Insensitive) of welfare in the introduction and conclusion, which should help the audience remember the message.

To achieve simplicity of structure, be sure your specific purpose, thematic statement, and main points are very clear to you so that you can express them with utmost economy. Keep in mind that some of the world's most magnificent structures are simple in design. Greek temples, which have been admired for thousands of years, are models of simplicity that impress observers with their strength, grandeur, and beauty. Think of simplicity as a major goal when building your speech.

Symmetry

Symmetry means proper balance. In a well-balanced speech all the major parts — the introduction, body, and conclusion — receive the right amount of emphasis and seem to fit together smoothly. Emphasis depends upon *timing*. The sense of proper fit, *coherence,* involves the logical relationship between parts.

Timing the Speech. Instructors frequently time speeches that are presented in class, and so you should plan with time limitations in mind. It can be very disconcerting to find yourself finishing the first main point of your speech with only one minute left and two more main points to go. Outside the classroom working within time limits is equally important. If you are asked to present a fifteen-minute report on a work project and instead take thirty minutes, you risk a poor reception. Time yourself as you practice, cutting and adding material to maintain the proper balance.

There is no clear rule of thumb that establishes time limits for the major parts of speeches. However, the following rules may be helpful:

1. *The body should be the longest part.* The body contains the essence of your message — the major ideas you want to communicate. If you spend three minutes on your introduction, a minute and a half on the body, and thirty seconds on the conclusion, your speech will seem badly out of balance.

2. *Your main points should be balanced with respect to time.* You might follow a principle of *equality,* in which each main point receives the same amount of attention. Or you could follow a principle of *progression,* in which successive main points receive increasing attention proportionate to their importance to your specific purpose. For example, to show that they build in importance, the first main point might receive one minute; the second, one and a half minutes; and the third, two minutes.

3. *The introduction and conclusion should be approximately equal in length.* Neither should seem abrupt, nor should either seem overly prolonged. The combined amount of time spent on the introduction and conclusion should be less than that spent on the body of your speech.

Making the Speech Coherent.   The coherence of a speech depends on how well the individual parts relate to each other. It is best to structure the body of your speech first so that you can be certain that your introduction and conclusion fit what you have to say. Your speech is also more coherent when you can tie together the introduction and conclusion. If the introduction asks a question, the conclusion could supply an answer based on the ideas developed in the speech. If you begin with a story of defeat, your conclusion might offer a related story of victory.

Orderliness

Orderliness suggests that you should follow a consistent pattern in developing your speech. For example, if you want to explore with your audience the solution to a problem, you would first present the problem and follow that with the solution. Why would you organize this way? Simply because this is how our minds typically work. We usually don't think first of solutions, then go in search of problems to fit them. This type of natural processing also explains the order of a question followed by an answer. We don't usually come up with answers, and then look for their questions.

Several other Gestalt principles are also helpful in ordering the main points in the body of your speech. We discuss them in the next section.

STRUCTURING THE BODY OF YOUR SPEECH

The body of your speech contains the *substance* of what you have to say. Here you pursue your purposes and develop your thematic statement. Because the body does the important work of your speech, you should organize it first, and then prepare the introduction and conclusion so that they help you realize your goals. In developing the body, you have three major tasks to accomplish.

1. You must determine what main points you will make.

2. You must arrange these points in the most effective order.

3. You must decide how to use supporting material to substantiate these points.

Determining Your Main Points

Preparing a speech is like building a bridge across a canyon so that communication can cross between speaker and listener. Each main point should be a pillar that supports the bridge. Your main points are the most important ideas related to your topic. Each main point should increase your audience's understanding of and interest in the topic.

As you do your research, you will find that certain ideas are stressed and repeated in the material you read or in the interviews you conduct. These ideas represent the most vital concerns and issues connected with your topic. By reflecting on them and how they affect your listeners, you can decide on the specific purpose and thematic statement of your speech. Shaped by your purpose, these featured ideas may well become the main points of your speech.

Let's look at how you might determine the main points for a speech on selecting a personal computer. To get the best overall picture, prepare a **research overview** that lists your main sources of information and the major ideas from each source. Figure 7.1 presents such an overview. Here the sources include personal experience, an article in *Consumer Reports*, a buyer's guide to personal computers, and an interview with the director of the computer lab on campus.

To find your main points, you would look for repeated ideas or themes across the sources. You might come up with the following themes (the initials refer to column headings in Figure 7.1):

1. Learning about computers [PE 1, 2, 3, and 4]

2. Matching the computer to your needs [PE 6; CR 1, 2, and 5; BG all; DM 1, 2, 3, and 5]

3. Investigating dependability and service [PE 5; CR 3 and 4; and DM 4, 5, and 6]

Constructing main points out of these themes now becomes relatively easy:

1. Learn the uses and limitations of personal computers.

2. Determine your needs and which computers might best serve them.

3. Consider the dependability of the computer and the availability of service.

Figure 7.1
Sample Research Overview

Personal Experience	Consumer Reports	Buyer's Guide	Interview (D. Madison)
1. Initial feelings about computers.	1. Check for software that meets your needs.	1. Compare costs vs. features.	1. Determine how you will use the PC (both present and future).
2. Some wrong impressions I had.	2. Compare for "user friendliness."	2. Decide what features you need/want.	2. Check possibility of upgrading/expanding system.
3. Some early mistakes in shopping.	3. Check for availability of local-dealer servicing.	3. Check software costs.	3. Check compatibility with campus services.
4. How I got on the right track.	4. Check on dependability/repair record.		4. Talk to other campus and local users; call local users group to check satisfaction with programs and service.
5. Talks with friends about dealer-service experiences.	5. Peripherals available?		5. Check for training/ troubleshooting help.
6. How the computer has helped me.			6. Check track record of company, time in business, availability of service if you move.

Arranging Your Main Points

Once you have determined your main points, you must decide how to arrange them in your speech. You need to come up with a way of ordering them that makes sense to your audience, is easy to follow, fits your material, and helps you realize your purpose. As you consider the order of your main points, remember the principles of good form: simplicity, symmetry, and orderliness. Additional Gestalt principles that will help you structure the body of your speech include proximity, similarity, and closure.

Principle of Proximity.   The **principle of proximity** suggests that things occurring together in time or space should be presented in the order in which they normally occur. If you are describing a process that involves three steps, you need to present these steps in their proper order using a *sequential design* that follows a chronological pattern. If you want to discuss events that led to a present-day problem you might also use a sequential design. Your research may show that the major incidents occurred in 1945, 1962, and 1975. If you follow this natural pattern, your speech will be easy to understand. But if you start talking about 1975, then jump back to 1945, then leap ahead to the present before doubling back to 1962, you will probably lose most of your listeners on one of these abrupt turns. You will have violated the principle of proximity.

If you are preparing a speech describing the scenic wonders of Yellowstone Park, your speech might best follow a *spatial design*. Such a design is based on physical relationships such as east-west, up-down, or points around a circle. You might begin with your audience at the south visitor's center, take them up the west side to Old Faithful, continue north to Mammoth Hot Springs, then down the east side through the Grand Canyon of the Yellowstone. This way your audience gets a verbal map to follow as well as a picture of the major attractions in the park.

Principle of Similarity.

The **principle of similarity** implies that people group together things that seem similar. This natural tendency underlies the *categorical design* for organizing speeches. Speakers use categorical designs when they discuss "three ways to stop smoking" or "the four characteristics of a good stereo system." Categories can be used to group *similar terms, concepts, or notions,* such as types of diets, or they can be used to represent *major divisions that exist in topics themselves,* such as the symptoms of a disease. Socrates may have been thinking of categories when he advised speakers to divide subjects "according to the natural formation, where the joint is, not breaking any part as a bad carver might."[3]

You can use a categorical design to talk about a person. For example, you might believe that the public image of Gloria Steinem has been distorted by poor press coverage; therefore, you decide to present a speech that will help the audience understand her feminism. You decide on a categorical design so that you can emphasize the factors leading to her activism. In such a design you might consider: (a) personal and family events, (b) professional events, and (c) political events. These categories generate the main points of your speech:

> *Specific purpose:* To inform my audience of critical events that contributed to Gloria Steinem's feminism.
>
> *Thematic statement:* To understand why Gloria Steinem is a feminist, one must examine the personal, professional, and political events that shaped her life.
>
> *Main points:*
> 1. Ms. Steinem's early home life laid the basis for her feminism.
> 2. Ms. Steinem's professional activities exposed her to sexual harassment.
> 3. Ms. Steinem's political experiences subjected her to discrimination.[4]

Principle of Closure.

We like to have things neatly tied up so that we feel we know the "whole story." This tendency explains the **principle of closure.** Have you ever become engrossed in a magazine article in a waiting room only to find that someone had torn out the last page of the story? Can you remember the annoyance you felt? Your need for closure had been frustrated.

The principle of closure suggests that we like to see patterns in speeches completed. If you omit an important category when developing your topic, listeners may notice its omission. If you leave out an important step in a sequence, audiences often sense the flaw. Although all speeches should have closure, there are two types for which closure is essential. These are *cause-effect* and *problem-solution* speeches. Because we need the world to seem purposeful, coherent, and controllable, we prefer that all events have clear causes and all problems have solutions.

A cause-effect speech can go in two directions: it can begin by focusing on a present situation and seek its causes, or it can look at the present as a potential cause of future effects. Sometimes these variations can be combined. You might take a current situation such as the budget deficit and develop a speech tracing its origins. If you had enough time, you might continue by predicting the future effects of the deficit. Understanding the causes could help your listeners see what needs to be done to reduce the deficit. Predicting future effects might make them *want* to reduce it. No matter which variation you use, the principle of closure suggests that you should include *both* the causes and effects in your speech.

The problem-solution design is closely related to the cause-effect design, and the two are often used in combination. The problem-solution design focuses the audience's attention on a problem, and then provides a solution to

---

SPEAKER'S NOTES

Determining and Arranging Your Main Points

1. Review your research notes to identify repeated ideas for possible main points.

2. Select as main points those most relevant to your specific purpose and most appropriate for your audience.

3. Limit the number of main points to three for a short speech and five for a longer effort.

4. Use the principle of proximity to arrange main points as they naturally occur in sequential or spatial patterns.

5. Apply the principle of similarity to arrange main points in a categorical design.

6. Use the principle of closure to assure completeness in cause-effect and problem-solution designs.

it. Such speeches often use motive appeals to bring the problem home to listeners. Once you have aroused strong feelings, your solutions must promise to satisfy them, or the audience will feel frustrated and resentful. Returning to our previous example, the budget deficit could be presented as a problem, a threat to national security and the well-being of future generations. The speaker then would look to the causes of the problem to find a solution. *Both* problem and solution must be discussed to satisfy listeners' need for closure.

Selecting Your Supporting Materials

Once you have determined and arranged your main points, you must decide how to develop and support them. Because your listeners will want good reasons for accepting what you have to say, you should strengthen each main point with *supporting materials:* facts, testimony, examples, or narratives. Like a flimsy bridge support, an undeveloped main point cannot carry much weight. There is no easy answer to the question of how much or what kind of supporting material is required to establish a main point. The following guidelines, however, may help:

1. *The more controversial the point you wish to make, the more you should use "hard" supporting material, such as statistical evidence and expert testimony.* When experts disagree on a subject or when expert opinion contradicts the ideas held by your audience, you must have more supporting material. Facts and figures add objectivity and authority to your message.

2. *The more complex or abstract a point, the more you should use examples as supporting materials.* Statistics are especially difficult to understand when presented in speeches, so you should supplement statistical information with examples that make the meaning clear. To heighten understanding, examples often use comparison and contrast to relate the unknown to the known. Calling an earthquake a "burp of the earth" — as we heard during media discussions of the 1989 California quake — illustrates this principle in miniature. Visual aids may also help clarify complex points.

3. *The more you ask from your listeners, the more you must reassure them with supporting material.* You should cite authorities the audience knows, trusts, and respects. Lay testimony may also reassure listeners because it comes from people like them.

4. *The less expertise you bring to an issue, the more you need objective supporting material.* Although your classmates may like you, your personal opinion of the Strategic Defense Initiative may not carry much weight with them. To speak credibly on important topics, your points should be buttressed with the best and most recent information and with expert opinion.

5. *The further a subject is from the lives of your listeners, the more you must use examples and narratives that build identification and human interest.* The impact of drought on human life in Africa cannot be conveyed by numbers alone. Only vivid images created by using examples or telling the stories of people involved will bring the main points to life.

Although the situation varies from topic to topic, speaker to speaker, and audience to audience, it is possible to set up an *ideal model* for the support of each main point. That model includes the main point plus the following supporting materials (not necessarily in this order):

- the most important relevant facts and figures;

- the most authoritative judgments about a situation, made by sources the audience will respect;

- at least one interesting story or example that helps humanize and clarify the situation.

Let us look at this model in action. Assume that you are making a speech in which your specific purpose is "to inform listeners of the impact of hunger in our city." Your thematic statement is "Hunger in our city causes widespread misery, robs us of human potential, and is a major cause of crime." One of your main points is "Hunger robs us of human potential." Here is one way you could use supporting materials to develop this point:

> Children in particular are affected by the grim reality of hunger. Each day hunger in our city robs us of their human potential. Dr. Paula Hoffman, director of research at Children's Hospital, told me that hunger is both a crisis in itself and the cause of many other social problems.
>
> "If you are born in certain areas of our city," Dr. Hoffman said, "you will have one chance in seven of being brain-damaged because of your mother's poor diet during pregnancy or inadequate food during the first year of life." That sort of damage never repairs itself.
>
> Dr. Hoffman introduced me to one of her patients, nine-year-old Lisa. Her eyes lacked sparkle, and her face was expressionless. I had the feeling that I was talking to the living dead. Lisa is a victim of the hunger in our city. How many Lisas are there?
>
> The *Report on Hunger,* prepared last year by a task force of the county medical society, tell us, "There may be 20,000 people in our county whose brains have been damaged by prenatal and postnatal malnutrition." That alone is a tragedy, but just think of the social problems it creates for all of us!

The first part of this example uses expert testimony to demonstrate that hunger is a major cause of diminished human potential. Note how the speaker's use of personal contact with an authority and an exact quotation strengthen the point. This expert testimony is then confirmed by a brief factual example that brings the message home. Finally, the use of data from the medical report shows the problem's magnitude.

All three forms of supporting material — expert testimony, example, and statistical information — work together to establish the main point. Each contributes its special strength. If each of your main points is buttressed by supporting materials that work together, your bridge of meaning should carry its message effectively to your listeners.

Once you have developed the body of your speech, you can then turn your attention to preparing an introduction and conclusion that join with the body to form a symmetrical, coherent message.

PREPARING AN EFFECTIVE INTRODUCTION

As you stand before your audience, you must quickly cope with two critical questions in your listeners' minds: *Why should I listen to this speech?* and *Why should I listen to this speaker?* The answers to these questions indicate two of the basic functions of speech introductions: to arouse the interest of your listeners and to establish your credibility. The third major function of an introduction is to preview the main points you will develop.

Capturing Attention and Interest

A speech that opens with "Good evening. Tonight I'm going to talk with you about organ transplants" has already created a problem for itself. It does little to make listeners really want to listen. Is there any way to avoid falling into the dullness trap? There are a number of ways in which you can attract, build, and hold the interest of your audience. These include (1) asking rhetorical questions, (2) beginning with a quotation, (3) telling a story, (4) involving the audience, (5) building suspense, (6) relating your subject to personal experience, and (7) shocking or startling the audience. Though these techniques may be especially helpful in the introduction, you can also use them throughout the speech.

Asking Rhetorical Questions. The usual function of a question is to seek information from others. However, the **rhetorical question,** which needs no answer, is different. Rather than seeking information, the rhetorical question attempts to arouse curiosity. Annette Berrington opened her classroom speech on safety belts by asking the audience:

> How would you like to have your name in the paper? I can tell you a good way to get it there. Don't wear your seat belt while you're riding in a car. Yesterday I called Nashville and talked to Linda Butler in the planning and research section of the Tennessee Highway Patrol. Ms. Butler shared some startling facts. Of the 899 people killed in automobile accidents in our state last year, 777 were *not* using their seat belts at the time of the crash. And how do you like these odds? You have a seven times greater chance of being killed if you don't wear your safety belt!

These rhetorical questions provided a provocative opening. The listeners' first reaction was to think that they *would* like to have their names in the paper — we all enjoy recognition. However, their positive response quickly changed as listeners realized the circumstances under which their names would appear. Needless to say, Annette had captured her audience's attention.

Beginning with a Quotation.

Starting your speech with a striking quotation or paraphrase from a well-known person or respected authority on your topic both arouses interest and gives you some borrowed ethos.

The most effective opening quotations are short and to the point. One student paraphrased a famous author to open his speech comparing and contrasting whole-grain and white breads.

> Henry Miller once said that you can travel 50,000 miles in America without tasting a good piece of bread.

If a quotation contains vital information or if the language is especially eloquent, you will want to cite the exact words. Susie Smith used the following quotation, attributed to the novelist William Faulkner, to introduce her classroom speech on job satisfaction:

> You can't eat for eight hours a day, nor drink for eight hours a day, nor make love for eight hours a day — all you can do for eight hours is work. Which is the reason why man makes himself and everybody else so miserable and unhappy.

Most books of quotations (see Chapter 5) are indexed by key words and subjects as well as by authors. They are excellent sources of quotations to introduce your topic.

Telling a Story.

Long ago around countless campfires, we humans began our love affair with stories. Through stories we remember the past, entertain and educate ourselves, and pass on our heritage to future generations. In introductions, stories help capture listener attention and depict a problem in vivid terms. Sandra Baltz, a premed major, introduced the issue of deciding who shall live and who must die with the following story:

> On a cold and stormy night in 1841 the ship *William Brown* struck an iceberg in the North Atlantic. Passengers and crew members frantically scrambled into the lifeboats. To make a bad disaster even worse, one of the lifeboats began to sink because it was overcrowded. Fourteen men were thrown overboard that horrible night. After the survivors were rescued, a crew member was tried for the murders of those thrown overboard.
>
> Fortunately, situations like this have been few in history, but today we face a similar problem in the medical establishment: deciding who will live as we allocate scarce medical resources for transplants. Someday, your fate — or the fate of someone you love — could depend on how we resolve this dilemma.

Humorous anecdotes are also often used in introductions. A touch of humor can put an audience in a receptive mood for your message. Humor is appropriate when your subject is light or the occasion is festive. But humor may also be the most frequently misused technique of introducing speeches. Thinking that being funny will assure success, novice speakers often search through joke books to find something to make people laugh. Unless carefully adapted, such material often sounds canned, inappropriate, or only remotely relevant to the topic or occasion. If you wish to use humor in your introduction, be certain the material is fresh and relevant to your topic.

Involving the Audience.   One of the most frequently used involvement techniques is complimenting the audience. People like to hear good things about themselves and their community. In 1962 John F. Kennedy delivered an address at a White House dinner honoring Nobel Prize winners. His opening remarks included this statement:

> I think this is the most extraordinary collection of talent, of human knowledge, that has ever been gathered together at the White House, with the possible exception of when Thomas Jefferson dined alone.[5]

With this elegant tribute Kennedy was able to pay homage to his guests without embarrassing them or going overboard with praise. His witty reference to the genius of Thomas Jefferson honored the past as well as the present and helped establish the nature of the dinner as a national celebration.

You can also involve listeners by relating your topic directly to their lives. This is especially important when your topic seems remote from the audience's immediate concerns or experiences. Beth Duncan wanted to speak to her college student audience on Alzheimer's disease, a topic that might have seemed distant to many of them. Beth helped listeners relate to her speech with the following introduction:

> I'd like to share with you a letter my roommate got from her grandmother, an educated and cultured woman. I watched her weep as she read it, and after she showed it to me, I understood why.
>
> "Dear Sally," it said. "I am finally around to answer your last. You have to look over me. ha. I am so sorry to when you called Sunday why didn't you remind me. Steph had us all so upset leaving and not telling no she was going back but we have a good snow ha and Kathy can't drive on ice so I never get a pretty card but they have a thing to see through an envelope. I haven't got any in the bank until I get my homestead check so I'm just sending this. ha. When you was talking on the phone Cathy had Ben and got my groceries and I had to unlock the door. I forgot to say hold and I don't have Claudette's number so forgive me for being so silly. ha. Nara said to tell you she isn't doing no good well one is doing pretty good and my eyes. Love, Nanny."
>
> Sally's grandmother has Alzheimer's disease. Over 2.5 million older people in the United States are afflicted with it. It could strike someone in our families — a grandparent, an aunt or uncle, or even our mother or father.

When Beth finished this introduction, her classmates were deeply involved with her topic. Realizing that this disease of older people could affect their families made them want to listen to Beth's speech. You too can involve your

An effective introduction should put you on good terms with your listeners. You can establish identification among yourself, the audience, and your topic by relating personal experiences that put your listeners in a receptive mood for your message.

listeners by relating your topic to their motivations or attitudes and by using inclusive words such as *we* and *our.*

Developing Suspense.   You can attract and hold your listeners' attention by arousing their curiosity, then making them wait before you satisfy it. The following introduction creates curiosity and anticipation:

> Getting knocked down is no disgrace. Champions are made by getting up just one more time than the opponent! The results are a matter of record about a man who suffered many defeats: Lost his job in 1832, defeated for legislature in 1832, failed in business in 1833, defeated for legislature in 1834, sweetheart died in 1835, had nervous breakdown in 1836, defeated for nomination for Congress in 1843, elected to Congress in 1846, lost renomination in 1848, rejected for land officer in 1849, defeated for Senate in 1854, defeated for nomination for Vice-President in 1856, defeated for Senate in 1858. In 1860 Abraham Lincoln was elected president of the United States. Lincoln proved that a big shot is just a little shot who keeps shooting. The greatest failures in the world are those who fail by not doing anything.[6]

Relating the Subject to Personal Experience.   An old adage suggests that people are interested first in themselves, next in other people, then in things, and finally in ideas. This may explain why relating a topic to personal experience heightens audience interest. When speakers have been personally involved with a topic, they also gain credibility. We are more willing to listen to others and take their advice if we know they have traveled the road themselves. Self-help groups such as Alcoholics Anonymous and Weight Watchers acknowledge this truth by restricting their leadership to members who have been through their programs.

Viola Brown effectively related her topic to personal experience. She began a speech urging her classmates to contribute to the United Cerebral Palsy Foundation by holding up a ten-dollar bill.

> This money means a lot to me, as I'm sure it would to most of you. College students who are working their way through school don't have money to burn. But I'm going to give this ten dollars away. It's my monthly contribution to the United Cerebral Palsy Foundation. This organization is very important to me because I have a cousin who has cerebral palsy. Today I want to tell you what it is like to have someone with this illness in your family. And I want you to know what the United Cerebral Palsy Foundation can do with this money.

Shocking or Startling the Audience.   Anything truly unusual draws attention to itself and arouses curiosity. Consider the headlines from the sensationalist tabloids: "TALKING BEAR SCARES COUPLE!" "SIXTY-YEAR-OLD WOMAN GIVES BIRTH TO TWINS!" "WHY I WENT FROM HERO TO HEROINE: EX-GI TELLS ALL!" When using this technique, you must be sure not to go beyond the bounds of propriety. You want to startle your listeners, not offend them.

Roberta Hobson used this **shock-and-startle technique** effectively in the opening of a persuasive speech:

> The world's oldest profession is alive and thriving. The *Star* estimates that the income for local female prostitutes in 1988 exceeded seven million dollars. This is tax-free income! Crackdowns to clean up our red-light districts are little more than a farce — a revolving door of arrest, bail, and release, often all in the same night. Since we obviously have not been able to control this illegal activity, it's

---

SPEAKER'S NOTES

Capturing the Attention of Your Audience

1. Ask rhetorical questions.

2. Use a quotation from a well-known person.

3. Tell a story that is related to your topic.

4. Show your listeners how your topic applies to them.

5. Create suspense and anticipation.

6. Call on your personal experience with the topic.

7. Startle the audience with something unusual.

time to try something else. I suggest that we follow the lead of Nevada and make prostitution legal in Indiana.

This opening quickly gained the attention and interest of the classroom audience. But it could have backfired and negatively affected Roberta's ethos had she not handled the topic with propriety and seriousness. She went on to present a well-researched and carefully prepared speech.

Whatever attention-arousing technique you use in your introduction, be sure that it is relevant to your topic. One student began with the following:

> Have you ever thought about what it might be like to die? Have you ever dreamed about death? Have you ever talked with someone who came close to death, yet survived?

These rhetorical questions gained the attention of the audience and prepared listeners for a speech on near-death experiences. Unfortunately, what followed was a speech on taxes. The student tried to tie his introduction to the topic by saying:

> Nothing is certain except death and taxes. This afternoon I want to tell you how you can save money on your income tax.

His speech was carefully prepared and effectively presented, yet the audience felt cheated. The introduction had prepared the audience for something the speech did not deliver. Be sure your attention-getting material is appropriate for your topic.

Establishing Your Credibility as a Speaker

The second major function of an effective introduction is to establish the credibility of the speaker. We tend to judge others early in our interactions with them. These initial impressions color our later perceptions, both of speakers and of their messages.[7] Therefore, it is important to establish early that you are qualified to speak on your subject.

Your credibility may come from personal experience. As she talked about the problems of a family member who suffered from cerebral palsy, Viola Brown relied on personal knowledge to establish her credibility. You do not have to have such personal experience, however, to be qualified to speak on a topic. In your introduction you can refer to your research to demonstrate your credibility.

> I was amazed to learn in psychology class that research does not support a strong link between exposure to persuasive communications and behavior. This discovery led me to do more reading on the relationship between advertising and consumer activity. What I found was even more surprising, especially when you consider that, according to *Parade* magazine, companies were willing to pay $700,000 for a thirty-second spot commercial during Super Bowl XXIV.

Such an approach creates more credibility (and is much more interesting) than had you said:

> The information for my speech came from my psychology class, two articles in the *Journal of Applied Psychology,* and a feature story in *Parade* magazine.

When you establish favorable ethos, you also create the grounds for one of the most powerful effects of communication: *identification* between you and your listeners. Identification occurs when people break through the walls that separate them as individuals and share thoughts and feelings as though they were one. When you seem attractive, friendly, competent, and dynamic, your listeners *want* to identify with you, and your effectiveness as a communicator is magnified.

Preview Your Topic

The final function of an introduction is to preview what is to follow in the body of the speech by presenting the thematic statement and the main points. The preview usually comes near the end of the introduction and may serve as a transition into the body. Because it establishes an agenda and helps the audience focus more clearly, a good preview is an aid to critical listening.

In the following speech on campus security problems, Martha Radner presented her thematic statement and then used a numbering system to preview her main points:

> Today I want to share with you a way to improve security on our campus, a way that would make life a lot safer for all of us. First, I want to show you how dangerous our situation has become. Second, I'll explore the reasons why current security measures on our campus are ineffective. And third, I'll present my plan for a safer campus.

By informing her listeners of her intentions as well as her speech's design, Martha helped her audience listen more intelligently.

DEVELOPING AN EFFECTIVE CONCLUSION

Many beginning speakers seem awkward when they come to the end of their speeches. "That's all, folks!" may be an effective ending for a Looney Tunes cartoon, but in a speech such conclusions violate the principles of good form and closure. Saying "That's it, I guess," or "Well, I'm done," accompanied by a sigh of relief, suggests that you have not planned your speech very carefully. You should spend at least as much time developing an effective ending for your speech as you spend on the introduction.

Functions of the Conclusion

Your conclusion is the final span in your bridge of meaning. Your concluding words should stay with listeners, remind them of your message, and, if appropriate, move them to action. Therefore, your conclusion should (1) summarize the meaning and purpose of your speech, (2) provide a sense of closure, and (3) in some persuasive speeches, motivate listeners to act.

The first task of an effective conclusion is to summarize the meaning of major ideas. This summary often functions as a transition between the body and the final remarks, as in this conclusion to a speech on choosing a personal computer:

> Now you should feel more comfortable about moving into the world of personal computers. Remember, begin by finding out what computers can do for you. Next, analyze your needs. Once you know what you need, you can look for a perfect match — the ideal computer for you. Finally, consider dependability and service in making your decision. Whatever you do, don't be taken in by the ads that promise something for nothing. Do some research so that you spend your money wisely.

Such a summary can itself offer listeners a sense of closure. To seal that effect, you can use any one of a number of special techniques.

Concluding Techniques

Many of the techniques that create effective introductions are also useful for developing memorable conclusions. Using the same technique to close a speech as you used to open it can make your speech seem balanced and elegant. This practice also increases the symmetry of form that we discussed earlier in this chapter.

Asking Questions.   When used in your introduction, questions help gain attention and excite curiosity. When used in conclusions, questions give your audience something to think about after you have finished. In persuasive speeches they can challenge listeners to action.

Annette Berrington opened her speech on the use of seat belts with a rhetorical question: "How would you like to have your name in the paper?" Her final words were, "Are you really sure you'd like to have your name in the paper?" This final question echoed the beginning and served as a haunting reminder to buckle up when you get in the car. Had Annette ended with "Remember, buckled seat belts save lives!" the effect would not have been as dramatic.

When used as a persuasive appeal, concluding questions may be more than rhetorical. They may actually call for a response from the audience. During his

Your concluding words should summarize your message in a memorable way. Vaclav Havel, president of the new democratic government in Czechoslovakia, inspired many as he addressed a joint session of the U.S. Congress in early 1990. The ovation he received as he concluded was more than just a courtesy; it was a tribute to the remarkable speech that is reprinted in Appendix B.

presidential campaigns, the Reverend Jesse Jackson often used this technique to register voters. He would end a speech by asking:

> How many of you are not registered to vote? Raise your hands. No, stand up so we can see you! Is that all of you who aren't registered? Stand up! Let me see you!

Such questioning and cajoling would be followed by on-site voter registration. Evangelists who issue an invitation to personal salvation at the end of their sermons often use concluding questions in a similar way. To be effective this technique must be the climax of a speech that has prepared its audience for action.

Closing with a Quotation.   Brief quotations that capture the essence of your message or purpose can make effective conclusions. If one literary quotation is used to open a speech, another on the same theme can provide balance in the conclusion. Susie Smith opened her speech on job satisfaction with a quotation from William Faulkner that linked work and unhappiness. She closed the speech with a more positive quotation from Joseph Conrad that summed up the meaning of satisfying work:

> I like what is in work — the chance to find yourself. Your own reality — for yourself, not for others — what no other . . . can ever know.

Telling a Story. Ending a speech with an anecdote that summarizes your message or purpose is also an effective concluding technique because the story tends to stick in listeners' memories. To conclude his student speech on converting waste materials into usable energy, Dan Martini told this story:

> Last week I was riding with a friend down Walnut Grove Road, and we could see the landfill area. The wind was stirring up paper and debris. It was a depressing sight. My friend shook his head and said, "You know, some archaeologist in the future may rediscover our civilization, buried under a pile of garbage."
>
> What I said to him is what I've said to you today: "Have more faith in our creative imagination. The same technology that makes waste can also show us how to use it productively. Like modern alchemy, our technology can transform garbage into gold — or at least into energy!"

Ending with a Metaphor. A concluding metaphor can end your speech effectively.[8] Metaphors combine things that are apparently unlike so that we see unexpected relationships. An effective metaphor reveals a hidden truth about the speaker's subject in a memorable way. As a conclusion to a speech, such a metaphor may provide lasting illumination. William S. Anderson, chairman of the board of NCR Corporation, used a sports metaphor to end a speech on the Japanese challenge to our economy. After discussing the problem and suggesting a solution, he concluded:

> The fact that Japan is entering the 1980s with its own agenda of difficult problems offers scant solace to the United States. Momentum still favors the Japanese. . . . And although the scoreboard at the moment may read 35 to 14, the home team still has time to revise its game plan, beef up its offense, and win the big one after all. It should be an interesting second half.[9]

The implied comparison of our economic rivalry with Japan to a football game makes an effective conclusion. It symbolizes our faith in competition and our belief that the underdog always has a chance to win.

Whatever concluding techniques you decide on should suit the material and structure of your speech. The conclusion should satisfy your audience that what was promised in the opening has now been delivered.

USING TRANSITIONS

To achieve coherence in your speech and to guide your listeners along, you will need connecting elements called **transitions.** Transitions link the various parts of a speech by showing why and how the main points relate to their subpoints and to each other. They also explain the connection between the body of a speech and its introduction and conclusion. Transitions signal listeners that the speaker is leaving one idea and moving on to another.

Some transitions are simple, short phrases such as "My next point is . . ." or "There is another important point that must be made. . . ." More often, however, transitions are worded as phrases that link ideas, such as "Having looked at why people don't pay compliments more often, let's consider. . . ." This type of transition sums up what you have just said while directing your audience to your next point.

Certain stock words or phrases can be used to signal other types of changes in a speech. For example, transitional words and phrases like *until now, twenty years ago, in the future,* and *only last week* can be used to point out time changes. Transitions can also be used to show that you are expanding on something you have already said. Transitions that signal addition include *furthermore, moreover,* and *in addition.* The use of the word *similarly* indicates that a comparison will follow. Phrases and words such as *on the other hand, unfortunately,* and *however* suggest that a contrast is imminent. Cause-and-effect relationships can be suggested with words like *as a result* and *consequently.* Introductory phrases like *in the distance* or *as we move west* indicate spatial relationships.

One special type of transition is the **internal summary.** An internal summary reminds listeners of the points you have already made before you move on to the next part of your speech. Internal summaries are especially useful in cause-effect and problem-solution speeches. An internal summary signals your listeners that you have concluded your discussion of the causes or problem and are ready to move on to the effects or solution. In addition, an internal summary condenses and repeats your ideas, which can help your listeners remember your message. Consider the following example:

> So now we see what the problem is. We know the cost in human suffering. We know the terrible political consequences and the enormous economic burden. The question is, what are we going to do about it? Let me tell you about a solution that many experts agree may turn things around.

The speaker condensed the three main points about the human, political, and economic aspects of a problem into an internal summary that prepared the audience for the next major phase of the speech. Internal summaries should be brief and to the point so that they highlight the major features of your message.

The lack of planned transitions is often apparent when beginning speakers overuse the words *well, you know,* or *okay* to replace transitions. Plan a variety of effective transitions that help your speech flow smoothly and clearly.

IN SUMMARY

A speech that is carefully structured helps the audience understand the message and enhances the ethos of the speaker.

Principles of Good Form.   A well-structured speech has *good form:* it is simple, symmetrical, and orderly. *Simplicity* can be achieved by limiting the number of main points and using clear, direct language. A speech has *symmetry* when the major parts receive proper emphasis and when they work together effectively. *Orderliness* means that a speech follows a consistent pattern of development.

Structuring the Body of Your Speech.   You should structure the body first, so that you can build an introduction and conclusion that fit well with the principal part of your speech. To develop the body, decide on your main points, determine how best to arrange them, and select effective supporting materials. To discover your main points, prepare a *research overview* of the information you have collected. This summary can help you spot major themes that can develop into main points.

You should arrange main points so that they follow natural perceptual patterns based on the principles of proximity, similarity, and closure. *Proximity* suggests that things should be discussed as they happen together in space or time. If they occur in a time sequence, use a sequential design for your speech. If they occur in physical relationship to each other, a spatial design might be appropriate. The *similarity* of objects or events may suggest a categorical design for structuring main points. The structure of the body satisfies the principle of *closure* when it completes the design it begins. Cause-effect and problem-solution designs require closure in order to be effective.

Supporting materials fill out the structure of the speech. The kind and type of supporting material you need depends on how controversial your point may be, its complexity, the risk it entails for listeners, your credibility, and its closeness to the actual experiences of listeners. In an ideal arrangement, you should support each main point with information, testimony, and an example or story that emphasizes its human aspects.

Preparing an Effective Introduction.   The introduction to a speech should arouse your listeners' interest, establish your credibility, and orient the audience to your message. Some useful ways to introduce a speech include asking *rhetorical questions,* beginning with a quotation, telling a story, involving the audience with the subject, creating suspense, relating the topic to personal experience, and startling the audience. As you build credibility, you also make possible identification between you and the audience. Your introduction is also the place to preview your topic.

Developing an Effective Conclusion.   An effective conclusion should summarize the meaning and purpose of your speech, provide a sense of closure, and, if appropriate, motivate listeners to act. Techniques useful for conclusions include asking questions, closing with a quotation, telling a story, and ending with a metaphor. Your speech will seem more symmetrical and satisfying to listeners if your conclusion ties into your introduction.

Using Transitions.   Effective *transitions* point up the relationships among ideas in your speech. *Internal summaries* remind listeners of the points you have made in one part of your speech before moving on to another.

TERMS TO KNOW

good form	**principle of similarity**
simplicity	**principle of closure**
symmetry	**rhetorical question**
orderliness	**shock-and-startle technique**
research overview	**transitions**
principle of proximity	**internal summary**

DISCUSSION

1. Working in small groups, share your research overviews for your next speeches. What main points are suggested by each overview? What can you learn about the selection of main points from these discussions?

2. Share the organizational plan of your next speech with a classmate so that you become consultants for each other. Help each other come up with alternative patterns for the main points, introductions, and conclusions. After the speeches are presented, each consulting team should explain the options it considered and why it chose the particular structures used for each speech.

APPLICATION

1. Select a speech from Appendix B and study its symmetry. Are its major parts — introduction, main points, and conclusions — coherent and properly balanced? If not, what would you suggest to improve it?

2. Analyze the structure of your favorite television advertisement. How does it gain attention and establish credibility? What design does it follow? Does the conclusion tie into the introduction? Present your analysis in class.

3. What kind of introductory technique would be most useful for each of the following specific purpose statements?

   a. To inform my audience of the role of student volunteers.
   b. To persuade my audience that it is better to marry than to live together.

  c. To inform my audience that fluorocarbons are destroying our atmosphere.
  d. To persuade my audience that *perestroika* holds the promise for world peace.

4. Develop a narrative you might use as an introduction for one of the topics in the preceding application. In small groups discuss how these stories might advance the purpose of the speech. Each group should select its best story and present it to the class as a whole.

5. Suggest an appropriate structural design for each of the following specific purposes:

  a. To inform listeners where they might see a grizzly bear in the wild.
  b. To inform my audience about sexist advertising practices.
  c. To inform listeners about the ideal way to prepare for an examination.
  d. To persuade my audiences to vote in the next election.
  e. To persuade listeners to vote Republican (or Democratic) in the next election.

NOTES

1. J. C. McCroskey and R. S. Mehrley, "The Effects of Disorganization and Nonfluency on Attitude Change and Source Credibility," *Communication Monographs* 36 (1969): 13–21.
2. Morton Deutsch and Robert M. Krauss, *Theories in Social Psychology* (New York: Basic Books, 1965), pp. 14–36.
3. Plato, "The Phaedrus," in *The Works of Plato,* ed. Irwin Edman (New York: The Modern Library, 1927), pp. 311–12.
4. Gloria Steinem, *Outrageous Acts and Everyday Rebellions* (New York: Holt, Rinehart & Winston, 1983).
5. Cited in Arthur M. Schlesinger, Jr., *A Thousand Days: John F. Kennedy in the White House* (Boston: Houghton Mifflin, 1965), p. 733.
6. Bob Lannom, "Patience, Persistence, and Perspiration," *The News Leader* (Parsons, Tenn.), 20 Sept. 1989, p. 9.
7. N. H. Anderson and A. A. Barrios, "Primacy Effects in Personality Impression Formation," *Journal of Abnormal and Social Psychology* 63 (1961): 346–50.
8. John Waite Bowers and Michael Osborn, "Attitudinal Effects of Selected Types of Concluding Metaphors in Persuasive Speeches," *Speech Monographs* 33 (1966): 148–55.
9. "Meeting the Japanese Economic Challenge," in *Representative American Speeches: 1980–1981,* ed. Owen Peterson (New York: H. W. Wilson, 1981), pp. 155–56.

*Our plans miscarry because they have no aim.
When a man does not know what harbor he
is making for, no wind is the right wind.*

— *SENECA*

8

OUTLINING

YOUR SPEECH

This Chapter Will Help You

◆ appreciate the importance of outlining your speeches.

◆ understand the process involved in developing an effective outline.

◆ develop a preparation outline to check the structure of your speech.

◆ prepare a formal outline following the conventions of coordination and subordination.

◆ condense your formal outline into a key-word outline for use in presenting your speech.

For several years our neighborhood was embroiled in zoning disputes. We lived on a cove surrounded by land that developers wanted rezoned for commercial use. Once when we were attending a zoning meeting prepared to protest a proposed automobile dealership, we discovered that a plan to operate a helicopter port was to be presented that same afternoon.

With only minutes to prepare, we began to organize our arguments against the helicopter port. Our specific purpose was clear: we wanted to defeat this proposal. Our thematic statement was: "A helicopter port in this neighborhood is both undesirable and illegal." We hastily outlined our main arguments on the back of a civil defense bulletin:

I. A helicopter port would be an undesirable intrusion into our neighborhood.
   A. It would disturb the peace and quiet of the residents.
   B. It would bother the patients in a nearby nursing home.

II. The applicants had shown disrespect for the law.
   A. They had not applied for a license before operating.
   B. They had violated FAA operating regulations.

Armed with this simple outline, which helped us focus and structure our speaking against the helicopter port, we were able to defeat *both* the port and the car dealership in the same afternoon!

As this example shows, outlining is not just an academic exercise, inflicted on students for no practical purpose. In the classroom as in real life, outlining is an essential phase of speech preparation. If we had spoken before the zoning board without first outlining our thoughts, we probably could have defeated *neither* proposal.

Outlining goes hand-in-hand with structuring, discussed in the previous chapter, in the preparation of a speech. As you make decisions on the main points in the body, it helps if you outline them so that you can see more clearly how they fit together. You can also check to see whether the main points cover everything you have proposed in your thematic statement. As you proceed to develop these main points, outlining can help you determine whether you have enough supporting material, whether it is sufficiently varied, and whether the subpoints flow logically out of the points above them. Moreover, the outline may help you see where you need transitions and if the introduction and conclusion tie together effectively.

In short, outlining helps to *discipline* the process of structuring and can point you in new creative directions. A good outline helps you control your material, organize and clarify your thinking, streamline your speech structure, and catch potential mistakes before you give voice to them. As you prepare your speech, you may develop the following outlines: a preparation outline, a formal outline, and a key-word outline.

Dᴇᴠᴇʟᴏᴘɪɴɢ ᴀ ᴘʀᴇᴘᴀʀᴀᴛɪᴏɴ ᴏᴜᴛʟɪɴᴇ

A **preparation outline** can help you develop and prepare your speech. You would not speak from such an outline, nor would it satisfy the requirements of a formal outline. It is strictly for your use during preparation and is a *tentative* plan of the speech you will eventually give. But it can show you how your ideas are evolving, whether they fit together, and whether you have enough supporting materials. You may need to make and discard several preparation outlines as you develop your speech toward its final form.

Why would you want to make a preparation outline? Assume that you will speak on "selecting a personal computer." You have done some reading and thinking on the topic but are not sure how your speech will develop. A preparation outline will help reduce your uncertainty.

The first thing you must do is be sure that you have your topic, specific purpose, and thematic statement clearly in mind. These constitute the foundation for the speech you will build, and if they are not clearly realized and firmly in place, your speech cannot develop satisfactorily. Write them out to assure your mastery of them:

> *Topic:* Selecting a personal computer
>
> *Specific purpose:* To inform my audience of steps to take in selecting a personal computer.
>
> *Thematic statement:* Choose a personal computer that will meet your needs and offer dependable service.

Keeping in mind that this is a tentative plan for your speech, you next will outline the body of your speech. Consult your research summary to identify the most important ideas. Decide which of these ideas are relevant to your purpose and thematic statement and how they might be stated as main points. Remember, you will want to limit your main points to no more than three in a short speech:

1. Learn what computers are capable of doing.

2. Select a computer that meets your needs.

3. Consider dependability and service.

To be certain you understand how these main points will develop, you must identify the subpoints that will go with them. **Subpoints** represent the major divisions of each main point: they break the main point down into more specific considerations. For example, on your first main point, you might list the following subpoints:

    A. Learn the basic vocabulary of "computerese."

    B. Learn what questions you should ask.

    C. Talk with PC owners to determine range of uses.

    D. Buy a good basic guide to PC's

Eventually, as you develop more refined preparation outlines, you will also develop **sub-subpoints,** which are divisions of subpoints. In your first preparation outline, sub-subpoints may not be necessary; your thinking might not be developed in sufficient detail to identify them adequately.

    Your next move will be to organize an introduction that fits the body of the speech you have planned. Remember, introductions should include attention-getting material, build your credibility, and preview your speech. Finally, you should plan a conclusion that will include a summary and concluding remarks. Figure 8.1 shows the final product when we fit these all together.

Figure 8.1
Sample Early Preparation Outline

PREPARATION OUTLINE

Topic: Selecting a Personal Computer
Specific purpose: To inform my audience of steps to take in selecting a personal computer.
Thematic statement: Choose a personal computer that will meet your needs and offer dependable service.

INTRODUCTION

    Attention-getting material: *Times Leader* ad: "Buy a Titan PC for $139!" Bargain or not? *Consumer Reports* quote: "A computer without software is no more useful than a doorstop."
    Establish credibility: Experience purchasing my own PC. Spent a lot of time learning how to get the most for my money.
    Preview: Explain the three things you should do before buying a PC.

BODY

    Main point #1: Learn what computers are capable of doing.
        Subpoints: Learn the basic vocabulary of "computerese."
                Learn what questions you should ask.
                Talk with PC owners to determine range of uses.
                Buy a good basic guide to PC's.

Let us assume that a day or so passes. You have done some more reading and thinking on your topic and are ready to refine your initial preparation outline. You may first notice that your thematic statement refers to only two main points, but you have plotted three main points in the outline. At this point you should revise the thematic statement to correct this problem:

> *Thematic statement:* Learn what computers can do, and then select one that will meet your needs and offer dependable service.

Next you should return to your main points to consider how the subpoints relate to them and to each other. You are now also ready to extend your thinking to the sub-subpoint level, should this be necessary. Consider the original version of the first main point:

Main point #1:	Learn what computers are capable of doing.
Subpoints:	Learn the basic vocabulary of "computerese."
	Learn what questions you should ask.
	Talk with PC owners to determine range of uses.
	Buy a good basic guide to PC's.

Main point #2:	Select a computer that meets your needs.
Subpoints:	Identify your immediate needs.
	Project your long-range requirements.
	Check a buyer's guide for PC's that satisfy your needs.
	Talk with local dealers about availability and cost.
Main point #3:	Consider dependability and service.
Subpoints:	Check ratings in *Consumer Reports.*
	Consult with dealers about service availability.
	Talk with users about their satisfaction with equipment and service.

CONCLUSION

Summary: When you invest in a PC, be sure that it meets your needs, that it is dependable, and that service is available.

Concluding remarks: Is that computer advertised for $139 a bargain? Thomas Jefferson: "Never buy what you do not want because it is cheap; it will be dear to you."

It is clear now that the above subpoints fall into two basic categories: (1) what a buyer should learn, and (2) how a buyer can learn them. You can now revise the preparation outline to reflect these categories.

Main point #1:	Learn what computers are capable of doing.
Subpoint A:	What you need to learn.
Sub-subpoints:	Basic vocabulary of "computerese."
	Questions to ask.
Subpoint B:	How you can learn this.
Sub-subpoints:	Talk with others who have PC's.
	Buy a good basic guide to PC's.

You examine the second main point in the same way:

Main point #2:	Select a computer that meets your needs.
Subpoints:	Identify your immediate needs.
	Project your long-range requirements.
	Check a buyer's guide for PC's that satisfy your needs.
	Talk with local dealers about availability and cost.

As you consider this cluster of ideas, two dominant subpoints again emerge: (1) deciding how you will use a personal computer, and (2) finding the right computer for your needs and your budget. Once more you can revise the preparation outline to show these subpoints:

Main point #2:	Select a computer that meets your needs.
Subpoint A:	Decide how you will use a computer.
Sub-subpoints:	Identify your immediate needs.
	Project your long-range requirements.
Subpoint B:	Find the right computer for your needs and budget.
Sub-subpoints:	Check a buyer's guide for PC's that satisfy your needs.
	Talk with local dealers about availability and cost.

Next you look at the third main point in the same careful way:

Main point #3:	Consider dependability and service.
Subpoints:	Check ratings in *Consumer Reports.*
	Consult with dealers about service availability.
	Talk with users about their satisfaction with equipment and service.

Again, two subpoints seem prominent: (1) check the dependability of equipment, and (2) check service availability. You adjust the preparation outline once more to reflect these categories.

Main point #3:	Consider dependability and service availability.
Subpoint A:	Check dependability of equipment.
Sub-subpoints:	Check ratings in *Consumer Reports.*
	Talk with users about any problems.
Subpoint B:	Check service availability.
Sub-subpoints:	Talk with users about service experiences.
	Consult with dealers about service availability.

Now you can put your revised points back together and look at the body of the speech as a whole. As you consider main points 1 and 2, some doubts begin to rise in your mind. Will it be enough to tell listeners they must learn the basic vocabulary of "computerese," or should you actually introduce them to some of this terminology? Will they be able to decide how they want to use a computer without a detailed knowledge of what computers can do? Can you give them enough background in a single short speech so that they can match computers to personal needs?

These questions bring the audience to center stage. You should always consider your listeners when you are planning, structuring, and outlining a speech. As you review your presentation outline, ask yourself questions, such as: "Will this information be clear to my audience?" "Will that example be meaningful to listeners?" "Does this testimony come from someone the audience respects?" As you begin to work on your speech, the audience can easily slip into the background. You may have to work up a complete preparation outline before you can see the limitations of an approach for your particular audience. At that point you may have to revise your outline. This means that speech preparation often proceeds in fits and starts, periods of frustration followed by moments of inspiration and revision.

As you consider your audience, the advice given to beginning journalists is appropriate: *Never overestimate your audience's information, and never underestimate its intelligence!* For example, assume the audience for your speech on computers includes 22 students — 16 freshmen and 6 sophomores, 14 males and 8 females — attending a small liberal arts college in the Midwest. The college has just announced that it will be setting up computer work stations on campus with direct access to library resources. You also know that most of the high schools in your state do not offer computer training. From this information you can assume that most of your audience members will know very little about personal computers, but they will soon need to. Although they may have heard terms like *byte, software,* and *modem,* they are not likely to understand what these words mean.

Figure 8.2
Revised Preparation Outline

REVISED PREPARATION OUTLINE

Topic: Personal Computers on Campus

Specific purpose: To inform my audience how a computer can help them in college.

Thematic statement: Computers can help with writing papers, organizing class notes, and handling mathematical problems.

INTRODUCTION

Attention-getting material: *Campus Inquirer* headline: We're going "high tech!" Will you be ready?

Establish credibility: Have been using a PC this past semester. Makes my work a lot easier.

Preview: Will show you how a PC can help write papers, organize notes and research materials, and do math homework.

BODY

Main point #1:   PC's are useful for writing themes and papers.

Subpoint A: They allow you to edit work easily.
   Sub-subpoints: Add, cut, and move single words or whole blocks of writing.
                Store your writing in the computer or on a disk until you are finished.

Subpoint B: They aid in proofreading manuscripts.
   Sub-subpoints: Check and correct spelling errors.
                Check and correct punctuation and grammar.
                Read manuscript back to you for final proofreading.

If you take these considerations into account, the specific purpose of the speech we have sketched seems overly ambitious. The preparation outline has helped you to see this problem. Not wanting to waste the time you have spent on research, you decide to keep the topic but to alter your purpose and to develop a new preparation outline. The question becomes: "How can I adapt my material so that the speech will serve my listeners and meet the time limits of the assignment?"

Because members of the anticipated audience know relatively little about personal computers, a starting point might be to inform them about what a personal computer can do for them as college students. As we think about this revised purpose, a new preparation outline begins to emerge (Figure 8.2).

Main point #2:   PC's help organize class notes and research materials.

    Subpoint A: Enter class notes into the computer while they are fresh in your mind.

        Sub-subpoints: Edit to group notes on same topic.
                        Edit to arrange material chronologically.
                        Use search command to find and highlight all material on a specific topic.

    Subpoint B: Enter research materials into computer.
        Sub-subpoints: Arrange research materials by topics.
                        Maintain bibliography as you go.
                        "Cut and paste" directly into term papers.

Main point #3:   PC's perform mathematical computations.

    Subpoint A: Computational programs simplify algebra and calculus.

    Subpoint B: Basic statistical analyses can be run on most PC's. Charts and graphs can be done automatically.

    Subpoint C: Tutorial programs are available.

CONCLUSION

Summary statement: A PC can save you time, increase your skills, and help organize your work.

Concluding remarks: Prairie College is going "high tech." I say it's "high time."

Had you not prepared a series of preparation outlines, you might have presented a speech that missed its target. It is not unusual for a speech to evolve through several such outlines before you settle on the right approach.

DEVELOPING A FORMAL OUTLINE

Some instructors require you to prepare a formal outline before presenting a speech in class. A **formal outline** is the final outline in a process leading from your first rough ideas for a speech to the finished product. The formal outline follows the established conventions of outlining. A basic model of the formal outline, illustrating many of these conventions, is shown in Figure 8.3.

The conventions of formal outlining include

1. an optional title, depending on the circumstances of the speech;

2. identification of speech topic, specific purpose, and thematic statement;

3. clear separation of speech parts: introduction, body, and conclusion;

Figure 8.3
Format for the Formal Outline

TITLE *(optional)*

Speech topic: _____

Specific purpose: _____

Thematic statement: _____

_____

INTRODUCTION

  I. Attention-getting material _____

_____

  II. Establish credibility _____

_____

  III. Preview _____

_____

[Transition into body of speech]

BODY

  I. Main point #1 _____

    A. Subpoint or supporting material _____

    B. Subpoint or supporting material _____

      1. Sub-subpoint or supporting material _____

      2. Sub-subpoint or supporting material _____

[Transition into point #2]

  II. Main point #2: _____

    A. Subpoint or supporting material _____

      1. Sub-subpoint or supporting material _____

      2. Sub-subpoint or supporting material _____

4. adherence to the rules of coordination and subordination;

5. proper wording of main points and subpoints;

6. indication of major supporting material;

7. a bibliography of major references.

Title

The need for a title for your speech varies with the circumstances. Classroom speeches may not require titles. When speaking outside the classroom, titles

B. Subpoint or supporting material _____

[*Transition into point #3*]

III. Main point #3: _____

   A. Subpoint or supporting material _____

   B. Subpoint or supporting material _____

     1. Sub-subpoint or supporting material _____

     2. Sub-subpoint or supporting material _____

       a. Sub-sub-subpoint or supporting material _____

       b. Sub-sub-subpoint or supporting material _____

[*Transition into conclusion*]

CONCLUSION

I. Summary: _____

_____

II. Concluding remarks: _____

_____

Bibliography

Books:

Articles:

Miscellaneous references:

are often useful for advertising speeches and attracting audiences. Therefore, it may be a good idea to experiment with titles for classroom speeches.

When properly chosen, titles prepare the audience for the speech. They can arouse curiosity, making people want to come and listen. A title can be stated early in the introduction, then repeated throughout the speech as a reminder of the central message. "Drinking and Driving Responsibly," the title Betty Nichols used for her speech, was a short form of her thematic statement (see the formal outline later in this chapter). Her title sparked curiosity because most people do not associate responsibility with drinking and driving.

Titles should not promise too much or deceive the audience. Titles that promise everything from the end of war to the end of obesity are too often followed by speeches that disappoint or frustrate listeners. Such titles often damage the trustworthiness of the speaker.

Topic, Purpose, and Thematic Statement

Although you won't necessarily state your topic, purpose, or thematic statement directly as you present your speech, the discipline of writing them out in a formal outline helps assure that you know what you want to accomplish with your audience. A clear realization of these elements can help you develop a cohesively structured message that moves with purpose from the opening to the closing words.

As noted earlier, this identification of speech topic, specific purpose, and thematic statement in preparation and formal outlines is very much like the foundation of a building: we may never actually see it *in* the speech itself, yet we know it must be present before speakers can build an effective structure of ideas.

Separation of Speech Parts

Separation of the major parts of the speech in the formal outline helps assure that you give each the full and careful attention it requires. Only when introduction, body, and conclusion are fully developed can they work together to achieve your specific purpose and fulfill the promise of the thematic statement.

Coordination and Subordination

Figure 8.3 illustrates the principles of coordination and subordination on which formal outlining is based. It demonstrates how you should use letters, numbers, and indentation to set up an outline. The actual number of main points and levels of subpoints you have in your outline depends on your topic, purpose, and design.

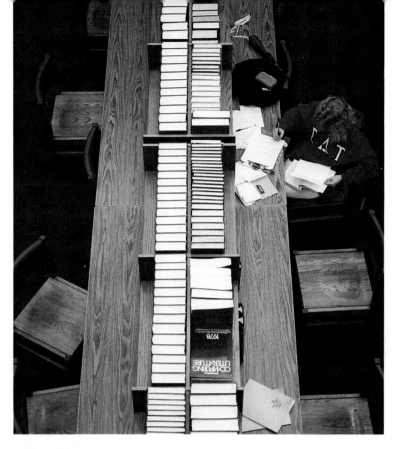

Outlining helps to discipline the process of structuring your speech; a good outline organizes and clarifies your thinking. You may need to make and discard several outlines as you develop your speech into its final form.

Coordination requires that statements that are approximately equal in importance (subpoints, sub-subpoints, etc.) should be placed on the same level in the outline. For example, your *I*'s and *II*'s, your *A*'s and *B*'s, and your *1*'s and *2*'s should seem about equally significant. In Figure 8.2 the main points (I, II, III) all identify major functions that computers might perform for students. They are approximately equal in importance. Think how strange it would be if the third main point in this outline was, "You can play games on your PC." That function would not be equal to word processing or organizing research, nor would it be relevant to your specific purpose or thematic statement. The subpoints for each main point also should be of about the same importance.

Coordination also requires that statements at the same level in an outline should receive approximately the same degree of support. If you back up one main point with strong testimony, then other main points should also be supported with important facts, testimony, examples, or narratives. Keep in mind that if you don't support statements equally, they will not seem equal in importance to your audience.

Subordination requires that material descend in importance from main points to subpoints to sub-subpoints. This arrangement follows a standard set of symbols: roman numerals, capital letters, arabic numbers, and small letters.

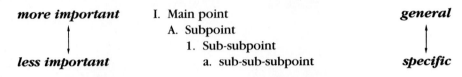

more important   I. Main point   *general*

A. Subpoint

1. Sub-subpoint

less important   a. sub-sub-subpoint   *specific*

The more important a statement is, the farther to the left it is positioned. If you turn an outline over so that it rests on its right margin, the "peaks" will represent the main points, the highest points of priority in the speech, with all other subpoints arranged under them according to significance.

Each level in your outline must be logically related to the level above it. In our earlier example, the main point "learn enough about PC's to make a wise choice" can be broken down into two logically related subpoints: "what you must learn" and "how you can learn it." As you can see, the main points are more general than the subpoints that follow. The subpoints become more specific as you move down the outline. To check your outline for proper subordination, ask yourself the following question: "Does each subordinate idea or each bit of subordinate material make the idea to which it is subordinate understandable or believable or compelling or enjoyable (depending on the purpose)?"[1]

The easiest way to demonstrate the importance of coordination and subordination is to look at a sample outline that violates these principles:

    I. Computers can help you develop writing skills.

        A. PC's can improve your schoolwork.

        B. PC's can be useful for organizing class notes.

    II. Computers can help you keep better financial records.

        A. They can help you plan personal time more effectively.

        B. They can be useful in your personal life.

        C. They can help organize your research notes for class projects.

This collection of thoughts is an outline in name only. It violates the principles of both coordination and subordination in that the levels are not equal in importance, nor are they logically related to each other in descending order. To straighten out this problem, let's look first at the main points. In this outline, they are not the most general, most important statements. The main points are actually I-A and II-B: the ideas that PC's can improve your schoolwork and be useful in your personal life. Putting these points where they belong allows us to correct the outline:

I. Computers can improve your schoolwork.

    A. PC's can help you develop writing skills.

    B. PC's can be useful for organizing class notes.

    C. PC's can help organize your research notes for class projects.

II. Computers can be useful in your personal life.

    A. PC's can help you keep better financial records.

    B. PC's can help you plan personal time more effectively.

Wording Your Main Points

The main points in your outline should be worded as simple, independent sentences. A main-point sentence that starts sprouting clauses should be broken down into subpoints. For example, the following does not make a good main-point sentence because it is too long and complex.

> Obesity endangers health and our feelings of self-worth, causing us to lose years off our lives and suffer unnecessary anguish.

It works better if changed and expanded into:

I. Obesity is a threat to our well-being.

    A. Obesity endangers health.
        1. Obesity results in increased heart disease.
        2. Obesity shortens the life span.

    B. Obesity damages self-image.
        1. Obese people often dislike themselves.
        2. Obese people may feel they have nothing of worth to offer others.

Breaking the complex sentence in the first example down into outline form helps you to focus what you are going to say. It simplifies both the structure and logic of your speech.

Look for opportunities to use **parallel construction** when wording the main points of your speech. If you were developing a speech on the need for reforms in election financing, you might word your main points as follows:

I. We need reform at the national level.

II. We need reform at the state level.

III. We need reform at the local level.

IV. But first we need to reform ourselves.

Parallel wording has many advantages. Each statement leads into a major area for development, and each statement helps build to the dramatic conclusion. Because each sentence has the same basic structure, the variations in each stand out sharply. The preceding example highlights the words *national, state, local, But first,* and *ourselves* because they are the only words that differ in important ways in otherwise similar sentences. The parallel structure emphasizes the way the speech narrows its focus like a zoom lens as it moves from a national to an individual perspective.

Parallel structure also helps to distinguish the main points from the subpoints. Since it involves repetition, parallel structure is easy to remember and may prolong the effect of the speech. Such structure satisfies the principles of good form and closure discussed in Chapter 7. Consider using parallel construction whenever this technique seems appropriate to the subject and to your purpose.

Supporting Your Main Points

The supporting material you plan to use should be included in the formal outline. Supporting materials often appear at the subpoint and sub-subpoint

---

SPEAKER'S NOTES

Developing a Formal Outline

1. Write out your topic, specific purpose, and thematic statement.

2. Outline your introduction, making sure that it contains attention-getting material, establishes your credibility, and previews your speech.

3. Outline your main points as complete simple sentences. Use parallel wording if possible.

4. Add appropriate subpoints under each main point in your outline. Be certain these are clearly related to their main points.

5. Include supporting material (as subpoints or sub-subpoints) for each main point.

6. Check the outline of the body of your speech for proper coordination and subordination.

7. Outline your conclusion, being sure that it contains a summary and concluding remarks to help your audience remember your message.

8. Prepare a bibliography, citing the articles, interviews, or books you used in the preparation of your speech.

levels, where they add credence to the subpoints and the main points above them. For example, a subpoint that states "PC's can improve writing skills" might rely on facts and examples, using charts to demonstrate that claim in dramatic visual form. At the sub-subpoint level one might find the following: "Chart A shows you how paragraphs can be reordered," and "Chart B shows how errors can be corrected."

Each main point in a speech requires some form of supporting material. The more controversial the point, the greater the need for supporting material. The following main point may require three different kinds of supporting material to make it acceptable to an audience:

Main point   I.   U.S. aid to anticommunist forces usually ends up working against us.

Expert testimony   A.   Professor Nathaniel Jones of the International Relations Department at Harvard University says U.S. aid often boomerangs.

Factual information   B.   According to a study by the Rand Corporation, in only two out of ten instances since 1960 has U.S. aid been successful.

Example   C.   These experts point to El Salvador, Honduras, and Guatemala, where, they say, we are paying a high price for the betrayal of our values.

Each of these types of supporting materials adds its own particular strength so that the main point can withstand possible objections.

As you prepare your formal outline, be sure to check that each main point receives the type and amount of supporting material it needs to be effective. If you cannot find or devise any effective supporting materials — any factual information, testimony, examples, or narratives — the claim probably does not deserve to be a main point in your speech. Figure 8.4 shows a sample formal outline that was prepared for an eight-to-ten-minute persuasive speech. The complete text of this speech may be found in Appendix B.

Reference Citations

A bibliography of works consulted in the preparation of your speech should appear at the end of a formal outline. If you conducted an interview, you should cite that information as well. The following guidelines will help you present your data:[2]

Books.   All references to books should be arranged alphabetically by the last name of the author(s). List the author's name, last name first, followed by the title and publication information (city of publication: publisher, date). For example:

> Booth, Wayne C. *A Rhetoric of Irony.* Chicago: University of Chicago Press, 1974.

Figure 8.4
Sample Formal Outline

DRINKING AND DRIVING RESPONSIBLY

Betty Nichols

Speech topic: Responsible Drinking and Driving

Specific purpose: To persuade my audience to accept the idea of *responsible* drinking and driving.

Thematic statement: We need to replace the old notion of "If you drive, don't drink" with a new idea of responsible drinking and driving.

INTRODUCTION

Betty uses the shock-and-startle technique to gain attention. Her thematic statement foreshadows the speech's problem-solution design. For credibility she relies on the ethos she had built in previous speeches.

I. During our lifetime half of us — I mean *us,* those of us in this room — will be involved in an alcohol-related accident.

   A. Chances are good that one of us won't make it — or will be crippled for life.

   B. Why don't we do something? Haven't we been warned repeatedly?

II. The old approach to drinking and driving simply does not work for most of us.

   A. We need to replace the traditional notion of "If you drive, don't drink" with a new idea of *responsible* drinking and driving.

   B. Today I want to discuss why the old approach to drinking and driving has not worked. And I want to spell out what I mean by responsible drinking and driving: managing our own drinking behavior, helping others manage theirs, and planning together to anticipate problems.

BODY

The first main point develops two basic reasons for the failure of the old approach. The first, that it ignores the psychology behind drinking and driving, depends on factual supporting materials, enlivened by a vivid metaphor. To support her second reason, that the old approach doesn't take into account the ignorance surrounding the subject, Betty might have used expert and prestige testimony.

I. The traditional approach — "If you drink, don't drive" — does not work.

   A. It ignores — and actually worsens — the negative psychology behind drinking and driving.
      1. Being surrounded by the steel and iron of a car gives us a false feeling of invincibility.
         a. The truth is, we run a much larger risk of being injured in an alcohol-related accident than of being assaulted or murdered (comparative statistics).
         b. The truth is, this false sense of security can turn our car into our coffin (metaphorical example).
      2. The traditional approach is based on an outmoded "Prohibition mentality."
         a. This mentality forbids us what we want — and makes us want it more!
         b. It also makes us want to violate sensible rules concerning drinking behavior, because it seems inconsistent with personal freedom.

   B. The prohibition approach ignores the real problem: *ignorance* itself, which results in irresponsible drinking behavior.
      1. Many of us are ignorant of the chemistry of drinking.
         a. We don't know that two beers an hour can result in a blood-alcohol level of .10.

        b. We don't know that this level qualifies us for a DWI charge.

   2. Many of us are ignorant of the legal risks.

        a. According to Jack Haley, director of the DWI school, a first conviction carries a mandatory jail term.

        b. Subsequent convictions carry even stiffer penalties.

The second main point relies on expert testimony for support. Betty makes her speech more interesting through narratives that ask her listeners to imagine themselves in drinking and driving situations.

II. The concept of *responsible drinking and driving* is the answer to this problem.

   A. We must learn to manage our drinking behavior.

      1. We must learn our tolerance level.

      2. We should know the alcoholic content of what we are drinking.

      3. We should limit ourselves to one drink an hour (expert testimony).

   B. We must help others manage their drinking behavior.

      1. Do not force liquor on friends who will be driving.

      2. Don't let a friend drive who has had too much to drink (narrative).

   C. We must help each other by developing contingency plans.

      1. We should talk with friends about the problem in advance.

      2. We should use the "designated-driver" system.

CONCLUSION

In her conclusion Betty summarizes her message and uses a rhetorical question to leave a haunting reminder in the minds of listeners.

I. It is clear that for most of us the old answer is no answer.

II. We need to learn to drink and drive responsibly: to manage our own drinking behavior, to help others manage theirs, and to work together to develop life-saving plans.

III. If we don't learn how to drink and drive responsibly, odds are that one of us will pay a large price for this problem. Look around you. And now look at yourself and at me. Who will it be?

Bibliography

Books:

Gusfield, Joseph R. *The Culture of Public Problems.* Chicago: University of Chicago Press, 1981.

Ray, Oakley. *Drugs, Society, and Human Behavior.* St. Louis: C. V. Mosby, 1983.

Articles:

"Drinking and Driving." *America* 151 (7–14 July 1984): 2.

"Drinking Limit — State Impact." *U.S. News & World Report* 97 (9 July 1984): 14.

Miscellaneous References:

Haley, Jack. Director of DWI School, Memphis. Telephone interview. 14 Nov. 1985.

Whalley, Anna. Alcohol and drug abuse counselor. Personal interview. 13 Nov. 1985.

Wrightsman, Lawrence S., and H. Sanford Fillmore. *Psychology: A Scientific Study of Human Behavior.* 4th ed. Monterey, Calif.: Brooks/Cole, 1975.

Articles.   All references to articles should be arranged alphabetically by the last name of the author, or by title if the author is not specified. List the author's name, last name first, followed by the title of the article, name of periodical, volume number, date of publication, and page numbers. For example:

Rushing, Janice Hocker. "The Rhetoric of the American Western Myth." *Communication Monographs* 50 (1983): 14–32.

"The Starry Sky." *Odyssey,* Jan. 1984, 26–27.

Miscellaneous References.   In this category you would list interviews, telephone calls, or other sources of information used in your speech. The formats are as follows:

Beifuss, Joan. Interview. *All Things Considered.* National Public Radio. WNYC, New York. 4 April 1986.

Frentz, C. R. Personal interview. 25 July 1986.

DEVELOPING A SPEAKING OUTLINE

You should not use formal outlines as prompts for the actual presentation of your speeches. If you try to speak from a formal outline, you will be tempted to read the outline rather than present your speech extemporaneously. Instead, use an abbreviated or **key-word outline,** which reduces the longer outline to a few key words that trace the sequence of your major points. This brief outline can be used to jog your memory as you are presenting your speech.

Even though you may never have to refer to the outline, it is comforting to know that it is there, just in case you need it. As a general rule, your key-word outline should fit on a single piece of paper or on two or three index cards. The outline should be written with large letters that can be read easily. Because it will be used strictly as a memory device, you may decide not to include the introduction, body, and conclusion headings from the formal outline. You want to keep it as simple as possible. A key-word outline adapted from the preparation outline for the speech on personal computers (Figure 8.2) is shown in Figure 8.5.

When you practice your speech, work first from your longer outline. Go through the speech two or three times, referring to this outline until you feel comfortable with what you are going to say and how you are going to say it. Then practice using your key-word outline until your speech flows smoothly. Put your outlines aside for a while, then come back and try giving the speech

Figure 8.5
Key-Word Outline

COMPUTERS ON CAMPUS

I. *CI:* GOING "HIGH TECH"
II. WRITING PAPERS AND REPORTS
    A. EDITING
    B. PROOFING
        1. SPELL CHECK
        2. GRAMMAR CHECK
        3. READ MANUSCRIPT
III. ORGANIZING NOTES AND RESEARCH
    A. CLASS NOTES
        1. EDIT
        2. REARRANGE
        3. HIGHLIGHT
    B. RESEARCH
        1. STORE BY TOPIC
        2. BIBLIOGRAPHY
        3. CUT AND PASTE
IV. HELPING WITH MATH PROBLEMS
    A. COMPUTATION
    B. STATISTICS
        1. CHARTS
        2. GRAPHS
    C. TUTORIALS
V. SAVE TIME, INCREASE SKILL, ORGANIZE.
    "HIGH TIME FOR HIGH TECH"

again, using only the key-word outline. If the key words still work as reminders, your preparation has been effective.

During the actual presentation of your speech you may want to have some material written out on separate cards. This is important with quotations or statistics that must be cited exactly. Some speakers find it best to have their introduction on one card, the key-word outline of the body of their speech on a second card, and their conclusion on a third.

You should not try to hide the key-word outline during your actual speech, nor should you feel self-conscious about using it. *The basic principle is that you should hold your outline in your hand or place it on a lectern in such a way that you minimize the loss of eye contact with listeners as you refer to it.* We shall have more to say about how to use the key-word outline in Chapter 11, "Presenting Your Speech."

IN SUMMARY

An outline gives you an overview of your speech and helps you organize your thoughts for maximum effectiveness.

Developing a Preparation Outline.   A *preparation outline* brings together the major parts of your message into a pattern that shows the relative importance of points and how they fit together. By developing preparation outlines you can judge the effectiveness of your initial preparations and determine where you may need more work or additional material.

Developing a Formal Outline.   *Formal outlines* follow a number of conventions, including coordination and subordination. *Coordination* requires that statements that are approximately equal in importance be placed on the same level in the outline. *Subordination* requires that statements descend in importance and that each level logically include the level below it. The main points should always be more general than those that are subordinate to them. The numbering, lettering, and indentation system should be consistent throughout the outline. A title may be useful to create interest in your speech.

The main points in a formal outline should be worded as simple, independent sentences. *Parallel construction* helps the main points stand out and helps the audience remember your message. All main points should be supported by either facts, testimony, examples, or narratives. These should be included in your outline. A formal outline usually requires a bibliography.

Developing a Speaking Outline.   A *key-word outline* can aid in the presentation of a speech. Such an outline reduces the speech plan to a few essential words that remind you of the content and overall design as you present the speech.

TERMS TO KNOW

preparation outline
subpoints
sub-subpoints
formal outline
coordination
subordination
parallel construction
key-word outline

DISCUSSION

1. Working in small groups, share a preparation outline for the next speech you will give in class. Explain the strategy of your structure and show how your outline satisfies the principles of coordination and subordination. Demonstrate that your supporting materials would be adequate. Revise as appropriate in light of the group discussion that follows.

2. Select one of the speeches from Appendix B (excluding Betty Nichols's speech) and prepare a formal outline of it. Does this outline make clear the structure of the speech? Does it reveal any structural flaws? Can you see any different ways the speaker might have developed the speech? Present your thoughts on these questions in class discussion.

3. If a successful speech is a bridge of meaning that joins speaker and listeners, as we discussed in Chapter 7, how would you describe the importance of an outline for the speech?

APPLICATION

1. Assume that the speeches you give in class this semester will be advertised in the campus newspaper. Develop titles that might be useful in attracting an audience to these speeches.

2. See if you can "unjumble" the following outline of the body of a speech using coordination and subordination appropriately. What title would you suggest for this speech?

Thematic statement: Deer hunting with a camera can be an exciting sport.

   I. There is a profound quiet, a sense of mystery.

      A. The woods in late fall are enchanting.
         1. The "film-hunter" becomes part of a beautiful scene.
         2. Dawn is especially lovely.

      B. Example of big doe walking under my tree stand.
         1. When they appear, deer always surprise you.
         2. Example of big buck after long stalk.

  II. Hunting from a stand can be a good way to capture a deer on film.

      A. The stalk method on the ground is another way to hunt with a camera.
         1. Learn to recognize deer tracks and droppings.
            a. Learn to recognize deer signs.
            b. Learn to recognize rubs on trees and scrapes on the ground.
         2. Hunt into the wind and move slowly.

B. There are two main ways to hunt with a camera.
   1. Stands offer elevation above the line of sight and line of scent.
   2. Portable stands are also available.
   3. Locating and building your permanent stand.

III. The right camera can be no more expensive than a rifle.

  A. Selecting the right camera for film-hunting is essential.

  B. Certain features — like a zoom lens — are necessary.

IV. Display slide of doe.

  A. You can collect "trophies" you can enjoy forever.

  B. Display slide of buck.

  C. Not all hunters are killers: the film-hunter celebrates life, not death.

NOTES

1. Robert T. Oliver, Harold P. Zelko, and Paul D. Holtzman, *Communicative Speaking and Listening* (New York: Holt, 1968), p. 125.
2. You can get more extensive directions on bibliographical form by consulting Joseph Gibaldi and Walter S. Achtert, *MLA Handbook for Writers of Research Papers,* 3rd ed. (New York: The Modern Language Association of America, 1988); or the *Publication Manual of the American Psychological Association,* 3rd ed. (Washington, D.C.: American Psychological Association, 1983). Your teacher may ask that you follow one of these or another guide.

III

DEVELOPING

PRESENTATION

SKILLS

Seeing . . . , most of all the senses, makes us know and brings to light many differences between things.

—*ARISTOTLE*

9

VISUAL AIDS

This Chapter Will Help You

- appreciate the advantages of using visual aids.

- understand what types of visual aids work best in different situations.

- learn the ways in which you can present visual aids.

- plan, design, and prepare visual aids that will enhance your message.

- use visual aids to give your speeches greater effectiveness.

If you are like most students, the first "public speech" you ever gave involved the use of a visual aid. In kindergarten or first grade, you probably participated in "Show and Tell." You may have brought an object that you were going to talk about — a new toy, something you made, the family pet — or you may have brought something to school that represented the object, such as a picture or a drawing. The visual aid helped you explain or describe your subject. Visual aids in later speech situations go far beyond "Show and Tell" in sophistication but still serve much the same purpose.

USES AND ADVANTAGES OF VISUAL AIDS

Visual aids give your audience direct sensory contact with your speech. Usually this contact is visual — hence the term *visual aids*. However, other senses, such as taste and hearing, can also provide such contact. In this chapter the term *visual aids* includes any and all supplemental materials you might use to increase the clarity and effectiveness of your speeches. Why are such aids so useful? The answer lies in a weakness of words as instruments of communication. As powerful as words can be when uttered by a skillful speaker, they are still essentially abstract. They represent objects and ideas, but they are not the objects and ideas they symbolize. Thus, words stand as a barrier between listeners and reality. To make sense of words, listeners must translate them into mental images, a process that can be difficult and confusing. Imagine how hard it would be to describe through words alone the carburetor system of a car. Even with effective graphics — models and charts — it would still be difficult for many of us to comprehend. It can require words *and* visual aids, blended skillfully, to explain some topics to some audiences.

Among the major advantages visual aids bring to a speech are the following:

1. *Visual aids enhance understanding.* Sometimes visual aids are superior to words in conveying meaning. It is easier to give directions if you can trace the route on a map. Similarly, when you are describing the auditory qualities of stereo-speaker systems, it can be more effective to let audiences actually *hear* the differences.

2. *Visual aids add authenticity.* When you show listeners the points you are making, you do more than just clarify your message. You authenticate or prove it. This type of proof is useful in both informative and persuasive speeches. Research confirms that "visual aids designed to supplement and clarify a persuasive message can affect attitude change and speaker credibility."[1] If audiences can actually hear the difference in stereo systems you have been describing, they are more likely to be convinced that one is

214

better than the other. When you show them the problem you are talking about, they should more readily accept your solution.

3. *Visual aids add variety.* Too much of a good thing, even a well-designed fabric of words, can get tiresome. The use of visual aids at critical points in a speech provides variety. Visual aids may even help improve your presentational skills. If communication apprehension is a problem for you, try using visual aids during your next presentation. As you identify the parts of a model or point to a graph, you may forget to be nervous. The physical movements needed to interpret a visual aid can channel your energy into a more effective presentation. Visual aids can make your speech more dynamic and interesting.

4. *Visual aids help your speech have lasting impact.* Because they are more concrete, visual aids are easier to remember than words alone. A photograph of a hungry child may stick in our memory, increasing the influence of a speech urging charitable contributions. Or we may remember the bright red markings signaling dangerous places on a map.

5. *Visual aids can help build your ethos as a speaker.* A neat, attractive visual aid reflects your commitment to communicate. It tells the audience you took time in the preparation of your speech. In some organizational settings, such as training and development workshops, audiences actually expect visual aids to be used. If you don't have them, the audience will be disappointed, and your credibility may suffer.

The skillful use of visual aids takes considerable creativity, planning, and preparation. In this chapter we describe the kinds of visual aids most frequently used in speeches, identify the ways in which they can be presented, offer suggestions for designing and developing them, and present guidelines for their use.

KINDS OF VISUAL AIDS

The number and kinds of visual aids are limited only by the speaker's imagination. We shall examine some of the more frequently used visual aids and the speech situations in which they are most helpful.

People

People themselves can function as visual aids. As the speaker, you cannot avoid being a visual aid for your own speech. Your body, clothes, grooming, actions, gestures, voice, facial expressions, and demeanor always provide an added dimension to your speech. Use these factors to help convey your message. For example, the best and easiest way to illustrate the proper stance for hitting a golf ball is to use your own body to demonstrate the stance. Even your clothes can function as a visual aid. If you will be talking about camping and wilderness adventures, blue jeans, a flannel shirt, and hiking boots might be appropriate attire for your speech. If you will be describing the joys of jogging, you might well wear a running suit.

You can also use other people as visual aids. Neomal Abyskera used two of his classmates to illustrate the line-up positions in the game of rugger, a game similar to rugby played in his native Sri Lanka. At an appropriate moment in his speech, Neomal said, "Peter and Jeffrey will show you how the opposing team members line up." While his classmates demonstrated the arm-locked shoulder grip position, Neomal briefly explained when and why the position was assumed. This visual demonstration was more interesting and effective than if he had tried to describe the position verbally or drawn it on poster-board with stick figures.

If you plan to use classmates for such a demonstration, be sure that they are willing to help you and will not distract from your speech. Rehearse with them so that they fit smoothly into the presentation. On the day of the speech they should sit on the front row so that they can come forward and then sit down again as quickly as possible.

Subjects and Models

Nothing can illustrate a subject more effectively than the subject itself. But some subjects — especially those that are very large or very small — are simply not practical for use in a speech. In such cases, scale models showing the subject reduced or enlarged may be your only option.

Subjects. When the subject of your speech can be carried easily to class and is large enough that listeners in the back of the room can see it without strain, you may decide to use it as a visual aid. Ideally, it should also be small enough to be kept out of sight until you are ready to use it. If you display the subject before you plan to use it, you risk being upstaged by your visual aid. If it is unusual, listeners may get involved in trying to figure out what it is and forget to listen to you. One of our students brought six different objects to class to illustrate an informative speech on the Montessori method of pre-school education. When it was her turn to speak, she lined up these objects across the desk in front of the lectern. They were such a distraction that during her speech a listener in the front row actually scooted his chair closer to the desk and picked up one of the objects to examine it. The speaker had to stop and ask him to put it back. She could have handled this situation more effectively by concealing the objects and bringing them out one at a time as they were being discussed.

Inanimate objects make better visual aids than living things, which you cannot always control. We once had a student present a speech on caring for puppies. She brought a six-week-old puppy to class as her visual aid. At the beginning of her speech, she removed the lectern from the speaker's table, spread some newspapers on it, placed the puppy on the table, and tried to give her speech. We are sure you have already guessed what happened. The first thing the puppy did was wet on the papers (including her note cards, which she had put down on the table while trying to control the puppy). The first thing the audience did was giggle. From there it was all downhill. The puppy squirmed and wiggled happily, tried to jump on the speaker, and alternately whined and yipped throughout the speech. The speaker was totally upstaged by her visual aid. When this fiasco was over, we asked the student why she had brought the puppy to class — what point she had wanted to make with its presence. She said she thought that because she was talking about puppies, it would be "nice to bring one along." Never create this kind of problem for yourself with a visual aid!

Objects are frequently used to illustrate speeches that demonstrate how to do something. Indeed, such speeches often cannot succeed without a visual aid. An engaging example of this type of use occurred near Halloween as part of a student speech on jack-o'-lanterns: both how to make them and the folk-lore behind them. The speaker demonstrated how to draw the face you want on a pumpkin with a magic marker and how to make a beveled cut around the stem so that the top won't fall in. As she was showing how to do these things, she was also telling stories of the ancient myths surrounding jack-o'-lanterns. Her visual aid and her words helped each other: the demonstration enlivened her speech, and the stories gave the demonstration depth and meaning. As she came to her closing remarks, she reached inside the lectern and produced a finished jack-o'-lantern, complete with lighted candle. The effect was dramatic.

Models. Sometimes your subject may be too large to carry, too small for the audience to see easily, too rare, expensive, or fragile to risk bringing to class, or simply unavailable. In such cases a model of the subject can serve as a visual aid. An additional advantage of a model is that you can also provide a cross section or cutaway example of the subject to show its interior.

George Stacey used a slightly smaller than life-size model of a person borrowed from the local Red Cross to demonstrate how to conduct cardiopulmonary resuscitation. The model folded neatly into a suitcase, so that it could be kept out of sight when not in use. When using a model as a visual aid, be sure that it is truly representative. It should be constructed to scale, maintaining the proper proportions between parts. The model should also be large enough for all listeners to see from their seats. Any visual aid that the audience must strain to see will be more of a distraction than a help.

Graphics

Graphics are representational visual aids that you prepare for use in a speech. They may include sketches, maps, graphs, charts, or textual graphics.

Sketches.   Sketches or diagrams that accompany a speech can offer simplified representations of what you are describing. They should be used to stress essential aspects of your message.

Mark Peterson prepared a sketch to illustrate his speech on factors to consider when buying a bicycle. Mark placed the poster board containing his sketch of a bicycle on the ledge of the chalkboard (blank side to the audience) before he began his speech. When he reached the point at which he wanted to talk about making bar-to-pedal and seat-to-handlebar measurements, he turned the poster around. Mark then showed his listeners how they should take these measurements to get a bike of the correct size. When he finished this demonstration, Mark turned the poster board around again to its blank side so that it would not be a distraction during the rest of his speech.

Maps.   Commercially prepared maps contain too much detail to serve as visual aids for speeches. Much of this detail is irrelevant, and the map will be difficult, if not impossible, for most listeners to read from their seats. The best maps are those that you make specifically for your speech so that they are large, simple, and relevant to your purpose. Maps are particularly useful in speeches based on spatial design. The map in Figure 9.1 was used to indicate the distance and routes between major attractions at Yellowstone National Park. Having such a map helps the audience put locations and spatial relationships into perspective and makes them easier to understand and remember. Stephen Huff used a map to help his listeners see precisely where a series of devastating earthquakes occurred along the New Madrid Fault, and to understand how a recurrence of such earthquakes might endanger them (see his speech and visual aids at the end of Chapter 12).

Whether a map works as a visual aid depends on the speaker's ability to integrate it into the verbal presentation. Elizabeth Walling used a map of the wilderness canoe area in northern Minnesota to familiarize her Memphis audience with that area. She made a double-sided poster that she was able to keep hidden behind the speaker's table until she was ready for it. On one side she highlighted the wilderness canoe area on an outline map of northern Minnesota, showing various points of interest to canoers. To illustrate how large the area is, Elizabeth then turned the poster over, revealing an outline map of western Tennessee. She had superimposed the wilderness area on a map familiar to her audience. At a glance we could see that this area would extend from Memphis to past Jackson, some eighty miles away. By using maps this way, Elizabeth created a striking visual comparison. She had taken an area that was unfamiliar and placed it in a familiar context.

Graphs.   Mrs. Robert A. Taft once commented, "I always find that statistics are hard to swallow and impossible to digest. The only one I can ever remember is that if all the people who go to sleep in church were laid end to end, they would be a lot more comfortable."[2] Many people may share Mrs. Taft's feelings about statistics. Masses of numbers recited in a speech may be at best

Figure 9.1
Map: Yellowstone Park

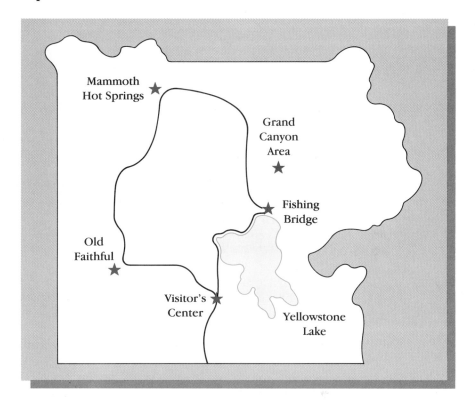

confusing and at worst overwhelming. A well-designed graph can help make statistical information easier for listeners to comprehend.

A **pie graph** or circle graph shows the size of a subject's parts in relation to each other and to the whole. The circle, or "pie," represents the whole, and the segments, or "slices," represent the parts. The two pie graphs in Figure 9.2 show the dramatic increase in the number of women earning college degrees, using the years 1950 and 1986 as bases of comparison. To use a pie graph effectively you should be able to break your material into five or fewer categories. Too many divisions of the pie make a graph cluttered and difficult to read.

A **bar graph** shows comparisons and contrasts between two or more items or groups. Bar graphs are easy to understand because each item can be readily compared with every other item on the chart. Figure 9.3 is a bar graph illustrating average revenues from campus fund-raising items. The speaker chose to label the bars in this graph with the names of the products. You might also distinguish the bars from one another through patterns or colors, but you must make it clear which color or pattern goes with which item.

Figure 9.2
Pie Graph: College Degrees Conferred, by Gender, 1950 and 1986

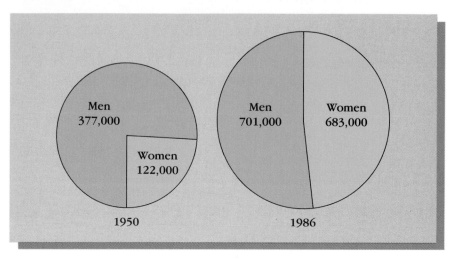

A **line graph** demonstrates changes across time and is especially useful for indicating trends of growth or decline. Because you can plot more than one item on a line graph, you can use it for complex and detailed representations. Consider, for example, how we might represent the information shown in Figure 9.2 in a line graph. Instead of showing college degrees earned by men and women for only two years, the line graph (Figure 9.4) allows us to show the intervening years as well. The upward-sloping lines confirm the dramatic rise in the number of women earning degrees.

Figure 9.3
Bar Graph: Average Revenue from Fund Raisers

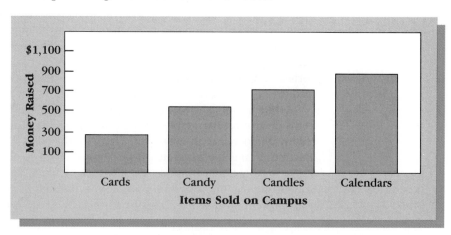

Figure 9.4

Line Graph: College Degrees Conferred, by Gender, 1950–1986

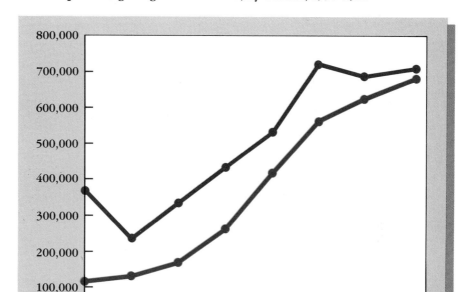

Whenever you plot more than one line on a graph, you must be certain that listeners can distinguish the lines. Use different colors or patterns, such as solid lines, dashes, and dots, to designate specific items. Different colors or patterns are preferable to labeling the lines because they keep the graph from becoming cluttered. Never try to plot more than three lines on a graph.

Charts.   Charts provide convenient visual summaries of processes and relationships that are not in themselves visible. However, they are more difficult to use as visual aids in speeches because they must often be oversimplified to keep them from being cluttered and distracting. Among the more frequently used types of charts are flow charts, tree charts, and stream charts.

Flow charts can show power and responsibility relationships, such as who reports to whom in an organization. Organizational flow charts usually place the most powerful office or person at the top of the chart, the next most powerful offices or people directly underneath, down through the least powerful offices or people. Flow charts can also be used to detail the steps in a process. Through the use of lines and arrows, such a chart indicates what steps

Figure 9.5
Flow Chart: Major Steps in the Preparation of a Speech

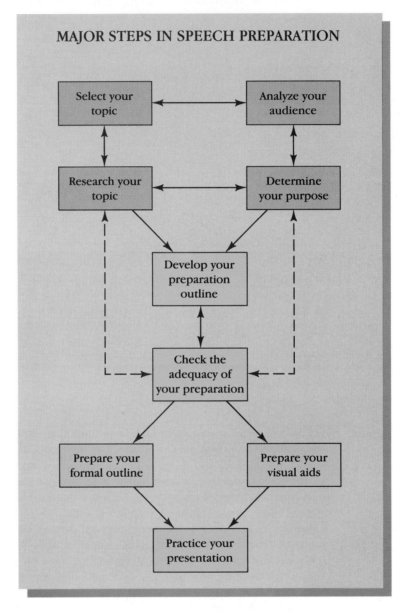

occur simultaneously and what steps occur sequentially. Figure 9.5 is a flow chart that traces the major steps in the preparation of a speech.

Tree charts show developments across time, such as the growth of families, language systems, or inventions. Generally a tree chart represents diffusion, the growth of the few into the many.

Stream charts also show development over time, but their purpose is different from that of a tree chart. Rather than indicating how the few become many, a stream chart shows how the many can come together to produce the few, just as many streams make up a river. Stream charts may be used to establish how forces converge to make up a person, product, or decision. The stream chart can offer a sophisticated visual projection of the cause-effect relationship.

The problem with most charts is that they are usually too complex and detailed for use in speeches, especially if your time is limited. Sequence charts, however, can be quite helpful, even in a brief speech. **Sequence charts,** which are presented in a series, show different stages of a process. You can create suspense by using sequence charts, as the audience anticipates what the next chart will reveal. For example, you could choose to present material on the awarding of college degrees, divided by gender, in a series of charts. On these charts you might want to use **pictographs,** images that symbolize the information they represent. In the first chart, representing 1950, you could show the figure of a man three times larger than the accompanying figure of a woman, indicating the 3:1 ratio in earned degrees. Intermediate charts prepared for decade years could show changes in the relative sizes of these figures, until the final chart would indicate the current 1:1 ratio with two figures of approximately equal size. Figure 9.6 indicates how the first and last charts in the sequence might look.

Figure 9.6

Sequence Chart: College Degrees Conferred, by Gender, 1950 and 1986

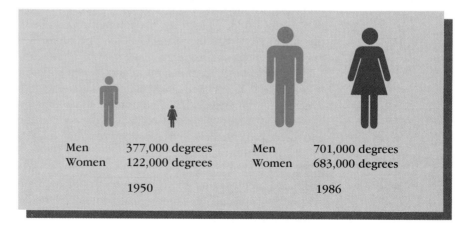

Men	377,000 degrees
Women	122,000 degrees

1950

Men	701,000 degrees
Women	683,000 degrees

1986

Textual Graphics. At times words may be the only symbols you need for a visual aid. In a speech of demonstration it is often helpful to list the steps in a process in order of occurrence: 1., 2., 3. A visual representation of key words can help an audience track the message of a complicated speech. Unfamiliar material can be emphasized and made clearer if the audience can both hear and see the message. You can prepare **textual graphics** using a chalkboard, poster board, flip charts, transparencies, slides, or handouts.

Photographs and Pictures

The old Chinese proverb that a picture is worth a thousand words is not always true in public speaking. Certainly a good photograph can help demonstrate or authenticate a point in a speech or can make a situation you are describing seem more vivid and realistic. For instance, if you were trying to describe the devastation caused by a flood, tornado, or hurricane, photographs *could* be quite useful. We say *could* carefully because photographs also have drawbacks as visual aids in speeches. They frequently include detail that is not relevant to the speech, so that they contain built-in distractions. Their very vividness can also be a disadvantage, especially when speakers rely on them too heavily to make a point, forgetting that language too must make points come alive through concrete examples and word pictures.

The major problem with using pictures as visual aids is their size. Unless a picture is large enough for everyone in the room to see with ease, it contributes nothing. We once had a student who tried to illustrate his speech on baseball by showing the audience pictures from a book. He used paper clips to mark the pages on which there were pictures he wanted to show the class. Unfortunately, the sequence of pictures in the book did not match the sequence of ideas in his speech, so he kept opening the book to the wrong pages. Additionally, the pictures in the book were too small to be seen except from the front row. This visual aid created considerable problems for the student, both diminishing the effectiveness of his presentation and damaging his ethos.

Finally, it is hard to resist the temptation to circulate photographs among the audience as you give your speech. The pictures then compete with you for the attention of listeners.

For all these limitations, photographs can still work well if they are carefully selected, controlled, and enlarged. They should be selected for their relevancy to your speech. They should be controlled just as you control charts, graphs, and maps, revealed only when they serve the point you are making and then put away. Color copiers can now make inexpensive eleven-by-seventeen-inch enlargements from snapshots. These are probably the minimally acceptable size for most classroom presentations. Because they are reproduced on copier paper, it is best to mount them on poster board.

Museum prints and commercial posters are made to be seen from a distance and are usually large enough to overcome the size problem. In his speech describing an extended camping trip, Michael McDonald used a print of

Thomas Moran's painting of the Green River in the American West to represent his feelings about that area. Paintings can often convey a mood or feeling, especially when used in combination with eloquent words. They can help speeches arouse emotion.

WAYS OF PRESENTING VISUAL AIDS

Chalkboards, flip charts, poster board, handouts, projections, films, videotapes, audiotapes, and computer-generated materials are often used as ways to present visual aids. Most corporate conference rooms, school classrooms, and public meeting places are equipped with chalkboards or flip charts. They are probably the most frequently used ways to present visual aids.

Chalkboard

The chalkboard serves well when the speaker wants to offer a step-by-step demonstration. Building a visual aid on the board one unit at a time creates suspense, which holds the attention of listeners. This spontaneous construction of a visual aid reinforces the impression that you are in command of a concept — you prove it by creating the visual aid right before the eyes of listeners. You can also use the chalkboard to emphasize certain words and ideas. Writing these terms or names on the board calls the audience's attention to their importance and helps your listeners remember them. This is especially important if the word or name is spelled differently from the way it is pronounced. For example, if you mentioned the leader of the undergound Christianity movement in China, Lin Xiangao, it would be advisable to write the name on the chalkboard.

A chalkboard also can be a good audience-adaptation tool. Despite your best preparation, there may be moments when you look at your listeners and realize that some of them have not understood what you have just said. By writing a few words on the board or drawing a simple diagram, you may be able to dispel their confusion.

A final advantage of using a chalkboard is that it keeps you from hiding behind the lectern while you are speaking. Once you have moved from the lectern to the chalkboard, you will feel freer to walk about, perhaps presenting your next point from the side of the speaking table or even moving in front of the table to reduce distance between yourself and listeners.

For all these strong advantages, chalkboards can hinder communication more than they help unless you use them carefully. If you are not artistically talented, your visual aids may look sloppy, and your audience may not be able to decipher what you have just put on the board. You can remedy this problem while preserving the appearance of spontaneity by lightly roughing out your designs in advance of your presentation. These should not be visible to listeners before your speech. Just be sure to warn earlier speakers not to erase your preparations!

Well-designed charts and graphs can make statistical information dramatic, colorful, and easier for audiences to understand. Here New York senator Daniel Patrick Moynihan uses a line graph to illustrate his argument that Social Security surpluses should not be used to offset the federal budget deficit.

Another possible disadvantage is that chalkboards can become cluttered with writing, which distracts from your speech. Be sure to erase any previous drawings on the board before you begin. As a courtesy to later speakers, erase your own visual aids when you have concluded.

A final problem with chalkboards is that speakers tend to overuse them and to use them poorly. Despite the most careful preparation, including lightly roughing out visual aids in advance, chalkboard visual aids are not as neat and polished as those constructed in advance on flip charts, poster boards, transparencies, slides, or handouts. Never use the chalkboard simply because you do not want to take the time to prepare a polished visual aid. When using the chalkboard, the speaker sacrifices eye contact. We have all witnessed speakers who end up talking more to the chalkboard than to the audience.

For these reasons chalkboard illustrations should be used sparingly in classroom speeches. Keep the designs or writing simple and to the point. Try not to turn your back on listeners. Stand to the side of your drawing, pause frequently, and regain eye contact with listeners as you explain what you are drawing. If the visual aid is too complex to permit you to maintain such contact, this is a clear sign that the aid should be prepared in advance on other materials.

There can be moments, however, when nothing matches the use of the chalkboard for dramatic effectiveness. As he ended his speech on local emergency services, Ralph Stanley wrote on the board in very large numbers, "526-3411," and said:

> So I want you to look at these numbers on the board until they are etched in your mind. 526-3411. Remember these numbers. 526-3411. They could save your life or the life of a loved one. 526-3411. In a real emergency you won't have time to look for the telephone book. 526-3411.

Here the verbal repetition combined with the visual representation increased the impact of his message and helped to drive home its importance.

Flip Chart

A flip chart is a large, unlined tablet. Most flip charts measure about two feet wide by three feet high and are made of newsprint. They are clipped to an easel so that pages can be flipped over the top once you are finished with them. You use broad-tipped felt markers to draw or write on the flip chart.

Flip charts offer many of the same advantages as chalkboard and minimize many of the disadvantages. They are convenient, inexpensive, and adaptable to most speech settings. With a flip chart you can produce a striking visual aid because felt markers are available in many vivid colors. And because flip-chart pads are portable, you can prepare your materials before your speech. This allows you to draw neater, more complex visual aids and to maintain audience contact throughout your speech. Like the chalkboard, the flip chart can also be used spontaneously should the need arise. Just be certain that you have blank pages left in the pad for this purpose and that you bring felt markers.

When preparing visual aid materials on a flip chart, try to keep each page as simple as possible. Write on every other page because the felt-marker ink may bleed through the paper. Back each page of prepared material with a blank page and join them together near the bottom with small paper clips. Leave the first page of the flip chart blank so that your written materials are hidden from audience view until you are ready to flip over the blank page and reveal your message or drawing.

Susan Larson used a flip chart effectively to illustrate a speech on nautical navigation. Figure 9.7 shows her first page of flip-chart material. The acronym POSH was her device for remembering how to navigate in relation to river markers. Susan kept her writing to a minimum so that the material stood out clearly and emphatically. Had she tried to write out the message "Keep the marker buoys to your left (port) as you leave the marina and to your right (starboard) coming home," the flip-chart page would have looked cluttered.

Susan's second and third flip-chart sheets each contained a color drawing of a Coast Guard navigation marker found in the inland waterways. Her fourth sheet was a simplified drawing of a navigational chart, showing the placement of buoys marking a river channel. As she talked, Susan drew the path a boat would have to navigate between the buoys. The flip-chart technique was less cumbersome than trying to handle four separate posters.

Figure 9.7
Flip Chart: Explanation of an Acronym

Poster Board

Poster board has many uses in the construction of visual aids. When you wish to make just one or two highly polished or complex visual aids or when flip charts are not available, poster board can be invaluable. You may be able to tack your poster to the cork border at the top of many chalkboards so that it can be seen more easily.

Even if you are not artistic, you can prepare an effective drawing on poster board. Most college bookstores or any office-supply store can provide all the materials you need to turn out a professional-looking product: the poster board, a straightedge or ruler, a compass, felt markers, and stick-on letters in a variety of colors and sizes. This basic equipment will enable you to prepare sketches, simplified maps, and charts or graphs.

On the day of your speech, be sure to conceal your visual aid until you need it. Only a moment is required to place the poster board on an easel, on the ledge in front of a chalkboard, or in front of the speaker's lectern. To be certain that things go smoothly, try to find a time when the classroom will not be in use so that you can practice your speech using the aid. As you practice, remember to stand to one side of the poster, facing the imaginary audience as much as possible while referring to your aid. Point to each feature as you speak about it. If you cannot get into the classroom for practice, come early on the day of your speech to be sure you can position the poster board as you want it. Bring masking tape and thumbtacks in case you should need them.

Handouts

Handouts that you distribute to the audience before your speech are a high-risk way to present a visual aid. The handout can compete with you for attention, and if your presentation is not compelling, the audience may opt to read instead of listen. Handouts do, however, have many advantages. They are especially useful when speech subjects are complex or contain much statistical information. Handouts are also helpful in speeches that introduce a new or technical vocabulary. When the speech is concluded, the handout remains to remind listeners of your message. Do not distribute handouts during your speech — do it before or after you speak, depending on whether the audience needs to refer to the material as you speak.

Dwight Davidson distributed the handout shown in Figure 9.8 for his speech entitled "Talking Computerese." Dwight's audience was able to follow him as he introduced and explained the terms in the handout. Without such a

Figure 9.8

Handout for Speech on Computerese

COMPUTER TERMINOLOGY

hardware: the physical equipment that makes up a computer; includes the computer itself, the monitor, the keyboard (if separate from the computer unit), and the printer.

software: programs, usually stored on disks, that make the computer function.

program: a set of instructions that tells the computer what to do. For example, a word processing program allows you to write and edit manuscripts.

modem: a telephone or direct line connection that allows you to tie in to other computers or sources of information. For example, with a modem you can connect your computer to the library card catalog or college computer printers.

disk: a revolving plate for storing information and data, similar to records you use with a stereo system or tapes for a tape recorder.

byte: a unit for measuring the computer and disk storage capacity. Each byte equals one letter, number, or space in computer print.

K (kilobyte): 1,024 bytes. If the average word is seven letters long, then 1K of storage equals 125 words, or approximately half a page of typed manuscript.

memory: the internal storage capacity of the computer.

language: the type of commands or instructions a computer is given to make it perform specific tasks. There are different languages for different computer systems.

visual supplement his listeners might have been lost. Stephen Huff distributed a handout called "Earthquake Preparedness Suggestions" after he concluded his speech so that the audience would be certain to remember that important information.

Slides and Transparencies

Slides and transparency projections allow the audience to see graphics or photographs more easily or to look at an outline of your main points while you are making them. This technique helps listeners remain on track during long or complicated presentations. Slides and projections are frequently used in organizational presentations.

Slides are difficult to handle in public speeches. The room must be darkened while they are being shown, and the illuminated screen — not you — becomes the center of attention. Unless you have remote-controlled equipment, you may have to stand behind or in the middle of the audience to run the projector. The result is that you will always be talking to someone's back. If you do not have remote-controlled equipment, your best solution may be to have a classmate change the slides on cue. You will need to practice coordinating your presentation with the showing of the slides. You will also need specialized equipment to prepare your slides. Check to see if your campus has an audiovisual media center that can help you.

Transparency projections have many advantages over slide presentations. A transparency projector enlarges and transmits an image from a clear celluloid original. Transparencies can be made on many copying machines and are quite inexpensive. You can draw, print, or type your original material on plain paper and have it converted to a transparency. Transparencies are also one of the best ways to use computer-generated graphics. Once the transparency has been made, you can highlight various parts with colored markers. The room need not be as dark for projections as for slides. You can also add material to a transparency as it is being shown. A pencil makes a convenient pointer to direct the audience's attention to features you want to emphasize. The major disadvantage of such projections is that you must speak from where your equipment is located. Again, you may find yourself addressing the backs of some listeners.

If you decide to use slides or transparencies as visual aids in a speech, be sure that you check the equipment ahead of time and familiarize yourself with its operation. Practice delivering your speech while using the equipment. It is always wise to have a spare light bulb taped inside the machine; many a presentation has been ruined by a burned-out light bulb. You should also have a heavy-duty extension cord so that you can position your equipment where you want it. Check the location of electrical outlets in advance and be sure the cord fits. Do not use too many slides or projections in a short speech. They should supplement your message, not replace it.

Computer-generated Materials

Many graphics programs are now available for use with personal computers. Given access to these programs, you can easily generate professional-looking visual aids. The graphs produced by a computer are much neater and more accurate than most of those drawn freehand. Computer programs can produce textual graphics that are clear, readable, and eye-catching. Some of the more sophisticated programs will even generate colored transparencies or slide masters when a laser color printer is available. Figure 9.9 shows an excellent computer-generated textual graphic for use as a transparency.

Figure 9.9
Computer-generated Transparency

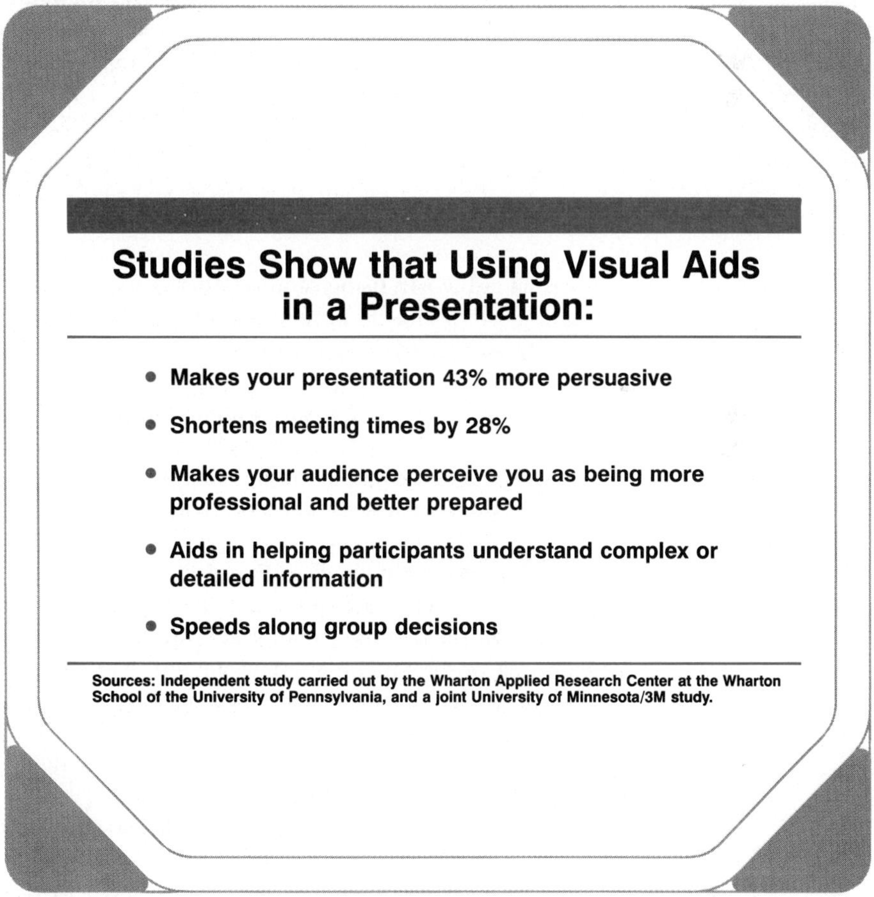

Studies Show that Using Visual Aids in a Presentation:

- Makes your presentation 43% more persuasive

- Shortens meeting times by 28%

- Makes your audience perceive you as being more professional and better prepared

- Aids in helping participants understand complex or detailed information

- Speeds along group decisions

Sources: Independent study carried out by the Wharton Applied Research Center at the Wharton School of the University of Pennsylvania, and a joint University of Minnesota/3M study.

Transparency generated by Microsoft® PowerPoint® Desktop Presentations Program. Reproduced with permission from Microsoft Corporation.

Computers can help you make handouts and slides as well as transparencies. Unless you have access to a blueprint-size enlarger/copier, computer-generated graphics are less appropriate for posters.

Films, Videotapes, and Audiotapes

Films, videotapes, and audiotapes can clarify and authenticate a speech and add variety to a presentation. The major problem is that they can be difficult to incorporate into a speech when time is limited. They also share many of the disadvantages of slide presentations, such as the need for a darkened room, special equipment, and operating skills. It is easy for a film or tape to dominate the speech, so that you are overwhelmed by your visual aid. When in doubt about the wisdom or practicality of using a film, consult your instructor.

Audiotapes may be more useful than films or videotapes and not as difficult to handle and integrate into the speech. If you wanted to describe the warning cries of various animals, for instance, an audiotape could be essential. Consult your instructor about the availability of equipment and materials if your speech would benefit from such a tape.

PREPARING VISUAL AIDS

Any visual aid worth using requires that you invest adequate time in planning, designing, preparing, and practicing its use. As you prepare, you should follow certain principles of design and color.

Principles of Design

The principles of design, including visibility, emphasis, and balance, are based on how a visual aid functions before an audience.

Visibility. As we have already noted, your visual aid must be easy for the audience to see without straining. The test is whether the visual aid can be seen from the back of the room. If not, the aid will become a distraction. When preparing a poster or flip-chart visual aid, you should use the following size letters for presentations in standard classrooms:

Titles:	3 inches high
Subtitles:	2 inches high
Other text:	1½ inches high

If you wish to use a computer to generate slides or transparencies, be certain that your computer can print large letters. Computer print is typically sized in

Figure 9.10
Standard Computer Print Sizes

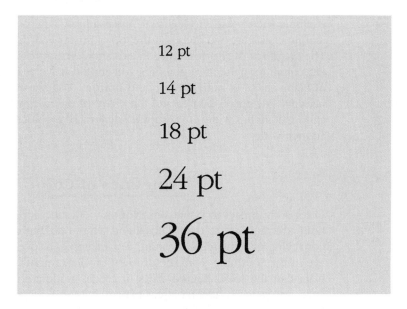

terms of points (pt). Figure 9.10 shows the standard computer print sizes appropriate for preparing transparencies, slides, or handouts.

Such visual aids should use the following sizes of letters:

	Transparencies	Slides	Handouts
Title	36 pt	24 pt	18 pt
Subtitles	24 pt	18 pt	14 pt
Other text	18 pt	14 pt	12 pt

Use boldface type when preparing computer-generated materials.

Emphasis.   Your visual aid should emphasize what the speech emphasizes. This means that you should keep visual aids relevant and simple. The eyes of your listeners should be drawn immediately to what you want to illustrate. The map of Yellowstone Park (Figure 9.1) eliminates all information except what the speaker wishes to stress. If the speaker had added unrelated information — such as pictures of bears to indicate grizzly-bear habitat or drawings of fish to show trout streams, the visual aid would have been more distracting than helpful. Graphics prepared for handouts may be more detailed than those used for posters, slides, or transparencies, but they should not contain extraneous material.

Balance.   Your visual aid should seem balanced and pleasing to the eye. The focal, or center, point of the aid can be the actual center of the chart or poster, or it can be deliberately placed off-center for the sake of variety. The POSH example shown earlier (Figure 9.7) has a high focal point. You should have a margin of at least two inches at the top of poster boards or standard flip charts. The margin at the bottom of such aids should be at least two and a half inches. On computer-generated graphics you should leave at least an inch and a half of blank space at both the top and bottom. You should also have equal side margins. For poster boards and flip charts these margins should be about one and a half inches wide. On computer-generated graphics they should be at least an inch wide.

Principles of Color

Color adds impact to visual aids. Not only does a colored visual aid attract and hold attention better than a black and white one, but color is a subtle way of conveying or enhancing meaning. For example, a speech detailing crop damage in the Southeast from the drought of 1986 might use an enlarged outline map showing least-affected areas in green, moderately damaged areas in orange, and severely affected areas in brown. In this way the colors express what they represent.

Color can also be used to reinforce certain moods and impressions. The color blue connotes power and authority (blue chip, blue ribbon, royal blue), for example. Using blue in your graphics can invest them with these qualities. Red is a highly emotional color and is used to connote crisis (in the red, red ink). Line graphs tracing the rise in cases of AIDS or the drop in sales for some company in financial trouble could be portrayed in red to suggest the urgency of the situation. On his map of the New Madrid Fault area, Stephen Huff showed the earthquake epicenters in red, thus emphasizing danger.

The manner in which colors are combined in graphics can also be used to convey subtle nuances of meaning. A **monochromatic color** scheme uses variations of one color to suggest changes in a subject. For example, using deeper shades of blue as you draw the figures representing increases in the number of women receiving college degrees could suggest growth in power.

An **analogous color** scheme uses colors that are adjacent on the color wheel, such as green, blue-green, and blue. Although this type of color scheme shows the differences among the components represented, it also suggests their connection and compatibility. For example, a pie graph could represent the students, faculty, and administration of a university, using analogous colors. The different colors suggest that these parts are indeed separate, but the analogous color scheme and the inclusion of these parts within a circle imply that they belong together. In this subtle way, the visual aid itself makes the statement that the components of a university ought to work together.

A **complementary color** scheme uses colors that are opposites on the color wheel, such as red and green. Complementary color schemes suggest tension and opposition among elements in a speech. Because they heighten the sense of drama, they may enliven informative speaking and encourage change in persuasive speaking. For example, one suggestion for developing the map accompanying the speech at the end of Chapter 12 would be to outline and color the New Madrid Fault area dark red and the surrounding area green, further dramatizing the danger of earthquake.

The colors you use for your graphics should always stand out from the background of the poster. Your best bet is to stay with white poster board and use strong colors, such as red, blue, and green, for contrast. Colors like pink, light blue, and pale yellow are not strong enough for good graphic emphasis.

Making Visual Aids

For charts, graphs, or other poster and flip-chart aids, you should begin with rough draft sketches that allow you to see how your aid will look when it is finished. If you will be using poster board, prepare a rough draft on cheaper paper of the same size. In this way you can see how the aid will actually look.

Don't try to crowd too much information into a single visual aid. With a light pencil mark off the margins to frame your aid. Divide your planning sheet into four equal sections to help you balance the placement of material. Use a

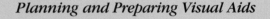

SPEAKER'S NOTES   *Planning and Preparing Visual Aids*

1. Be certain your visual aid enhances the meaning or impact of your speech.

2. Limit the number of aids you will use. Keep the focus on your message.

3. Make a rough draft of your visual aid to check out how well it works.

4. Be sure your aid is simple, balanced in design, and easy to see from the back of the room.

5. Use color in your visual aid to increase its effectiveness.

6. Prepare a *neat* visual aid. A sloppy one can damage your credibility and reduce the effectiveness of your speech.

Figure 9.11
Ineffective Computer-generated Graphic

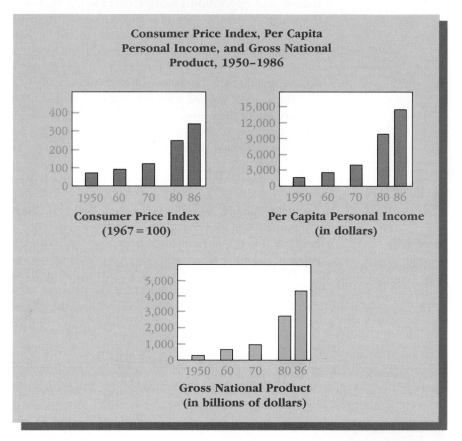

wide-tipped dark felt marker to rough in your design and your words. Step back to view your visual aid from a distance. Is your eye immediately drawn to the most important elements in the poster? Have you positioned your graph or chart so that it will be most effective? Is the poster balanced, or does it look lopsided? Will your audience be able to read words without straining? Is there anything you can eliminate? If the poster looks cluttered, consider making a series of visual aids instead of just one.

Once you have decided that your rough draft is what you want your finished product to look like, practice presenting your speech while using the aid. Does it enhance what you have to say? Is it easy for you to use? When you have settled on a layout and design, take time to prepare a polished final product. If an art room with equipment is available on campus, see if you can get permission to prepare your final product there.

With computer-generated graphics for use as slides, transparencies, or handouts, you might experiment with several different designs, printing yourself copies so that you can see the entire page at one time. Don't get so caught up with what the program can do that you try to incorporate everything into a visual aid. If you do, you will wind up with something that is so "busy" it will detract from your message, rather than supplement it. The computer-generated graphic in Figure 9.11 is too cluttered to be effective for use in a speech. Too much information is crammed into it, and the multiple colors are distracting. The visual aid would have been much more effective had the information been separated into three different graphs.

USING VISUAL AIDS

As we discussed each of the specific kinds of visual aids, we offered suggestions on how to use them in presentations. Here we review these suggestions and extract some basic guidelines.

When you are using a visual aid, stand to the side of it and point directly at what you are talking about. Maintain eye contact with your listeners. Before you begin the speech, check out the equipment to be sure that it is working properly.

- Practice your presentation using your visual aid. Be sure that it is smoothly integrated into your speech.

- Go to the room where you will be speaking to decide where you will place your aid both before and during your speech. Determine what you must bring to display it (thumbtacks, masking tape, etc.).

- Check out any electronic equipment you will use (slide projector, overhead projector, VCR, etc.) in advance of your presentation. Be certain that you can operate it smoothly and that it is working properly.

- Do not display your visual aid until you are ready to use it. When you have finished with it, cover or remove the aid so that it does not distract your audience.

- Don't stand directly in front of your visual aid. Stand to the side of it and face the audience as much as possible. Maintain eye contact with listeners. You want them to see both you and your visual aid.

- When you refer to something on the visual aid, point to what you are talking about. Don't leave your audience searching for what you are describing.

- Do not distribute materials during your speech. If you have prepared handouts, distribute them before or after you speak.

IN SUMMARY

Visual aids are tools to enhance the effectiveness of speeches. They can increase comprehension, authenticate a point, add variety, and help a speech have lasting impact.

Kinds of Visual Aids.   Every speech has at least one visual aid: the speaker. Your appearance, clothing, and body language must all be in concert with your message. Other people may also be used in demonstrations. Another form of visual aid is the actual speech subject. Unless it is large enough to be seen, small enough to be portable, and strictly under your control, you may have to use a model or a sketch instead.

Maps are useful in speeches based on spatial designs. Draw them specifically for your speech so that they contain only the material you wish to emphasize. Graphs can help make complex data more understandable to an audience. *Pie graphs* illustrate the relationships between parts and a whole. *Bar graphs* highlight comparisons and contrasts. *Line graphs* show changes over time. Charts give form to abstract relationships. Among the most frequently used are *flow charts, tree charts,* and *stream charts. Sequence charts* can be especially effective in speeches to emphasize and illustrate various stages in a process.

Photographs and pictures can add authenticity to a speech if handled correctly. Photographs provide slice-of-life realism but can also include irrelevant detail. Any photograph used in a speech should be enlarged so that everyone in the audience can see it.

Ways of Presenting Visual Aids. Chalkboards and flip charts are popular ways of presenting visual aids. Chalkboards permit step-by-step demonstrations that can build suspense and hold attention. Unless carefully designed and roughed in ahead of time, such spontaneous visual aids may confuse listeners. A better option may be to use flip charts or poster board.

Handouts are effective in explaining complex or unfamiliar material; these should be distributed either before or after a speech. Slides and transparency projections can help the audience stay on track, but they also can be awkward to handle and may compete with you for attention. Though they add variety, films and videotapes can be difficult to integrate into a brief classroom speech. You may find that audiotapes are easier to use. Many visual aids can be generated with special computer software.

Preparing Visual Aids. As you plan your visual aid, be aware of basic principles of design. The visual aid must be easy for the audience to see. It should emphasize what the speech emphasizes, excluding all extraneous material. It should seem balanced and pleasing to the eye. Striving for simplicity, plan your layout before you begin working on the finished product. Consider using strong colors to add interest and impact.

Using Visual Aids. Practice using the visual aid until it seems a natural part of your presentation. Always talk to your audience and not to your visual aid and keep the aid out of sight when not in use.

TERMS TO KNOW

visual aids
pie graph
bar graph
line graph
flow chart
tree chart
stream chart
sequence chart
pictograph

textual graphics
monochromatic color
analogous color
complementary color

DISCUSSION

1. Watch news programs on television and observe how graphics and pictures are combined with words to convey meaning clearly and effectively. What techniques are most useful? Be prepared to discuss examples of effective and ineffective usage in class.

2. Recall classes in which your instructors used visual aids. Did these aids serve one or more of the four functions of visual aids (aid understanding, authenticate a point, add variety, or give greater impact to the message)? Why or why not?

3. Describe situations in which speakers either would or would not be effective visual aids for their own speeches. Have you ever seen examples outside your classroom in which speakers as visual aids worked against their own speeches?

4. Look through a recent popular magazine and analyze the advertisements according to the principles of design discussed here. Do the visual aspects of the ads work in concert with the words to emphasize the message? Which of the ads seem most balanced and pleasing to the eye? Do any of the ads violate the rules of simplicity and ease of comprehension? Which of the ads use color most and least effectively? Bring the most interesting ads to class and discuss your findings.

APPLICATION

1. Select a speech in Appendix B and prepare the rough draft of a visual aid that might have been used with it. Would the aid have helped the speech? What other options did you consider?

2. What kinds of visual aids might be most useful for the following speech topics?
   a. Nuclear-waste disposal sites in the United States
   b. What to do in case of snake bite
   c. History of the stock market over the last decade
   d. How the federal budget is divided into major categories
   e. Development of weapons systems in the Soviet Union and the United States

f. Administering your university: who has the power to do what?

g. How we got the modern telephone: the growth of an invention

h. Hunger in Africa: the human story

i. The sounds of navigation and what they mean

NOTES

1. William J. Seiler, "The Effects of Visual Materials on Attitudes, Credibility, and Retention," *Speech Monographs* 38 (1971): 334; and Douglas R. Vogel, Gary W. Dickson, and John A. Lehman, "Persuasion and the Role of Visual Presentation Support: The UM/3M Study," 3M Corporation (1986), pp. 1–20.

2. Cited in Laurence J. Peter, *Peter's Quotations: Ideas for Our Time* (New York: Bantam, 1979), p. 478.

> *Colors fade, temples crumble,*
> *empires fall, but wise words endure.*
>
> —*EDWARD THORNDIKE*

10

THE SPEAKER'S LANGUAGE

This Chapter Will Help You

- understand the power of words to influence behavior.

- express ideas clearly and simply.

- dramatize events through powerful images.

- use language to bring listeners together.

- choose words that move people to action.

- follow the rules of correct and effective language use.

A legislator was asked how he felt about whiskey. He replied, "If, when you say whiskey, you mean the Devil's brew, the poison scourge, the bloody monster that defiles innocence, dethrones reason, creates misery and poverty — yes, literally takes the bread from the mouths of little children; if you mean the drink that topples Christian man and woman from the pinnacle of righteous, gracious living into the bottomless pit of degradation, despair, shame and helplessness, then certainly I am against it with all my power.

"But if, when you say whiskey, you mean the oil of conversation, the philosophic wine, the ale that is consumed when good fellows get together, that puts a song in their hearts and the warm glow of contentment in their eyes; if you mean Christmas cheer; if you mean the stimulating drink that puts the spring in an old gentleman's step on a frosty morning; if you mean that drink, the sale of which pours into our treasury untold millions of dollars which are used to provide tender care for our crippled children, our blind, our deaf, our dumb, pitiful, aged and infirm, to build highways, hospitals, and schools, then certainly I am in favor of it.

"That is my stand, and I will not compromise."[1]

Clearly, language can be double-faced, deceptive as well as richly expressive. As the preceding example shows, the sheer use of words — often cascades of words — can help a speaker escape a tough question even while seeming to answer it! Yet words are the basic material of speeches, and how well you use language often determines your success as a speaker. This chapter describes the power of language in speeches, identifies certain tools of language that can be especially helpful, and establishes standards for the effective use of spoken language.

THE POWER OF LANGUAGE

Words can shape attitudes. Was a certain action *murder, justifiable homicide,* or *self-defense?* The act itself does not change, but the words we choose to describe it can influence how we see it. Language can focus our feelings, deflect our attention, and excuse our behavior to ourselves and others. This power of words has led one modern critic, Kenneth Burke, to conclude that persuasion begins with the names we decide to give things.[2]

Oral language differs somewhat from written language, requiring different approaches and techniques to achieve its ends.[3] Oral language has a more spontaneous quality; it is often less formal, more colloquial, and more fragmentary than its written counterpart. Pauses and vocal emphasis act as punctuation marks. Because listeners cannot go back and reread a statement, oral language must be simpler in construction than written language and should make greater use of repetition to assure understanding. Examples and illustrations are vital in oral communication. In this section we discuss five significant ways in which oral language can influence listeners.[4]

The Power to Make Listeners See

When we listen to the words of successful speakers, we see the world as they see it. Their words are like windows that reveal subjects with startling clarity. But, as the Renaissance scholar Francis Bacon once suggested, the glass in these windows may be "enchanted." The perspective they provide can be tinted and distorted by the speaker's interests, values, and preoccupations. Thus, words can color the subjects they reveal with the speaker's personal feelings.

For example, how should we identify the human fetus? Is it simply a mass of living tissue, or is it a human being? At what point does one become the other? These are the legal and moral issues at the heart of the ongoing controversy over women's right to choose abortion. The issues are established by the way a speaker *depicts* the fetus, by what the speaker's language allows us to see. One side depicts the fetus as "an unborn child," calling abortion "legalized murder."[5] The other side suggests that the early fetus is simply a mass of cells, not yet a viable human being. Who is right and who is wrong? It is hard to decide by simply looking at the early fetus — *it is words that determine how we identify and classify it.* And the words used are usually charged with intense feelings. Each word becomes both a claim and a conclusion that need to be justified with evidence and argument.

The power of words to make you see is fundamental, for it affects your awareness of subjects. It influences how you encounter the world. Your perceptions will in turn predetermine your attitudes, values, and actions.

The Power to Awaken Feelings

Not only can language control perceptions, it can also excite intense feelings. In persuasive and ceremonial speeches, language can touch us, move us to action, and even convert us to new ways of thinking. To arouse appropriate feelings language must often overcome three major barriers: time, distance, and apathy.

Overcoming Time. When events depicted by a speaker lie in the remote past or in the distant future, it can be very difficult to awaken feelings. Listeners tend to be oriented toward the present. They are concerned more with immediate events in which they have direct involvement. However, the language of feeling has a time-machine quality — it can bring past and future events into the present and make them seem real.

Let's see, for example, how large corporations can use the power of narrative to evoke the past and overcome one of their major problems: the loss of identity, the impression among both employees and customers that the company is impersonal. Narratives that recapture the feelings of the past, often told at company meetings or special events, can preserve identity and establish a sense of heritage and corporate culture. It is easier to work for a company when it seems to have human qualities. Note how the words in the following story awaken feeling. Reconstructed from oft-told legend, these words capture the heritage of the Federal Express Company, pioneer in overnight delivery[6]:

> You know, we take so much for granted. It's hard to understand now how Federal Express was once literally just a fly-by-night dream, a mad idea in which a few people had invested — not just all their time and all their money, but their futures, their lives. But I can remember one time early on . . . things weren't going so well. . . . We were really up against it — couldn't even make the payroll. Looked like we were going to crash and lose everything. Fred [Smith, founder of the company] was in despair — never seen him quite like that. "What the hell," he said, and flew off to Las Vegas. The next day he flew back and his face was shining. "We're going to make it," he said. He had won $27,000 at the blackjack table! And we did make it. We made the payroll, and shortly after that, things turned around, and Federal Express began to grow into the giant it is today. . . .

Language can also make a bridge to the future. In his inaugural address, John F. Kennedy addressed future Soviet-American relations in these terms:

> Let both sides seek to invoke the wonders of science instead of its terrors. Together let us explore the stars, conquer the deserts, eradicate disease, tap the ocean depths, and encourage the arts and commerce. . . .
>   And if a beachhead of cooperation may push back the jungle of suspicion, let both sides join in creating a new endeavor, not a new balance of power, but a new world of law, where the strong are just and the weak secure and the peace preserved.[7]

Such language builds images that come alive in the mind, making the future seem both possible and real. Because language can cross the barrier of time, we are able to have both a sense of tradition and a vision of tomorrow to guide us through the present.

Overcoming Distance.   The closer subjects are to our lives, the easier it is to develop feelings abut them. But what if speakers must discuss events that occur far away? Again, language can close the distance between listeners and events. Language can act like a telescope to bring distant events up close so that we can develop feelings about them. Consider how this student reduced the psychological distance between her urban audience and her rural subject by introducing an interesting character and describing his meaning to her life. Her excellent use of graphic language allows her audience to share her feelings and experiences:

> James Johnson knows the loveliest, most sparkling springs in Fentres County. He has lived all eighty-four years of his life there, and he taught me the most important things I know: why the mist rises on a lake at night, how to make the best

blackberry jam you've ever tasted, and how to take care of baby wild rabbits that are abandoned. Today, I want to tell you more about James — and about myself through him.

By focusing on certain details, which helped the audience envision the place she was describing, the speaker used language to conquer distance and arouse feelings about a subject that otherwise might have seemed remote.

Overcoming Apathy.

We live in an age of communication overkill. The modern audience has become jaded by an endless supply of information, persuasion, and entertainment, making it harder to arouse feelings. But with the personal contact public speaking makes possible, speakers can reach out directly to listeners and touch them with language. Jesse Jackson stirred the audience of the Democratic National Convention in 1988 with the following words:

> America's not a blanket woven from one thread, one color, one cloth. When I was a child growing up in Greenville, South Carolina, and grandmother could not afford a blanket, she didn't complain and we did not freeze. Instead, she took pieces of old cloth — patches, wool, silk, gabardine, crockersack on the patches — barely good enough to wipe off your shoes with.
>
> But they didn't stay that way very long. With sturdy hands and a strong cord, she sewed them together into a quilt, a thing of beauty and power and culture.
>
> Now, Democrats, we must build such a quilt. Farmers, you seek fair prices and you are right, but you cannot stand alone. Your patch is not big enough. Workers, you fight for fair wages. You are right. But your patch, labor, is not big enough. Women, you seek comparable worth and pay equity. You are right. But your patch is not big enough. Women, mothers, who seek Head Start and day care and pre-natal care on the front side of life, rather than jail care and welfare on the back side of life, you're right, but your patch is not big enough.
>
> Students, you seek scholarships. You are right. But your patch is not big enough. Blacks and Hispanics, when we fight for civil rights, we are right, but our patch is not big enough. Gays and lesbians, when you fight against discrimination and [for] a cure for AIDS, you are right, but your patch is not big enough. Conservatives and progressives, when you fight for what you believe, right-wing, left-wing, hawk, dove — you are right, from your point of view, but your point of view is not enough.
>
> But don't despair. Be as wise as my grandmama. Pool the patches and the pieces together, bound by a common thread. When we form a great quilt of unity and common ground we'll have the power to bring about health care and housing and jobs and education and hope to our nation.[8]

Here the references to the poverty of his youth and to his grandmother's loving care aroused sympathetic feeling from many viewers. The image of a quilt — suggesting warmth, the home, and the human power to create things of lasting worth and beauty from humble materials — gave delegates and viewers a vision of unity to strive for and sparked thunderous applause.

Appealing images can overcome the apathy of jaded audiences. In his speech to the 1988 Democratic National Convention, Jesse Jackson used a quilt metaphor to suggest unity, warmth, family ties, and the power people have to create something of value out of nothing.

Clearly, language can overcome the barriers of apathy, time, and distance to make us care about a subject.

The Power to Bring Listeners Together

On many issues, individual action is not enough, as the previous example from Jesse Jackson suggests. Only groups, acting together, can make a difference. The speaker must create a feeling of group identity among members of the audience so that they feel they can do something about this problem together. In addition, a speaker needs to build a sense of closeness with listeners. Fortunately, humans have a natural tendency to band together, and language can intensify this impulse.

Images of heroes and adversaries are especially important to feelings of group closeness. Heroes, often portrayed as performing unusual deeds or enduring special sacrifices for the benefit of the group, offer leadership models. Identifying adversaries or enemies, who represent what the group is *not*, helps the group define itself. In persuasive speeches you may want to transform your audience into an action group. You can help this process by providing images of heroes and adversaries for the action you urge.

For example, assume that you will speak to fellow students on a proposed rise in tuition costs. You oppose this increase for a number of reasons. Your specific purpose is to urge your audience to sign petitions protesting the increase, which you will present to legislators, your college president, and the editor of the local newspaper. To build group solidarity you could start with a quotation from a sympathetic local legislator that points out the injustice and the negative consequences of the tuition increase. You could then cite statements of adversaries — perhaps college administrators or unsympathetic legislators — that will arouse resentment in your audience. The language of heroes and adversaries should help your listeners develop a sense of group identity and cohesiveness. In your zeal, however, be careful not to present a false picture of others as friends or foes by unfairly quoting them out of context.

The Power to Encourage Action

Even though a speaker may bring listeners together through effective language, they may not feel compelled to act. Speakers must also be able to use words that make people *want* to take action. Successful speakers often create real-life dramas that involve listeners.[9] Such social melodramas draw clear lines between right and wrong and push listeners into making commitments. In the words of an early union organizing song, the audience may be asked, "Which side are you on?"[10] In your speech on tuition costs, for example, you may want to picture many college administrators and state legislators as unresponsive to student needs:

> Who wants tuition raised? The same administrators and legislators who ignore our pleas for better teaching. Until we organize and speak with a louder, more unified voice, those in power will continue to take advantage of us. They must hear us say: "Give us what we pay for! Give us good teaching! And don't keep raising the price on us!"

If you want your words to lead to action, you should try to picture the results of change for your listeners.

> Our college can be a great center for learning, but only if the faculty *and* the students *and* the administration really want it to be. Learning happens when good, highly motivated teachers and students take each other seriously. It can happen here. But only if we care enough to make it happen.

Whether words move us to action often depends on our trust in the speaker, which underscores again the importance of ethos.

The Power to Help Listeners Remember

Ceremonial speeches that revive traditions reveal the power of words over how we remember. One classic example in our society is the presidential inaugural address. In his second inaugural address, President Reagan evoked memories of American heroes and patriotic myths to help his listeners rekindle a sense of their shared heritage:

> ... Hear again the echoes of our past.
> A general falls to his knees in the harsh snow of Valley Forge; a lonely President paces the darkened halls and ponders his struggle to preserve the Union; the men of the Alamo call out encouragement to each other; a settler pushes West and sings a song, and the song echoes out forever and fills the unknowing air.
> It is the American Sound. It is hopeful, big-hearted, idealistic — daring, decent and fair. That's our heritage. That's our song.[11]

Whenever you need to revive a sense of shared history in your listeners, whenever it is important for them to recall treasured group memories, remember the power that certain words can have. Often these words are names that symbolize great events or that trigger vivid scenes in the minds of listeners. When used artfully in a speech, they are like the few deft brush strokes of an artist sketching an entire scene. The right words and phrases, used in the right places, can create a lasting picture in the minds of listeners.

The power of language is great, ranging from shaping perceptions to revitalizing group memories. How can speakers harness this power in ways that are ethical and elevating? We turn now to the special tools or techniques of language you can use to achieve these effects.

THE TOOLS OF LANGUAGE

A number of techniques serve the purposes of language we have mentioned. Properly used, they help you tap the potential of spoken language to influence the lives of listeners.

Tools to Help Listeners See

Language helps us "see" things by overcoming barriers to perception. Such barriers occur when subjects are abstract, complex, or vast and when listeners already hold opposing views.

Abstract Subjects.   *Abstract* words refer to ideas, intangible qualities, beliefs, or values. Abstract words like *justice* pose special problems for communication. Because they don't represent concrete objects, it is easy for people to react to them in different ways. *Honor* may mean one thing to one person, something entirely different to another. Under such conditions communication becomes problematic. Fortunately, techniques exist to help overcome this difficulty.

One such technique is to show a *relationship* between an abstract subject and a concrete object of comparison. Thus, we might say, "His courage turned on and off like a faucet — first cold, then hot" or "She wore her victory as though it were her favorite dress," in which the abstract subjects *courage* and *victory* are related to the concrete objects *faucet* and *dress.* The words that bridge the gap between the abstract and concrete are usually the terms *like* or *as* or their equivalents. This tool of language is called **simile** (sim′-uh-lee): it works if it helps listeners understand your point more clearly and vividly. For example, Soviet leader Mikhail Gorbachev stated his hope that initial agreements with the United States might "cause *a kind of* peaceful 'chain reaction' in the field of strategic offensive arms" reduction.[12]

When using similes, keep in mind that the object you select for comparison can either improve or worsen your listeners' impression of a subject. Aristotle observed that if you want to praise a subject, you should relate it to something better. You might say, "She writes like Hemingway." If you wish to diminish a subject, you should select an inferior object for comparison, such as "This novel reads like a soap opera." To use simile ethically you should be able to back up your comparison with supporting material.

Another tool for overcoming abstraction replaces ordinary or expected words with unusual, surprising, or graphic language. In this technique of *replacement* or **metaphor** (met′-uh-for), we superimpose words that describe concrete objects upon abstract subjects. The effect can be to bring those subjects into focus, often in startling and insightful ways. During the Senate hearings on the Watergate burglary committed during President Nixon's 1972 reelection campaign, L. Patrick Gray, who had been director of the Federal Bureau of Investigation, was questioned relentlessly. What did it mean to have one's reputation destroyed in such a prolonged, public way? John Ehrlichman, who was a member of the White House team surrounding the president, used a metaphor to describe that experience. Gray, Ehrlichman said, had been left to "twist slowly, slowly in the wind" — a graphic description of the kind of death Gray's reputation had suffered. Earlier in this chapter, when we examined the "quilt" image in Jesse Jackson's speech, we saw what a powerful conceptual device metaphor can be.

When using replacement, be careful not to stretch your metaphors too far. If you say that the recent flu epidemic was a tornado that devastated your campus, then go on to talk about the need for better storm warnings from doctors, disaster insurance from the administration, and disaster relief from teachers, you risk straining the metaphor. You can seem more in love with your own verbosity than concerned with your subject, and that kind of vanity can damage your ethos. Instead, keep your metaphors brief: don't dwell on them too long. You should also be wary of mixing metaphors. The speaker who intoned, "Let us march forward into the seas of prosperity" got a laugh he didn't want and hadn't intended.

Also guard against using trite similes and metaphors, such as "brave as a lion" or "dead as a doornail." Overuse has dimmed these comparisons to the point where people no longer pay attention to them. They may also harm your ethos because a speech filled with clichés can suggest a mind that is dull and stale.

Complex Subjects.   Many subjects are so complex that it is hard to describe them in their entirety. We are forced to concentrate on those aspects that are most appropriate to our purpose. If our descriptions are too complicated, we may confuse listeners with too much detail. With such subjects language must *select* and *simplify,* spotlighting relevant features.

One technique of language that helps us deal with complex subjects *focuses upon a part of the subject to represent the whole of it.* For example, an antihunting television documentary, in portraying the guilt of a hunter, focused upon his bloody hands. Such *representation* is called **synecdoche** (sin-eck′-duh-kee). It can direct our attention to a strategic part of the subject and thus help us make our point about it.* An important synecdoche of our time is the word *movement,* often used to characterize campaigns of reform such as the civil rights movement, the women's movement, and the Chinese freedom movement. In this use of synecdoche, the word itself is a strategy, because it selects the marching and demonstrating aspects of reform campaigns in order to emphasize their mass appeal, activity, and strength. It can be used to attract recruits or even to intimidate opponents.

A related technique directs our attention to something closely associated with a subject that represents its nature. This technique is called **metonymy** (muh-tahn′-uh-me). In the television example mentioned above, the camera zoomed in to feature not just the bloody hands of the hunter, but also the knife he was holding. This combined synecdoche and metonymy reinforced the association of both guilt and brutality with the idea of hunting. Traditional metonymies in American rhetoric are the frontier, the cowboy, and the pioneer woman, used as symbolic representations of American character.

In addition to these specific techniques, language has a tendency to simplify moral issues by reducing them to contrasts such as good versus evil, war versus peace, or right versus wrong. These add drama to communication and make it easier to urge action. However, the price of such simplification can be distortion. Be wary when speakers depict the world in black and white.

Vast Subjects.   Some subjects are so vast that they seem to defy description. For example, war correspondents often find it difficult to describe the effects of war on civilians. How can one convey a sense of thousands of displaced people fleeing into refugee camps? Merely stating numbers does not describe the subject adequately.

---

*Synecdoche can also present the *whole,* of which the subject is part. In this secondary use, synecdoche stresses the significance of the subject, such as referring to a police officer as "the law."

In situations like this, effective communicators must rely on examples to show us representative instances. In Chapter 6 we noted that examples may be used to arouse and sustain attention and interest, clarify major ideas, and emphasize specific points. The use of examples also helps to make vast subjects easier for your audience to comprehend by evoking vivid images in the minds of your listeners. If you are trying to describe the effects of war on civilians, you could talk about an old man and his granddaughter, the only survivors of their family, and describe them trudging wearily down a dusty road to nowhere.

The word *trudge* in this example also demonstrates the tendency of certain words, like *buzz, hiss,* or *bump,* to imitate by their sound the object or action they signify. This technique is called **onomatopoeia** (ah´-nuh-mat´-uh-pea´uh). The word *trudge* suggests the weary, discouraged walk of the survivors and makes the imagery more dramatic.

Opposing Views.   Occasionally you may come before an audience that holds a view of a subject different from the one you want them to accept. When this happens, you may have to resort to a technique called **perspective by incongruity.**[13] This technique works like verbal shock treatment to make people see a subject in a radically new way. Roger Tory Peterson, the noted author of bird identification guidebooks, used perspective by incongruity to emphasize the importance of environmental awareness:

SPEAKER'S NOTES   *How Language Helps Us See: The Three R's*

1. Drawing *relationships* between abstract subjects and concrete objects of comparison ("Her heart was as big as a Montana sky" — *simile*).

2. *Replacing* expected, abstract words with surprising, concrete words ("Fear was the rope that choked him" — *metaphor*).

3. *Representing* complex subjects by focusing on selected features or associations ("There's blood on her hands" — *synecdoche.* "The number-crunchers are taking over the field" — *metonymy*).

4. *Representing* vast subjects by selected examples that imitate mass actions ("Among the countless refugees was an old man, who *trudged* down the dusty road to nowhere" — *onomatopoeia*).

5. *Replacing* a conventional view with a radically different perspective ("You may think you're bright, but your bulb has burned out" — *perspective by incongruity*).

Many people go through life as though they are wearing blinders or are sleep-walking. Their eyes are open, yet they may see nothing of their wild associates on this planet. Their ears, attuned to motor cars and traffic, seldom catch the music of nature — the singing of birds, frogs, or crickets — or the wind. These people are *biologically illiterate — environmentally illiterate —* and yet they may fancy themselves well informed, perhaps sophisticated.[14]

Perspective by incongruity often depends on extreme uses of metaphor. One student speaker, after describing what she alleged were various incidents of discrimination against women on campus, concluded: "Why, this campus is a stinking pigpen for male chauvinism!" Many in the audience were shocked, and a few protested, but the image lingered and caused more than one listener to rethink the situation. The verbal techniques of relationship, replacement, and representation can help us climb the walls that separate us so that we can share perceptions of our world.

Tools to Make Listeners Feel

As we noted in Chapter 3, there are two major types of meaning. The *denotative meaning* of a word is its dictionary definition, its generally agreed-upon objective usage. For example, the word *alcohol* might be defined denotatively as "a colorless, volatile, flammable liquid, obtained by the fermentation of sugars or starches, which is widely used as a solvent, drug base, explosive, or intoxicating beverage."[15] How different this definition would be from the two extremely connotative definitions of alcohol quoted in the example at the beginning of this chapter! *Connotative meaning* invests a subject with emotional associations, the remains of positive or negative past experiences. Thus, *alcohol* in the form of whiskey is no longer just a chemical substance but either "the poison scourge" or "the oil of conversation." Connotative language intensifies feelings, whereas denotative language encourages audience detachment.

The same techniques of language that make you see things in certain ways can also trigger connotative meaning. Simile and metaphor can kindle feelings by the objects they select for relationship and replacement. If the perspective they provide is shocking, as in the "pigpen" example, these feelings can be transferred to the speaker as well as to the subject. Synecdoche and metonymy can also arouse us by the speaker's choice of focus. For example, during the Vietnam War, demonstrators often chanted: "Hey, hey, LBJ, how many kids did you kill today?" The effect of this metonymy was to concentrate emotional attention on one outcome of American involvement in Southeast Asia.

Finally, well-chosen examples can make us feel as well as see. It is easier to identify emotionally with a frail old man and a hungry little girl than with great masses of people. As John Steinbeck observed: "It means very little to know that a million Chinese are starving unless you know one Chinese who is starving."[16] This is why Save the Children ads present the story of a single child who needs your help rather than overwhelming you with the number of starving children in Third World nations. With a problem so vast, the little we can do seems hardly worth the effort. But tell us about little Maria, who lives in a barrio outside Managua and for whom twenty dollars a month will provide food, shelter, clothing, and an opportunity to attend school. We can relate to this desperate child. We can help *her.* The example acts as a lens to bring the subject into clear and compelling focus.

Such use of example is closely associated with the concept of **image,** which the Roman rhetorician Longinus described some two thousand years ago as the natural language of the passions. According to Longinus, the image works when "you think you see what you describe, and you place it before the eyes of your hearers."[17] During the grim days of World War II, when London was bombed every night, the British people needed a strong vision to reassure and sustain them. Sir Winston Churchill often talked to them on the radio. During those speeches he developed an image of defiance and hope for Western civilization. Note how he builds this image upon a metaphor of fire.

> What he [Hitler] has done is to kindle a fire in British hearts ... which will glow long after all traces of the conflagration he has caused in London have been removed. He has lighted a fire which will burn with a steady and consuming flame until the last vestiges of Nazi tyranny have been burnt out of Europe.[18]

Another technique of language useful for arousing feeling is exaggeration, or **hyperbole.** Speakers sometimes exaggerate to encourage action or to force listeners to confront moral problems. Note the use of hyperbole in this speech given by Martin Luther King, Jr., on the night before he was killed:

> Men for years now have been talking about war and peace, but now no longer can they just talk about it. It is no longer the choice between violence and nonviolence in this world, it's nonviolence or nonexistence.... And in the human rights revolution, if something isn't done and done in a hurry to bring the colored peoples of the world out of their long years of poverty, their long years of hurt and neglect, the whole world is doomed.[19]

Are the choices really that simple, the consequences that inescapable? Perhaps not, but King wanted his listeners to understand in their minds *and* hearts what would happen if they neglected their moral responsibility. His hyperbole was meant to make his audience think and feel simultaneously.

You should be careful when using hyperbole. The line between exaggerating slightly for the sake of effect and telling a lie is all too easy to cross. You do not want to acquire a reputation as a speaker who habitually exaggerates. Save hyperbole for those moments when it is vital for listeners to get your message.

A final technique that helps to awaken feeling, especially when the subject is abstract, is **personification.** Personification involves treating nonhuman subjects, such as ideas or institutions, as though they had human form and feeling. When the Chinese students demonstrating for freedom marched into Tiananmen Square carrying a statue of the "Goddess of Liberty," they were borrowing a personification that has been used in the Western world for about four hundred years: the representation of liberty as a woman.[20] Here is how an American student used personification effectively in a classroom speech:

> This university must be more caring. It must see that its investments make a statement to others about its morality. When it supports companies that invest in South Africa, it endorses apartheid. It becomes a silent partner in global inhumanity. It lashes the backs of black people one more time.

By treating an institution as if it were human, the speaker emphasized its moral responsibility. Personification makes it easier to arouse feelings about values and policies that might otherwise seem far removed from the lives of listeners.

Tools to Create Togetherness

Words can create a sense of group belonging by the use of inclusive pronouns, by developing cultural narratives, by building a vocabulary of group-specific symbols, or by relying on universal images.

Speakers rarely refer to *my* feelings, *my* values, *my* plans, or *my* cause but rather *our* feelings, *our* values, *our* plans, *our* cause. Similarly, they do not suggest that *I* will do something or that *you* will do something, but that *we* will do it together. These inclusive pronouns encourage a sense of group unity. They minimize differences within the group and sometimes emphasize differences between group members and those on the outside.

As any group interacts, it develops a history, which is usually passed on to new members as a narrative.[21] One traditional American story pictures our country as a melting pot for immigrant groups. Another, derived from a series of popular books written by Horatio Alger at the end of the nineteenth century, emphasizes that the humblest person can succeed in America by being ambitious, energetic, and thrifty. Many of our narratives derive from experiences on the Western frontier. These stories, with their heroes, villains, and martyrs, establish a sense of social reality for us. When they are repeated or referred to in speeches, they confirm our national identity. In a very effective student speech Martha Porter praised one of her friends, a Cambodian refugee, for overcoming cultural barriers and poverty to graduate with high honors. Much of the power of her speech stemmed from its references to such traditional cultural narratives:

> When Ang Sok came to this country, she owned only the clothes she was wearing — and they were pretty ragged. She could not speak English. She wanted only a chance to learn, to work, and to succeed — only the opportunity to become an American. Our country gave it to her. Now, in three weeks she will graduate from our university magna cum laude. Isn't it ironic that she should have to come all the way from Cambodia to show us what it means to be an American?

The longer groups exist, the more they must rely on a special language to sustain their identity. Language provides two powerful tools, culturetypes and archetypal metaphors, to serve these needs.

Culturetypes.

Culturetypes.   Words that are specific to a group's culture, that express its values, goals, heroes, and enemies, we call **culturetypes.**[22] Richard Weaver, a commentator on communication in the 1950s, described such words as "god and devil terms."[23] He suggested that *progress* was the primary "god term" of American culture in the 1950s. When used in speeches, *progress* became a rallying cry. People were willing to do almost anything to achieve the benefits the word suggested. Other related god terms of the 1950s, according to Weaver, were *science* (the favored methodology of our time, the way to determine truth), *scientist* (the priestlike practitioner who brings us truth); *fact* (truth as discovered by science); *modern* (in a world devoted to progress, the newest is always the best); and *efficient* (a progressive world manages cause and effect relationships to hasten a better future). On the other hand, words like *Communist* and *un-American* were "devil terms." Devil terms cast a subject into disfavor and strengthen our sense of group belonging by defining what we are not.

Culturetypes change and evolve with the passing scene. By the mid-1970s words like *natural, peace,* and *communication* had become god terms, *nuclear* and *pollution* devil terms. During President Reagan's years in office there was an attempt to promote business terms as culturetypes (*entrepreneur* became heroic) and to revive a strong patriotic sense of the word *American.*

Michael Calvin McGee, a scholar at the University of Iowa, has identified a special subgroup of culturetypes that express the basic political faith or system of beliefs — the *ideology* — by which people live.[24] He calls these terms **ideographs** and argues that words such as *freedom, liberty,* and *democracy* are especially potent because they express and celebrate our American political identity.

In addition to these national culturetypes, you should also consider whether there may be special culturetypes that express group identity at your school and that might be effective with your audience. In what does your school take great pride? Who are its rivals and adversaries? The answers to these questions could alert you to special language that may help advance your purpose. One student at Indiana University strengthened her arguments by noting: "Purdue has done it — why can't we?" Presumably, students at Purdue could use Indiana in the same culturetypal way.

Culturetypes can strengthen your speech when used ethically. These words remind us of our identity, make us proud of who we are, and suggest that we must be true to that identity. However, because they are so potent, culturetypes can easily be misused. People often react to them without thinking. To use culturetypes ethically, be sure to show their application to your topic and defend their relevance to your position.

Archetypal Metaphors.   These metaphors draw upon human experience that is common, enduring, and intensely felt. Their appeal is constant over time and across cultures. Because they are rooted in basic, intense experience, these metaphors have the power to arouse strong feelings. They can be an important means of increasing the audience's identification with speakers and their topics.

Archetypal metaphors draw upon sources such as light and darkness, storms, the sea, disease and cure, war and peace, structures, the family, and space. A brief look at several of these sources suggests their potential power in communication.[25]

1. *Light and darkness.* From the beginnings of time, people have been conditioned to negative associations with darkness. The dark is cold, unfriendly, and dangerous. On the other hand, the light brings warmth and safety. It restores one's sense of control. When speakers use the light-darkness archetype, they usually equate problems or bad times with darkness and solutions or recovery with light.

   President Bush's reference to a "thousand points of light" dramatized his appeal to the positive spirit of volunteer service in America. Wuer Kaixi, a leader of the Chinese freedom movement, expressed his horror over the Tiananmen Square massacre of June 4, 1989, by describing a "black sun that rose on the day in June that should have belonged to a season of fresh flowers."[26] Because this source is so often used, it poses a challenge to imaginative speakers who wish to avoid triteness. But if you can discover creative ways to frame your topic in terms of darkness and light, you will find your audience listening with special feeling and appreciation.

2. *Storms and the sea.* The archetypal image of the storm is often used to depict catastrophes. Frequently, the storm occurs at sea — a dangerous place under the best of conditions. The student speaker who argued that "our society is cut adrift — it has lost its moorings, and we don't seem to see the dark nuclear storm threatening on our horizon" was using an effective combination of archetypes to give dramatic expression to his fears of the future.

3. *Disease and cure.* This archetypal metaphor reflects our fears of illness and our ongoing search for cures. The plague was the great symbolic disease of the past; more recently, cancer is the metaphoric illness that dominates discourse. The speaker usually offers a cure. If the disease has progressed too far, radical surgery may be the only answer. After a very bitter and divisive campaign, Bill Allain was elected governor of Mississippi in 1983. In a speech shortly after the election, Allain suggested that he saw himself as "a doctor" whose job was "to get rid of some of the ills we've got in Mississippi."[27]

SPEAKER'S NOTES   *Using Language to Create*
                                                Group Togetherness

1. Emphasize inclusive words such as *we* and *our*.

2. Present group narratives and legends.

3. Use culturetypes that express group values and increase identification.

4. Use archetypal metaphors to intensify the meaning of common experiences and create identification.

Similarly, metaphors of *war and peace* reflect our fascination with war and our yearning for peace.[28] *Structural* images emphasize the human urge to create better conditions by constructing better policies and institutions. *Family* metaphors often express the dream of a loving relationship among people through such images as "the family of humanity."[29] And *spatial* metaphors reflect striving upward and forward toward goals and the wish to avoid falling or retreating into failure.

Culturetypes and archetypal metaphors can help you develop a speech that appeals to group consciousness and that sets the stage for group action. *Be careful not to overdo such language.* If you strain to use these images, they will seem artificial. But if such language fits naturally, it can make your speech both appealing and unifying.

Tools to Make Listeners Act

Action requires time and trouble and may also involve cost and risk. These barriers may make listeners cautious about accepting a speaker's recommendations and unwilling to act, even when the need for action is urgent. Fortunately, there are language resources that can overcome audience reluctance.

The same tools that awaken feeling can also incite action. Hyperbole, imagery, and personification can make us want to undertake action by helping us see the possible consequences of acting or not acting. Synecdoche and metonymy encourage action by simplifying complex situations. Similarly, certain archetypal metaphors, such as disease and war, can encourage aggressive behavior. Other language techniques that can spur an audience to action include alliteration, anaphora, inversion, and antithesis.

Alliteration. **Alliteration** is the repetition of initial consonant sounds in closely connected words: "Rather than *m*ilitary *m*adness, we need to offer the world *p*eace and *p*rosperity." The repetition of sounds captures attention and reinforces the thoughts contained in the words. This technique can be very effective in the introductions and conclusions of action-oriented speeches. Be careful not to overdo alliteration — it can sound pretentious if it is too obvious.

Anaphora. Using the same initial wording in a sequence of phrases or sentences is called **anaphora** (uh-naf'-uh-ruh). This technique is especially suited for formal conclusions, when it seems to seal the thoughts developed in the speech. The speaker who ended with the words "Freedom yesterday, freedom today, freedom tomorrow" was using anaphora.

Inversion. In **inversion** the normal word order is changed to make statements more memorable and emphatic. One student speaker concluded with a paraphrase based on a sermon by John Donne, "Ask not for whom the bell tolls. It tolls for thee." The "ask not" was inversion.

Antithesis. When a speaker combines opposing elements in the same sentence or adjoining sentences so that listeners can see their choices clearly, the technique is called **antithesis** (an-tih'-thuh-sis). Antithesis suggests a decisive mind that has a clear grasp of options. The student speaker who summarized her persuasive speech in the following way used antithesis well:

> So now we see the problem of quality in higher education more clearly. It is not the lack of funding that cheats us as much as the lack of leadership. It is not dwindling state support as much as shrinking commitment by those who represent us. One of Shakespeare's characters said it well: "The fault," he said, "is not in our stars but in ourselves."

The following quotation, from the inaugural address of President Kennedy, is a famous example combining antithesis, inversion, and anaphora. See if you can find these techniques at work:

> And so, my fellow Americans: Ask not what your country can do for you — ask what you can do for your country.
> My fellow citizens of the world: Ask not what America will do for you, but what together we can do for the freedom of man.[30]

Tools to Help Listeners Remember

Some language is particularly appropriate for ceremonies and special occasions, when groups celebrate past events, recognize outstanding achievements, remember their values, and revive their sense of identity. Often speakers make the past come alive by recalling specific people or events. Reference to the

The language of ceremonial speeches helps audiences remember their heritage by revitalizing culturetypes such as *freedom* and *liberty*. President Ronald Reagan was admired for ceremonial speeches such as his presentation at Pointe du Hoc, Normandy, commemorating the Allied invasion of Europe during World War II.

midnight ride of Paul Revere evokes memories of the bold, resourceful spirit of American colonists. Great intellectual or sports accomplishments are often used to represent the spirit of a university.

Ceremonial speeches help revitalize group culturetypes. Words like *freedom, liberty,* and *progress* can gain new meaning when connected to other language tools. The following example, drawn from a speech presented in class by John Washburn, illustrates this process well.

> What is freedom in our time? I'll tell you how I see it. Freedom is our right to take risks on our own, our right to climb the mountain, and if necessary, our right to fall. Freedom is our right to pick up and go, to decide our own destiny. Freedom is our right to open our mouths and make fools of ourselves without going to jail for our thoughts. Freedom is our right to laugh if we want to, to pray if we want to. Freedom means a nation that aims at those elusive targets of respect and fairness and tolerance for all. It doesn't mean that we always hit those targets — what nation has? The most important thing is that in our wonderful and naive way, we keep trying.

This excerpt from a ceremonial speech uses the techniques of metaphor, synecdoche, anaphora, image, and personification in an effort to revitalize the culturetype *freedom*. Can you find them at work in the example?

Because group identity is important for its own sake as well as for what it can accomplish, language that evokes a sense of heritage can be very effective. Archetypal metaphor can help us appreciate who we are and what we represent in the great scheme of things. "So we survived the storm of war, came out of the darkness, and watched the sun rise on a new day" is the kind of language that helps us recall, understand, and celebrate the meaning of group experiences.

All such tools of language can help you put the power of words to work for the sake of good causes and effective leadership.

USING LANGUAGE EFFECTIVELY

No one can tell you exactly how you should use language because your style is an expression of your individuality. **Rhetorical style** is the unique way you choose and arrange words in a speech. Your rhetorical style may vary according to the topic, audience, and situation. Formal situations call for more formal language. Words and expressions appropriate to a celebrity roast would be out of place at a memorial service. Your language for a speech on the dangers of nuclear power might be different from that for a speech warning about what one student called "power shopping." Your style for an audience of accountants may well vary from that for an audience of artists.

Nevertheless, there are certain standards for language usage you should strive to achieve whenever you communicate. We refer to these standards as the five *C*'s of language: clarity, color, concreteness, correctness, and conciseness.

Clarity

To make your listeners see, your language should be clear and simple, drawn from familiar, everyday life. Although this advice may seem obvious, it is often ignored. Some speakers forget that audiences may not share their technical vocabularies, so they don't translate difficult terms into lay language. Senator Albert Gore, Jr., showed his sensitivity to this problem in a speech he presented to the National Academy of Sciences. To make the rather complex point that a gradual deterioration of the environment might prove worse than a sudden catastrophe, Senator Gore told a simple narrative about a frog. *U.S. News & World Report* summarized his story as follows:

> If dropped into a pot of boiling water, a frog will quickly jump out. But if the same frog is put into a pot and the water is slowly heated, the frog will stay put until boiled alive. Just so with pollution, the senator told the National Academy of Sciences last week: if we do not wake up to the slow heating of our environment, we may jump too late.[31]

Like Senator Gore, tell people what they need to know in language they can understand.

A major enemy of clarity is jargon. All of us have been exposed to language that seems purposefully befuddling. Television commentator Bill Moyers warned his audience at the University of Texas against the dangers of jargon:

> If you would . . . serve democracy well, you must first save the language. Save it from the jargon of insiders who talk of the current budget debate in Washington as "megapolicy choices between freeze-feasible base lines." (Sounds more like a baseball game played in the Arctic Circle.) Save it from the smokescreen artists, who speak of "revenue enhancement" and "tax-base erosion control" when they really mean a tax increase. . . . Save it from . . . the official revisionists of reality, who say that the United States did not withdraw our troops from Lebanon, we merely "backloaded our augmentation personnel."[32]

Often such jargon is used because people don't really want to communicate. In contrast, effective speaking is clear and direct.

One special technique to achieve clarity is strategic repetition. In your writing classes you may have been cautioned against redundancy. In oral communication, however, you frequently have to repeat to be understood. Your listeners cannot pause to savor an expression, nor can they glance back over your words. They must understand instantly, or they will not understand at all.

Amplification, the art of strategic repetition in speeches, allows you to dwell on an important or difficult point. You amplify when you rephrase points rather than simply repeating them verbatim. Using a good example is another way to amplify a point. In effect, you tell listeners something, you tell them another way, and then you show them what you have been telling them. In his classroom speech "Football as an Art," George Anderson used the techniques of amplification:

> Football is an art enacted by eleven persons playing as one [*statement*]. Each of the eleven must have a role, and each role must fit into an overall action [*restatement*]. On a long run or completed pass the art is enacted superbly. A fumble, an interception, or a loss behind the line of scrimmage indicate breakdowns in the art [*illustrative examples*].

Although clarity is important to every language function, it is especially vital to listener understanding. This makes clarity the basic standard of language use.

Color

Color refers to the emotional intensity or the vividness of language. Therefore, this standard relates directly to the power of words to arouse feeling. Colorful language stands out in our minds and is apt to be remembered. Consider the following passage from a speech by Malcolm X, the well-known human rights activist of the 1960s:

> What can the white man use now to fool us? After he put down that march on Washington, and you see all through that now. He tricked you. Had you marchin' down to Washington. Yeah! Had you marchin' back and forth between the feet of a dead man named Lincoln and another dead man named George Washington singin' "We Shall Overcome." He made a chump out of you! He made a fool out of you! He made you think you were goin' somewhere and you ended up goin' nowhere but between Lincoln and Washington.[33]

What makes this statement colorful? First, it is very direct, very conversational. It uses the fragments and rhythms of everyday street language. The words are simple and graphic, such as *fool, trick,* and *chump.* They hit with special force. Although deceptively simple, the passage is really quite artful. It uses the contrast between the living, active, singing marchers and the statues of the "dead men," Lincoln and Washington. It also uses a striking antithesis: "He made you think you were goin' somewhere and you ended up goin' nowhere. . . ."

Colorful language often creates sensory images for the audience. We saw this technique at work in our earlier excerpt from a speech about James Johnson: [He] knows the loveliest, most sparkling springs. . . . He taught me . . . why the mist rises on a lake at night, how to make the best blackberry jam you ever tasted, and how to take care of baby wild rabbits. . . . " This speaker selected her images deliberately to awaken several of her listeners' senses — to make them "see" the mist, "taste" the jam, "feel" the rabbits' fur. She used adjectives sparingly but with striking pictorial result ("sparkling springs" — notice how the alliteration contributes to the pleasing effect). Adjectives should not be strewn about a speech extravagantly but saved so that they really count when you use them.

Color can also be achieved through synecdoche and metonymy, which direct our attention to exciting aspects of subjects. Color can be created as well by hyperbole, personification, and the imaginative use of archetypal metaphor. When speakers use colorful language well, we are drawn to them. Therefore, color is an important standard for effective language usage.

Concreteness

It is virtually impossible to discuss anything of significance without using abstract language. However, if the language in your speech is overly abstract, listeners may lose interest. Moreover, because abstract language is more ambiguous than concrete language, a speech full of abstractions also invites misunderstanding.

Concrete language refers to things that listeners can apprehend through their senses. The more concrete a word is, the more specific information it conveys. For example, consider this continuum of terms describing a cat.

Mehitabel is a/an

| creature | animal | mammal | cat | Persian cat | gray Persian cat |

abstract ──▶ *concrete*

A similar continuum can be applied to active verbs. If we wanted to describe how a person moves, we could use any of the following terms:

Jennifer
moves   walks   prances
abstract ──▶ *concrete*

Again, we see that the more concrete our language, the more pictorial and precise the information we can convey. Concrete words are also easier for listeners to remember. Therefore, your language should be as concrete as the subject permits.

Correctness

Nothing can sink your ship more quickly than a glaring misuse of language. Mistakes in grammar or word selection can be disastrous to your ethos because most audiences connect such errors with incompetence. They are likely to reason that anyone who misuses language can hardly offer good advice. When you select your words, be careful that they say exactly what you mean to say.

Use your dictionary when you have any doubts about word choice. Even words that are classified as synonyms have slightly different meanings. For example, the words *disorganize* and *derange* are sometimes listed as synonyms, yet their meanings are different enough that to use them interchangeably could cause serious problems. Just try referring to a disorganized person as deranged, and you will see what we mean.

People often err when using words that sound similar. Such confusions are called **malapropisms,** after Mrs. Malaprop, a character in a play by Richard Sheridan. William J. Crocker of Armidale College in New South Wales, Australia, collected the following samples from student speeches:

A speaker can add interest to his talk with an *antidote.*

The disagreements can arise from an unintended *conception.*

The speaker hopes to arouse *apathy* in his audience.

Good language can be reinforced by good *gestation.*

The speaker can use either an inductive or a *seductive* approach.[34]

Students are not the only ones who make such blunders. Elected officials are not above an occasional malapropism. One former United States senator declared that he would oppose to his last ounce of energy any effort to build a "nuclear waste suppository" in his state.[35] And a former mayor of Chicago once introduced the poet Carl Sandburg as "the poet lariat of the United States."[36] The lesson is clear. To avoid being unintentionally humorous, check the meaning and pronunciation of any word you feel uncertain about in a current dictionary.

Conciseness

In discussing clarity we talked about the importance of dwelling on certain points. Although it may seem contradictory, you must also be concise, even while you are amplifying. Typically, speakers must meet specified time limits, especially in the classroom setting. Most students worry at first about how to fill five minutes, and then are amazed at how rapidly the time passes when they are speaking. You must make your points quickly and efficiently. Follow the advice given by Franklin Delano Roosevelt to his son James: "Be sincere . . . be brief . . . be seated!"

Even if you have unlimited time for speaking, conciseness is a virtue. It helps listeners to see more clearly and to feel more powerfully. Long, drawn-out speeches lose audience interest. They can kill the impulse toward action that persuasive speaking must cultivate.

To achieve conciseness strive for simple, direct expression. Thomas Jefferson once said, "The most valuable of all talents is that of never using two words when one will do." Use the active voice rather than the passive in your verbs: "We demand action" is more concise — and more direct, colorful, and clear — than "Action is demanded by us."

You can also be succinct by using comparisons that reduce complex issues to the essentials. Sojourner Truth, a nineteenth-century human rights activist, once had to dispute the argument that society should not educate blacks and

SPEAKER'S NOTES   *The Five C's of Effective Language Usage*

1. Strive for *clarity* by using familiar words in a simple, direct way.

2. Use *colorful,* vivid language to make your message memorable.

3. Develop *concrete* images so the audience can picture what you're talking about.

4. Check the *correctness* of the words you use.

5. Be *concise.*

women because of their "inferiority." She destroyed that then-powerful position with a simple parable: "If my cup won't hold but a pint, and yours holds a quart, wouldn't you be mean not to let me have a little half-measure full?"[37]

The goal of conciseness encourages the use of **maxims,** those wise but compact sayings that summarize the beliefs of a people. During the Chinese freedom demonstrations of 1989, a sign carried by students in Tiananmen Square adapted the maxim of Patrick Henry, "Give Me Democracy or Give Me Death." Similarly, demonstrators at a nuclear plant in Colorado carried a sign reading, "Hell No, We Won't Glow!" This maxim was a variation on a chant often heard in antiwar rallies of the 1960s, "Hell no, we won't go!" As these examples suggest, maxims can have special power in attracting mass-media attention. When printed on posters, they can be easily photographed and filmed and thus can satisfy the hunger of the press for visual messages. Their brevity makes them ideally suited to the rigid time constraints of television news. One problem with the use of maxims might arise should you allow them to substitute for careful, well-supported arguments. However, once you have developed a responsible speech, consider how you might use maxims to emphasize your message.

IN SUMMARY

The Power of Language.   Language is a powerful instrument of communication. Words enable us to share our perceptions and feelings with others and to develop values and goals together. Words can promote togetherness among people and help launch programs of action to accomplish worthy goals. Words may also preserve the memories of our heritage and help stabilize our culture.

The power to affect perceptions with words carries a great ethical obligation: we must be able to justify the names we give to things. If we want to share feelings with listeners, we must overcome barriers of time, distance, and apathy. Language that builds a sense of group belonging for the sake of action often relies on images of heroes and enemies. Language can also trigger action by showing the consequences of acting and not acting. Finally, language helps us remember our heritage by preserving heroes and patriotic stories.

The Tools of Language.   Language offers the speaker special tools. To help us see and feel, successful speakers use techniques based on the three *R*'s: relationship, replacement, and representation. *Simile* helps clarify abstract subjects by relating them to things that are concrete and familiar. *Metaphor* offers new perspectives by replacing anticipated words with surprising, unexpected language. *Synecdoche* and *metonymy* help simplify complex subjects by focusing on certain representative features or associations. Well-chosen examples can reduce vast subjects to representative instances. Such examples can add authenticity through the use of *onomatopoeia,* words that sound like their subjects. *Perspective by incongruity* can sometimes shock listeners into new ways of understanding.

To assist the sharing of feelings, effective speakers emphasize connotative over denotative language. The same tools that assist seeing in common may also promote feeling in common. The *image* is the natural language of the emotions. *Hyperbole* can help overcome audience lethargy and kindle powerful feelings. *Personification* helps develop emotions about abstractions or impersonal institutions.

To develop group identity speakers should use inclusive pronouns, such as *our* and *we.* A speaker can also promote identity by telling stories that illustrate cultural values and goals. In addition, speakers may use the special vocabulary of symbols — *culturetypes* and *archetypal metaphors* — to promote group feeling. Culturetypes express group values in a compact way, and archetypal metaphors remind us of our common humanity. When properly used, such techniques as *alliteration, anaphora, inversion,* and *antithesis* can enhance appeals for action. Ceremonial language helps us remember our heritage.

Using Language Effectively.   *Rhetorical style* is the unique way you choose and arrange words while speaking. Although style varies with the user and with different topics, audiences, and situations, you should strive to satisfy the five major standards of *clarity, color, concreteness, correctness,* and *conciseness.* Clear language is simple and direct and draws its comparisons from everyday life. *Amplification* promotes clarity by dwelling on important, difficult points. Color refers to the emotional intensity and vividness of our language and is especially vital to the sharing of feeling.

The more concrete a word is, the more specific the information it conveys. Your language should be as concrete as the subject permits. Correctness is vital to ethos because grammatical errors and improper word choices can lower perceptions of your competence. *Malapropisms,* confusions among words based on similarities of sound, can be very damaging. Concise speakers strive for brevity, often using comparisons that reduce complex issues to the essentials. *Maxims* are the ultimate in conciseness.

TERMS TO KNOW

simile	ideograph
metaphor	archetypal metaphor
synecdoche	alliteration
metonymy	anaphora
onomatopoeia	inversion
perspective by incongruity	antithesis
image	rhetorical style
hyperbole	amplification
personification	malapropism
culturetype	maxim

DISCUSSION

1. The example that opens this chapter presents arguments for and against whiskey, using connotative language. Rephrase these arguments, using denotative language. How does this change affect the power of the arguments? Which speech situations call for more denotative language? How can connotative language be misused? Under what circumstances is it most appropriate?

2. In the 1950s, Richard Weaver suggested that *progress* was the primary culturetype of American society. What words do you nominate as culturetypes in contemporary society? Why? How are they used now in public communication? Find and share examples from speeches, essays, editorials, cartoons, or advertisements.

3. How can specific language techniques be abused in public communication? Bring examples to class.

4. Analyze how you used the power of language in your last speech. What, if any, barriers to perception or feeling did you have to overcome, and what techniques did you use? Could you have improved the effectiveness of your language? How?

APPLICATION

1. Use archetypal metaphors to describe the following abstract concepts:
   friendship
   freedom
   justice
   brotherhood
   democracy
   poverty
   Present your descriptions in class. Which work most effectively and why?

2. Study the language customs and strategies in a speech from a political campaign. How is the power of language exercised? What special tools are used? Evaluate the effectiveness of this usage according to the standards discussed here.

3. Using published pamphlets and speeches determine the heroes and villains of the Chinese freedom, peace, anti-apartheid, gay rights, and women's liberation movements.

4. To explore and help develop stylistic techniques, your instructor will assign different language tools to members of the class and then present a subject. Your task will be to make a statement about this subject using the technique you have been assigned. Share these statements in class. Try this

exercise several times, using different subjects and different tools of language. Evaluate in class what this exercise reveals about the power, techniques, and standards of language.

5. Identify and discuss the language techniques used by Elie Wiesel in his Nobel Prize acceptance speech in Appendix B. Specifically discuss what techniques were used to reawaken group memory and identity, and whether and why they were effective for you as an audience.

NOTES

1. William Raspberry, "Any Candidate Will Drink to That," *Austin American Statesman* 11 (May 1984): A-10. The "Whiskey Speech," a legend in Southern politics, was originally presented by N. S. Sweat, Jr., during a heated campaign for liquor-by-the-drink in Mississippi. Because about half of his constituents favored the question and the other half were vehemently opposed, Representative Sweat decided to defuse the issue with humor.

2. Kenneth Burke, *Language as Symbolic Action: Essays on Life, Literature, and Method* (Berkeley: University of California Press, 1966), pp. 44–80.

3. John F. Wilson and Carroll C. Arnold, *Public Speaking as a Liberal Art,* 3rd ed. (Boston: Allyn and Bacon, 1974), pp. 225–28.

4. These five powers of language were first explored in Michael Osborn, *Orientations to Rhetorical Style* (Chicago: Science Research Associates, Inc., 1976), and are developed further in Michael Osborn, "Rhetorical Depiction," in *Form, Genre, and the Study of Political Discourse,* ed. Herbert W. Simons and Aram A. Aghazarian (Columbia: University of South Carolina Press, 1986), pp. 79–107.

5. *The Silent Scream,* documentary film produced by American Portrait Films, 1984. For a detailed analysis of this conflict, see Celeste Michelle Condit, *Decoding Abortion Rhetoric: Communicating Social Change* (Urbana: University of Illinois Press, 1990).

6. Based on the account in Claire Perkins, "The Many Symbolic Faces of Fred Smith: Charismatic Leadership in the Bureaucracy," *The Journal of the Tennessee Speech Communication Association* 11 (1985): 22.

7. John F. Kennedy, "Inaugural Address," in *Presidential Rhetoric, 1961–1980,* ed. Theodore Windt (Dubuque, Iowa: Kendall Hunt, 1980), p. 10.

8. Jesse Jackson, "Common Ground and Common Sense," *Vital Speeches of the Day* 54 (15 Aug. 1988): 649–53.

9. Listeners whose lives seem dull and unrewarding are especially susceptible to such dramas. See the discussion in Eric Hoffer, *The True Believer: Thoughts on the Nature of Mass Movements* (New York: Harper, 1951).

10. Union organizing song written in 1932 by Florence Reece, wife of a leader of the National Miners Union in Harlan County, Kentucky.

11. Ronald Reagan, "Second Inauguration Address," *Vital Speeches of the Day* 51 (1 Feb. 1985): 226–28.

12. Mikhail Gorbachev, "USSR Foreign Relations," *Vital Speeches of the Day* 54 (15 Dec. 1987): 130–33.

13. Kenneth Burke, *Permanence and Change: An Anatomy of Purpose* (New York: New Republic, 1935), pp. 118–64.

14. Roger Tory Peterson, "Commencement Address," presented at Bloomsburg University, Bloomsburg, Pa. Cited in *Time,* 17 June 1985, p. 69.

15. Adapted from *The American Heritage Dictionary,* 2nd ed. (Boston: Houghton Mifflin, 1985), p. 92.

16. John Steinbeck, preface to *The Forgotten Village,* as cited in Peter Lisca, "*The Grapes of Wrath* as Fiction," in *The Grapes of Wrath: Text and Criticism* (New York: Viking, 1977), p. 736.

17. Longinus, "On the Sublime," in *The Great Critics: An Anthology of Literary Criticism,* trans. W. Rhys Roberts and ed. James Harry Smith and Edd Winfield Parks (New York: Norton, 1951), p. 82.

18. Winston Churchill, *Blood, Sweat, and Tears* (New York: Putnam, 1941), pp. 367–69.

19. Martin Luther King, Jr., from a transcription of "I've Been to the Mountaintop," delivered in Memphis, Tenn., 4 Apr. 1968. For complete text see *Texts in Context: Critical Dialogues on Significant Episodes in American Political Rhetoric,* ed. Michael C. Leff and Fred J. Kauffeld (Davis, Calif.: Hermagoras Press, 1989), pp. 311–21.

20. Michael Calvin McGee, "The Origins of Liberty: A Feminization of Power," *Communication Monographs* 47 (1980): 27–45.

21. Ernest G. Bormann, "Fantasy and Rhetorical Vision: The Rhetorical Criticism of Social Reality," *Quarterly Journal of Speech* 58 (1972): 396–407.

22. Osborn, *Orientations to Rhetorical Style,* p. 16.

23. Richard Weaver, "Ultimate Terms in Contemporary Rhetoric," in *The Ethics of Rhetoric* (Chicago: Henry Regnery, 1953), pp. 211–32.

24. Michael Calvin McGee, "The Ideograph: A Link Between Rhetoric and Ideology," *Quarterly Journal of Speech* 66 (1980): 1–16.

25. For further insights into the function of archetypal metaphors, see Michael Osborn, "Archetypal Metaphor in Rhetoric: The Light-Dark Family," *Quarterly Journal of Speech* 53 (1967): 115–126; and "The Evolution of the Archetypal Sea in Rhetoric and Poetic," *Quarterly Journal of Speech* 63 (1977): 347–63.

26. *Time,* 10 July 1989, p. 32.

27. *Commercial Appeal,* 10 Nov. 1983, p. A-3.

28. See Robert Ivie, "Images of Savagery in American Justifications for War," *Communication Monographs* 47 (1980): 279–94.

29. See another side of this image in J. Vernon Jensen, "British Voices on the Eve of the American Revolution: Trapped by the Family Metaphor," *Quarterly Journal of Speech* 63 (1977): 43–50.

30. Kennedy, "Inaugural Address," p. 11.

31. David R. Gergen, "The Boiling Pot," *U.S. News & World Report,* 15 May 1989, p. 76.

32. Bill Moyers, "Commencement Address," presented at the Lyndon B. Johnson School of Public Affairs, University of Texas, Austin. Cited in *Time,* 19 June 1985, p. 68.

33. Malcolm X, from a transcription of "The Ballot or the Bullet," delivered in Cleveland, Ohio, 3 Apr. 1964.

34. "Malapropisms Live!" *Spectra,* May 1986, p. 6.

35. Richard Lacayo, "Picking Lemons for the Plums?" *Time,* 31 July 1989, p. 17.

36. *New York Times,* 30 Jan. 1960. Cited in James B. Simpson, *Simpson's Contemporary Quotations* (Boston: Houghton Mifflin, 1988), p. 208.

37. Sojourner Truth, "Ain't I a Woman?" in *Feminism: The Essential Historical Writings,* ed. Miriam Schneir (New York: Random House, 1972), p. 95.

Whosoever hath a good presence and a good fashion carries continual letters of recommendation.

—FRANCIS BACON

11

PRESENTING
YOUR SPEECH

This Chapter Will Help You

- ◆ become aware of what makes an effective presentation.

- ◆ learn the four major methods of presentation.

- ◆ understand how to use your voice and body to communicate.

- ◆ learn how to practice presenting your speech.

Jean felt strongly about U.S. policy in Central America. When her instructor assigned a persuasive speech, she felt morally bound to speak on that subject. So she went to the library and read deeply to expand her knowledge. Following her research Jean analyzed her audience, carefully narrowed her topic, determined her speech strategy, and outlined her speech. For several days she practiced at least an hour each afternoon, working to make her normally quiet voice more emphatic and expressive and developing forceful gestures to reinforce her message. Finally, she felt comfortable presenting her speech.

On the day of her presentation, Jean walked to the front of the room, displaying a confidence she did not really feel. As she began her speech, she lost herself in her desire to communicate. All she could think about was sharing her message with those in front of her. Her nervousness was transformed into energy that made her face and voice compelling, her movements decisive and emphatic. Though they were impressed by her manner, all her listeners could think about was her sincerity and how much sense she made. When she finished, there was a moment of silence, then a burst of applause. Jean and her listeners had shared a moment of real communication.

This vignette reminds us that a successful speech represents the integration of a number of skills, involving both *what* you say and *how* you say it. In this chapter we turn our attention to "how you say it," or **presentation.** We consider what makes a presentation effective, the different methods of presentation, the development of an effective speaking voice, using the body to communicate, and the importance of practice.

Skills for effective presentation also can help you in other communication situations. They will be useful in job interviews, meetings, and social situations. Once you gain a sense of poise, or platform presence, it tends to stay with you over the years. It allows you to carry what Francis Bacon called "continual letters of recommendation."

WHAT IS EFFECTIVE PRESENTATION?

A speech is not a speech until it has been presented by the speaker and received by the audience. The essence of communication is sharing. As we noted earlier, the word *communicate* derives from the Latin word meaning *common.* Effective presentation makes it possible for the speaker and audience to hold ideas and feelings in common. Ineffective presentation can widen the gap between speaker and listener.

Your attitude is the starting point for effective presentation. You must want to share with the audience. We have purposely used the term *presenting* the speech rather than *delivering* it to help you keep this in mind. The speech you prepare is your gift to the audience. You have invested a great deal of yourself in the preparation of this gift, so the manner in which you give it is important.

If you have selected a topic that is important to you, one that excites you and that you want to share with others, then you have taken the first step to an effective presentation. Your enthusiasm should color your presentation with energy and forcefulness. It should tell your audience that you really care about your topic and about them.

A skillful presentation does not call attention to itself or distract from the message you intend to communicate. A formal, "oratorical" style, with broad, sweeping gestures and grandiloquent vocal patterns, may leave your audience wondering more about where you got your acting training than about what you have to say. Mumbling your way through your speech is equally distracting. Your speech should be readily intelligible and loud enough to be heard in all parts of the room.

An effective presentation sounds natural and conversational, as though you are talking *with* people, not *at* them. When you speak to a group, you should be a bit more formal and deliberate than when you talk informally with your friends, but not too much so. Good speech presentation also sounds spontaneous, as though the words and ideas are coming together for the first time. Your vocal tone, loudness, and rate of speaking should be appropriate to your material and to the size of your audience.

Methods of Presentation

There are four major methods of speech presentation: impromptu speaking, memorized text presentation, reading from a manuscript, and extemporaneous speaking. Extemporaneous speaking, which combines careful planning with a direct, conversational, seemingly spontaneous style of utterance, is the method preferred in most speaking situations. It is emphasized in most of our discussion in this chapter and throughout the book. Here, however, we shall address briefly the other types and the situations in which they are appropriate.

Impromptu Speaking

Impromptu speaking is often referred to as speaking "off the cuff," an idiom that suggests you could put all the notes for your speech on the cuff of your shirt or blouse. Impromptu speaking situations give you little or no time for preparation or practice. The incident we described at the beginning of Chapter 8, in which we learned shortly before a city zoning hearing that developers were proposing a helicopter port in our neighborhood, called for an impromptu speech. At work you might find yourself being called to make a presentation "in fifteen minutes." In meetings you may be asked to "say a few words" on a subject about which you are knowledgeable. Impromptu speaking situations are also frequent in college classes, when you are asked to respond

Group meetings often call for impromptu presentations. The ability to organize your ideas and present them confidently puts you at a great advantage in civic or business situations.

to a question or to comment on a point your professor has just made. Whatever the situation, you must rely on your previous knowledge and experience to carry you through.

When you have just a few minutes to prepare, begin by determining the main points you want to cover. If you have access to any type of writing material — a note pad, the back of a used envelope, even the proverbial cuff of your shirt — jot down a memory-jogging word for each of these main ideas, either in the order of their importance or as they seem to follow each other in natural order. This skeleton outline will keep you from rambling or forgetting something that is important. Stick to the main points, verbally enumerating them as you go: "My first point is.... Second, it is important to observe.... Finally, it is clear that...." Illustrate each point with some type of supporting material: information, stories, or examples. Examples are especially useful since they help clarify the slight confusion that often accompanies impromptu speaking. Keep your presentation short and summarize to conclude your remarks.

An impromptu speech usually occurs in a context of other speeches. As we noted in Chapter 4, these previous speeches can create an atmosphere for your presentation. Take your cues from other speakers and from the demands of the situation. If others stood at the front of the room to speak and this seems to satisfy audience expectations, you should do so as well. On the other hand, if earlier speakers remained seated, you may wish to follow suit and adjust the tone of your message to this more relaxed setting. Much may depend on whether preceding speakers have been successful. If these speakers offended listeners while making standing presentations, you may wish to remain seated. The contrast created by this approach can help distance you from those less successful speakers.

Remember that standing to speak is a form of emphasis. It suggests that what you are going to say is important and affects the formality of your manner. If you remain seated, the audience may expect less from your message and anticipate an informal manner of presentation. If you think that you may be making several impromptu statements during the course of a discussion, you may wish to reserve the more formal standing mode of presentation for that moment when you make your most important statement.

Fortunately, most impromptu speaking situations are relatively casual. No one expects a polished speech on a moment's notice, but the ability to gather your ideas quickly, organize them effectively, and present them confidently puts you at a great advantage in both social and business interactions. The principles of structuring, developing, and supporting ideas that you are learning for more carefully prepared presentations can also help you become a more effective impromptu speaker.

Memorized Text Presentation

You may choose to memorize certain parts of an extemporaneous speech such as your introduction and conclusion. Because these parts of a speech are so important in gaining audience attention and leaving a lasting impression, their wording should be carefully planned. You might also want to memorize short congratulatory remarks, a toast, or a brief award acceptance speech. In general, however, you should avoid trying to memorize entire speeches because this method of presentation poses many problems.

Memorized text presentations require considerable skill. Often, novices who try to memorize speeches get so caught up with "remembering" that they forget to communicate with their audience. The memorized presentation then becomes more of a soliloquy than a public speech and can sound either stilted or "singsongy." Because it binds speakers to a prepared text, the memorized approach inhibits adjusting to audience feedback. It can prevent speakers from amplifying points that need clarification or from following up on ideas that have been especially effective. This kind of presentation can also end up with speakers staring up at the ceiling, at the wall or out the window, as they strain to remember the exact words. Needless to say, these behaviors reduce audience contact.

Another problem with memorized speeches is that they must be written out in advance. Most people do not write in an oral language style because they have been trained to use a written style. The major differences between oral and written language were mentioned in Chapter 10 but bear repeating here. Good oral style utilizes short, direct, conversational patterns. Even sentence fragments are acceptable. Repetition, rephrasing, and amplification are more necessary in speaking than in writing. Imagery should be used to help the audience visualize your subject.

If you feel you must memorize a speech, be sure that you compose the speech using good oral style. Then commit the speech so thoroughly to memory that you can communicate confidently with the audience. Should you experience a "mental block" during a memorized presentation, remember that the audience will not know about your difficulty unless you show signs of distress. *Keep talking.* Talk your way through your block. Go back and restate the point you have just made (chances are it may need repetition anyway!). Most of the time, going back to summarize a previous point will put your mind back on track. If it doesn't, you may find yourself *forced* to adopt the preferred extemporaneous style of speech.

Reading from a Manuscript

Manuscript presentation requires at least as much skill as making a memorized presentation. It also shares many of the same problems and creates some of its own. Most people do not read aloud well to others, as accomplished actors and actresses prove each year at the Academy Awards when they try to read their acceptance speeches. Additionally, when speakers plan to read from a manuscript, they frequently do not spend enough time practicing. If the

SPEAKER'S NOTES

Suggestions for Using Different Methods of Presentation

1. When making an *impromptu speech,* enumerate your main points, support each point with information, an example, or a story, and then conclude with a summary.

2. Memorize only very short remarks. If you experience a "mental block" during a *memorized presentation,* go back over your last point.

3. Read material only when accurate wording is important or time constraints are severe. Practice a *manuscript presentation* until you are thoroughly familiar with your material.

4. Use an *extemporaneous presentation* to make your speech sound spontaneous. Plan, prepare, and practice extemporaneous presentations.

speech is written out in front of them, it does not seem as important to become familiar with the ideas. But unless speakers are comfortable with the material, they find themselves glued to their manuscripts rather than communicating with listeners. They may first lose eye contact and then mental contact with their audiences.

Reading from a prepared manuscript may be necessary when accurate wording is imperative or when time constraints are severe. Official proclamations, legal announcements, professional papers, or mass media presentations that must be timed within seconds usually call for manuscript presentation. Additionally, extemporaneous presentations may include quotations or statistical data that require you to read those parts of the speech.

To make reading work for you rather than against you, be certain that you write your message in an oral style. If possible, use a large-print typewriter or word processor to prepare the final draft of your manuscript so that you can see it clearly without straining. Double or triple space the print. Mark pauses in the manuscript with slashes. Underline words or phrases you want to emphasize. Practice presenting your speech from the manuscript so that you become familiar with it. Then you can more easily maintain eye contact with your audience.

Record yourself as you practice; then review these tapes to evaluate your own presentation. If you have access to videotape equipment, by all means use it. Do you sound as though you are reading instead of talking with someone else? Are you able to maintain eye contact with your audience? If you are stumbling over the phrasing or pronunciation of certain words, either revise the manuscript or practice until these words flow naturally. Strive for a conversational style of presentation.

This exercise may help you read more effectively: Practice reading any written prose, increasing your vocal force at the end of each sentence. This imitates the natural way we converse. It also will help you avoid the drab, end-of-the-sentence "blahs" that often plague oral reading. The energy you generate at the end of sentences will impel you into your next sentence, moving your speech forward.[1]

Extemporaneous Speaking

Extemporaneous speaking is prepared and practiced but not written out or memorized. When you speak extemporaneously, you may use a brief outline to serve as a memory jogger. This key-word outline is a streamlined version of the formal outline for your speech. It helps you work from a pattern or sequence of ideas that should be a vivid presence in your mind. Each time you practice from your outline, your wording will differ slightly. Because your speech is not written out in advance, the language seems more spontaneous and natural. Additionally, this mode of presentation allows you to adjust to your audience as you observe their responses. Do they understand you? Do you need to define a word you have just used? Do you need an example to make something clearer? Are you holding their interest? When speaking extemporaneously, you can monitor the responses of the audience and make changes on the spot.

Because preparation and practice are involved, extemporaneous speaking is more polished than impromptu speaking. Preparation and practice are revealed by the more careful organization of your material, the more complete support you are able to bring to your points, and the greater ease with which you present your speech. And because the wording is not preset, the extemporaneous mode allows more flexibility and spontaneity than a memorized or read presentation. It is easier to sound conversational when you have the direct contact with listeners that extemporaneous speaking allows. Because it combines the best characteristics of the forms we have discussed, many instructors prefer that you use extemporaneous presentation for most of your classroom speeches. We offer much of our advice in this chapter and elsewhere with this style in mind.

USING YOUR VOICE EFFECTIVELY

How well your speech comes across to your audience depends a great deal on the adequacy of your voice. *A good speaking voice conveys your meaning fully and clearly in a manner that enhances your ethos.* This means that you do not cultivate a good speaking voice for its own sake. The age of the golden-voiced orator, in which speakers took more pride in how they sounded than in what they said, has pretty much passed into oblivion. Some of the more famous speakers of our time have had less than perfect voices and articulation. Franklin Delano Roosevelt had a rather raspy, strident voice, yet his "fireside chats" on the radio comforted many during the Depression and the early days of World War II.

Nevertheless, you should be concerned with vocal characteristics because of the close connection between voice and ethos. Your voice is very personal; in fact, your voice may represent your personality to many people. Someone who talks in a soft, breathy voice may be labeled "sexy"; another, who speaks in a deep, resonant, and forceful voice, may be considered "authoritative." In other words, minor adjustments in the way you speak can bring about changes in the way you are perceived by others. No one can give you a new voice, but you may be able to utilize more fully what nature has provided.

The sad truth is that a truly effective speaking voice is a distant goal for many people. Many of us picked up bad vocal habits when we were young: as children we may have learned *not* to talk freely. ("Children should be seen and not heard.") As adolescents we may have discovered that expressing ourselves freely opened us to ridicule in the cruel interpersonal games teenagers sometimes play. Consequently, we may have developed flat, inexpressive voices as a shield against such pain. As we encounter the stresses and pressures of modern life, we may react with strained, strident voices. Finally, we are tossed into a public speaking class, which only increases our stress. The result? Voices that do not communicate freely and naturally. In such situations the advice "Just be natural" or "Just be yourself" may not be very useful. The problem is, *we don't know how to be natural.* That's where work on the voice comes into the picture. We exercise our voices to recover the lost vocal potential within ourselves.

To function most expressively, your voice needs careful attention. As one voice specialist put it, "Though speech is a human endowment, how well we speak is an individual achievement."[2] We should mention, however, that unsupervised vocal exercises are not the answer for speech impairments. If you have such a problem, contact the speech pathology clinic on your campus or in your community for professional help.

If you doubt that your voice can play a vital role in the meaning a listener attaches to your words, consider the following simple sentences.

> I don't believe it.
>
> You did that.
>
> Give me a break.

How many different meanings can you create, just by varying the pace, emphasis, and rising and falling inflections of your voice?

The first step in learning to use your voice more effectively is to evaluate how you usually talk. Tape-record yourself both speaking spontaneously (talk about what you did last night) and reading a short selection (any three or four consecutive paragraphs from this book will do). When you first hear yourself, you may say, "Is that really me?" Ask yourself the following questions:

1. Does my voice convey the meaning I intend?

2. Would I want to listen to this voice if I were in the audience?

3. Does this voice present me at my best?

If your honest answers to any of these questions are negative, then you are a candidate for vocal improvement. You may be able to improve by paying special attention to the following: pitch, rate, loudness, variety, articulation, pronunciation, or dialect. Save your original tape so that you can hear yourself improve as you practice.

Pitch

The **pitch** of your voice refers to its placement on the musical scale. For effective speaking, you need to find a pitch level that is comfortable and allows maximum flexibility and variety in your speech.

Each of us has a **habitual pitch,** or level at which we speak most frequently. Additionally, we all have an **optimum pitch,** or a level at which we can produce our strongest voice with minimal effort and that allows variation up and down the scale.

You can use this exercise to help determine your optimum pitch:

> Sing the sound *la* down to the lowest pitch you can produce without feeling strain or having your voice break or become rough. Now count each note as you sing up the scale to the highest tone you can comfortably produce. Most people have a range of approximately sixteen notes. Your optimum pitch will be about one-fourth of the way up your range. For example, if your range extended for twelve notes, your optimum pitch would be at the third note up the scale. Again, sing down to your lowest comfortable pitch, and then sing up to your optimum pitch level.

Tape-record this exercise, and compare your optimum pitch to the habitual pitch revealed during your first recording. If your optimum pitch is within one or two notes of your habitual pitch, then you should not experience vocal problems related to pitch level. If your habitual pitch is much higher or lower than your optimum pitch, you may not have sufficient flexibility to raise or lower the pitch of your voice for changes in meaning and emphasis. Additionally, a voice that is habitually pitched too low sounds harsh or gravelly; one that is pitched too high may sound shrill or thin. You can change your habitual pitch by practicing speaking and reading at your optimum pitch.

Once you have determined your optimum pitch, use it as a base or point of departure in your practice. Read the following paragraphs from John F. Kennedy's inaugural address at your optimum pitch level, using pitch changes to provide meaning and feeling. To make the most of your practice, tape-record yourself so you can observe both problems and progress.

> Let the word go forth from this time and place, to friend and foe alike, that the torch has been passed to a new generation of Americans — born in this century, tempered by war, disciplined by a hard and bitter peace, proud of our ancient heritage — and unwilling to witness or permit the slow undoing of those human rights to which this nation has always been committed, and to which we are committed today at home and around the world.
>
> Let every nation know, whether it wishes us well or ill, that we shall pay any price, bear any burden, meet any hardship, support any friend, oppose any foe to assure the survival and the success of liberty.[3]

The intention of this exercise is to explore the full range of variation around your optimum pitch and to make you more conscious of the relationship between pitch and effective communication. Therefore, you should exaggerate the variation during practice, going beyond what you *think* might be normal. If you have a problem with a constricted pitch range, you may discover as you listen to your recorded voice that the exaggeration actually makes you more effective!

When you speak before a group, do not be surprised if your pitch seems higher than usual. Your voice is sensitive to your emotional state and generally goes up in pitch when you are under pressure. If there is a large gap between your habitual and optimum pitch, hum the latter to yourself as you start rehearsing your speech. Set the right pattern for your voice as you set the right pattern for your ideas.

Rate

Your **rate** of speaking, or the speed at which you utter words, should vary with the type of material you are presenting. Rate contributes to the mood of your speech. Serious, complex topics call for a slower, more deliberate rate; lighter topics can be handled best by a faster pace. Variety of rate includes the relative duration of syllables in words and the use of pauses, as well as the overall speed of presentation.

Beginning speakers may encounter problems with tempo if they are intimidated by the situation. They may react by speeding up and running their words together as though they were onejumpaheadofthesheriff. What they communicate is not the meaning of their speeches, but rather their desire to finish as quickly as possible and sit down! Other speakers may become so slow or deliberate that they sound as though they were frozen in time. They plod through their speeches. Neither extreme lends itself to effective communication.

As we noted in Chapter 3, the typical rate for extemporaneous speaking is about 125 words per minute. You can check your speed by timing your reading of the excerpt from the Kennedy inaugural. If you were reading at the average rate, you would have taken about forty-five seconds to complete that material. If you allowed time for pauses between phrases, appropriate for such formal material, your reading may have run longer. If you took less than forty seconds, you were probably going too fast or not using pauses effectively. Your tape recording should reveal this problem.

Pauses can emphasize meaning very effectively. You can pause to underscore the importance of an idea you have just presented. Pausing before and after a word or a phrase gives it added emphasis. Pausing also gives your listeners time to contemplate what you have said. Moreover, pauses can clarify the relationships among ideas, phrases, and sentences. They are oral punctuation marks, taking the place of commas and periods in written communication. Read the following passage aloud again, using pauses where indicated by the slash marks. This exercise will give you an idea of how President Kennedy used pauses to emphasize and clarify the flow of his ideas:

> Let the word go forth from this time and place, / to friend and foe alike, / that the torch has been passed to a new generation of Americans — / born in this century, / tempered by war, / disciplined by a hard and bitter peace, / proud of our ancient heritage — / and unwilling to witness or permit the slow undoing of those human rights / to which this nation has always been committed, / and to which we are committed today / at home and around the world. /

President John F. Kennedy's speaking voice was unusual but effective, marked by a distinct dialect that became his oral signature. Kennedy used pause and emphasis to communicate his ideas with special force.

> Let every nation know, / whether it wishes us well or ill, / that we shall pay any price, / bear any burden, / meet any hardship, / support any friend, / oppose any foe / to assure the survival and the success of liberty.

When practicing your next speech, be sure that you are using pauses to emphasize and clarify ideas.

If your natural tendency is to speak too slowly, you can work to develop a faster rate in practice sessions by reading light material aloud. The following selection by Mark Twain calls for a lively pace. (Reading at between 160 and 175 words per minute, you should take about 70 seconds to complete this selection.) In the story Twain (the narrator) knows absolutely nothing about farming but must write a story to meet a deadline for an agricultural newspaper. In his desperation he fabricates an advice column that causes a farmer to burst into his office.

> "There, you wrote that. Read it to me — quick! Relieve me. I suffer." I read as follows:
>
> "Turnips should never be pulled, it injures them. It is much better to send a boy up and let him shake the tree.
>
> "Concerning the pumpkin, the custom of planting it in the front yard with the shrubbery is fast going out of vogue, for it is now generally conceded that the pumpkin as a shade tree is a failure.

"Now, as the warm weather approaches, and the ganders begin to spawn. . . ."

The excited listener sprang toward me and said: "There, that will do. I know I am all right now, because you read it just as I did, word for word. But stranger, when I first read it I said to myself, now I believe I *am* crazy: and with that I fetched a howl that you might have heard for two miles, and started out to kill somebody, because I knew it would come to that sooner or later, and so I might as well begin. I burned my house, crippled several people, and have one fellow up a tree where I can get him if I want him. Then I thought I should stop in here to check with you. I tell you, it is lucky for that chap up in the tree that I did. Good-bye, Sir. *Good*-bye."[4]

Loudness

No presentation is effective if the audience cannot hear you. Similarly, your presentation will not be successful if you overwhelm the audience with a voice that is too loud. When you speak before a group, you usually need to speak louder than you do in general conversation. The size of the room and background noise also may call for adjustments. Take your cues from the audience. If you are not loud enough, you may see listeners leaning forward in their seats, straining to hear you. If you are speaking too loudly, your listeners may unconsciously lean back in their seats, pulling away from the source of the booming irritation.

In order to speak at a proper level of loudness, you must have good breath control. If you are breathing improperly, you may not have enough force to project your voice so that you can be heard in the back of a room. Breathing improperly can also cause you to run out of breath before you finish a phrase or come to an appropriate pause. To check whether you are breathing properly for speaking, do the following exercise:

> Stand with your feet approximately eight inches apart. Place your hands on your rib cage (thumbs to the front, fingers to the back) directly above your waist. Take a deep breath — in through the nose and out through slightly parted lips. If you are breathing correctly, you should be able to feel your ribs move *up and out.* Your breathing is being controlled by your diaphragm, the band of muscles that encloses the lower portion of your rib cage.

Improper breathing can affect more than the loudness of your speech. If you breathe by raising your shoulders, the muscles in your neck and throat will become tense. The result may be a high pitch and a harsh quality in your voice. Moreover, you probably will not take in enough air to sustain your phrasing, and it will become difficult to control the release of air. The air and sound then all come out with a rush when you drop your shoulders, leading to unfortunate oral punctuation marks when you neither want nor need them.

To see if you have a problem, try this exercise:

> Take a normal breath and see how long you can count while exhaling. If you cannot reach fifteen without losing volume or feeling the need to breathe, you need

to work on extending your breath control. Begin by counting in one breath to a number comfortable for you, then gradually increase the count over successive tries. Do not try to compensate by breathing too deeply. Deep breathing takes too much time and attracts too much attention while you are speaking. Use the longer pauses in your speech to breathe, and practice the rhythm of your breathing during rehearsal.

You should seek to vary the loudness of your speech, just as you strive for variety in pitch and rate. Changes in loudness are often used to express emotion. The more excited or angry we are about something, the louder we tend to become. But don't let yourself get caught in the trap of having only two options: loud and louder. Decreasing your volume, slowing your rate, pausing, or dropping your pitch can also express emotion quite effectively.

To acquire more variety in loudness, practice the following exercise recommended by Hillman and Jewell: "First, count to five holding on to your optimum pitch but at a very soft volume, as if you were speaking to one person. Then holding the same pitch, count to five at medium volume, as if to ten or fifteen people. Finally, holding the same pitch, count to five, as if to thirty or sixty people."[5] If you tape-record your practice, you should be able to hear the clear progression in loudness.

Variety

In our discussions of pitch, rate, and loudness we have stressed the importance of variety to effective presentation. Nothing is more boring than speakers who drone on and on in a monotone. What they are saying seems to have no meaning for them. Vocal variety adds color and interest to a speech. It can make a speaker more attractive and encourages identification between speaker and audience. One of the best ways to achieve this goal is to practice reading aloud materials that demand variety to express meaning and feeling. As you read the following selection from *the lives and times of archy and mehitabel* by Don Marquis, strive for a maximum variety of pitch, rate, and loudness. Incidentally, archy is a cockroach who aspires to be a writer. He leaves typewritten messages for his newspaper-editor mentor but, because he is a cockroach, archy cannot type capital letters and never uses punctuation marks. His friend mehitabel, whom he quotes in this message, is an alley cat who has grandiose dreams and a dubious reputation. Have fun!

> archy what in hell have i done
> to deserve all these kittens
> life seems to be just one damn litter after another
> after all archy i am an artist
> this constant parade of kittens
> interferes with my career
> its not that i am shy on mother love archy
> why my heart would bleed if anything happened to them

and i found it out
a tender heart is the cross i bear
but archy the eternal struggle between life and art
is simply wearing me out[6]

Tape-record yourself while reading your favorite poems or dramatic scenes from plays or novels. Work toward greater variety of expression. Compare these practice tapes with your initial self-evaluation tape.

Patterns of Speaking

People often make judgments about others based on their speech patterns. Those who slur words together or have faulty speech sounds, who make gross mispronunciations, or who have an unusual dialect may be labeled as "outsiders" or may even be thought uneducated or socially undesirable. If you sound "odd" to your listeners, their attention will be distracted from what you are saying to the way you are saying it. If you sound "different" to them, your speech patterns may become a barrier to identification. One of your authors recently taught a large lecture class at the University of California, Davis. After the initial lecture, I asked the class if there were any questions. The first student question was, "Where are you from?" I then had to spend some time with the class exploring our stereotypes of "southerners" and "Californians" in order to develop identification and establish ethos in the classroom.

In this section we cover articulation, enunciation, pronunciation, and dialect as they contribute to or detract from speaking effectiveness.

Articulation.   Your **articulation** refers to the way you produce individual speech sounds. Some people have trouble making certain sounds. They habitually substitute a *d* for a *th* so that they say "dem" instead of "them." Other sounds that are often misarticulated include *s, l,* and *r.* Severe articulation problems can interfere with effective communication, especially if the audience cannot understand the speaker or if the variations are perceived as signs of low social or educational status. Such problems are best treated by a speech pathologist, who retrains the individual to produce the sound in a more acceptable manner. Minor articulation problems may not disrupt communication and may even add distinctiveness to one's speech pattern. They can be part of a person's oral signature. Barbara Walters's speech is immediately recognizable by her "weak" *r* and *l* sounds, yet these have not hindered her success in television.

Enunciation.   **Enunciation** refers to the way you articulate and pronounce words in context. In casual conversation it is not unusual for people to slur their words, saying, for example, "gimme" for "give me." But improper or careless enunciation can cause credibility problems for the public speaker. Are you guilty of saying "Swatuh thought" for "That's what I thought"; "Harya?" for

"How are you?", or "Howjado?" for "How did you do?" Such lazy enunciation patterns are not acceptable in public communication settings. Equally unacceptable are inflated, pompous, pretentious articulation patterns in which speakers meticulously enunciate each and every syllable, affecting a language pattern they think is stylish or sophisticated. Very few speakers can make this kind of speech pattern work without sounding phony. You should strive to be neither sloppy nor overly precise.

Pronunciation.   Your **pronunciation** refers to whether you say words correctly. Pronunciation includes both the use of correct sounds and the proper stress or accent on syllables. Because written English does not always indicate the correct pronunciation of spoken English, we may not be sure how to pronounce words that we first encounter in print. For instance, does the word *chiropodist* begin with an *sh,* a *ch,* or a *k* sound?

If you are not certain how to pronounce a word, consult a dictionary. A useful reference work is John S. Kenyon and Thomas R. Knott's *A Pronouncing Dictionary of American English* (Springfield, Mass.: Merriam, 1953), which contains regional variations of acceptable pronunciations. Also helpful is W. Cabell Greet's *World Words: Recommended Pronunciations* (New York: Columbia University Press, 1948), which shows how 25,000 foreign words should be pronounced in English. Additional useful references are the *NBC Handbook of Pronunciation,* 3rd ed. (New York: Crowell, 1964), which is very easy to use, and *Webster's New World Guide to Pronunciation* (New York: Simon & Schuster, 1984), which is both recent and inexpensive. When international stories and new foreign leaders first appear in the news, newspapers frequently indicate the correct pronunciation of their names. Check front-page stories in the *New York Times* for such guidance.

In addition to problems pronouncing unfamiliar words, you may find that there are certain words you habitually mispronounce. For example, how do you pronounce the following words?

government	**February**
ask	**nuclear**
athlete	**library**
picture	**secretary**
just	**get**

Unless you are careful, you may find yourself slipping into these common mispronunciations:

goverment	**Febuary**
ast or aks	**nuculer**
athalete	**liberry**

pitchur	**sekaterry**
jist	**git**

Mispronunciation of common words can damage your ethos. Most of us know the words we chronically mispronounce and are able to pronounce them correctly when we think about it. The time to think about it is when you are practicing your speech.

Dialect.

Dialect. A **dialect** is a particular speech pattern associated with an area of the country or a cultural or ethnic background. Your dialectal pattern usually reflects where you were raised or have lived for any length of time. In the United States there are three commonly recognized dialect patterns: eastern, southern, and midwestern. Additionally, there are local variations within the broader dialects: Tidewater Virginians speak differently from Arkansans, Vermonters differently from New Yorkers.

Insofar as dialect is concerned, there is no such thing as right or wrong, superior or inferior. There can be occasions, however, when a distinct dialect may be an advantage or disadvantage. Listeners have aesthetic preferences for dialects based largely on their familiarity to the ear. Audiences may also have stereotyped preconceptions about people who speak with certain dialect patterns. For example, those raised in the South often associate a northeastern dialect with brusqueness and abrasiveness, and midwesterners may associate a southern dialect with slowness of mind and action. You may have to work to overcome these prejudices against your dialect.

If your dialect blocks communication between you and your audience, you can plan your speech to overcome this difficulty. Sometimes the best way to tackle such a problem is to acknowledge it. Get it out in the open early in the speech, then move on in a spirit of good will. This kind of direct, disarming approach to a problem may not remove it but should reduce it until it is no longer important:

> We sound different. I know that. I just didn't have the good fortune to be born in Philadelphia. But we laugh the same way. We care the same way about our families. And when crime comes to our communities, we often cry the same way.

If your dialect represents the best standards of your own community, you should not rush to tamper with your speech. Only when your dialect creates barriers to understanding for a significant portion of your audience should you be deeply concerned. Then you may want to work toward softening your dialect so that you lower these barriers for the sake of your message. If others share your dialect problem, you may be able to form a self-help group in which you help each other identify specific problems and work together to correct them. If you can combine these sessions with actual practice for the speeches you will give in class, so much the better.

USING YOUR BODY EFFECTIVELY

Communication with your audience begins before you ever utter a single word. Your facial expression, personal appearance, and air of confident command all have something to say. How do you walk to the front of the room before you begin to speak? Do you step forward with poise and purpose? As you begin to speak, do you look listeners directly in the eye? Do you seem relaxed and enthusiastic about your speech? While you are speaking, do you move and gesture as freely and naturally as you would in social conversation? These visible behaviors form your **body language,** a nonverbal but extremely significant system of cues. For public speaking to be effective, your body language must reinforce your verbal language. If your face is expressionless as you urge your listeners to feeling and action, you are sending inconsistent messages. Be sure that your body and words both "say" the same thing.

Facial Expression and Eye Contact

I knew she was lying the minute she said it. There was guilt written all over her face!

He sure is shifty! Did you see how his eyes darted back and forth? He never did look us straight in the eye!

Have you ever made statements like these? Most people believe that they can judge people's character, determine their true feelings, and tell whether they are being honest from facial expressions. If there is a conflict between what listeners see and what they hear, they will usually believe their eyes rather than their ears.

Our eyes are the most important feature of facial expressiveness. In our culture, frequent and sustained eye contact suggests honesty, openness, and respect. We tend to think of a person's eyes as a window into the real self. If you avoid looking at your audience while you are talking, you are drawing the shades on these windows of communication. The lack of eye contact suggests either that you do not care about listeners, that you are putting something over on them, or that you are afraid of them.

When you reach the place where you are going to speak, pause and make direct eye contact with listeners. This signals that you want to communicate and prepares your audience to listen. As you speak, be sure to include all sectors of your audience in eye contact. Don't just stare at one or two people. You will make *them* uncomfortable, and other members of the audience will feel left out. Look first at people at the front of the room, then shift your focus to audience members sitting in the middle, finally look at those in the rear. You may find that those sitting in the back of the room are your most difficult audience. They may have selected the back of the room because they don't *want* to listen, because they don't want to be involved with your message. Their physical distance from you creates a special problem in establishing favorable identification. You may have to work harder to hold their attention, and eye contact is one way you can reach them.

As you begin your speech, smile at your audience if this is appropriate to your message. Your face should be an animated projection of the meaning of your words. An expressionless face is an advantage only in a game with deuces wild. A frozen face in public speaking is often a sign of fear and can be a serious barrier to communication. Additionally, listeners may interpret an expressionless face as a sign that the speaker is indifferent. The frozen face can be a mask behind which the speaker hides. The solution to this problem lies in selecting a topic that makes you enthusiastic, concentrating on sharing your message with your audience, and having the confidence that comes from being well prepared.

You can also try the following exercise:

Utter these statements, using a dull monotone and keeping your face as expressionless as possible:

This is the hardest thing I've ever done.
I am absolutely delighted by your gift.
I don't know when I've ever been this excited.
We don't need to beg for change — we need to demand change.
All this puts me in a very bad mood.
All this puts me in a great mood.

Now utter the same statements, using vocal variety and making your face *express* the appropriate feelings. Exaggerate your expressions as you practice. You will probably find that your hands and body want to get involved as well, to emphasize the strong emotions. Encourage such impulses because you need to develop a fully integrated system of body language.

Movement and Gestures

Most actors learn — often the hard way — that if you want to steal a scene from someone who has more lines than you, all you have to do is move around, develop a twitch, or swing a leg. Before long, all eyes will be focused on you and not on the person who is delivering the lines. This nasty little theatrical trick shows that physical movement can command attention even more than words. All the more reason that your words and gestures should work in harmony and not at cross-purposes! This means you should avoid random movements such as pacing back and forth and hair or mustache curling. Once you are aware of such mannerisms, it is easy to control them.

Gestures and movement should always appear natural and spontaneous, prompted by the speaker's ideas and feelings. They should never appear contrived and artificial. For example, you should avoid the ludicrous practice of making a gesture fit each word or sequence of words you utter. Perhaps every speech instructor has encountered speakers like the one who stood with arms circled above him as he said, "We need to get *around* this problem." That's taking body language too far!

To appreciate the effective uses of movement during speeches, we need to consider two important principles of **proxemics,** the study of how humans use space during communication. The first of these principles involves the *distance* between you as speaker and your listeners. If you stand too far from your listeners, you will make identification, that desirable feeling of closeness between speaker and listener, difficult to achieve. This problem can be even worse if you stand behind a lectern, imposing a physical barrier between you and your listeners. If you are short, you may almost disappear from view! If this is a problem, you should speak either beside or in front of a lectern; then your body language can work in your favor. A different problem arises if you move so close to listeners that you sense them growing uncomfortable. When this happens, you know you have violated their sense of personal space. Such discomfort can be a distraction that interferes with your message, so you need to find a happy medium concerning distance between you and listeners.

A second principle of proxemics you need to consider is that of *elevation.* When you speak, you often stand above your seated listeners in a "power position." Some speakers find this arrangement at odds with their purpose of achieving identification. Often they will sit on the edge of the desk in front of the lectern in a more relaxed and less elevated position. If your message is informal and requires close identification, you might want to give this a try.

Just as bad habits can prevent us from realizing our best potential voice, they can also block our use of full and expressive gestures. Many of us must rediscover — or even discover for the first time — this unrealized potential of our body language. The time for this discovery is during practice because during the speech itself all your concentration must be on the ideas you are presenting.

Effective gestures involve three phases: readiness, execution, and return. In the readiness phase you must be prepared for movement. Your hands and body should be in a position that does not inhibit free action. For example, you cannot gesture if your hands are locked behind your back. We have often watched students' arms strain to move in a gesture while their hands are stuffed in their pockets. As you execute a gesture, let yourself move naturally and fully. Don't raise your hand halfway, then stop in the middle with your arm frozen in an awkward position. Finally, when you have completed your gesture, let your arms return naturally to a relaxed position, resting in front of you or at your sides or on the lectern, where they will be free to move again when the next impulse to gesture arises.

Personal Appearance

Your clothing and grooming have a definite impact on how you are perceived by your audience. Not only does your appearance affect the way others perceive you, it also affects the way you see yourself and consequently the way you behave. A policeman out of uniform may not act as authoritatively as when dressed in blue. A doctor without a white jacket on may behave like just another person. You probably have a certain type of clothing that makes you feel comfortable and relaxed. You may even have a special "good luck" outfit that raises your social confidence.

When you are scheduled to speak, you should dress in a way that puts you at ease and makes you feel good about yourself. Outside the classroom most speakers prefer to follow audience custom concerning grooming and dress. However, your speech is a special occasion, and you should treat it as such. By dressing a little more formally than you usually do, you emphasize both to yourself and the audience that your speech is important. As we noted in Chapter 9, your appearance can serve as a visual aid that complements your message. Like any other visual aid, it should never compete with your words for attention or be distracting. The best rule is to dress in good taste for the situation you anticipate.

THE IMPORTANCE OF PRACTICE

It takes a lot of practice to sound natural. Although this statement may seem paradoxical, it should not be that surprising. Making a presentation before a group is not your usual way of communicating. You may not have had a great deal of experience speaking in this kind of situation. Even though most people seem spontaneous and at ease when talking with a friend or small group of acquaintances, something can happen when they walk up to the front of a room and turn to face a larger audience of less familiar faces. Instantly, they may feel that there is an icy wall between themselves and listeners and become stilted, awkward, unnatural. The vital flow of communication is blocked, and the frustration felt by both speaker and listeners increases the strain.

The key to melting this ice and opening the vital flow of communication is effective rehearsal. Practice concentrating on your ideas until you have a vivid sense of them. As you develop this awareness, you will begin to respond to your ideas as you present them. Your voice, face, and body will express your feelings. On the day of your speech, your expressiveness will help overcome the distance that separates you from listeners. As your audience responds, that distance will disappear.

To develop an effective extemporaneous speaking style, practice presenting your speech from an outline. Even experienced speakers practice until they feel the speech is part of them. During practice you can actually hear what you have been preparing and can try out the words and techniques you have been considering. What looked like a good idea on paper may not seem to work as well when it comes to life in spoken words. It is better to discover this fact in rehearsal than before an actual audience.

The first two or three times that you run through your speech you will probably want privacy while you practice. Even then you should try to simulate the conditions under which the speech will be given. Stand up while you practice. Imagine your listeners in front of you. Picture them responding positively to what you have to say. Address your ideas to them, and think of those ideas as having impact.

If possible, go to your classroom to practice. If this is not possible, find another empty room where the speaking arrangements are similar. Rehearsing your speech under conditions close to those of actual presentation allows you to get a better feel for the situation you will face. Then the situation will not seem quite as strange when you make your actual presentation.

You may begin practice by working from your formal outline. Once you feel comfortable, you can switch to a key-word outline and practice speaking from that. If you have practiced sufficiently, the outline will transfer from the paper to your head. Nonetheless, it can be comforting to have the key-word outline in front of you as you actually present the speech.

Keep material you must read to a minimum. Type or print quotations in large letters so you can see them easily. Put each quotation on a single index card or sheet of paper. If using a lectern, position this material so that you can maintain some eye contact while reading. If you will speak beside or in front of the lectern, hold your cards in your hand and raise them when it is time to read so that you can reestablish eye contact easily. Practice reading your quotation until you can present it naturally.

While you are practicing, you can serve as your own audience by recording your speech and playing it back for self-evaluation. If videotaping equip-

SPEAKER'S NOTES   *Practicing for Presentation*

1. Read your formal outline to fix the main points in your head.

2. Present the speech, using the formal outline.

3. Practice again, using your outline less and increasing eye contact.

4. Now practice with a key-word outline, reading only direct quotations.

5. Work on integrating verbal and nonverbal communication.

6. Check the timing of your speech.

7. Practice before friends, listen to their advice, and make changes if necessary.

8. Practice some more until you feel comfortable and confident.

ment is available, arrange to record your speech so that you can see as well as hear yourself. It is sometimes better to review your taped speech at a later time so that you can be more objective in judging it. If you try to evaluate yourself immediately after you make your practice presentation, you may be hearing what you think you said rather than what you actually said. Always try to be the toughest critic you will ever have, but also be a constructive critic. Never put yourself down or give up on yourself. Work on specific points of improvement.

In addition to evaluating yourself, it sometimes is helpful to ask a friend or friends to listen to your presentation. This outside opinion should be more objective than your self-evaluation, and you will get a feel for speaking to real people rather than to an imagined audience. Seek constructive feedback from your friends. Was it easy for them to follow you? Do you have any mannerisms (such as hair twisting or saying "you know" after every other sentence) that distracted them? Were you speaking loudly and slowly enough? Were your ideas clear and soundly supported?

On the day that you are assigned to speak, get to class early enough to look over your outline one last time so that it is fresh in your mind. If you have devoted sufficient time and energy to your preparation and practice, you should feel confident about communicating with your audience.

IN SUMMARY

What Is Effective Presentation?   An effective *presentation* successfully integrates the skills of nonverbal communication, especially those of voice and body language, with the words of your speech. Such presentation allows speakers and listeners to share ideas and feelings. It is characterized by enthusiasm and naturalness. Your voice and manner should project your sincere commitment but should not call attention to themselves. You should sound and look spontaneous, not contrived and artificial.

Methods of Presentation.   The four major methods of speech presentation are impromptu speaking, memorized presentation, reading from a manuscript, and extemporaneous speaking. In *impromptu speaking* you talk with minimal or no preparation and practice. Both *memorized* and *manuscript presentations* require that your speech be written out word for word. An *extemporaneous speech* requires a carefully planned sequence of ideas, but the wording is not predetermined. Instructors usually require that you present speeches extemporaneously.

Using Your Voice Effectively.   A good speaking voice conveys your meaning fully and clearly to all listeners in a manner that enhances your ethos. Maximum vocal expressiveness depends on your ability to control pitch, rate, loudness, and variety. Your *optimum pitch* is the level at which you can produce a clear, strong voice with minimal effort. Speaking around your optimum pitch gives your voice flexibility. The rate at which you speak can affect the impression you make on listeners. You can control rate to your advantage by using pauses and by changing your pace to match the moods of your material. To speak loudly enough, you need proper breath control. Vary your loudness for the sake of emphasis. Vocal variety adds color and interest to a speech, makes a speaker more attractive, and encourages identification between speaker and audience.

Articulation, enunciation, pronunciation, and dialect refer to the unique way you give voice to words. *Articulation* concerns the manner in which you produce individual sounds. *Enunciation* refers to the way you utter words in context. Proper pronunciation means that you say words correctly. Your *dialect* may identify the area of the country in which you learned language and your cultural or ethnic background. Occasionally, dialect can create identification and comprehension problems between a speaker and audience.

Using Your Body Effectively.   You communicate with *body language* as well as with your voice. Eye contact signals listeners that you want to communicate. Your facial expressions should project the meanings of your words. Movement attracts attention; therefore, your movements and gestures must complement your speech, not compete with it. *Proxemics* is the study of how humans use space during communication. Two proxemic principles, distance and elevation, can affect your identification with an audience as you speak. Be sure your grooming and dress are appropriate to the speech occasion and do not detract from your ability to communicate.

The Importance of Practice.   You should practice your speech until you have the sequence of main points and supporting materials well established in your mind. It is best to practice your presentation under conditions similar to those in which you will give your speech. Keep citations or other materials that you must read to a minimum. Tape-recording or videotaping can be useful for self-evaluation during rehearsal.

TERMS TO KNOW

presentation	rate
impromptu speaking	articulation
memorized text presentation	enunciation
manuscript presentation	pronunciation
extemporaneous speaking	dialect
pitch	body language
habitual pitch	proxemics
optimum pitch	

DISCUSSION

1. Attend a public speaking event in your community, such as a lecture at your college, a political speech, or a church service. Did the speaker read from a manuscript, make a memorized presentation, or speak extemporaneously? Was the speaker's voice effective or ineffective? Why? How would you evaluate the speaker's use of body language? Discuss your observations with your classmates.

2. Observe nonverbal communication among small groups at a social gathering. Look at people's facial expressions, their gestures, their movements in communication. How are these similar or dissimilar to what you have observed during speeches in class? Record your observations and discuss them in class.

3. Look for examples in live or televised speeches in which the speaker's appearance played a positive or negative role. Discuss and analyze your observations in class.

4. Form small groups in class and discuss the following questions: Can you remember factors in your own personal background that may have taught you bad vocal habits or restricted your body language? What can you do to correct these habits and free your natural expressiveness? Can the group and the class as a whole help you make these changes?

APPLICATION

1. Exchange your self-evaluation tape with a classmate and write a critique of the other speaker's voice and articulation. Emphasize the positive but make specific recommendations for improvement. Work on your classmate's recommendations to you, and then make a second tape to share with your partner. Do you see signs of improvement in each other's performance?

2. Make a list of words you often mispronounce. Practice saying these words correctly each day for a week. See if you carry over these changes into social conversation.

3. Experiment with reading the same material aloud at different rates of speed and with varying loudness. Do these differences seem to affect the meaning of the material?

4. As you practice your next speech, deliberately try to speak in as dull a voice as possible. Stifle all impulses to gesture. Then practice speaking with as colorful a voice as possible, giving full freedom to movement and gesture. Notice how a colorful and expressive presentation makes your ideas seem more lively and vivid as you speak.

5. Form small groups and conduct an impromptu speaking contest. Each participant should supply two topics for impromptu speeches, and participants should then draw two topics (not their own). Participants have five minutes to prepare a three-minute speech on one of these topics. Each student then presents the speech to the group, which selects a winner.

NOTES

1. This exercise was suggested by Professor Jo Lenhart, Memphis State University, who uses it in teaching voice and articulation for theater students.
2. Jon Eisenson, *Voice and Diction: A Program for Improvement* (New York: Macmillan, 1974), p. vii.
3. John F. Kennedy, "Inaugural Address," in *Presidential Rhetoric: 1961–1980,* ed. Theodore Windt (Dubuque, Iowa: Kendall Hunt, 1980), p. 9.
4. Mark Twain, adapted from "How I Edited an Agricultural Paper," in *Sketches: Old and New* (Hartford, Conn.: American, 1901), pp. 307–15.
5. Ralph Hillman and Delorah Lee Jewell, *Work For Your Voice* (Murfreesboro, Tenn.: Copymatte, 1986), p. 63.
6. Don Marquis, adapted from "mehitabel and her kittens," in *the lives and times of archy and mehitabel* (Garden City, N.Y.: Doubleday, 1950), pp. 76–80.

IV

TYPES

— OF —

PUBLIC SPEAKING

The improvement of understanding is for two ends: first, our own increase of knowledge; secondly, to enable us to deliver that knowledge to others.

—*JOHN LOCKE*

12

THE NATURE

— *AND* —

KINDS OF INFORMATIVE SPEAKING

This Chapter Will Help You

- ◆ understand the basic functions of informative speaking.

- ◆ learn how to motivate listeners, attract and sustain attention, and make your message easy to remember.

- ◆ distinguish among speeches of description, demonstration, and explanation and learn the major designs appropriate to each.

- ◆ prepare and present effective informative speeches.

Perhaps the most pervasive element of language is that, through communicating with others, not just about practical affairs, but about feelings, desires and fears, a "shared consciousness" is created. . . . Language is without doubt an enormously powerful force holding together the intense social network that characterizes human existence.[1]

Without the sharing of information there would be no civilization as we know it today. Although other animals may share food, engage in primitive social behaviors, and use signal language to warn of dangers or express emotions, humans alone have developed a complex language that has allowed knowledge to accumulate and be shared across generations.

Because we cannot experience personally everything that may be important or interesting to us, we must rely on language and pictures to expand our understanding of the world. *The essence of informative speaking is the sharing of knowledge to create understanding.*

Shared information can be vital to survival. Early detection and warning systems alert us to impending severe weather problems like hurricanes and tornadoes. Civil defense agencies use the media to warn us of environmental accidents. News of medical breakthroughs and information on nutrition and hygiene practices that can increase our life span must be communicated so that we can take advantage of them.

Beyond simply enabling us to live, information helps us to live better. Having friends in to visit this weekend? What will you talk about with your guests? Preparing a special treat for them? How did you learn to prepare it? Starting a new job? How will you find out what you are supposed to do at work? How will you learn to do it? How many of your classes rely primarily on lectures for instruction? How many learning experiences have you had in which the sharing of information was not vital?

Information is power. It can help us operate machines, control the environment, even manage people. Information is therefore a valued commodity. Companies pirate other companies for employees with know-how and creativity. Graduate schools look for students who have the background of knowledge necessary for success. Countries engage in espionage activities to learn what their friends and enemies are doing. An incompetent manager who fears the loss of power may even try to withhold information in an effort to maintain control (a strategy that usually fails).

Throughout our lives we are constantly exchanging information. In this chapter we look at the functions of informative communication, the relationship between informative communication and learning, and three basic types of informative speeches (speeches of description, speeches of demonstration, and speeches of explanation). We also discuss six speech designs appropriate to these types — spatial, categorical, comparison and contrast, sequential, historical, and causation — and how more than one design can be combined in a speech.

FUNCTIONS OF THE INFORMATIVE SPEECH

We refer in this section to "the informative speech" as though it were a distinct and separate type of speaking, but speeches rarely break down into such neat categories. In the same speech, you might introduce yourself, provide vital information, advocate a course of action, and celebrate cherished values. However, any given speech can usually be characterized by its major purpose. *If the main purpose of the speech is to share knowledge, then we call the speech informative.*

Four basic functions characterize the informative speech. First, informative speaking involves the sharing of information and ideas. Second, informative speaking shapes perceptions. Third, informative speaking helps set our mental agenda of what is important in the world. Finally, informative speaking clarifies options.

Sharing Information and Ideas

An informative speech *gives* rather than asks or takes. The demands on the audience are relatively low. Listeners are asked to attend, to comprehend, to assimilate, but not to change their beliefs and behaviors. An informative speech provides knowledge for listeners to use however they may wish. It does not advocate programs of action. For example, one student speaker gave an informative speech in which she revealed the most dangerous local intersections in terms of traffic accidents, but she did not urge listeners to use the bus or walk instead of driving. Although the demands on the listener are modest in informative speaking, the demands on the speaker are high. The speaker must have a thorough understanding of the subject. It is one thing to know something well enough to satisfy yourself. It is quite another to know something well enough to function as a public speaker.

By sharing information, an informative speech helps reduce critical areas of ignorance. An informative speech does not simply repeat material the audience already knows. Rather, *the informative value of a speech is measured by how much new information or understanding is provided for the audience.*

You begin building the informative value of a speech with your audience analysis and topic selection. Can you add to listeners' knowledge or give them a fresh perspective? Have you selected a vital, novel, and interesting topic, avoiding those that have been overworked? Unless you can answer yes to these questions, you should rethink your topic selection.

In informative speaking, the speaker functions basically as a teacher. To teach people effectively, you must arouse and maintain attention by adapting your message to the interests and needs of your audience. You must make your listeners aware of how important the new information is. Present your material clearly, so that listeners can understand and retain it with minimal effort. When you have finished, your listeners should feel that they have benefited from the communication transaction.

Shaping Perceptions

It would be a mistake to assume that informative speaking, because it does not attempt to persuade listeners, has no influence over them. Clearly, what speakers share is not just raw information, but their *interpretations* of information. They share points of view. Because no subject of any significance can be covered completely in a short presentation, speeches must be selective. Speakers must highlight the examples and images they feel best represent their subject. If the subject is new to the audience, the initial presentation will influence how listeners receive and respond to the topic in the future. Thus, informative speeches, because they reveal subjects in ways distinctive to the speaker, perform the dynamic task of shaping how listeners *see* subjects (a function also discussed in Chapter 10). This is a "pre-persuasive" function of informative speaking because how we see subjects may also determine how we *feel* and eventually *act* concerning them.

Let us suppose that you know very little about political campaigns or the role that student volunteers might play in them. Further suppose that you hear *one* of the following speeches on political campaigning:

A speech by an enthusiastic, politically active student who describes volunteer campaign activities in an exciting way;

or

A speech by a disgruntled student reporting how college volunteers are given menial and meaningless jobs in political campaigns.

Neither of the speakers suggests that you should or should not volunteer to work in the upcoming election. Each provides what he or she believes to be an accurate picture of the role of student volunteers in political campaigns. Yet each description leaves you with a different predisposition for future behavior. If you were exposed only to the first speaker, you might be more inclined to respond later to a persuasive appeal for helpers than if you heard only the second speaker.

As you prepare an informative speech, be aware that you may be shaping perceptions. *How* you shape listeners' perceptions should be consistent with later persuasive speeches you might give. You must also be careful that your strong feelings about a subject do not cause you to present a biased or distorted perspective. If listeners feel you are manipulative or if they believe that your biases prevent you from making a responsible informative presentation, they may dismiss your message and lower their estimation of your ethos.

Setting the Agenda

Appreciation for the role that information plays in our lives is rapidly expanding. One important contemporary research program in communication concerns how the mass media function in **setting the agenda** of our public concerns.[2] As they present the "news," the mass media also tell us what we should be thinking about.

Informative speaking performs such an agenda-setting role. Because it directs our attention to certain subjects and shapes our perceptions about them, informative speaking influences what we regard as important. The act of selecting one topic for attention, and not selecting others, creates a hierarchy of importance among subjects.

Cecile Larson's speech, "The 'Monument' at Wounded Knee," which appears in Appendix B, illustrates both the perception-shaping and agenda-setting functions of informative speeches. Cecile's description of the monument etches a graphic picture in our minds: she both *shapes* and *intensifies* our perceptions so that they are hard to forget. These perceptions can set the stage for future action. After hearing her speech, we may want to know more about the treatment of Native Americans, past and present. And we may be predisposed to be receptive to persuasive speeches urging reform and better treatment of these "first" Americans. Thus, as it sets our mental agenda, informative speaking can prepare us for persuasion.

Clarifying Options

An informative speech can reveal and clarify our options for action. Information expands our awareness, opening new horizons and fresh possibilities. Information can also help us discard irrelevant or unworkable options. The better we understand a subject, the more intelligent the choices we can make on important issues that surround it.

What should we know about obesity? Informative speakers may tell us about the consequences of doing something or nothing to correct this problem. They may tell us about different diets and their medical soundness. They may also inform us about the roles of exercise and counseling in weight control. Such information would expand our knowledge of options for dealing with this problem.

A responsible informative speech covers a topic so that all major positions are fairly represented. Speakers may see the same subject in different ways, but it is unethical to deliberately omit or distort information that is vital to audience understanding. Similarly, speakers who are unaware of options because they have not done the research that will *make* them aware are irresponsible. Try to find material from sources that represent different perspectives. A responsible, ethical, informative speaker carefully seeks out and presents all relevant material that may be important for an audience to know.

The two speeches on student political activity mentioned earlier demonstrate possible abuses of the option-clarifying function of informative speaking. If the speeches are presented as *representative* of student political activities, then both speakers are guilty of overgeneralization from limited personal experience. A more responsible approach would include surveying the *Reader's Guide to Periodical Literature* for articles on college-student volunteers in political campaigns, interviewing students who have been active in politics, and talking with local campaign managers to determine how student volunteers might assist in upcoming elections.

INFORMATIVE SPEAKING AND THE LEARNING PROCESS

Because the ultimate goal of informative speaking is the sharing of knowledge to create understanding, we turn now to some basic principles of learning. The three factors we will consider are motivation, attention, and retention.

Motivation

In Chapter 4 we introduced the concept of motivation as an element of audience analysis. Now we show you how motivation applies specifically to learning in informative speaking.

Learning requires some work from listeners. If you want them to remember and use the information you provide, you must motivate them to learn. You must show them how they may benefit from this information. Will it make them more secure, happier, healthier, or more successful? Will it make them feel better about themselves? Can you show them how your topic relates to their needs?

You can relate your subject to the satisfaction of audience needs and interests either by direct statements or indirectly by the use of examples. In a speech on job-interviewing suggestions, you might decide to use a direct approach. In your introduction you could talk about the problems of finding a job in today's economy and how a good interview can make a difference in who gets hired. For supporting materials you might use information from magazine articles on interviewing and a quotation from the personnel manager of a well-known local company. As a transition into the body of your speech, you might say, "Today, I'm going to describe four factors that can determine whether you get the job of your dreams. First. . . ." In this case you have given your audience a reason for wanting to listen to the remainder of your speech. In short, you have begun the learning process by motivating your listeners.

Attention

In Chapter 7, we noted the importance of engaging audience attention in the introduction of your speech. For a speech to be successful, you also must sustain this attention throughout the presentation. In this section we examine six basic perceptual factors that attract and sustain attention: intensity, repetition, novelty, activity, contrast, and relevance. We also explain how to use these factors to sustain interest and promote learning.

Intensity.   Our eyes are drawn automatically to the brightest lights in our environment, and we turn our heads to investigate the loudest noises. In public communication intense language and vivid images can be used to attract and hold attention. You can emphasize a point by supplying examples or illustrations that magnify its importance. You can also achieve intensity through the use of visual aids and vocal variety. In his televised speech describing his national drug policy (see Appendix B), President Bush gained attention through the intensity of his first sentence: "This is the first time since taking the oath of office that I felt an issue was so important, so threatening, that it warranted talking directly with you, the American people."

Repetition.   Sounds, words, or phrases that are repeated attract our attention and embed themselves in our consciousness. Skillful speakers frequently repeat key words or phrases in their speeches to stress the importance of a point, to furnish listeners with cues to keep them moving in the right direction, or to balance or unify their message.

Repetition is the strategy that underlies the language tools of alliteration and anaphora. As we saw in Chapter 10, alliteration can lend vividness to the main ideas of informative speeches: "Today, I will discuss the *m*eanderings of the *M*ississippi River, from *M*innesota to the sea." The repetition of the *m* sound catches our attention and emphasizes the statement. In a like manner, anaphora can establish a pattern that sticks in memory. Used in the form of a repeated rhetorical question, such as, "What is our goal? It is to . . . ," anaphora focuses and sustains attention.

Strategic repetition also may involve parallel construction or a similar pattern of wording. President Bush's speech provides another example:

> Who's responsible? Let me tell you straight out. Everyone who uses drugs. Everyone who sells drugs. And everyone who looks the other way.

Novelty.   Our minds are attracted to anything new or unusual. A novel turn of phrase can have such a striking impact that the words even become slogans. In recent history "the New Frontier," "the Great Society," and "Star Wars" (used to refer to the Strategic Defense Initiative) have gained such status. Metaphors can provide different perspectives. To speak of the college experience as a "war against ignorance" is totally different from referring to it as a "journey out of darkness." However, both metaphors could be used to spark and sustain the attention of an audience.

Activity.   Our eyes are attracted to moving objects. This attraction to activity can be used productively to gain attention in speeches. Gestures, physical movement, and visual aids can all add the element of activity to your speech. You can also increase a sense of activity in your speeches through the use of concrete action words, vocal variety, and a narrative structure that moves your speech along. Note the sense of action and urgency, as well as the invitation to act, in the conclusion of this student's speech:

> I don't know what you're going to do, but I know what I'm going to do. I'm going to march right down tomorrow and register to vote. There's too much at stake not to. Want to come with me?

A lively example or an exciting story can also bring a speech to life and engage your listeners.

Contrast.   Opposites attract attention. If you live or work in a noisy environment and it suddenly becomes quiet, the stillness can seem deafening. Similarly, if you abruptly change the pitch of your voice or your rate of speaking, the contrast draws attention. Presenting the pros and cons of a situation creates a similar effect. You can also highlight contrasts by speaking of opposites such as life and death, light and dark, or the highs and lows of a situation.

In a speech dramatizing the need to learn more about AIDS, we once heard a speaker introduce two or three specific examples with the statement, "Let me introduce you to *Death.*" Then, as the speech moved to the promise of medical research, the speaker said, "Now let me introduce you to *Life.*" This example combined both repetition and contrast to create a dramatic effect.

Surprise is necessary for contrast to be effective. Once people become accustomed to an established pattern, they no longer think about it. They take notice of any abrupt, dramatic change from the pattern.

Relevance.   Things that are personally related to our needs or interests attract our attention. Research has indicated that sleepers respond with changes in brain-wave patterns when their names are mentioned. Mothers have been known to sleep through severe thunderstorms, yet to awaken abruptly at the faint sound of their infant crying. Relevance is essential to public speaking as well.

Darren Wirthwein made his speech on how to select running shoes relevant as well as humorous for his Indiana University audience by stressing the distance between places on campus. Darren pointed out that his early morning speech class was held in a campus building over a mile from the freshman dormitory — without his running shoes he might have missed his speech! Because his listeners shared his situation, they chuckled, then listened attentively. Follow Darren's lead and increase relevance by using examples close to the lives of audience members.

Retention

Information is useless unless your listeners remember and use it. Repetition aids retention as well as attention. The more frequently we hear or see anything, the more likely we are to retain it. Advertisers bombard us with slogans

Listeners measure the informative value of a speech by how much important new information or understanding it provides them. A well-organized speech helps them retain this information.

to keep their product names in our consciousness. These slogans may be repeated in all of their advertisements, regardless of the visuals or narratives of the individual messages. We can even remember slogans from our childhood years: "Ivory soap is ninety-nine and forty-four one hundredths percent pure." The repetition of key words or phrases within a speech helps the audience remember the message. In his famous civil rights speech in Washington, D.C., Martin Luther King's repetition of the phrase, "I have a dream . . ." became the hallmark of the speech and is now used as its title.

Relevance is also important to retention. According to the Dutch scholar Erasmus, efficient minds are like a fisherman's net, able to keep all the big fish while letting the little ones slip through. Our minds filter new information as we receive it, associating it with things we already know and unconsciously evaluating it for its potential usefulness or importance. The advice that follows seems simple but is profoundly important. *If you want listeners to remember your message, tell them why and how your message relates to their lives.*

Structural factors also affect how readily a message can be understood and retained. Suppose you were given the following list of words to memorize:

north, man, hat, daffodil, green, tulip, coat, boy, south, red, east,
shoes, gardenia, woman, purple, marigold, gloves, girl, yellow, west.

SPEAKER'S NOTES   *Helping Listeners Learn*
                                        New Information

1. Approach your topic in a way that is fresh and interesting.

2. Show listeners how they can benefit from your information.

3. Attract and sustain attention by using vivid examples, novel images, exciting stories, and contrasts.

4. Help listeners remember your message by using strategic repetition and clear organization.

It looks rather difficult, but see what happens when we rearrange the words.

> north, south, east, west;
> man, boy, woman, girl;
> daffodil, tulip, gardenia, marigold;
> green, red, purple, yellow;
> hat, coat, shoes, gloves.

In the first instance you have an apparently random list of twenty words. In the second the words have been organized by categories: now you have five groups of four related words to remember. Material that is presented in a consistent and orderly fashion is much easier for your audience to understand and retain.

The way you organize the information in your informative speeches depends on your purpose and material. In the remainder of this chapter we look at three functional types of informative speeches and six designs that are frequently used to structure them.

TYPES OF INFORMATIVE SPEECHES

As we noted earlier, the major purpose of any informative speech is the sharing of knowledge to create understanding. Such sharing typically takes one of three forms: description, demonstration, or explanation.

Speeches of Description

Often the specific purpose of an informative speech is to describe a particular activity, object, person, place, or concept. When you have presented a **speech of description,** the audience should carry away in their minds a clear idea of your subject, such as the picture Stephen Huff painted of the gigantic New Madrid earthquakes of 1811 (see the text of his speech at the end of this chapter). This lingering image is more than just a reflection of the subject; it also conveys its meaning. Before television was widely available, the ability to use language to help the audience "see" what was happening was important for radio broadcasting. One of the most successful reporters was Edward R. Murrow. The following excerpt from one of his programs describes the nightly bombing of London in the fall of 1940:

> This is London at 3:30 in the morning. This has been what might be called a "routine night" — air-raid alarm at about nine o'clock and intermittent bombing every since. I had the impression that more high explosives and few incendiaries have been used tonight. Only two small fires can be seen on the horizon. Again the Germans have been sending their bombers in singly or in pairs. The anti-aircraft barrage has been fierce but sometimes there have been periods of twenty minutes when London has been silent.... That silence is almost hard to bear. One becomes accustomed to rattling windows and the distant sound of bombs, and then there comes a silence that can be felt. You know the sound will return. You wait, and then it starts again. That waiting is bad. It gives you a chance to imagine things.[3]

This excerpt from the Murrow broadcast is rich in specific detail — it is not just early morning but "3:30 in the morning." The language is concrete; the sentences are short, clear, and stark. The descriptions of the actual events of the night are colored with the reporter's personal reactions to them. We are aware that we are seeing through his eyes, and we share his uneasiness. This makes the description especially vivid.

The subject of your descriptive speech should suggest the appropriate pattern for its arrangement. The Murrow example above, because it was in the form of a news report, follows a sequential design, in which events are reported in the natural time order in which they occurred. Other frequently used forms for descriptive speeches are spatial designs, categorical designs, and comparison and contrast designs, which are discussed later in this chapter.

Speeches of Demonstration

The **speech of demonstration** shows the audience how to do something or how something works. We all hear speeches of demonstration frequently. Professors inform you how to write term papers for their classes, sales representatives explain how to use computers for word processing, managers instruct their employees on the way to do their jobs, and hucksters tell you how to get rich overnight. Self-help books flood the market, offering advice on everything from how to lose ten pounds in two weeks to how to study for the Law School Admission Test. What all these examples have in common is that they demonstrate a process.

Speeches of demonstration aim either at *understanding* or *application,* showing listeners how something is done, or instructing them so that they can perform the process themselves. In a short presentation you can usually demonstrate more complex processes if your goal is understanding rather than application. For example, you might be able to prepare a seven-minute speech on how grades are collected, recorded, averaged, and distributed at your university, but you certainly would not expect your audience to be able to set up a grade-processing system after your presentation. Instead, you hope they will *understand* how the grade process works. On the other hand, in the short time allotted for a classroom speech, you might be able to teach your classmates how to mat pictures for their rooms or how to read a textbook efficiently. These are skills they can *apply* to their lives. Stephen Huff's speech demonstrated to his classmates how to protect themselves in case of a major earthquake. Regardless of whether your specific purpose is to foster understanding or to teach application, most speeches of demonstration follow a sequential design, discussed in the section on speech designs.

Speeches of demonstration are almost always helped by the use of visual aids, especially when your purpose is to teach your listeners how to perform the process themselves. For instance, if you were giving the speech on matting pictures, you might bring some of the knives used, a piece of matting material, and a sample of the finished product. Stephen Huff distributed a handout that listed the steps to follow in case of an earthquake (he circulated this *after* his speech so that it would not compete for his listeners' attention). When demonstrating a process, "show and tell" is usually much more effective than just telling.

Speeches of Explanation

The **speech of explanation** is used to inform the audience about ideas or policies — subjects that tend to be more abstract than those dealt with through description or demonstration. "Rape by Any Other Name" by "Jane Doe," which appears in Appendix B, explained an idea that may have surprised some of her listeners — that rape can occur between friends or even intimates. In this frank and courageous speech, "Jane" explained the causes of "date rape," its devastating effects, and the ways it can be avoided. She also illustrated how a speech of explanation can use vivid description to make its subject come alive in human terms.

George Bush's speech on drugs, referred to earlier in this chapter, was primarily a speech of explanation. In this speech the president described his program in terms of its four major emphases:

1. increasing enforcement of drug-use laws

2. stopping the flow of drugs from foreign sources

3. improving drug-treatment facilities

4. providing more effective drug education

Bush's speech illustrates how a speech of explanation on an abstract topic must get down to specifics. First, he divided the program into its major parts, following a categorical design. Then he described each of these parts in more specific terms. He grounded his speech by using all the basic supporting materials discussed in Chapter 6: facts, testimony, examples, and narratives.

By translating the abstract and unknown into the concrete and recognizable, the speech of explanation attempts to produce understanding of ideas or policies in the minds of listeners. Speeches of explanation may use any of the designs described in the following section.

SPEECH DESIGNS

In this section we focus on six designs often used in informative speeches: spatial, categorical, comparison and contrast, sequential, historical, and causation designs. These may also be used in persuasive and ceremonial speeches.

Spatial Design

A **spatial design** is especially appropriate for speeches that describe places or that locate subjects within some physical arrangement. Most people are familiar with maps and can readily visualize directions. Once you have determined a starting point and direction of movement, you simply take your audience on an *orderly* imaginary journey to some destination. Cecile Larson used a spatial design for much of her speech describing the monument at Wounded Knee. After giving the audience a brief account of what happened there, Cecile located this historic site geographically, then took her audience with her through the Sioux Indian reservation in search of the monument. She concluded by describing the monument and its setting.

In using a spatial design, you should decide on a starting point — from the top or bottom, right or left, north or south, etc. — and then proceed in a *systematic way.* You should develop your speech so that it builds interest as you go along. Cecile's speech progressed so that she and her listeners *arrived* at Wounded Knee; she did not start there. Once you begin a pattern of movement for a spatial design, you should stay with it to the end of the speech. If you change directions abruptly in the middle, the audience may get lost on one of your turns.

Categorical Design

Some subjects have natural or customary divisions that suggest **categorical designs.** For example, taxes may be classified as federal, state, county, and city — or as income, property, sales, and excise. In speeches on such subjects, these divisions often provide the main points for development. Such categories may represent actual divisions of your subject. More often, however, categories represent customary ways of thinking. Thus, we have the conscious and the unconscious minds, primary and secondary factors, reason and emotion. Categories are the mind's way of ordering our world. They help us to reduce and organize information so that it is meaningful and does not overwhelm us.

Thressia Taylor used a categorical design for an informative speech explaining nutrition. She discussed the five elements of food that are essential to our well-being. Five is probably the maximum number of categories that can be effectively handled in a short presentation. Any subject that breaks down into more categories will be too complex for most classroom speeches. Unless you can condense these categories into a manageable number, you should probably consider another way to approach the speech or else narrow its focus.

Thressia's speech illustrated another important point: a categorical design should begin and end with the most important categories in the design. She started her speech by discussing protein and ended with water. The strategy behind such order is clear: the important first category gains attention, the important final category gives the speech a sense of climax.

Comparison and Contrast Design

When your topic is new to your audience, a **comparison and contrast design** can be very effective. Such design creates understanding by relating an unfamiliar subject to something the audience already knows and understands. A comparison and contrast design can be especially useful in speeches of description. Our Sri Lankan student described the game of rugger as played in his homeland by comparing and contrasting it with American football.

Such designs often make use of **analogy.** Analogies are helpful for scientific subjects that are difficult for most of us to understand or for topics remote from ordinary experience. Analogy comes in two forms: literal and figurative. In a **literal analogy,** the subjects are drawn from the same field of experience: rugger and football, for example, are two forms of contact sport, so the comparison between them is literal. In a **figurative analogy,** the speaker draws together different fields of experience: for example, a speaker might relate the body's constant struggle against infection to a military campaign, identifying the nature of the armies, how they fight, and the consequences of victory or defeat. The basis for a figurative analogy is metaphor, which we discussed in Chapter 10. Because comparison and contrast require imagination on the part of the speaker, audiences admire such designs when they are successful. But an analogy can harm the speaker's ethos and the speech if the comparison

When your topic is new to your audience, a comparison and contrast design may be most effective. You can explain a highly technical or scientific subject by comparing and contrasting it with something your listeners know and understand.

seems too far-fetched. The advice we gave for metaphor also holds for design by figurative analogy: avoid stretching the comparison too far, or the design will seem strained.

Sequential Design

A **sequential design** presents the steps involved in the process you are demonstrating. The first task in developing a sequential design is to determine the essential steps in the process. For example, in a speech on matting a picture you might come up with the following steps:

1. Deciding what color mat to use

2. Getting the right equipment

3. Determining the size of your mat

4. Cutting the mat

5. Matting the picture

6. Deciding between a straight and bevel cut

7. Drawing the lines before you cut

8. Backing the picture

Looking over this list, you discover that you have identified eight steps — at least three too many for a short presentation. At this point you should arrange these steps in the order in which they occur to see if any of them can be compressed into more general steps. Your revised order of steps might take this form:

1. Planning the project
   a. Deciding on color
   b. Determining size
   c. Selecting a type of cut
2. Obtaining equipment
   a. Drawing equipment
   b. Cutting equipment
   c. Matting materials
3. Cutting the mat
   a. Drawing the lines for cutting
   b. Making the actual cut
4. Matting the picture
   a. Attaching the picture to the mat
   b. Backing the picture

Presenting the steps in this orderly manner helps you "walk and talk" the members of your audience through the process. They now understand how to begin and what to do in the proper order.

Historical Design

Historical designs place a subject in a time perspective and, like sequential designs, follow an orderly progression. But whereas a sequential design is best suited to speeches of demonstration or description, the historical design is most appropriate for speeches of explanation. When using historical designs, you may start with the beginning of an idea or issue and trace it up to the present, or you may start with the present and trace the concept back to its origins. For example, if you wanted to present a historical perspective on Unitarianism, you would probably begin by talking about the beliefs of Emerson and the early transcendentalists. Similarly, a speech on contemporary feminism might trace its beginnings to the suffrage movement of the nineteenth and early twentieth centuries.

Because of time limitations, you must be careful to narrow your topic to manageable proportions. Then you must scan the past and select those events that are most relevant to your point. In this way you telescope time into sequences of vital moments that have contributed to the present state of affairs. Although any rhetorical account of the past will always be selective, be certain that the examples you choose are representative of the situation. Avoid biased or one-sided explanations.

Causation Design

Speeches of explanation often focus on causes and effects in trying to make the world understandable for us. A speech that tries to show how some things create others is following a **causation design.** Such a speech may begin with a description of an existing condition, then probe for its causes. Or the speech may begin with the present state of affairs and try to predict effects in the future. Causation designs are frequently used to inform people about economic issues. For example, you might prepare a speech on the effects of the late spring freeze on the quality, availability, and price of peaches, or the potential impact on college students of proposed changes in federal aid to education. Causation designs may also be used to explain why hurricanes occur, why wars have been fought, or why exercise makes a person healthier.

Speeches of causation are subject to one very serious limitation — the tendency to oversimplify. Any complex condition will generally have many underlying causes. Be wary of overly simple explanations.

Combined Speech Designs

Although we have presented these designs as simple patterns for speeches, effective speeches sometimes combine two or more of them. If you believe that a combined design will work best for your material, be certain to plan it carefully so that you do not appear to be rambling or jumping helter-skelter from one design type to another.

SPEAKER'S NOTES   *Designing an Informative Speech*

1. In a spatial design, move in a consistent direction.

2. In a categorical design, limit the number of categories to five or fewer.

3. In comparison and contrast designs, relate unfamiliar subjects to something well known.

4. In a sequential design, present the steps in the order in which they normally occur.

5. In a historical design, focus on relevant events and present them in a systematic way.

6. In a causation design, do not oversimplify cause and effect.

7. When combining designs, provide clear transitions between designs.

Alan Dunnette presented an informative classroom speech, "The Moscow Summer Games," that combined historical and categorical designs. He opened his speech by providing a historical view of how these "games" originated as a joking response by the citizens of Moscow, Tennessee (population 583), to the American boycott of the 1980 Summer Olympic Games, scheduled for the *other* Moscow. After presenting this historical background, Alan went on to describe the different types of events that make up the games: the serious events, such as the ten-kilometer run and the canoe and kayak races, and the fun events, such as the Great High Noon Tobacco Spitting Showdown, the Women's Skillet Throw, and the Invitational Cow Milking Contest ("invitational because Moscow cows are particular about who grabs them and where"). Alan was able to make this combined pattern work effectively because he planned it carefully. He also used a transition to cue the audience to the shift in design by saying, "So that's how the Moscow games got started. Now what kinds of events take place there?"

IN SUMMARY

Informative speaking shares knowledge to create understanding. Information sharing is important to survival and to effective living. In short, information is power.

Functions of the Informative Speech.   Four functions characterize the informative speech. First, informative speaking reduces ignorance by providing insight or understanding. Second, informative speaking shapes perceptions that affect later responses. Third, informative speaking *sets the agenda* of what we consider to be important. Finally, informative speaking clarifies options for decision making. In short, informative speaking teaches people something about a subject they need to know better.

Informative Speaking and the Learning Process.   From the perspective of the audience, the informative speech is a learning experience. You can motivate listeners to learn by showing them how your subject relates to their needs or interests. You must also sustain their attention throughout your speech. Six factors that contribute to attention are intensity, repetition, novelty, activity, contrast, and relevance. You will also want your audience to remember your message. Repetition, relevance, and structural organization are important factors in retention.

Types of Informative Speeches.   Informative speeches may be classified as speeches of description, demonstration, and explanation. *Speeches of description* create word pictures that help the audience visualize a subject. *Speeches of demonstration* show the audience how something is done. They may give listeners an understanding of a process or teach them how to perform it. Speeches of demonstration are often more effective when visual aids are used. *Speeches of explanation* inform the audience about abstract and complex subjects, such as concepts or programs.

Speech Designs.   The patterns most frequently employed in informative speeches are spatial, categorical, comparison and contrast, sequential, historical, and causation designs. A *spatial design* orders the main points as they occur in physical space. Spatial designs are especially appropriate for describing objects or places. *Categorical designs* may represent actual divisions of your subject or traditional ways of thinking. In a short speech you should limit your number of categories to no more than five. *Comparison and contrast designs* are especially effective when your topic is new to the audience. These designs are based on *literal* or *figurative analogies,* depending on whether the compared subjects are drawn from the same or different fields. Most speeches of demonstration use a *sequential design,* which presents the steps in a process in their proper order. A *historical design* always develops your subject chronologically by following the order of events. Because such history is selective, you must be careful not to present a distorted perspective. A *causation design* explains how one condition generates or is generated by another.

Sometimes you may decide to incorporate two or more designs into a speech. In that case be certain to provide transitions so that listeners are not confused by the changing patterns.

TERMS TO KNOW

setting the agenda	analogy
speech of description	literal analogy
speech of demonstration	figurative analogy
speech of explanation	sequential design
spatial design	historical design
categorical design	causation design
comparison and contrast design	

DISCUSSION

1. Analyze the speech of "Jane Doe" in Appendix B in terms of its functions, type, and design. Discuss how it gains and holds attention and motivates learning. Can you think of different designs for the speech? Would they be better or worse?

2. Select your nominations for the "best" and "worst" lecturers you have as instructors this semester, excluding your speech instructor. Without naming these individuals, discuss how they design their presentations and encourage or discourage learning in their classes.

3. Discuss the relationship between information and power. Find specific examples of the use and misuse of such power.

4. Watch a television program that purports to be informative. Which informative functions does it fulfill? Does it seem to have a persuasive purpose as well? Is it ethical in the way it proceeds?

APPLICATION

1. Select an informative topic, determine a specific purpose, and develop two different outlines for the speech you might give, each illustrating a choice among the six design options (spatial, categorical, comparison and contrast, sequential, historical, and causation). In each design explain how you would motivate listeners to learn.

2. Plan the informative speech you prepare for class to be sure you use at least three of the six factors of attention (intensity, repetition, novelty, activity, contrast, and relevance). Turn in a short statement specifying the techniques you will use and why you believe they will be effective.

3. Read the speech by Vaclav Havel in Appendix B and describe its function as an informative speech. Discuss the major stylistic techniques used in the speech and discuss how they contribute to its effectiveness.

NOTES

1. Richard E. Leakey, *The Making of Mankind* (New York: Dutton, 1981), p. 141.
2. Shearon A. Lowery and Melvin L. De Fleur, *Milestones in Mass Communication Research,* 2nd ed. (New York: Longman 1988), pp. 327–52.
3. *In Search of Light: The Broadcasts of Edward R. Murrow 1938–1961,* ed. Edward Bliss, Jr. (New York: Alfred A. Knopf, 1967), p. 35.

SAMPLE INFORMATIVE SPEECH WITH VISUAL AIDS

The New Madrid Earthquake Area

—— *Stephen Huff* ——

Stephen's introduction sets the scene in graphic detail. He opens with a rhetorical question and further involves his audience by repeating, "If you're like me." He motivates listeners by tying the San Francisco quake to the New Madrid Fault area where they live. He provides a skillful preview that indicates he will develop a categorical design, combining descriptive, explanatory, and demonstrative functions. His admission of ignorance allows his audience to identify with him as an attractively modest person, and also suggests his substantial preparation for the speech — both important benefits for his ethos.

How many of you can remember what you were doing around seven o'clock on the evening of October 17th? If you're a sports fan like me, you had probably set out the munchies, popped a cold one, and settled back to watch San Francisco and Oakland battle it out in the World Series. Since the show came on at seven o'clock here in Memphis for its pregame hype, you may not have been paying close attention to the TV — until — until — until both the sound and picture went out because of the Bay Area earthquake.

If you're like me, you probably sat glued to the TV set for the rest of the evening watching the live coverage of that catastrophe. If you're like me, you probably started thinking that Memphis, Tennessee, is in the middle of the New Madrid earthquake area and wondering how likely it would be for a large earthquake to hit here. And if you're like me, you probably asked yourself, "What would I do if a major earthquake hit Memphis?"

As I asked myself these questions, I was surprised to admit that I didn't know very much about the New Madrid earthquake area or the probability of a major quake in Memphis. And I was really upset to discover that I didn't have the foggiest idea of what to do if a quake did hit. So I visited the Center for Earthquake Research and Information here on campus; talked with Dr. Arch Johnston, the director; and read the materials he helped me find. Today, I'd like to share with you what I learned about the New Madrid earthquake area, how likely it is that Memphis may be hit by a major quake in the near future, what the effects of such a quake might be, and — most important — what you can do to be prepared.

Stephen's first main point concerns earthquakes in general and the New Madrid area in particular. The magnitude chart puts the intensity of earthquakes into perspective. His comparisons and contrasts with the atomic bomb and the recent San Francisco quake help make the numbers meaningful, as do his descriptions of the great New Madrid quakes. He uses facts and statistics as primary supporting material, enlivened by vivid examples and stories.

Let's start with a little history about the New Madrid earthquake area. During the winter of 1811 to 1812, three of the largest earthquakes ever to hit the continental United States occurred in this area. Their estimated magnitudes were 8.6, 8.4, and 8.8 on the Richter Scale. [He reveals magnitude chart.] I have drawn this chart to give you some idea of how much energy this involves. To simplify things, I have shown the New Madrid quakes as 8.5. Since a one-point increase in the Richter Scale equals a thirtyfold increase in energy release, the energy level of these quakes was over nine hundred times more powerful than the Hiroshima atomic bomb and more than thirty times more powerful than the 7.0 quake that hit San Francisco last October. [He conceals magnitude chart.]

Most of the reports of these early earthquakes come from journals or Indian legends. The Indians tell of the night that lasted for a week and the way the "Father of Waters" — the Mississippi River — ran backwards. Waterfalls were formed on the river. Islands disappeared. Land that was once in Arkansas — on the west bank of the river — ended up in Tennessee —

on the east bank of the river. Church bells chimed as far away as New Orleans and Boston. Cracks up to ten feet wide opened and closed in the earth. Geysers squirted sand fifteen feet into the air. Whole forests sank into the earth as the land turned to quicksand. Lakes disappeared and new lakes were formed. Reelfoot Lake — over ten miles long — was formed when the Mississippi River changed its course. No one is certain how many people died from the quakes because the area was sparsely settled with trappers and Indian villages. Memphis was just an outpost village with a few hundred settlers.

[He shows map of epicenters.] As you can see on this map, Memphis itself is not directly on the New Madrid Fault line. The fault extends from around Marked Tree, Arkansas, northeast to near Cairo, Illinois. This con-

Stephen's simplified map of the New Madrid Fault area helps his audience see the

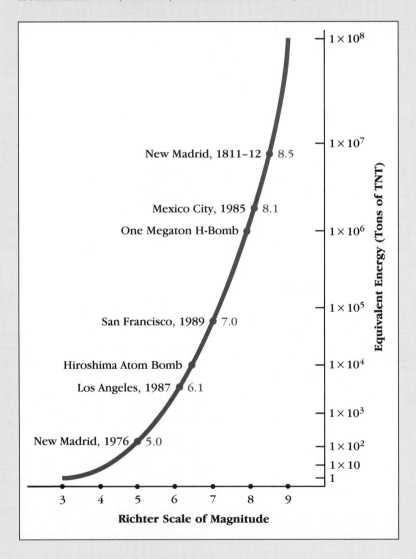

322

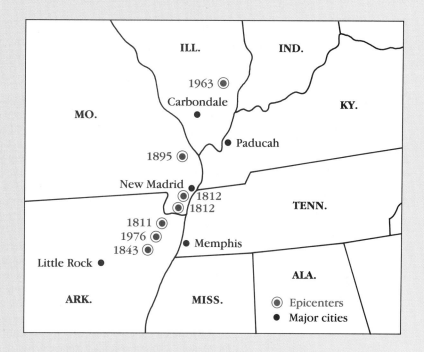

tinues to be a volatile area of earthquake activity. According to Robert L. Ketter, director of the National Center for Earthquake Engineering Research, between 1974 and 1983 over two thousand quakes were recorded in the area. About 150 earthquakes per year occur in the area, but only about eight of them are large enough for people to notice. The others are picked up on the seismographs at tracking stations. The strongest quake in recent years occurred here in 1976. [He points to location on map.] This measured 5.0 on the Richter scale.

The New Madrid earthquake area is much different from the San Andreas Fault in California. Because of the way the land is formed, the alluvial soil transmits energy more efficiently here than in California. Although the quakes were about the same size, the New Madrid earthquakes affected an area fifteen times larger than the "great quake" that destroyed San Francisco in 1906.

Although scientists cannot predict exactly when another major quake may hit the area, they do know that the *repeat time* for a magnitude-6 New Madrid earthquake is seventy years, plus or minus fifteen years. The last earthquake of this size to hit the area occurred in 1895 north of New Madrid, Missouri. [He points to epicenter on map.] According to Johnston and Nava of the Memphis Earthquake Center, the probability that one with a magnitude of 6.3 will occur somewhere in the fault area by the year 2000 is 40 to 63 percent. By the year 2035 this probability increases to 86 to 97 percent. The probabilities for larger quakes are lower. They estimate the probability of a 7.6 quake within the next fifty years to be from 19 to 29 percent. [He conceals map of epicenters.]

323

What would happen if an earthquake of 7.6 hit Memphis? Allan and Hoshall, a prominent local engineering firm, prepared a study on this for the Federal Emergency Management Agency. The expected death toll would top 2,400. There would be at least 10,000 casualties. Two hundred thousand residents would be homeless. The city would be without electricity, gas, water or sewer treatment facilities for weeks. Gas lines would rupture, and fires would sweep through the city. Transportation would be almost impossible, bridges and roads would be destroyed, and emergency supplies would have to be brought in by helicopter. The river bluff, midtown, and land along the Wolfe River would turn to quicksand because of liquification. Buildings there would sink like they did in the Marina area during this past year's San Francisco quake. If the quake hit during daytime hours, at least 600 children would be killed and another 2,400 injured as schools collapsed on them. None of our schools have been built to seismic code specifications.

In fact, very few buildings in Memphis have been built to be earthquake resistant, so it would be difficult to find places to shelter and care for the homeless. The major exceptions are the new hospitals in the suburbs, the Omni Hotel east of the expressway, the Holiday Inn Convention Center, and two or three new office complexes. The only municipal structure built to code is the Criminal Justice Center. The new Memphis Pyramid, being built by the city and county, which will seat over twenty thousand people for Memphis State basketball games, is not being built to code. I'd hate to be in it if a major quake hit. The prospects are not pretty.

What can we do to prepare ourselves for this possible catastrophe? We can start out by learning what to do if a quake does hit. When I asked myself what I would do, my first reaction was to "get outside." I've since learned that this is not right. The "Earthquake Safety Checklist" published by the Federal Emergency Management Agency and the Red Cross makes a number of suggestions. I've written them out and will distribute them after my speech.

First, when an earthquake hits, if you are inside, stay there. Get in a safe spot: stand in a doorway, stand next to an inside wall, or get under a large piece of furniture. Stay away from windows, hanging objects, fireplaces, and tall unsecured furniture until the shaking stops. Do not try to use elevators. If you are outside, get away from buildings, trees, walls, or power lines. If you are in a car, stay in it; pull over and park. Stay away from overpasses and power lines. Do not drive over bridges or overpasses until they have been inspected. If you are in a crowded public place, do not rush for the exit. You may be crushed in the stampede of people.

When the shaking stops, check for gas, water, or electrical damage. Turn off the electricity, gas, and water to your home. Do not use electrical switches — unseen sparks could set off a gas fire. Do not use the telephone unless you must report a severe injury. Check to see that the sewer works before using the toilet. Plug drains to prevent a sewer backup.

There are also some things you can do in advance to be prepared. Accumulate emergency supplies: at home you should have a flashlight, a transistor radio with fresh batteries, a first-aid kit, fire extinguishers, and enough canned or dried food and beverages to last your family for 72 hours. Identify hazards and safe spots in your home — secure tall heavy furniture; don't hang heavy pictures over your bed; keep flammable liquids in a garage or outside storage area — look around each room and plan where you would go if an earthquake hit. Conduct earthquake drills with your family.

There's one more suggestion that I would like to add. One that is specific to Memphis. Let our local officials know that you are concerned about the lack of preparedness. Urge them to support a building code — at least for public structures — that meets seismic resistance standards.

In preparing this speech, I learned a lot about the potential for earthquakes in Memphis. I hope you have learned something too. I now feel like I know what I should do if an earthquake hits. But I'm not really sure how I would react. Even the experts don't always react "appropriately." In 1971 an earthquake hit the Los Angeles area at about six o'clock in the morning. Charles Richter, the seismologist who developed the Richter Scale to measure earthquakes, was in bed at the time. According to his wife, "He jumped up screaming and scared the cat."

Stephen's conclusion is rather brief. Although his final story is amusing, he might have summarized his major points to make the ending more effective.

Because there has been implanted in us the power to persuade each other . . . , not only have we escaped the life of the wild beasts but we have come together and founded cities and made laws and invented arts. . . .

— *ISOCRATES*

13

The Nature

—— *and* ——

Kinds of Persuasive Speaking

This Chapter Will Help You

- appreciate the importance of persuasion in our society.

- understand the characteristics of persuasive speaking.

- recognize the steps in the persuasive process.

- meet the challenges of persuasive speaking.

- understand the different types of persuasive speeches
  and the designs best suited to each.

You may awaken to a radio announcer selling tickets to a rock concert. On the morning news a weather forecaster urges you to carry an umbrella. You step out into a world of persuasion. Politicians plead for your vote. Billboards along highways tout everything from bourbon to church attendance. The novels, movies, music, and television shows you encounter may promote social or political causes.

For your part, you may have to convince your parents that you deserve a trip to Florida over spring break. (Just look at how good your grades were last term!) Or you may have to convince a scholarship committee that you deserve financial aid. When you are looking for a job, you must sell yourself to an employer. If you want to advance, you must successfully promote your ideas at work.

Whatever path your life takes, you can't avoid persuading and being persuaded.

Beyond its daily importance to you, persuasion is vital to the way our society works. The right to persuade and be persuaded is the cornerstone of our social and political system, guaranteed by the First Amendment to the Constitution. According to the late Supreme Court Justice Louis D. Brandeis, "Those who won our independence believed that the final end of the State was to make men free to develop their faculties; and that in its government the deliberative forces should prevail over the arbitrary."[1] Free and open persuasion is required for these "deliberative forces" to prevail.

Deliberation occurs when audiences allow all sides of an issue to have their say before coming to a decision on how to proceed. In contrast, when decisions are imposed on us, they may require force to back them up. Our political system is based on the belief that persuasion is more ethical than force. We should make commitments because we are persuaded, not because we are coerced.

On certain issues you may object to the expression of opposing views, but the freedom to express unpopular views is what liberty is all about. The English philosopher John Stuart Mill put the matter eloquently:

> If all mankind, minus one, were of the one opinion, and only one person were of the contrary opinion, mankind would be no more justified in silencing that one person, than he, if he had the power, would be justified in silencing mankind.
>
> . . . We can never be sure that the opinion we are endeavoring to stifle is a false opinion; and if we were sure, stifling it would be an evil still.[2]

Other reasons for tolerating minority opinions are more practical in nature. Research suggests that exposure to different viewpoints can stimulate listeners and produce better, more original decisions.[3] For example, even though I may never agree with your view that we should abolish all labor unions, your arguments may cause me to reexamine my position, to understand my own convictions better, or perhaps even to modify my views.

Important as persuasion may be, many people are apt to ask: "What difference can one person make? I'm not very important, and my words won't carry much weight." Perhaps not, but words do make ripples, and ripples can come together to make waves. Just ask Anna Aley, whom we first introduced in Chapter 1. Anna was a student at Kansas State University when she gave the persuasive speech on substandard student housing that is reprinted at the end of this chapter. Her speech, first presented as a class assignment, was heard again in a public forum featuring outstanding student speeches on the KSU campus. It made such an impression that it was reprinted in the local newspaper, the *Manhattan Mercury,* which followed it up with a series of investigative reports and a sympathetic editorial. Brought to the attention of the mayor and city commission, Anna's speech helped promote substantial reforms in the city's rental housing policies. Her words are still reverberating in Manhattan, Kansas.

Perhaps your persuasive speech will not have such dramatic impact, but be assured that our words can affect the quality of lives around us. All the more reason for us to understand persuasion and its workings. This chapter will consider the characteristics of such speaking, the process of persuasion, the challenges of persuasive speaking, the types of persuasive speeches, and the designs appropriate for them.

CHARACTERISTICS OF PERSUASIVE SPEAKING

The characteristics of persuasive speaking are most clear when viewed in contrast with informative speaking.

Informative speaking reveals and clarifies options; persuasive speaking urges us to make a choice among options. One of the basic strategies of persuasive speaking is to eliminate alternatives systematically until only one choice remains. The informative speaker might say, "Here are different ways to deal with Iran"; the persuasive speaker would urge, "We should pursue *this* course of action in dealing with Iran."

Informative speaking calls for little commitment from the audience; persuasive speaking asks for a great deal. Although there may be some risk in exposing yourself to new information and ideas, you have much more at stake in listening to a persuasive speaker. You risk little as you listen to the informative speaker describe off-campus living conditions. But the persuasive speaker asks you *to do something* about these conditions. What if he or she is not being honest? What if the course of action you are persuaded to follow turns out to be a mistake? *Doing* always involves a greater risk than simply *knowing* or understanding. The world of persuasion is filled with uncertainty, and your commitment could cost you.

The ethical obligation for informative speakers is great; the ethical obligation for persuasive speakers is even greater. When you influence the lives of others or ask them to take risks, you must assume responsibility for your words. Whenever you want people to invest their time, talents, or money, you must be cautious. Would your plan for off-campus housing result in actual improvement, or would it merely raise the rent? As speaker, you carry the ethical obligation to see that any reforms you urge are sound and well considered.

The informative speaker acts as teacher; the persuasive speaker acts as a leader. The informative speaker will describe, explain, or demonstrate. The persuasive speaker will influence, convince, or inspire an audience to adopt certain attitudes or behaviors. Because of the greater risk involved, an audience will evaluate a persuasive speaker more carefully with respect to competence, sincerity, strength, and self-interest. As you stand before others to lead them against the slumlords of student housing, your character and ability will be on public display. Ethos is especially crucial in persuasive situations.

Informative speaking stresses understanding; persuasive speaking often depends on exciting emotion. Strong feelings are natural when much is at stake. The arousal of feelings also may be necessary to overcome the audience's hesitation over the risks involved in making a commitment. For example, the statement "Studies show that a 10 percent rise in tuition costs will reduce the student population by about 5 percent next fall" may be useful in an informative speech but would be feeble in persuasion. Now look at this way of putting the matter:

> Those who plan tuition increases are well paid, so they think a few hundred dollars more each term will have little effect on students. Most of us will survive a 10 percent rise in tuition costs, they say. Only one in twenty won't be back because of it, and that will just decrease the surplus enrollment!
>
> Well, let me tell you about a friend of mine — let's call him Joe. Joe's family is Mexican-American — very poor. Joe is their pride and joy, their hope for making it. Joe is on the Dean's List, and he can look forward to a successful career in accounting when he graduates. But with this rise in tuition, Joe won't be back next fall. Another dream deferred — another dream denied! What do the planners care about that? What do they care about Joe?
>
> Perhaps you are a Joe. But even if you are not, he is one of us, and he needs our help *now*.

The emotional language of persuasion is often necessary to help us see the human truth of situations and to stir us to action.

Informative speaking usually addresses listeners as individuals; persuasive speaking frequently appeals to groups. Persuasion often requires concerted action for its success. If you want your audience to protest a proposed increase in tuition, you must address them as members of a group — in this case, as student-victims. As we noted in Chapter 10, language can be used to create a sense of group identity. Persuasive communication can encourage individuals to act together as a powerful force for change.

THE PROCESS OF PERSUASION

How can we explain how Betty Nichols broke through the audience apathy surrounding her subject, drinking and driving? (See her speech in Appendix B.) Or how Anna Aley stirred her student audiences to protest the poor housing conditions to which many were subjected?

We must understand how persuasion works before we can hope to practice it successfully. William J. McGuire, professor of psychology at Yale University, suggests that there may be up to twelve steps in successful persuasion.[4] For our purposes, these twelve steps may be grouped into four categories: reception, orientation, acceptance, and integration. *These categories boil down to the simple principle that in successful persuasion people listen, learn, agree, and change as a result of what they hear.*

Reception

The first group of factors in the persuasive process concerns how we receive messages. These factors include exposure, attention, and involvement.

Exposure.   According to McGuire, persuasion begins with exposure to a persuasive message. You must see an ad or hear a speech before it can have an effect. That is why advertisers pay enormous sums for prime-time exposure of their messages on television. In the world outside the classroom, advance publicity must convince audiences to attend speeches. For example, Anna Aley's title, "We Don't Have to Live in Slums," might entice those living in substandard off-campus housing to attend the open forum.

Although as a student speaker you have a captive audience, not all your listeners will actually be exposed to your message, especially if they are worrying about their own upcoming speeches or are daydreaming. At a minimum, to expose your ideas you must speak loudly enough to be heard. However, to secure genuine exposure to your message, you must make listeners *want* to hear what you say.

Attention.   When listeners perk up at your opening words, you have begun to build attention. To increase and sustain this attention, you can use the techniques described in Chapters 7 and 12, such as telling a story, using a striking quotation, or startling the audience. Anna Aley's vivid description of serious health and safety hazards in her off-campus apartment quickly gained the attention of her listeners. In addition to such techniques, your voice, facial expressions, and gestures should reinforce the impression that your words deserve attention.

Involvement. As audience attention grows, listeners become increasingly involved with the message. Speakers help this process when they *motivate* listeners by showing them what is at stake. "What I'm going to tell you today could make it possible for you to retire comfortably — with all the money you need for travel — by the time you are fifty!"

As messages achieve exposure, attention, and involvement, the momentum toward persuasion increases.

Orientation

The second group of factors in McGuire's explanation of persuasion concerns whether listeners understand, learn information, and know how to act in order to carry out the persuader's proposals. All these critical factors come under the heading of orientation.

Comprehension. Listeners are quickly discouraged if they don't understand the speaker's message. A clear structure, adequate definitions and examples, and familiar language are all necessary for comprehension. "For example" is often heard in persuasive speeches, where the technique works much like an internal visual aid. Transitions, previews, and summaries can also promote understanding. If you tell your audience you will cover three ways to lower car insurance rates, and then enumerate them as you speak ("First. . . . Second. . . . And finally. . . ."), your speech will be much easier to follow and understand.

Information. Ethical and effective persuasion builds on a foundation of information, often called *evidence.* Listeners want to know the facts before they risk a commitment. They should also understand the human dimensions of a problem, which can best be communicated by examples or narratives. The information provided must be credible — listeners must be satisfied that you have described the situation fully and accurately. Expert testimony is usually essential to verify information. Anna Aley's speech uses all these types of supporting materials — facts and figures, examples, narrative, and expert testimony — to establish her base of evidence. In addition, listeners want good reasons for action. Reasons tell us how to interpret information. In the form of *proof* and *argument,* discussed in the next chapter, they point us toward certain attitudes and behaviors.

Implementation. It does little good to bring people to the point of acceptance if they don't know *how* to put your plan into effect. Therefore, you should help the audience learn the skills and procedures necessary to implement your proposal. Effective public health campaigns against smoking must not only convince people that smoking is bad for them but must provide them with ways to stop smoking.

If your persuasive message is understandable, offers listeners the information and incentives they need for acceptance, *and* clarifies how they can comply with your proposal, you will have increased the odds in favor of persuasion.

Acceptance

Levels of acceptance for a speaker's persuasive message can range from small concessions to total commitment. According to McGuire, acceptance involves agreeing with the message, retaining it, and remembering both your agreement and the reasons for it.

Agreement.   Agreement comes when listeners react by saying or thinking, "This speaker has a point," or "She's probably right," or "I'm convinced — no doubt about it." Although you may aim for total commitment, even lesser forms of agreement could mean success, especially when your listeners have to give up previous convictions or if your proposal involves much risk.

Retention.   You can help listeners remember your message by telling stories and painting vivid word pictures. Narratives and images will remain after abstract reasons are forgotten. It also helps if your speech has a striking conclusion. The story of her neighbor's accident, used at the conclusion of Anna Aley's speech, helped embed her message in the minds of her listeners.

SPEAKER'S NOTES

Applying McGuire's Model of the Persuasive Process to Your Speeches

1. Arouse attention with an effective introduction.

2. Involve listeners by relating your message to their interests and needs.

3. Ensure understanding by defining complex terms, using concrete examples, and organizing your material clearly.

4. Build your persuasive efforts on a base of solid information.

5. Be sure listeners know how to carry out your proposal.

6. Help the audience remember your message by using vivid word pictures and a striking conclusion.

7. Ask for a public commitment from your listeners. Give them something to do that starts them on the path to change.

8. Ensure enduring change by stirring deep feelings and connecting them with powerful reasons.

Remembering Agreement.   More than just remembering your message, you want listeners to remember their commitment and the reasons for it. If you can induce listeners to make a public statement by signing a petition, raising their hands, or even voicing agreement, you strengthen their commitment and help them remember it. The student speaker who mobilized the audience against a proposed tuition increase (a) brought a petition to be signed, (b) provided the addresses of local legislators to be contacted, and (c) urged listeners to write letters to campus and local newspapers.

Integration

For your persuasive speeches to have a lasting impact, listeners must use your message when they make decisions, must change their behavior in response to it, and must consolidate their new attitudes and actions into their total belief systems. These steps represent the integration phase of successful persuasion.

Utilization.   Persuasion is more easily accomplished if there is some immediate benefit in adopting the attitude or course of action you propose. Beyond this direct advantage, the best persuasive speeches help us understand

In 1989 Eastern Europeans yearning for freedom and reform heard powerful persuasive speeches. To inspire lasting change, speakers evoked both deep feeling and strong reason.

and interpret our overall experience. They equip us to make better future decisions. As you protest a proposed tuition increase, you may also create a sense of community and caring among your student listeners that will endure and enrich their lives.

Demonstration.   Just as the test of pudding is in the tasting, the test of persuasion is often a change in behavior. Even though listeners may express agreement, do what you ask, and even use what they learn to make future decisions, you achieve genuine persuasion only when such changes persist. Antismoking campaigns illustrate the point. One of our students wryly observed that it was easy to quit smoking — he had done it many times! It is one thing for listeners to agree to stop smoking, another for them to stop for a short period of time, and quite another for them to quit forever. To secure long-lasting change, persuasion usually has to evoke deep emotions in listeners and connect those feelings with powerful reasons.

Consolidation.   Occasionally, persuasion attempts to transform the belief systems of listeners. Rare is the speaker and rarer still the speech that can achieve such change in a single persuasive effort. Such fundamental changes in belief systems usually require many powerful appeals, heard over time, to have an effect. Usually, classroom speeches do not even attempt such basic changes of listeners' lives. It can happen, however. In the 1960s, the civil rights speeches delivered by students (especially in southern classrooms, where the risk was high and the atmosphere tense) sometimes succeeded in helping listeners integrate new information, attitudes, and behavior into their total belief systems.

THE CHALLENGES OF PERSUASION

Many challenges confront a persuasive speaker, ranging from enticing a reluctant audience to listen to moving a sympathetic audience to action. As you plan a persuasive speech, you need to consider the audience's position on the topic, how listeners might react to you as speaker, and the situation in which the speech will be presented.

Where do your listeners stand? Does the audience hold varying attitudes about the topic, or is it united? If listeners are divided, you might hope to unify them around your position. If listeners are already united — in opposing your view — you might aim to divide them and hope to attract some toward your position. How will listeners regard you as a speaker on the subject? If you do not already have their respect, trust, and good feeling, you must strive to enhance your ethos by using testimony from highly regarded sources. What about the occasion? Even classroom speech situations may occur at a sensitive time. For example, you might use the anniversary of the *Challenger* space-shuttle disaster to present a speech urging renewed exploration of outer space.

Evaluating the relationships among the audience, the topic, you as speaker, and the occasion will tell you how far you can hope to go in a particular persuasive speech. These relationships also may suggest the strategy of your speech and the kind of supporting material you need to convince your listeners.

Enticing a Reluctant Audience to Listen

Attitudes and beliefs are often hard to change, especially when they are important to listeners. If you are facing an audience that opposes your position, success may be measured in small achievements, such as getting thoughtful attention. When facing a reluctant audience, your first job may be to dispel any suspicion or anger that could block exposure to your message. One way of handling such an audience is to adopt a **co-active approach** to persuasion.[5] The major steps in this approach include

1. Establish identification and good will early in the speech.

2. Start with areas of agreement before you tackle areas of disagreement.

3. Work toward the acceptance of general values before proposing specific changes.

4. Use experts and evidence the audience will respect and accept.

5. Set modest goals for change; don't strive for too much through any single effort.

6. Offer a **multisided presentation,** in which you discuss the advantages of your position in comparison with others.

Let's look at how you could apply these steps in a speech against capital punishment. You could begin by *building identification,* pointing out the common beliefs, attitudes, and values you share with the audience, such as "We all believe in fairness, in respect for human life." At the same time you would be *starting with areas of agreement* and *working toward the acceptance of general values.* It might also help to take an indirect approach, presenting your evidence and reasoning before announcing your purpose.

> What if I were to tell you that we are condoning unfairness, that we are condemning people to death simply because they are poor and cannot afford a good lawyer? What if I were to show you that we are sanctioning a model of violent behavior in our society that invites more violence, more victims, more heartbreak?

As you present your evidence, cite authorities that *your audience will respect and accept.* "FBI statistics tell us that if you are poor and black, you are three times more likely to be executed for the crime of murder." *Keep your goals modest.* Hope only that your audience will listen all the way through your presentation and give it a fair hearing. Your objective might be to give the audience information that could *eventually* change their minds.

> I know that many of you may not like to hear what I'm saying, but think about it. If capital punishment does not deter violent crimes, if indeed it may encourage *more* violent crimes, isn't it time we put capital punishment itself on trial?

Finally, *make a multisided presentation* by acknowledging the arguments in favor of capital punishment, showing that you respect and understand that position, even though you cannot accept it.

> I know that the desire for revenge can be all-powerful. If I had a loved one who had been brutally killed, I would want the killer's life in return. I wouldn't care about the unfairness of capital punishment. I wouldn't care that capital punishment actually condones brutality. I would simply want an eye for an eye. But that does not mean you should give it to me. It does not mean that society should base public policy on my anger and hatred.

Research suggests that a multisided approach is effective when the audience opposes you and also helps to make those whom you persuade resistant to later counterattacks.[6] When you acknowledge and then refute the arguments of the opposition, you help your credibility in two ways. First, you enhance your *trustworthiness* by showing respect for your opposition. You suggest that their position merits consideration, even though you have a better option. Second, you enhance your *competence* by showing your knowledge of the opposing position and of the reasons why people accept it.

After your speech, you should continue to show respect for the audience. Even if some listeners want to argue or heckle, keep your composure. Others may be impressed by your self-control and may be encouraged to rethink their positions in light of your example.

There may be times when you and your audience are so far apart that you wish to adopt more radical strategies. Candor can be such a strategy. You could begin by acknowledging that you are not in agreement with your listeners, but you respect their right to their position and hope they will respect yours. Such openness may help establish the beginnings of trust. Even if audience members do not see you as a friend, they may at least start to see you as an honest opponent and may give you a hearing. If you emphasize that you will *not* be asking them to change their minds, simply to hear you out and to listen to the reasons why you believe as you do, you may be able to have your day in court.

We once heard a student make a speech opposing abortion to a class that was sharply divided on that issue. She began with a personal narrative, the story of how her mother had taken thalidomide (an experimental drug that induced birth defects) by mistake and was faced with a decision on terminating the pregnancy. The student concluded the story by saying that if her mother had chosen the abortion route, she would not be there speaking to

SPEAKER'S NOTES

Meeting the Challenge of a Reluctant Audience

1. Establish good will and build arguments based on shared values.

2. Present evidence from sources the audience will accept.

3. Set modest goals. Do not strive for too much change at one time.

4. Use a multisided approach to show respect for the opposition while demonstrating that your position is better.

them that day. She paused, smiled, and said, "Although I know some of you may disagree with my views on abortion, I must say I am glad that you are here to listen and that I am here to speak. Think about it." If your reasons are compelling and your evidence is strong, you may soften the opposition and move "waverers" toward your position.

Another technique that is helpful in handling opposition involves modifying your specific purpose. Do not try to accomplish too much in a single speech. Attitudes and opinions rarely develop out of one listening experience. They are more often developed over time through accumulated experiences and information. If too much change is advocated, you may create a **boomerang effect,** in which the audience reacts by opposing your position even more strongly.[7] To hope for a major change on the basis of any single persuasive effort is what McGuire calls the **great expectation fallacy.**[8] Instead, be patient. Try to move the audience a step at a time in the direction you want them to go.

Do not despair if the change you seek does not happen immediately. Often there is a delayed reaction to persuasion, a **sleeper effect,** in which change shows up later after listeners have had time to integrate the message into their belief systems.[9] Even if no change is apparent, your message may serve a **consciousness-raising function,** sensitizing your listeners to the issue and making them more receptive to future persuasion.[10] It may require a series of messages to move people through all the steps in the persuasive process.

Facing a reluctant audience is never easy. But you can't predict what new thoughts your speech might stimulate among listeners or what delayed positive reactions to it there might be. Even if it only keeps alive the American tradition of dissent, it will have served a valuable function. Just as Olympic divers often earn higher scores for attempting difficult dives, persuasive speakers can win added credit for confronting reluctant audiences intelligently, courageously, and constructively.

Removing Barriers to Commitment

Speaking to listeners who have not yet committed themselves also presents a challenge. These listeners may hesitate because they lack important information, or they may not see the connection between their values and interests and what you propose, or they may not be certain they can trust what you say. To deal with these challenges you should provide vital information, show them how your proposal relates to their values or interests, or strengthen your credibility so that you gain increased trust.

Provide Vital Information.   Often a single missing fact or unanswered question can stand in the way of commitment. "I know that many of you agree with me but are asking, 'How much will this cost?'" Anticipating audience reservations and supplying such vital information can help move listeners toward your position.

Affirm and Apply Values.   Persuasive speeches that threaten audience values are not likely to be effective. You must establish that what you urge agrees with what listeners already believe or with their vital interests. For example, if your listeners resist a proposed educational program for the disadvantaged because they think people ought to take care of themselves, you may have to show them that your program represents "a *hand up,* not a *handout.*" Show the audience how people will be able to take care of themselves once the program goes into effect. It is also helpful if you can demonstrate that your proposal will lead to other favorable consequences, such as reductions in public assistance, unemployment compensation, and criminal activities.

As we noted in Chapter 4, values are often resistant to change. If you can reason from the perspective of your listeners' values, using them as the basis

SPEAKER'S NOTES   *Meeting the Challenge of*
                                                an Uncommitted Audience

1. Provide documented information from reputable sources.

2. Show listeners how your proposal is consistent with their needs and values.

3. Acquire borrowed ethos by citing authorities the audience respects.

4. Be careful not to overstate your case or rely too heavily on emotional appeals.

SPEAKER'S NOTES

*Meeting the Challenge of
Moving an Audience to Action*

1. Remind listeners of the values and beliefs that are at stake.

2. Stress the need for action by picturing and comparing the results of acting and not acting.

3. Present a specific step-by-step plan of action.

4. Urge public commitment to your proposal.

for your arguments, you will create identification and remove a barrier to commitment.

Strengthen Your Credibility. When audiences hesitate because they question your credibility, you must rely heavily on borrowed ethos from expert testimony to make your case. Cite sources that your listeners trust and respect. Uncommitted audiences will scrutinize both you and your arguments carefully. Reason with such listeners, leading them to the conclusion you want them to reach. Provide supporting material for each step along the way. Adopt a multisided approach, in which you consider all options fairly, to confirm your ethos as a trustworthy and competent speaker.

When addressing uncommitted listeners, don't overstate your case. Let your personal commitment be evident through your sincerity and conviction, but be careful with emotional appeals to guilt or fear. These appeals could backfire, causing listeners to reject both you and your message.[11] It is also important not to push uncommitted listeners too hard. Help them move in the desired direction, but let them make the final step themselves.

Moving from Attitude to Action

When listeners share your position and accept your leadership, they may be ready for a speech proposing action. However, it is one thing to agree with a speaker and quite another to accept all the inconvenience, cost, and risk that a commitment to action may require. You may have to present a powerful justification for what you propose. At the least, you may have to remind listeners of their beliefs, demonstrate the need for their involvement, and present a clear plan for them to follow.

Revitalize Shared Beliefs.   When persuasive speakers and audiences celebrate their shared beliefs, the result is a renewed commitment. Such occasions often involve retelling traditional stories and resurrecting heroes, giving them new life and meaning. At political conventions Jefferson, Lincoln, Roosevelt, and Kennedy are often remembered in speeches. Such stories and examples recall our heritage and show how it relates to the present.[12]

Justify Action.   The law of inertia suggests that bodies at rest tend to remain that way until compelled into movement by a sufficient force. So it is with audiences. Listeners may resist action by exaggerating the difficulty of a proposal or insisting that it is impossible. To overcome such resistance, use examples or narratives that picture the audience undertaking the plan of action successfully. Stress that "we *can* do it, and this is *how* we will do it."

A second technique for justifying action is to present vivid images of the *need* for it. Show your listeners how the quality of their lives — how even survival — depends on prompt action. Demonstrate how the new situation they will create will be satisfying. It often helps if you can associate the change with a vision of the future. In his final speech, Martin Luther King, Jr., said, "I may not get there with you, but I can see the Promised Land." King's vision of the Promised Land helped justify the sacrifice called for in his plan of action.

Explain the Plan of Action.   To get listeners to act, you must give them a plan and get them to take the first step. A speaker hoping to persuade classmates to work to defeat a proposed tuition raise might say something like this:

> How many of you are willing to help defeat this plan to raise our tuition? Good! I see your heads nodding. Now, if you are willing to sign this petition to protest this injustice, hold up your hands. Hold them higher so I can see you! O.K.! Good! I'm going to circulate this petition, and I want each of you to sign it. If we act together, we can make a difference.

The plan you present must show listeners what has to be done, who must do it, and how to proceed. Try to anticipate and refute excuses listeners might offer to avoid responsibility. Strong feelings aroused through vivid images are often necessary to move people to action. If you can get one person in the audience to make a commitment, others will often follow. Once people have openly voiced their commitment, they are more likely to follow through on it.[13]

TYPES OF PERSUASIVE SPEECHES

In this section we discuss three major types of persuasive speeches: those that address attitudes, those that urge action, and those that contend with opposition. Although a speech may perform all these functions, most of the time one will dominate.

Speeches Addressing Attitudes

The basic goal of **speeches addressing attitudes** is to form, reform, or reinforce audience attitudes. Sometimes a speaker may simply wish to raise discontent by addressing a topic such as "what's wrong with the income tax system." Later speeches can then build on this discontent and urge specific programs of reform. Thus, speeches addressing attitudes often prepare the way for speeches urging action.

When they are most ambitious, speeches addressing attitudes aim for a total change of conviction. A speech on the topic "we need a new way of thinking about taxation in America" might attempt such far-reaching influence. These speeches can be appropriate when the problems they address require more than surface remedies.

Obviously, the greater the change of attitude you aim for, the more difficult it will be to achieve your goal. As we noted in Chapter 4, beliefs, attitudes, and values are an integral part of our personality. Deep changes in any of these can have a revolutionary impact on lives, so audiences are usually highly resistant to proposals calling for such reform. There is always the possibility that such persuasive efforts will cause audiences to reject the speaker and cling even more stubbornly to their previous beliefs.

To be effective, speeches addressing attitudes must begin on common ground. Betty Nichols's speech on responsible drinking and driving began by assuming that she and her listeners shared the belief that drunk driving is a serious problem. Betty reinforced that shared belief and then offered a change in attitude as part of a solution for the problem. To encourage such change, offer audience members good reasons for modifying their convictions.[14]

Speeches Urging Action

Speeches urging action go beyond attitude change and encourage listeners to take action either as individuals or as members of a group. Sometimes such speeches urge an immediate, specific action in response to a pressing situation. At other times the action requested may be ongoing. When a speech advocates group action, the audience must see itself as having common identity and purpose. As we noted in Chapter 10, the speaker can reinforce group identity by using inclusive pronouns (*we, our, us*), telling stories that emphasize group achievements, and referring to common heroes, enemies, or martyrs. Anna Aley used an effective appeal to group identity as she proposed specific actions:

> ... What can one student do to change the practices of numerous Manhattan landlords? Nothing, if that student is alone. But just think what we could accomplish if we got all 13,600 off-campus students involved in this issue! Think what we could accomplish if we got even a fraction of those students involved!

In contrast, Betty Nichols called for ongoing individual action as she appealed for new approaches to the drinking and driving problem. When a persuasive speech urges individual commitment, audience members must see the value or necessity of action in personal terms.

Speeches advocating action may involve some degree of risk. Therefore, the speaker must present compelling reasons to overcome the listener's natural caution. The consequences of acting and not acting must be clearly spelled out. The plan presented must seem practical and reasonable, and listeners should be able to see themselves enacting it successfully.

Speeches of Contention

In **speeches of contention** you directly refute opposing arguments to clear the way for attitudes and actions you are proposing. "There are those who say that we cannot afford to land explorers on Mars in this century," said Marvin Andrews to his public speaking class. "I say we can't afford not to." Marvin then went on to describe the costs of a space journey to Mars and the benefits we might expect from such exploration. "But we really can have no idea of all the benefits, any more than Queen Isabella could have foreseen all the results of the voyage of Columbus. Fortunately, she did not listen to advisers who said his trip would cost too much," Marvin concluded.

If some audience members hold opposing views, a speech of contention may offend them, placing them on the defensive and making them all the more difficult to persuade. Why, then, would you give such a speech?

On controversial topics such as gun control or the legalization of drugs, you often can't avoid a speech of contention. The attitude change or action you propose may instantly arouse opposition from those who feel equally strongly on the other side of the issue. We have already described one tactical strategy to use when facing reluctant listeners: aim to get a fair hearing and to establish common ground. However, in situations when danger threatens and immediate action is needed, such mild persuasive tactics may be inappropriate. You may have to address opposing beliefs directly and discredit the arguments that support them.

Additionally, speeches of contention may be the best strategy when you suspect there are uncommitted listeners or reasonable opponents in the audience. These are the listeners you may reach with tactful counterarguments. If you can change them, they could influence others. Even among your supporters there may be those who need assurance that an opposing argument can be effectively countered. Your refutation may strengthen their resolve.

Finally, some situations, as when one must discuss our government's policies toward South Africa before a reluctant audience, may call for speeches of contention as a last-ditch tactic. You may believe that your listeners are so strongly entrenched in their opposition that your only hope is to shock them with a direct, frontal attack that shows them why they are wrong. You hope for a positive delayed effect after their first negative reaction. Or you may even

Moral and ethical issues, such as those surrounding the practice of apartheid in South Africa, often call for speeches of contention. A refutative design that counters the opposition point by point, starting with the weakest claim, can be the best strategy for speeches like those given at this antiapartheid rally.

decide that your chances for persuasion are small but that your position deserves to be heard with all the power, reason, and conviction you can muster. You can have your say and feel better for it.

DESIGNS FOR PERSUASIVE SPEAKING

As you consider the type of persuasive speech you will develop, you must decide how to structure your speech. Many of the designs used for informative speeches are also appropriate for persuasive speeches. The categorical design can provide reasons for accepting changes in attitude, taking action, or rejecting the arguments of others. The sequential design may be used to specify the steps in a plan of action. Similarly, the comparison and contrast design works well for speeches of contention in which you contrast the weaknesses of an opposing argument with the strengths of your own. In the remainder of this chapter, we look at designs especially suited to persuasive speeches. Figure 13.1 explains the relationship between types of persuasive speeches and their major design options.

Problem-Solution Design

The **problem-solution design** first convinces listeners that they have a problem, then shows them how to deal with it. The solution can involve changing an attitude or taking an action and is particularly appropriate for those types of persuasive speeches. Although this approach sounds simple, it is sometimes difficult to convince listeners that they have a problem. People often ignore problems until they reach a critical stage. You can counteract this tendency by depicting the crisis that surely will emerge unless your audience makes the changes you suggest.

When you prepare a problem-solution speech, do not overwhelm your listeners with details. Cover the most important features of the problem, then show the audience how your solution will work. A problem-solution speech opposing a proposed tuition increase might use the following design:

Thematic statement: We need to defeat the proposal to raise tuition next fall.

Figure 13.1

Types of Persuasive Speeches and Major Options for Designing Them

Type	Major Design Options	Summary of Procedures
Form, reform, or reinforce attitudes	Categorical	Justifies attitudes or change in attitude by presenting categories of reasons.
	Problem-solution	Reveals an attitude as central to a problem, and a change in attitude as the key to its solution.
	Analogy	Creates favorable or unfavorable attitude shifts by associating a topic with an object of comparison.
Urge action	Sequential	Shows how a proposed plan will work as a systematic sequence of actions.
	Problem-solution	Promotes the need for action to solve some serious social or personal problem.
	Motivated sequence	Calls for action as the final phase of a process that encompasses arousing attention, demonstrating need, satisfying need, and visualizing results.
Contend with opposing views	Comparison/contrast	Attacks an opposing position by comparing and contrasting its weaknesses with the strengths of one's own.
	Refutative	Follows a systematic five-step method of attacking an opposing position.
	Analogy	Justifies rejection of an opposing approach by connecting it with some disliked similar proposal or situation.

I. Problem

    A. The plan will create serious hardships for many students.
        1. Many current students may have to drop out.
        2. New students will be discouraged from coming.

    B. The plan will be self-defeating.
        1. Decreased attendance will mean decreased revenue.
        2. Decreased revenue will reduce the university's service to the community.
        3. Reduced service will mean reduced support from the state.

II. Solution

    A. Get signatures on a petition against the tuition increase.
        1. Send copies to state legislators.
        2. Deliver to the president of the university (alert TV stations).

    B. Start a letters-to-the-editor campaign.

    C. Organize a rally on campus.

When the problem can be identified clearly and the solution is concrete and simple, the problem-solution design works well in persuasive speeches.

Analogy Design

In a persuasive speech using an **analogy design,** the body of the speech consists of an extended comparison supporting the speaker's proposal. We have already seen how analogies can serve informative speeches by relating the unknown to the known to increase understanding. In a persuasive speech, analogies go beyond this function to affect attitudes as well. Therefore, analogy design is well suited for persuasive speeches urging changes of attitude. Because this design can also cast an opposing position in an unfavorable light, it can also serve persuasive speeches that contend with other views.

For analogy to work as a persuasive design, the audience must have an attitude toward the object of comparison that will serve your purpose. For example, if your audience has a positive attitude toward the efficiency of Japanese industry, then drawing an analogy between Japanese management techniques and an open management style for American industry might be an effective technique. Of course, if your audience has negative feelings about Japan, the analogy could backfire. On the other hand, if you wish to discredit an opposing position, you can connect it to something that your listeners are likely to reject. When you compare a proposed plan to "taxation without representation," you are using a negative analogy to the conditions that inspired the American Revolution. Because you can develop both positive and negative analogies, this can be a very useful design for persuasive speeches.

As we observed in the previous chapter, analogies may be either literal or figurative, depending on whether you are comparing things of the same or different kinds. A speech based on an extended analogy between American and Japanese business cultures would follow a literal analogy design. Such a speech would emphasize a rational pattern of persuasion, based on precise points of similarity and difference. On the other hand, speeches based on figurative analogy design are often quite emotional, based on the transfer of attitudes and feelings. Let us see how our speech against a proposed tuition increase might be structured using a figurative analogy. Arguing that "the proposal to raise tuition treats students more like slaves than like members of a free society," you might follow this plan:

I. A slave state does not consult slaves: who consulted you?

    A. How the proposal originated.

    B. When it was planned.

    C. Who planned it.

II. A slave state does not care about the welfare of slaves: who cares about your welfare?

    A. How students in general will be affected.

    B. Specific cases of hardship in our class.

III. A slave state does not see the consequences of its acts: who has measured the impact on our university?

    A. Prospect of diminished revenue.

    B. Loss of outstanding faculty and programs.

    C. Decreased support from state.

In this example the speaker hopes for a transfer of emotion — from the behavior of a "slave state" to the unjust conduct of the university. If the analogy works, it is likely to have a profound impact on listener attitudes. When using the figurative analogy design, the speaker must still be able to demonstrate that the analogy fits the situation, or it will seem far-fetched and inappropriate.

Motivated Sequence Design

The **motivated sequence design,** introduced by Alan Monroe,[15] concentrates on stimulating an awareness of need, then showing how it can be satisfied. This design has five steps, beginning with the arousal of attention and ending with a call for action. Therefore, it has special usefulness in persuasive speeches that have action as their goal.

1. *Arousing attention.* As in any speech, you begin by stimulating interest in your subject. In Chapter 12 we discussed six factors related to attention:

intensity, repetition, novelty, activity, contrast, and relevance. These same techniques may be used in persuasive speeches.

2. *Demonstrating a need.* Show your listeners what they might win or lose if they accept or reject your proposal. Tie your demonstration to the basic needs discussed in Chapter 4.

3. *Satisfying the need.* Present a way to satisfy the need you have demonstrated. Set forth a plan of action and explain how it meets the needs of the audience. Provide evidence that your plan will be effective through examples showing how it has worked in other places.

4. *Visualizing the results.* You can visualize results with either positive or negative images. You could show your listeners how their lives will be changed for the better when your plan is enacted. A positive image of the future can help overcome resistance to action. You could also present a dire picture of what life will be like if they do not go along with your plan. You might even put these positive and negative verbal pictures side by side to strengthen their impact through contrast.

5. *Calling for action.* Your call for action may be a challenge, an appeal, or a statement of personal commitment. The call for action should be short and to the point. Give your listeners something specific that they can do right away to start the process of change. If you can get them to take the first step in the proposal, the next will come more easily.

Let's look at how this model might work in a persuasive speech:

Arousing attention	How would you like to finish college with $5,000 in the bank rather than $5,000 in the hole?
Demonstrating need	Housing — along with food — is probably your major college expense, costing you thousands of dollars a year. Every year the costs go up. The money you spend on a dorm room or apartment rental is lost to you forever.
Satisfying the need	Investing in a mobile home can help reduce your housing costs. Monthly payments will be lower than apartment rent. When you graduate, you can sell the home and get back a good part of your investment.
Visualizing the results	Today's mobile homes are attractive and comfortable places to live. They come complete with air-conditioning and the newest kitchen and laundry appliances. Some even have fireplaces and Jacuzzi tubs. Each month part of your payment goes to accumulating equity in the home. When you sell the home, you recover this equity money.
Calling for action	The Campus View Mobile Home Park, just three miles from this building, sells new and used mobile homes. Go out there and look around. Ask John Bentley what kind of a deal you might make. Save yourself some money and live better at the same time.

To use the motivated sequence correctly, first consider where your listeners stand on the issue as you begin your speech. Then emphasize the steps that will carry persuasion forward. If you were speaking to an audience that was already convinced of the need for a change but lacked a plan to make it work, you could focus on Step 3, "satisfying the need." However, if you faced an audience that contested the need, your emphasis should be on Step 2, "demonstrating the need." In the latter situation, you might simply mention that ways to satisfy the need are available and stop short of a call for action. These final steps could be addressed in later speeches.

The major problem with the motivated sequence design is that it may tempt a speaker into trying too much in a single speech. If you expect to move from introducing a problem, to showing how it can be solved, to energizing listeners to solve it — all in one short speech — you may be committing the great expectation fallacy we mentioned earlier. This is especially true if the problem is complex and much risk is involved. Also, when beginning speakers use such a rigid model to structure their speeches, they may be tempted to follow the formula as though they were baking a cake using a generic mix. Just as the best cooks turn out culinary masterpieces by modifying recipes, the best speakers adapt designs to fit their subjects, audiences, purposes, and their own personalities.

Refutative Design

In the **refutative design,** used in speeches of contention, the speaker tries to raise doubts about, damage, or even destroy an opposing position by pointing out its inconsistencies and absurdities. To bring off an effective refutation, you must understand the opposition's motivations, arguments, and evidence. It is often wise to attack the opposition's weakest point first. If this works, it may cast doubt on other opposing arguments. The point of attack may be illogical reasoning, flimsy or insufficient evidence, or even the self-interest of an opposing speaker. However, to keep the dispute as constructive as possible, avoid personal attacks unless credibility issues are inescapable.

There are five steps in developing an effective refutation. These five steps should be followed in sequence for each argument or point you plan to refute.

1. State the point you are going to refute and explain why it is important.

2. Tell the audience how you are going to refute this point.

3. Present your evidence using facts and figures, examples, and testimony. Cite sources and authorities the audience will accept as competent and credible.

4. Spell out the conclusion for the audience. Do not rely on listeners to figure out what the evidence means. Tell them directly.

5. Explain the significance of your refutation — show how it discredits or damages the position of the opposition.

For example, you might refute an argument against sex education in public high schools in the following manner:

State the point you will refute and explain its importance.

Our well-intended friends would have you believe, and this is their biggest concern, that birth-control information increases teen-age sexual activity.

Tell how you will refute this point.

I want to share with you some statistical evidence that contradicts this contention — a contention that is simply not supported by the facts.

Present your evidence using credible sources.

The latest study on this issue, conducted in 1989 by the National Department of Human Services, compared sexual activity rates in sixty high schools across the United States — thirty with sex education programs and thirty without. Their findings show that there are no significant differences in sexual activity rates between these two groups of schools.

State your conclusion.

Therefore, the argument that access to birth-control information through sex education programs increases sexual activity simply does not hold water.

Explain the significance of your refutation.

That's typical of the attack on sex education in the schools — a lot of sound and fury, signifying nothing.

SPEAKER'S NOTES   *Designing Your Persuasive Speech*

1. In a categorical design, provide reasons for changing attitudes or actions.

2. In a sequential design, specify the steps in a plan of action.

3. In a comparison and contrast design, contrast the weaknesses of an opposing position with the strengths of your own.

4. In a problem-solution design, focus on the main features of a problem, and then present a simple, clear solution.

5. In an analogy design, compare your proposal with something listeners favor to encourage acceptance. Attack an opposing position by comparing it to something listeners dislike.

6. In a motivated sequence design, consider your listeners' stand on the issue; then emphasize the most relevant points in a five-step process from "arousing attention" to "calling for action."

7. In a refutative design, attack the weakest points of the opposition first, concentrating on defects in evidence, proof, and argument. Avoid personal attacks unless credibility issues are inescapable.

You can strengthen this design if you follow your refutation by proving a similar point on your own, thus balancing the negative effect of refutation with the positive effect of demonstration. The result is to supply the audience with an alternative belief to substitute for the one you have refuted. Use the same five-step sequence to support your position. For example, you might follow the preceding refutation with the following demonstration:

State the point you will support and explain its importance.

I'm not going to try to tell you that birth-control information reduces sexual activity. But I want to tell you what it does reduce. It reduces teen-age pregnancy.

Tell how you will support this point.

There is reliable evidence that fewer girls become pregnant in high schools with sex education programs.

Present your evidence using credible sources.

The same study conducted by the National Department of Human Services demonstrated that in high schools with sex education programs the pregnancy rate dropped from one out of every sixty female students to one out of ninety within two years of the program's going into effect.

State your conclusion.

Therefore, sex education is a good program. It attacks a devastating social problem — teen-age pregnancy.

Explain the significance of your demonstration.

Any program that reduces unwanted teen-age pregnancy is valuable — valuable to the young women involved, valuable to society. We all pay in so many ways for this personal and social tragedy — we should all support a program that works to reduce it. And we should reject the irrational voices that reject the program.

IN SUMMARY

Persuasive communication is inescapable. Persuasion is also vital to our political system, which is based on the principle of rule by *deliberation* and choice rather than by force. The right to express one's opinions — no matter how unpopular — also serves practical goals. Groups that have been exposed to different positions usually make better decisions because they are stimulated to examine a situation and to think about their options.

Characteristics of Persuasive Speaking.   In contrast to informative speaking, persuasive speaking urges a choice among options and asks for a commitment. The persuasive speaker acts as a leader and often emphasizes group over individual action. Persuasive speeches rely more on emotional involvement than informative speeches do, and they carry a heavier ethical burden.

The Process of Persuasion.   When persuasion is successful, people listen, learn, agree, and change as a result of what they hear. These behaviors parallel McGuire's categories of reception, orientation, acceptance, and integration of persuasive material. Reception includes exposure, attention, and involvement with persuasive messages. Orientation means comprehending, learning information and ideas, and acquiring skills needed for compliance. Acceptance includes agreeing with and retaining a message and remembering one's agreement. Integration involves using the persuasive message in later decision making, changing one's behavior, and consolidating the message into one's total belief system.

The Challenges of Persuasion.   Persuading others poses many challenges. You must assess the situation to determine the exact nature of your challenge. You may have to entice a reluctant audience to listen, remove barriers that block commitment, or move listeners from agreement to action.

Types of Persuasive Speeches.   The three major types of persuasive speeches address attitudes, urge action, and contend with opposition. *Speeches addressing attitudes* may aim for small changes or radical conversion. The latter kind is difficult, and risks a *boomerang effect. Speeches urging action* call for actual participation in enacting change. Such speeches may strive for group action, emphasizing identification, or for individual action, emphasizing self-interest. *Speeches of contention* confront the opposition by systematically refuting its claims. You usually do not speak to convert opponents but rather to win over the uncommitted and to influence opinion leaders.

Designs for Persuasive Speaking.   Problem-solution, analogy, motivated sequence, and refutation designs are particularly suited for persuasive speeches. In a *problem-solution design,* you must first convince the audience that a problem exists, and then advance a solution that corrects it. In an *analogy design,* construct an extended comparison that will transfer attitudes favoring your position. The *motivated sequence design* has five steps: arousing attention, demonstrating a need, satisfying the need, visualizing the results, and calling for action. To use the *refutative design,* state the point you intend to refute, tell how you will refute it, present your evidence, draw a conclusion, and explain the significance of the refutation. Refutation is often followed by demonstration, in which you prove a point to replace the one you have disproved.

TERMS TO KNOW

deliberation	speeches addressing attitudes
co-active approach	speeches urging action
multisided presentation	speeches of contention
boomerang effect	problem-solution design
great expectation fallacy	analogy design
sleeper effect	motivated sequence design
consciousness-raising function	refutative design

DISCUSSION

1. Examine magazine ads and newspaper articles for examples of persuasion cloaked as information. What alerts you to the persuasive intent? In what respects does such pseudo-information possess the characteristics of persuasion discussed in this chapter? In what respects does it possess the characteristics of informative discourse discussed in Chapter 12?

2. The letters-to-the-editor section of the Sunday newspaper is often a rich (and raw!) source for the study of persuasive material. Using a recent Sunday paper, analyze the persuasion attempted in these letters. Which do you think are most and least effective and why?

3. The speech on slum housing that appears at the end of this chapter was prepared for a student audience at Kansas State University. What changes might you suggest in this speech if it were to be presented to a luncheon meeting of realtors in Manhattan, Kansas? Why?

4. When should a speaker give up trying to persuade a hostile audience and simply confront listeners directly with the position they oppose? Why would a speaker bother to do this? Is it possible that both speaker and audience might gain something from such a confrontation? Find an example of such a speech. Do you agree with the strategy used in it? Discuss in class.

APPLICATION

1. Keep a diary of your day, identifying all the moments in which you confront and practice persuasion. Evaluate your adventure in persuasion. When were you most and least persuaded and most and least persuasive? Why? Did you encounter (or commit!) any ethical abuses?

2. Read one of the persuasive speeches in Appendix B and identify the following:
   a. the challenge the speaker confronted
   b. the type of persuasive speech
   c. the design of the speech

   Analyze the speech using the McGuire model of the persuasive process.

3. Select a controversial subject and outline the persuasive speeches you would present on the subject to
   a. an uncommitted audience
   b. an audience in agreement
   c. an audience in opposition

   Discuss the differences among your approaches.

4. A public forum is being held on campus on the issue of drinking and driving. The first speaker on the program is Betty Nichols, who will present the speech included in Appendix B. You have been asked to refute her position. Outline the speech you will present.

NOTES

1. *Whitney* v. *California,* 274 U.S. 357, 375 (1927).
2. *On Liberty* (Chicago: Henry Regnery, 1955 [originally published 1859]), p. 24.
3. Charlan Jeanne Nemeth, "Differential Contributions of Majority and Minority Influence," *Psychological Review* 93 (1986): 23–32.
4. William J. McGuire, "Attitudes and Attitude Change," in *The Handbook of Social Psychology,* ed. Gardner Lindzey and Elliot Aronson, vol. 1 (New York: Random House, 1985), pp. 258–61.
5. Herbert W. Simons, *Persuasion: Understanding, Practice, and Analysis* (New York: Random House, 1986), p. 153.
6. Carl I. Hovland, Arthur A. Lumsdaine, and Fred D. Sheffield, "The Effects of Presenting 'One Side' versus 'Both Sides' in Changing Opinions on a Controversial Subject," in *Experiments on Mass Communication* (Princeton, N.J.: Princeton University Press, 1949), pp. 201–27; and William J. McGuire, "Inducing Resistance to Persuasion," in *Advances in Experimental Social Psychology,* ed. L. Berkowitz (New York: Academic Press, 1964), pp. 191–229.
7. N. H. Anderson, "Integration Theory and Attitude Change," *Psychological Review* 78 (1971): 171–206.
8. William J. McGuire, "Attitudes and Attitude Change," p. 260.
9. T. D. Cook et al., "History of the Sleeper Effect: Some Logical Pitfalls in Accepting the Null Hypothesis," *Psychological Bulletin* 86 (1979): 662–79.
10. M. E. McCombs, "The Agenda-Setting Approach," in *Handbook of Political Communication,* ed. D. D. Nimmo and K. R. Sanders (Beverly Hills, Calif.: Sage, 1981), pp. 121–40.
11. T. W. Milburn and K. H. Watman, *On the Nature of Threat: A Social Psychological Analysis* (New York: Praeger, 1981).
12. Michael Osborn, "Rhetorical Depiction," in *Form, Genre, and the Study of Political Discourse,* ed. Herbert W. Simons and Aram A. Aghazarian (Columbia: University of South Carolina Press, 1986), pp. 79–107.
13. R. A. Wicklund and J. W. Brehm, *Perspectives on Cognitive Dissonance* (Hillsdale, N.J.: Erlbaum, 1976).
14. See Karl R. Wallace, "The Substance of Rhetoric: Good Reasons," *Quarterly Journal of Speech* 49 (1963): 239–49; and Walter R. Fisher, "Toward a Logic of Good Reasons," *Quarterly Journal of Speech* 64 (1978): 376–84.
15. This design was introduced in Alan Monroe's *Principles and Types of Speech* (New York: Scott, Foresman, 1935) and has been refined in later editions.

SAMPLE PERSUASIVE SPEECH

We Don't Have to Live in Slums

—— *Anna Aley* ——

Anna's speech uses a problem-solution design to urge action. She gains attention and involves her listeners by asserting that slum conditions exist and that they pose a threat. Anna supports these assertions by describing her personal experience through a superb selection of concrete examples.

Slumlords — you'd expect them in New York or Chicago, but in Manhattan, Kansas? You'd better believe there are slumlords in Manhattan, and they pose a direct threat to you if you ever plan to rent an off-campus apartment.

I know about slumlords; I rented a basement apartment from one last semester. I guess I first suspected something was wrong when I discovered dead roaches in the refrigerator. I definitely knew something was wrong when I discovered the leaks: the one in the bathroom that kept the bathroom carpet constantly soggy and molding and the one in the kitchen that allowed water from the upstairs neighbor's bathroom to seep into the kitchen cabinets and collect in my dishes.

Then there were the serious problems. The hot water heater and furnace were connected improperly and posed a fire hazard. They were situated next to the only exit. There was no smoke detector or fire extinguisher and no emergency way out — the windows were too small for escape. I was living in an accident waiting to happen — and paying for it.

The worst thing about my ordeal was that I was not an isolated instance; many Kansas State students are living in unsafe housing and paying for it, not only with their money, but their happiness, their grades, their health, and their safety.

Here Anna shows that hers was not an isolated experience but a general problem requiring reform. She orients her audience by citing factual supporting material on the magnitude of the problem. Then she appeals to her listeners' own observations. Anna also describes students as a likely group of victims, whom slumlords will take advantage of because of their vulnerability. She cites the number of renters' complaints to reinforce this conclusion.

We can't be sure how many students are living in substandard housing, housing that does not meet the code specifications required of rental property. We can be sure, however, that a large number of Kansas State students are at risk of being caught in the same situation I was. According to the registrar, approximately 17,800 students are attending Kansas State this semester. Housing claims that 4,200 live in the dorms. This means that approximately 13,600 students live off-campus. Some live in fraternities or sororities, some live at home, but most live in off-campus apartments, as I do.

Many of these 13,600 students share traits that make them likely to settle for substandard housing. For example, many students want to live close to campus. If you've ever driven through the surrounding neighborhoods, you know that much of the available housing is in older houses, houses that were never meant to be divided into separate rental units. Students are also often limited in the amount they can pay for rent; some landlords, such as mine, will use low rent as an excuse not to fix anything and to let the apartment deteriorate. Most importantly, many students are young, and

Presented at Kansas State University. Used by permission.

consequently, naive when it comes to selecting an apartment. They don't know the housing codes; but even if they did, they don't know how to check to make sure the apartment is in compliance. Let's face it — how many of us know how to check a hot water heater to make sure it's connected properly?

Adding to the problem of the number of students willing to settle for substandard housing is the number of landlords willing to supply it. Currently, the Consumer Relations Board here at Kansas State has on file student complaints against approximately one hundred landlords. There are surely complaints against many more that have never been formally reported.

There are two main causes of the substandard student housing problem. The first — and most significant — is the simple fact that it is possible for a landlord to lease an apartment that does not meet housing code requirements. The Manhattan Housing Code Inspector will evaluate an apartment, but only after the tenant has given the landlord a written complaint and the landlord has had fourteen days to remedy the situation. In other words, the way things are now, the only way the Housing Code Inspector can evaluate an apartment to see if it's safe to be lived in is if someone has been living in it for at least two weeks!

A second cause of the problem is the fact that campus services designed to help students avoid substandard housing are not well known. The Consumer Relations Board here at Kansas State can help students inspect apartments for safety before they sign a lease, it can provide students with vital information on their rights as tenants, and it can mediate in landlord-tenant disputes. The problem is, many people don't know these services exist. The Consumer Relations Board is not listed in the university catalogue; it is not mentioned in any of the admissions literature. The only places it is mentioned are in alphabetically organized references such as the phone book, but you have to already know it exists to look it up! The Consumer Relations Board does receive money for advertising from the student senate, but it is only enough to run a little two-by-three-inch ad once every month. That is not large enough or frequent enough to be noticed by many who could use these services.

It's clear that we have a problem, but what may not seem so clear is what we can do about it. After all, what can one student do to change the practices of numerous Manhattan landlords? Nothing, if that student is alone. But just think of what we could accomplish if we got all 13,600 off-campus students involved in this issue! Think what we could accomplish if we got even a fraction of those students involved! This is what Wade Whitmer, director of the Consumer Relations Board, is attempting to do. He is reorganizing the Off-Campus Association in an effort to pass a city ordinance requiring landlords to have their apartments inspected for safety before those apartments can be rented out. The Manhattan code inspector has already tried to get just such an ordinance passed, but the only people who showed up at the public forums were known slumlords, who obviously weren't in favor of the proposed ordinance. No one showed up to argue in favor of the ordinance, so the city commissioners figured that no one wanted it and voted it down. If we can get the Off-Campus Association organized and involved, however, the commissioners will see that someone does want the ordinance, and they will be more likely to pass it the next time it is proposed. You can do a great service to your fellow students — and to yourself — by joining the Off-Campus Association.

A second thing you can do to help insure that no more Kansas State students have to go through what I did is sign my petition asking the student senate to increase the Consumer Relations Board's advertising budget. Let's face it — a service cannot do anybody any good if no one knows about it. Consumer Relations Board's services are simply too valuable to let go to waste.

An important thing to remember about substandard housing is that it is not only distasteful, it is dangerous. In the end, I was lucky. I got out of my apartment with little more than bad memories. My upstairs neighbor was not so lucky. The main problem with his apartment was that the electrical wiring was done improperly; there were too many outlets for too few circuits, so the fuses were always blowing. One day last November, Jack was at home when a fuse blew — as usual. And, as usual, he went to the fuse box to flip the switch back on. When he touched the switch, it delivered such a shock that it literally threw this guy the size of a football player backwards and down a flight of stairs. He lay there at the bottom, unable to move, for a full hour before his roommate came home and called an ambulance.

Jack was lucky. His back was not broken. But he did rip many of the muscles in his back. Now he has to go to physical therapy, and he is not expected to fully recover.

Kansas State students have been putting up with substandard living conditions for too long. It's time we finally got together to do something about this problem. Join the Off-Campus Association. Sign my petition. Let's send a message to these slumlords that we're not going to put up with this any more. We don't have to live in slums.

Bibliography

Kansas State University. *K-State! Campus Living.*

Registrar's Office, Kansas State University. Personal interview. 10 Mar. 1989.

State of Kansas. Residential Landlord and Tenant Act, 1975.

Whitmer, Wade, director, Consumer Relations Board. Personal interview. 10 Mar. 1989.

Anna concludes her speech with a true-life narrative to help assure that listeners will retain her message and integrate it into their belief systems. Her speech ends with a forceful appeal to action.

Speech is power: Speech is to persuade, to convert, to compel.

— *RALPH WALDO EMERSON*

14

Evidence, Proof,
— *and* —
Argument

This Chapter Will Help You

- ◆ use supporting materials as evidence in persuasive speeches.

- ◆ develop powerful proofs based on effective evidence.

- ◆ form compelling arguments by selecting and combining proofs.

- ◆ recognize and avoid fallacies of evidence, proof, and argument.

Nineteen eighty-nine was a spectacular year for persuasion — a year of powerful speeches to millions hungry for reform and change. In Poland, in East Germany, in Czechoslavakia, the people spoke and the people listened. Old walls fell and were replaced by new political systems — new conceptions of what it means to be human. The people lit countless candles and marched and sang in honor of their newfound freedom. In China's Tiananmen Square and on the bloody streets of Romania, many of these persuasive speakers and persuaded listeners died.

When persuasion is effective, it often shows us the errors of the past, how we should feel and behave, and how to proceed systematically to our new-found goals. Persuasion can improve the quality of our lives, but it can also have a cost. Changing our minds can require a painful admission — that we have been wrong! The new way of doing things can be expensive both in material and spiritual ways. It can involve risks, perhaps social disapproval from friends and family who are *not* persuaded. It may mean that we have to change a lifestyle that we found comfortable and enjoyable. At its most extreme, as our opening vignette indicates, the cost of persuasion may even be life itself.

Knowing the possible risks involved, why do we expose ourselves to persuasion? Why do we listen to speakers with whom we disagree? Why do we absorb facts and testimony that contradict our attitudes? What compels us to integrate new convictions into our belief systems and adopt a change in outlook? In short, what is it that *drives* the process of persuasion discussed in Chapter 13?

To answer these questions, we must introduce three new terms: evidence, proof, and argument. **Evidence** consists of supporting materials as they are used in persuasion. **Proofs** use evidence to produce reasons for accepting a speaker's recommendations. Finally, **arguments** combine evidence and proofs into strategic patterns designed to persuade undecided or reluctant listeners and to reinforce the views of those who already support the speaker's position. Together, these elements form an integrated system — from the simplest piece of evidence to the most complex array of arguments — that drives the persuasive process and explains its power. In this chapter we discuss the nature of evidence, proofs, and arguments; show how they work together; explain how you can use them ethically and effectively; and demonstrate how to avoid some of the major mistakes that can rob persuasion of its power.

USING EVIDENCE EFFECTIVELY

In Chapter 6 we discussed the functions of supporting materials and the ways they could be used in all kinds of speeches. When supporting material is used in persuasive speaking, it becomes evidence. Here we will examine the special functions of evidence to supplement our earlier discussion.

Evidence is the most simple, most basic component of the integrated system that drives persuasion, yet it is absolutely vital. Consider a hypothetical situation. A speaker stands and says, "I want us all to sign up as organ donors." A listener responds, "Why?" The speaker replies, "Well, I just think we should. I'm entitled to my opinion." Now consider a different approach. Paul B. Fowler was a student at Alderson-Broaddus College when he presented the speech, "The Gift of Life," reprinted in Appendix B. In this powerful and moving speech, Paul said:

> According to the *Transplant Organ Procurement Foundation Manual,* more than 25,000 kidney transplants have been performed since 1963. Pittsburgh surgeons alone transplant over 100 kidneys per year. However, only 25 percent of kidney patients can receive a kidney from a living family member. Most must wait for several years for an organ from a donor. In the Pittsburgh area alone, over 120 patients are waiting right now for a phone call telling them a kidney has become available. Nationwide, over 5,000 people are waiting.

The contrast is clear. The person listening to our hypothetical speaker might respond, "You are entitled to your opinion, but I am also entitled to ignore it." Paul Fowler's audience *had* to listen and take his message seriously, even if it did not agree with all his recommendations. The combination of facts and testimony lifted his message above mere personal opinion. His evidence added strength, authority, and objectivity to his speech. *Evidence, therefore, is the essential ingredient in the persuasiveness of a speech.*

Because you are asking your listeners to take a risk when you present a persuasive speech, audiences will demand support for your assertions. As you do research, look for evidence that is relevant, recent, and derived from sources your audience will respect and accept.

To understand better the distinct uses of evidence, let us look briefly at each of the forms of supporting material identified in Chapter 6 and contrast the work they do in informative and persuasive speeches.

Facts and Figures

In informative speeches, facts and figures illustrate and clarify points. In persuasion, facts and figures justify the conclusions and recommendations speakers ask listeners to accept. Facts and figures are especially vital during the orientation phase of persuasion to prepare listeners for the conclusions that follow. Information is the foundation for the structure of persuasion; without it that structure will be shaky and may tumble when challenged by opposing speakers. Juli Pardell, arguing for more effective safety regulations in air travel, showed how a judicious use of facts, figures, and testimony can lay the foundation for persuasion:

> In order to fully comprehend the problem of congested skies, we can focus on a specific airport's situation. The Los Angeles airport deserves special attention.

The *Christian Science Monitor* of October 29, 1985, contends that it "exemplifies the growing congestion that decreases safety margins." Thirty other airports lie within a ninety-mile radius of Los Angeles airport, creating a hubbub of planes in the sky. Within a forty-five-mile radius, 197 planes vie for space in the skies at any given moment. Overcongestion only enhances the chance for planes to crash, such as they did last October.

By the time Juli finished presenting these and other carefully documented facts and figures, her audience felt she was justified in recommending reforms in air safety regulation. The text of her speech is reprinted in Appendix B.

Examples

In informative speeches, examples illustrate ideas and create human interest. In persuasive speeches, examples may also move listeners by exciting emotions such as sympathy, fear, or anger. Factual examples are especially useful. When you can say, "This really happened," you strengthen the power of the example. Hypothetical examples are less powerful because they did not actually occur. LaDell Patterson demonstrated the value of factual examples in a speech opposing discrimination against women in news organizations. In her speech she cited the experiences of Laura Stepp, a reporter for the *Washington Post*:

> Ms. Stepp recalled an incident that happened to her. She said while a *Washington Post* lawyer was reading one of her stories, she commented that she hoped it would land on the front page because of its importance. His reply to her was, "All you have to do is shake your little fanny and they'll put it on the front page." When she objected, he said he had no idea that the remark was offensive.

This example, one of many in LaDell's speech, helped arouse the indignation of her listeners against such behavior and prepared them emotionally for the reforms she recommended.

Narratives

Narratives serve informative speeches by illustrating the meaning of major points. In persuasive speeches, narratives create a sense of reality and build identification between listeners and the speech subject. Narratives may also carry listeners to the scene of a problem. They can engage listeners in a living drama. Kirsten Lientz illustrated this function when she opened her persuasive speech with the following narrative:

> It's a cold, icy December afternoon. You hear a distant crash, then screams, and finally the unending moan of a car horn fills the silence. You rush the short distance to the scene of the crash where you find a Ford Bronco overturned with a young woman and two small boys inside. The woman and one of the boys climb

from the wreckage unhurt; the other boy, however, is pinned between the dashboard and the roof of the car, unconscious and not breathing. Would you know what to do? Or would you stand there wishing you did? These events are real. Bob Flath saved this child with the skills he acquired at his company's first aid workshop.

After this dramatic narrative introduction, Kirsten's listeners were ready to listen to her speech urging them to take the course in first aid offered at her university.

Testimony

Testimony is even more critical in persuasive than in informative speaking. When you use testimony in a persuasive speech, you are calling upon witnesses to confirm your position. Introduce these witnesses carefully, describing their credentials. To support her call for air safety improvements, Juli Pardell cited eight authoritative sources of information. Paul Fowler in his plea for organ donors cited four reputable books. It was not just Juli and Paul speaking — it was all these sources of testimony together.

If the witnesses you cite testify against their apparent self-interest, the evidence is even more powerful. For example, if student reform leaders admit that the latest street demonstrations have gone too far or when government

---

SPEAKER'S NOTES   *Using Evidence*

1. *Have enough facts and figures.* The more you ask of listeners, the stronger your base of information must be.

2. *Find the most recent facts and figures available.* People want the latest information before they commit themselves.

3. *Emphasize factual examples to add authenticity.* Use examples to arouse emotions when appropriate.

4. *Use narratives to create identification.* Stories help the audience relate to you and your subject.

5. *Emphasize expert testimony.* Document the qualifications of the experts you use as sources.

6. *Use multiple sources and types of evidence.* Develop a blend of evidence that combines the strengths of various forms.

officials confirm that mistakes have been made, their statements provide strong evidence for opposing speakers to use.

Rely on expert testimony as your major means of support, drawing on prestige and lay testimony as secondary sources of evidence. Use prestige testimony to stress values you want listeners to embrace; use lay testimony to relate your subject to the lives of listeners. Remember that when you quote others in your speeches, you are associating yourself with them — for better or for worse. Be careful with whom you associate!

PROVING YOUR POINTS

Proofs are interpretations of evidence that provide listeners with compelling reasons for changing attitudes or behaviors.[1] The work of proofs has been studied since the Golden Age of Greece. Aristotle suggested in his *Rhetoric* that there are three types of proofs: **logos,** which emphasizes rational evidence; **pathos,** which appeals to *personal* motives and emotions; and **ethos,** based on the perceived competence, character, and attractiveness of the speaker. In our time the work of many scholars has revealed the possibility of a fourth major form of proof, which we call **mythos.**[2] Appeals to mythos rely on the *social* traditions and values important to an audience and the stories and legends that express them.

A persuasive speech rarely relies on a single type of proof. Each kind of proof brings its own special strength to a speech, and the different kinds are often even stronger in combination. Figure 14.1 summarizes the relationships between forms of evidence and types of proof.

Logos

Logos rests on a foundation of facts and figures. Proof by logos assumes that people act rationally most of the time. If they are given facts and shown how to interpret them, they will then process this information to reach an appropriate conclusion.

How does such proof use evidence to develop compelling reasons? To understand this process, we must consider how all proofs are structured. As a general rule, proofs follow a simple basic pattern:

1. a *statement* that must be proved;

2. *evidence* that supports the statement;

3. a *conclusion* that ties together the statement and evidence.

In the third paragraph of her speech, "Drinking and Driving Responsibly" (see Appendix B), Betty Nichols wants to establish the idea that driving is dangerous, despite the sense of security that some may feel in a car. To prove this

Figure 14.1

Basic Relationships between Evidence and Proof

Form of Evidence	Type of Proof
Facts and figures ◄───────► (justify as well as clarify)	Logos (builds rational appeals)
Example ◄───────► (moves as well as illustrates)	Pathos (builds emotional appeals)
Testimony ◄───────► (witnesses as well as confirms)	Ethos (rests on credibility)
Narrative ◄───────► (creates identification as well as interest)	Mythos (shows connection to culture and tradition)

statement, Betty presents these facts: "Drunk driving causes 24,000 deaths per year and 65,000 serious injuries." Although this evidence is strong, Betty recognizes that these facts alone may not be vivid enough to establish the statement forcefully in the minds of her listeners. She therefore uses a dramatic contrast to make these figures come to life: "Let's compare these numbers with the risk of being a homicide victim. We have a 1 in 150 chance of being murdered, but we have a 1 in 33 chance of being killed or crippled in an alcohol-related accident." This evidence enables her to come to this striking conclusion: "Our car, which makes us feel so safe, so secure, so powerful, can become our assassin, our coffin."

Betty's example demonstrates how proof by logos can add power to a speech, especially when it is combined with colorful language, skillful technique, and good audience contact. *The practical result is that the evidence allows the speaker not just to support a statement, but to establish it decisively in the minds of the audience.*

Pathos

Proof by pathos recognizes that we are creatures of feeling as well as thought. People usually react strongly when they feel angry, afraid, guilty, excited, or compassionate toward others. Properly engaged, these feelings can promote attitudes and advance causes. Examples and narratives are the types of evidence most often used to arouse such feelings. One classroom speaker appealed to sympathy and compassion by using herself as an example and by telling a moving story:

Why should you sign the organ donor pledge on the back of your driver's license? Let me tell you about a thirty-four-year-old teacher and mother of two — a woman whose kidneys were irreparably damaged by undiagnosed high blood pressure. For three years she went through expensive and painful dialysis treatments. She had to quit her full-time job and work as a substitute teacher because of her health. Then one night she received a call from the University Hospital. A young man had died in a motorcycle accident. His kidney was available for transplant. Since then she has regained the fullness of her life. Without that organ transplant, she would either still be on dialysis or dead. If that man — in a moment of true thoughtfulness — had not signed the back of his driver's license, *I* might not be here to speak tonight.

This introduction and the persuasive speech that followed moved many listeners. After this student finished her speech, several classmates signed the organ donor pledge on their drivers' licenses.

Appealing to emotion this way can help overcome audience inertia. Often, proof by pathos is the only way to convince people of the human dimensions of a problem or of the need for immediate action. Still, as powerful as emotional proofs may seem, they must be used with caution. If the appeal to feeling is too obvious, audiences may suspect that the speaker is trying to manipulate their feelings and may resent the effort. Appeals to negative emotions such as fear or guilt are especially tricky since they can boomerang, discrediting both the subject and speaker.

During the late spring of 1986, President Reagan presented several speeches urging Congress to approve aid to the counterrevolutionary forces in Nicaragua, whom he identified as "freedom fighters." The first of these speeches used pathos as the major form of proof, exciting fear to convince the public that Nicaragua posed a threat to the United States. In the first seven sentences of this speech, the president used nine fear appeals, ranging from a rather mild reference to the situation as a "mounting danger" to the more extreme contention that "desperate Latin peoples by the millions would begin fleeing north into the cities of the Southern United States."[3] He accused the Sandinistas of crimes ranging from drug trafficking to international terrorism and associated them with a host of villains, including the PLO, Arafat, Qaddafi, and the Ayatollah Khomeini. Examples used in the speech made the fear appeals especially vivid:

> Evangelical pastor Prudencio Baltodano found out he was on a Sandinista hit list when an army patrol asked his name. "You don't know what we do to the evangelical pastors. We don't believe in God," they told him. Pastor Baltodano was tied to a tree, struck in the forehead with a rifle butt, stabbed in the neck with a bayonet — finally, his ears were cut off, and he was left for dead.

Later that week, Congress turned down the aid President Reagan requested. Some observers felt that he had simply gone too far, that his appeals to anger and fear were too obvious, and that his conclusions strained credibility. You can learn from this example. If you use proof by pathos, be sure you can back up what you say. Bolster pathos with logos as you develop the proof pattern of your speech.

Ethos

Proof by ethos assumes that people may be persuaded by the personal influence of the source of a message. In persuasion there are two types of ethos that you must be concerned with — your personal credibility as speaker and the credibility of the sources you cite in your speech.

In Chapter 2 we discussed ways to establish your personal ethos. Here we are more concerned with the ethos of your sources of information. As audiences evaluate your evidence, they also will consider where you got your information. Listeners will evaluate your sources with respect to competence, integrity, attractiveness, and power. If the sources are highly respected, audiences will be more inclined to accept the information or opinion.

Appeals based on ethos are popular in advertising. When the credibility of Tylenol suffered after several product-tampering incidents, the company relied heavily on proof by ethos to overcome marketing problems. Its public relations people developed an aggressive advertising campaign that featured lay testimony, showing ordinary people "witnessing" that they trusted Tylenol. The company also introduced prestige and expert testimony stressing the use of Tylenol by doctors and in hospitals. Other advertisers rely on source attractiveness to sell their products. The pictures of Jim Palmer in his Jockey shorts, featured in women's magazines, have influenced many a woman to purchase them for her mate (perhaps on the outside chance that he will look just as attractive).

How might proof by ethos work in your speeches? Let's look at how Heide Nord used such proof to persuade her listeners to change their attitudes about suntanning. To support the statement "We should avoid prolonged exposure to the sun," Heide emphasized expert testimony supplemented with lay testimony:

> The April 24, 1988, *Consumer Report* of the Food and Drug Administration tells us that "Prolonged exposure to sunlight without protection is responsible for about 90 percent of skin cancer." It describes the case of Wendell Scarberry, a skin cancer patient with over a hundred surgeries behind him. Wendell talks about the seriousness of the disease and urges that we be careful about sun exposure. "You can't cure skin cancer," he says, "by just having the doc whack it off." Finally, the American Cancer Society in its pamphlet *Fry Now Pay Later* says that skin cancer most often occurs among people who spend a lot of time in the sun, especially if they have been exposed in their teens or twenties. Well, that's where most of us are right now.

This combination of expert and lay testimony empowered Heide as she urged listeners to protect themselves from prolonged exposure to the sun.

Proofs based on the testimony of reliable, competent, and trustworthy sources are extremely important in persuasive speaking. Identify your sources and stress their credentials to speak on the subject. It is also helpful if you can say that their testimony is the most recent on the subject. For maximum effect, quote key statements directly, without paraphrase.

Mythos

Proof by mythos assumes that people value their membership in a society and share in its cultural heritage. As we saw in Chapter 4, our attachment to traditions and social values can motivate our actions. *Mythos refers to the stories and sayings that illustrate the values, faith, and feelings that make up the social character of a people.* Martha Solomon, a communication scholar, has noted, "Rhetoric which incorporates mythical elements taps into rich cultural reservoirs."[4]

Proof by mythos often calls upon patriotism, cultural pride, and heroes or enemies as evidence. For example, an Olympic coach might tell a team that has fallen behind, "Don't give up! Americans have never been quitters!" You would find yourself using a similar type of proof if you asserted, "Students at WVU have too much pride to tolerate lax standards."

In the United States we are raised on political narratives, such as those that stress the hardships of the Pilgrims and Washington's winter at Valley Forge. These stories impress on us the meaning and price of religious and political freedom. We may think of our country as "a frontier" or "the melting pot of the world."[5] Proof by mythos also may be based on economic legends, such as the stories of success through hard work and thrift made popular by the Horatio Alger books of the late nineteenth century. Proof by mythos can also arise from religious narratives. The Bible provides a rich storehouse of parables, which are often used as proofs — not just in religious sermons but in political persuasion as well.[6]

Although the type of evidence most often used in proof by mythos is the narrative, stories need not be retold in their entirety each time they are invoked. Because they are familiar, allusions to them may be sufficient. In his speech accepting the Democratic presidential nomination in 1960, John F. Kennedy called on the myth of the American frontier to move Americans to action:

> The New Frontier of which I speak is not a set of promises — it is a set of challenges. It sums up not what I intend to offer the American people, but what I intend to ask of them.[7]

This proof by mythos emerged as a central theme of Kennedy's presidency. He didn't need to refer directly to the legends of Daniel Boone and Davy Crockett or to the tales of wagons pushing west to meet the dangers and challenges that lay ahead — he was able to conjure up those thoughts in his listeners with the phrase "the New Frontier."

The Western frontier is a major source of proof by mythos in our culture. The frontier offered pioneers the opportunity to begin life anew and represents such values as freedom, individualism, initiative, and courage.

How can you use proof by mythos in a classroom speech? Let us look at how Robert Owens used such proof as he urged more effective action against drug traffic in urban slums. Robert wanted to establish the statement "We must win the battle against drugs on the streets of America." He supported this statement by creating a sense of outrage in listeners over the betrayal of the American dream in urban America:

> Read *Time* magazine of September 11, 1989, and you'll meet an America you never sang about in the songs we learned in school. It's an America in which hope, faith, and dreams are nothing but a bitter memory. They call America a land of hope, but it's hard to hope when your mother is a cocaine addict on Susquehanna avenue in North Philadelphia. They call America a land of faith, but what faith can you cling to when even God seems to have abandoned the street corners to the junkies and the dealers! They call America a land of dreams, but what kind of dreams can you have when all you hear at night as you lie in bed are the curses and screams of the players in the deadly game.
>
> We might be able to redeem the hope, the faith, and the dream Americans like to talk about. But we're going to have to move in a hurry. President Bush said we've got to declare war on drugs, but we need to do more than declare war. We've got to *go* to war, and we've got to win! If we don't, the crack in the Lib-

erty Bell may soon symbolize — not freedom — but a deadly drug that is destroying the American spirit all over this land.

These appeals to a betrayed mythos justified Robert's concluding plea for a broad-based, aggressive campaign to rid America of its drug culture. Such proof by mythos is powerful when you invoke traditions that are important to listeners and when the action you advocate seems consistent with cultural values. *The unique function of proof by mythos is to help listeners understand how the speaker's recommendations fit into the total belief and behavior patterns of the group.* This gives it a special role in terms of the persuasive process model we discussed in the last chapter. It can help integrate new attitudes and action into the group's culture.

Proof by mythos is similar to proof by pathos in that it is a powerful form, capable of both great good and considerable evil. At its best it heightens our appreciation for our social identity and promotes consistency between community values and public policy. It makes us want to act in a way that is worthy of our heritage. But when it is abused, appeals to mythos can justify harm to those who may not wish to conform to group values. In our enthusiasm for the values dramatized by speakers, we may allow other important values to be ignored or subverted. Had Robert Owens followed his indignant attack on the drug culture with the conclusion that we ought to muzzle those who wish to see drugs legalized, he would have violated another important social value: freedom of speech. There is a delicate ecology among all our social values — they live together in sometimes difficult and fragile harmony. Speakers may do grave damage by their careless use of proof by mythos.

Using Proofs in Combination

Much of the art of persuasion lies in the way speakers combine proofs to make their points convincing. Two considerations are important in this regard: (1) determining which form of proof is most appropriate to your situation, and (2) understanding how the proofs can work together effectively.

Logos lays the foundation for persuasion, but different situations can increase the importance of other forms. If your situation calls for human understanding of a problem, proof by pathos, supported by moving examples, may become essential. If the situation is uncertain or confusing, proof by ethos, supported by expert testimony, may take priority. If the situation calls for realizing how traditions and values make certain actions imperative, proof by mythos, using cultural narratives, may be necessary. You should also consider how combining different forms of proofs can increase the persuasive power of a message. Although logos reassures listeners that they are dealing with facts, pathos extends the human meaning of the facts. Ethos makes an audience more confident of a speaker's recommendations, and mythos shows how these recommendations fit into the overall culture of the group. Using different forms of proofs in combination in a particular speech is usually superior to using one form alone.

FORMING ARGUMENTS

People rarely argue about matters they already agree on. Rather, the word *argument* suggests those special persuasive efforts speakers make to defend their positions or convince others about issues that are complex or undecided. An argument suggests that contending positions exist and that listeners have the power to favor one side or the other or even to resolve the dispute by vote. An argument also implies that there is an opportunity to solve a disagreement with words, rather than force.

Although the word has many meanings, we shall use "argument" to describe *an arrangement of proofs designed to form a compelling case on one side of an undecided issue.* A successful argument shapes the reasons drawn from these proofs into a justification for accepting the speaker's advice. There are three major forms of argument based on the nature of human reasoning: deduction, induction, and analogy. For each of these forms there also exists a **counterargument** or a way of weakening the argument using the refutational design discussed in the previous chapter.

Deductive Argument

Deductive argument starts with a generally accepted truth, connects some specific issue with that truth, and then draws a conclusion based on that connection. Because it usually begins on common ground, deductive argument can be useful in speeches of contention presented before reluctant audiences. Examples of deductive arguments abound in the controversies that surround us daily. One of the most interesting episodes in the ongoing public debate over abortion occurred in 1984 with the appearance of a film called *The Silent Scream.* The film confronted viewers with what it called the "grisly reality" of abortion, and even opponents acknowledged that it was powerful. The film was narrated by Dr. Bernard Nathanson, a self-confessed former abortionist who has become an antiabortion activist. At one point in his narration of the film, Dr. Nathanson pauses, addresses the camera, and argues as follows:

> Now this book is Williams' *Obstetrics,* the 16th edition, written in 1980. It is a standard textbook used throughout every medical school in the United States. The preface of this book . . . cautions us as follows: "Happily we have entered an era in which the fetus can be rightfully considered and treated as our second patient. Who would have dreamed even a few years ago that we could serve the

fetus as physician?" Traditional medical ethics and precepts command us that we must not destroy our patients, that we are pledged to preserve their lives. Now let's see what abortion does to this our second patient.[8]

The basic structure of deductive reasoning, the **syllogism,** is implied in this statement. The syllogism consists of a major premise, a minor premise, and a conclusion. The **major premise** is some general truth, in this case, *doctors should not destroy their patients.* Here, the major premise seems self-evident—who would contend with it? Note, however, that Dr. Nathanson supports it with proof by mythos, anchoring it in "traditional medical ethics and precepts." Most of his audience would have been aware of the Hippocratic Oath, a pledge taken by physicians to preserve human life. Dr. Nathanson's own ethos as a physician also helps to prove the premise.

As in most controversies, the abortion argument centers on the claim made about a related subject or situation. This claim is called the **minor premise** of the syllogism. Here the minor premise is that *the fetus is a patient.* Implied in this claim is the related idea that the fetus is a human being. The minor premise is supported with proof by pathos, relying heavily on emotional language. Phrases such as "unborn child" create identity and sympathy for the fetus. In his ongoing narration Dr. Nathanson asserts, "Beyond question the unborn child is simply another human being, another member of the human community, indistinguishable in every way from any of us."[9] By attributing human consciousness to the fetus, personification heightens the audience's identification with it. This technique gives the film its title, suggesting that the endangered fetus senses its doom and opens its mouth in a "silent scream."

The minor premise is also supported with proof by ethos drawn from our respect for physicians and the language of science. For example, Dr. Nathanson says that the humanity of the fetus is confirmed by "great new technologies, such as ultrasound imaging, electronic fetal heart monitoring, fetology, hysteroscopy, radio immuno-chemistry, and a host of other dazzling technologies which today constitute in fact the corpus of the science of fetology."[10]

When the minor premise can be proved, the deductive argument carries through to its **conclusion,** in this example: *therefore, doctors should not perform abortions.* The conclusion ties together the major and minor premises and directs the audience to what you want it to believe or do. If your listeners accept the premises as you have supported them with proof and evidence, then they should also accept the conclusion. Deductive argument works well when audiences share beliefs and values that the speaker can use as major premises for reasoning.

As we noted earlier, for each form of argument there is a counterargument. Deductive counterarguments usually concentrate on discrediting the proofs and evidence that support the major and minor premises. Their intention is to weaken the argument until it loses its power. Let us examine how Planned Parenthood, a group that supports elective abortion as a last resort in family planning, responded to *The Silent Scream.* In a PBS documentary, *The Abor-*

tion Battle, Planned Parenthood relied on the testimony of several University of Washington Medical School staff physicians.[11] The response first attacked the proof by ethos in *The Silent Scream,* suggesting that Dr. Nathanson was an irresponsible and unethical physician who misused semantic and cinematic techniques to support his position. They also charged that the use of Williams's *Obstetrics* was incomplete and taken out of context; they argued that Williams has a full chapter on abortion as well and thus recognizes its legitimacy.

Most of Planned Parenthood's counterarguments, however, were directed at the proofs by pathos supporting the minor premise. The doctors used charts to show the differences in brain development between the early fetus and the fully developed infant. Here they countered pathos with logos, arguing that there are no neural pathways in the fetal brain that can produce either the awareness of danger or the consciousness of pain. Planned Parenthood also charged *The Silent Scream* with sensationalism; the doctors argued that phrases such as "the unborn child" were verbal tricks that did not prove the humanity of the early fetus. Sophisticated technologies, they said, could show us the two-inch fetus in the womb but could not answer the moral question of when human life actually begins. Thus, the University of Washington physicians attacked both specific evidence and what they alleged were lack of adequate proofs. Finally, Planned Parenthood charged that in *The Silent Scream'*s concern for the "second patient," it ignored the medical community's responsibility to its first patient, the woman. The effect of the film, they argued, was to divert attention from what they saw as the "real" issue: the fate of living people whose lives are caught up in desperate situations.

It is clear from this extended view of deductive arguments and counterarguments that the effectiveness of proofs is vital. *Both advocates and opponents must concentrate upon the proof structure of deductive arguments.* The soundness, power, and appeal of that structure will determine whether the argument stands up under scrutiny.

Inductive Argument

Inductive argument works from specific instances to general conclusions. Because it begins with the careful gathering of observations, it is the basis of scientific investigation. It is the exact opposite of deductive argument because it begins with particulars rather than with some general truth used as a major premise. But in the best persuasive situations inductive argument works hand-in-hand with deductive argument. Inductive argument is used to develop major premises that have been verified rather than simply handed down as items of faith. The syllogisms based on premises drawn from inductive investigation may lead us to more reliable conclusions. Therefore, a combined inductive/deductive argument may provide the strongest form of reasoning.

Inductive argument is perhaps our most popular and useful form of persuasion. It is the basis for the problem-solution design. Consider, for example, how Paul Fowler used this kind of argument in his speech, "The Gift of Life."

To win support for a national organ transplant program, Paul first examines three categories of acute need: kidney, heart, and liver transplants. In each category he presents an impressive array of facts and testimony from medical experts. Indeed, the forms of proof most useful in inductive argument are logos and ethos based on expert testimony.

As he proves these categories of need, Paul builds an impressive sense of the magnitude of the problem and heightens and humanizes it with examples. Having concluded this survey of particulars, he is ready to move on to the solution phase of his speech, which includes his general recommendations.

Paul's speech demonstrates two major advantages of inductive argument: (1) *Inductive argument can build a powerful sense of need by accumulating evidence and proofs until any reasonable listener can no longer deny the urgency of the situation;* and (2) *because inductive argument is based on factual observations, its conclusions seem authentic and reliable.*

"The Gift of Life" also shows how inductive argument can carry a persuasive speech through to its conclusion. The powerful sense of need that Paul develops leads into a careful account of the barriers blocking an effective solution: inadequate funding and poor communication. He then subdivides each of these barriers into their component problems, supporting his analysis at every step of the way.

Although proof by pathos is typically secondary in most inductive arguments, Paul demonstrates how it can operate in conjunction with logos and ethos to strengthen a case. His speech concludes with a moving story told by a mother whose son's suicide became a "gift of life" to others. Proof by pathos adds the human dimension to the solid factual and authoritative base of proofs Paul has established.

In addition to its usefulness in problem-solution and categorical designs, inductive argument can also be used in refutative and comparison and contrast designs to develop speeches of contention against opposing positions. Comparison and contrast persuasive speeches proceed by pointing out particular strengths and weaknesses of the positions before drawing the general conclusion that one is superior to the other. Refutative speeches subject opposing positions to close examination, searching out specific weaknesses in the evidence supporting those positions before concluding that they are without merit.

The usefulness of inductive argument is so widespread that it seems the very foundation of reasonableness in public discussions. Perhaps it is grounded in the common sense "show-me" and "seeing-is-believing" attitudes of healthy skepticism that many people carry with them when they listen to debate over public controversies.

How can you determine if inductive argument will work in your persuasive speech? The major test of such argument is the adequacy of your observations to support the conclusion drawn from them. Have you read and observed enough? Are your observations recent and reliable? Are you objective enough to see the situation clearly? Are your observations representative of the situation, reflecting the usual rather than the unusual? Do you draw the right conclusion? Do you carefully qualify the strength of your conclusion with words such as "possibly," "probably," or "certainly"? These are the kinds of questions that critical listeners and counterarguers will ask as they put your inductive argument to the test. Ask them first of yourself, and your argument should withstand scrutiny.

Argument by Analogy

Argument by analogy creates a strategic perspective on a subject by relating it to a similar situation in a way that is helpful to your case. To connect the subject with the parallel situation you may wish to use similes or metaphors. For example, in a speech urging the values of study, you could argue analogically that study "is *like* athletic training. It takes hard work and discipline" or that "when you study, you take flight. You see things that you could not see before." If listeners accept these analogies as you prove the points of connection, they may then accept your conclusions. Argument by analogy is the form we encounter in the analogy design for persuasive speeches.

One type of argument by analogy associates your subject with something that already has strong positive or negative feelings attached to it. Another type associates a plan of action with one that has already worked or not worked, depending on your purpose. In the debate over our nation's drug policy, for instance, those who favor the legalization of "recreational" drug use frequently base their arguments on an analogy to Prohibition.[12] They contend that the constitutional amendment that made liquor sales illegal caused more problems than it solved, that it led to the rise of a vast criminal network that provided Americans with the alcoholic beverages they desired. Our efforts to outlaw recreational drugs, they suggest, have had the same dire consequences.

In developing their argument by analogy, prolegalization advocates claim that it is impossible to ban a human desire — to do so merely encourages contempt for the law. Moreover, they assert, legalizing drugs would help put the international drug dealers out of business just as the relegalization of alcohol helped bring about the demise of the gangsters of the 1930s. They further suggest that legalization would reduce the corruption of public officials, as happened after the repeal of Prohibition. Finally, they argue, if drug sales were legal it would be easier to control the quality of drugs, thus reducing the danger to users (parallel to the health problems associated with bootleg whiskey during Prohibition).

As this example shows, argument by analogy begins with the identification of strategic points of comparison between similar situations. These comparisons are then supported with evidence and proofs. Those making counterarguments emphasize the dissimilarity between the compared situations and try to invalidate the evidence and proofs. Opponents to legalizing drugs claim that there are many important differences between drugs and alcohol.[13] Alcohol, they say, is not as addictive for casual users as heroin or cocaine. The antilegalization forces contend that the result of legalization would be to multiply the drug problem, not reduce it. Moreover, they suggest that because drug abusers are sometimes prone to paranoia and violence, the cost to society would be magnified. Finally, the antilegalization proponents argue, the campaign against drugs can point to some successes, whereas enforcement of the Prohibition laws was a disaster from the outset. Thus, the public debate rages on, argument clashing with counterargument.

What makes argument by analogy work? This type of argument may be similar to induction, since we try to gain insight through careful observation. However, analogy differs from induction in that our observations are concentrated on *one* similar situation rather than ranging across many. This means that although argument by analogy may seem more concrete and more interesting than inductive argument, it also can be less reliable. When using argument by analogy, be certain that the critical similarities outweigh the dissimilarities.

The Importance of Defining Terms

All of the argumentative forms we have identified depend on the adequate definition of terms. Have you ever found yourself in a heated discussion with a friend, only to find out later that you were not even talking about the same thing? Socrates suggested that all persuasive messages should start with definitions of terms, so that speakers and listeners could share understanding from the beginning. The advice is sound. Opening definitions clarify what you mean, reveal your intentions, and show the audience how you perceive a subject. When the speaker and audience come from different backgrounds, careful definitions are even more imperative.

Many problems of definition, however, arise more from fundamental issues than from semantic misunderstandings. Is alcohol a drug? Is the fetus a human being? Such questions often lead speakers to argue that a concept should have a certain *ethical* definition. Emmeline Pankhurst, an early British feminist, relied on such argument in the following excerpt:

> We women, in trying to make our case clear, always have to make a part of our argument, and urge upon men in our audience the fact — a very simple fact — that women are human beings. It is quite evident you do not all realize we are human beings or it would not be necessary to argue with you that women may, suffering from intolerable injustice, be driven to adopt revolutionary methods.[14]

This sort of argument relies heavily on proof by pathos. In the 1968 Memphis sanitation strike leading to the assassination of Dr. Martin Luther King, Jr., the workers often marched carrying signs that read, "I am a Man." This simple-looking statement was actually one small part of a complex ethical argument. The strikers, all of whom were black, were claiming that they were not treated like men, either in social or economic terms. This example suggests that definition itself can sometimes be highly compressed persuasion, calling on listeners to fill in its meaning for themselves.

SPEAKER'S NOTES   *Developing Powerful Arguments*

1. Deductive arguments are effective when you begin with an accepted truth as a premise, then lead your audience to the desired conclusion.

2. Deductive argument requires that you supply strong proofs and evidence for your minor premise.

3. In inductive argument you must base your conclusions on an authoritative array of representative observations.

4. You can build inductive arguments through the use of categorical, problem-solution, comparison and contrast, and refutative designs of persuasion.

5. In argument by analogy, you create a strategic perspective on a subject by relating it to a similar situation.

6. Argument by analogy may be less reliable than inductive argument.

7. The effectiveness of all arguments depends on adequate definition of basic terms to achieve clarity.

It is not easy to resolve such problems of definition, but at least we as listeners can interpret them for what they often are: *fundamental issues at the very heart of controversy.* As speakers, we should be careful that our key terms are as clear as they can be from the outset.

AVOIDING DEFECTIVE PERSUASION

It takes hard work to prepare a persuasive speech — analyzing your audience, researching your topic, and planning your strategy. Do *not* ruin the effectiveness of this work or cause listeners to question your credibility by committing **fallacies,** or errors in persuasion. These mistakes may crop up at any point in the persuasive process: in the evidence you use, the proofs you develop, or the reasoning of your arguments. There are also fallacies that are particular to some of the specific persuasive speech designs discussed in the previous chapter. In this section we identify some of these major errors so that you are able to guard against them, as both a producer and consumer of persuasive messages.

Defective Evidence

Evidence is defective when the speaker misuses facts, statistics, or testimony.

Misuse of Fact.   A major misuse of evidence involves the confusion of fact and opinion. As we noted earlier, a fact is verifiable information. An opinion is a personal interpretation of information: a statement of belief, feeling, attitude, or value. "The university lost $200,000 last year" is a statement of fact. Anyone can look at the records and verify it. "The university is mismanaging its budget" is a statement of opinion, a personal interpretation that may or may not be correct. Opinions can be useful in persuasive speeches, but treating an opinion as though it were a fact, or a fact as though it were an opinion, can be the source of many problems. It can make you seem to claim too much or too little and can raise real questions about your competence and ethics.

A second misuse of factual evidence is the **slippery slope fallacy,** which assumes that once something happens it establishes an inevitable trend leading to disastrous results. During the Vietnam War government officials often argued that if Vietnam fell to the Communists, all of Southeast Asia would be lost. In the slippery slope fallacy it is not logic that drives the prediction of events, but rather our darkest fears.

Another abuse of factual evidence occurs when irrelevant material is introduced into an argument to divert attention from the issues. This technique — called the **red herring** — is often used when speakers are not comfortable with the actual issue. Usually the diverting material is so sensational or emotional that it confuses listeners about the real issue. In 1952 Senator Richard M. Nixon, then candidate for vice president, spoke on national television to refute charges that he had used $18,000 of campaign contributions for personal expenses. In this speech Nixon diverted attention by talking about his dog Checkers, a gift that he would not return, he said, because his children loved it. Nixon also related his financial life history in terms of what he owned and what he owed, matters at best vaguely related to the $18,000. He then launched a counterattack on the Democrats, accusing his opponent of having his wife on the payroll and suggesting that Adlai Stevenson, the Democratic presidential candidate, was "soft on communism." These techniques were red herrings because they diverted attention from what happened to the $18,000.

Statistical Fallacies.   Audiences are often intimidated by numbers. We've all been taught that "figures don't lie" without being advised that "liars figure." Speakers sometimes exploit our weakness by creating statistical deceptions. For example, consider the **myth of the mean,** or the "illusion of the average." If you've ever vacationed in the mountains, you are well aware that a stream may have an "average depth" of six inches, yet a person could drown in one of its deep pools. The Chamber of Commerce reports that the "average July temperature" in Memphis is eighty-five degrees, but this includes the low nighttime as well as the high daytime temperatures and omits any consideration of humidity. A speaker could tell you not to worry about poverty in Plattsville because the average income is well above the poverty level. Yet this average could be obtained because a few families are very wealthy whereas the majority have incomes below the poverty level. Such "average-income" information creates an illusion of well-being that does not reflect reality. Averages can be useful to summarize important statistical information, but be sure they do not hide the reality of a situation.

Another statistical fallacy involves the use of **incomparable percentages.** It is misleading to compare percentages *when the bases of comparison are unequal.* We once heard a speaker argue, "The gross national product of the United States is growing at an annual rate of only 6 percent, while that of the Soviet Union is growing at a rate of 14 percent. Therefore, the Russians are rapidly overtaking us." The speaker had fallen prey to misinterpretation: a 6 percent rise in the American GNP represented more actual economic growth than a 14 percent rise in the Russian GNP: 6 percent of $500 billion is greater than 14 percent of $200 billion. It was not the Americans who were losing ground! Figure 14.2 illustrates these defective uses of facts and figures.

Defective Testimony.

There are many ways in which testimony can be abused. Speakers misuse testimony when they omit the date a statement was made to hide the fact that the evidence is obsolete. Speakers deceive us when they leave out important facts about their experts, intimidating us instead with impressive titles such as "*Dr.* Michael Jones of *Harvard University* tells us that smoking does not harm health." What the speaker *doesn't* reveal is that Dr. Jones was talking (erroneously) about pipe smoking, or that he is a history professor, or that he was writing public relations material for the Tobacco Growers Association. Speakers also abuse testimony when they cite words that are not representative of a person's position but are taken out of context. As we noted in Chapter 6, prestige and lay testimony can be misused if they replace expert opinion when facts must be established. Finally, the "voice of the people" can be easily misrepresented, depending on *which* people you choose to quote.

Inappropriate Evidence.

Other abuses occur when speakers deliberately use one form of evidence when they should be using another. For example, you might use facts and figures when examples would bring us closer to the human truth of a situation. Welfare statistics are sometimes misused in this way. It is as though the speaker preferred to talk about poverty in the abstract, distancing listeners from its concrete reality. On the other hand, speakers may give examples to arouse emotions when what is needed is the dispassionate picture of a situation established by facts and figures. Testimony is abused when it is intended to compensate for weak or inadequate facts. Narratives may also be used inappropriately. Calling someone a "Robin Hood who steals from the rich to give to the poor" has been used to justify more than one crime.

Figure 14.2
Examples of Defective Evidence

1. **Slippery Slope:**
   "an event will become
   a trend"

2. **Red Herring:**
   "diversion of attention"

3. **Myth of the Mean:**
   "averages can create
   illusions"

4. **Incomparable Percentages:**
   "unequal bases make for
   defective comparisons"

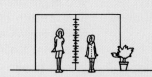

Defective Proofs

Any form of proof can have defective relationships among its statements, evidence, and conclusions. Proof by ethos seems the most prone to misuse. This kind of abuse can occur when persuaders try to discredit a position by presenting false images of opponents. Such images are especially misleading when they are built on derogatory stereotypes. In a recent environmental dispute, for instance, one side attacked the other by charging that its supporters were "little old ladies in tennis shoes" and "outside agitators." Not to be outdone, the opposition countered that its opponents were "rapists of public parkland."[15] Such attacks are known as the fallacy of **argument *ad hominem,*** an attack not on the issues but on the people who advance them.

Proof by ethos can also be abused when speakers overuse it — when they try to intimidate listeners by citing an overwhelming number of authorities and neglect to present information and good reasons for accepting their claims. Avoid such practices in your own persuasive efforts.

The final abuse of proofs we shall mention occurs when persuaders simply do not present them, claiming what they have not really established. Often this abuse is disguised by the colorful use of language, so that the words themselves *seem* to establish the conclusion. Some antiabortion advocates may be guilty of this practice when they refer to the fetus as the "unborn child," without bothering to address first the difficult moral question of when human life actually begins. President Reagan's description of the Nicaraguan contras as "freedom fighters" substituted the semantic power of the ideograph "freedom" for effective proof of the contras' actual character and intentions. This fallacy is called **begging the question.**

Defective Arguments

Major fallacies may be found in all forms of argument.

Errors of Deduction.   Because the major premise is the foundation of deductive reasoning, an argument can be only as good as the premise is sound. Therefore, each word in the major premise should be carefully considered when you design your argument. If the major premise suffers from **categorical imprecision,** or vagueness in its key terms, the entire argument is in jeopardy. Consider the speaker who began an argument based on the premise "college athletes are dumb." This speaker was instantly in trouble. When his speech was over, his listeners assailed him with questions. How did he define *athletes*? Was he talking about intercollegiate or intramural athletes? Did he include women as well as men? How about the tennis players? What did he mean by *dumb*? Was he talking about grade-point average? Was he referring to the athletes' graduation rate or to the quality of their conversation? Did he have sufficient evidence to support such an unqualified premise? It is safe to say that

The 1989 publication of Salman Rushdie's *Satanic Verses* was controversial. When arguing, avoid contradictions like the one characterizing this protest, in which freedom of speech was used to support censorship.

the speaker did not persuade too many people that day. To avoid such a fiasco, be sure that you know what you mean by each word in your major premise and that you have evidence to support what each word claims.

Another type of deductive error involves the **confusion of probability and certainty.** Suppose a friend from the Tau Alpha sorority calls you to set up a blind date. If the premise "Tau Alphas are attractive" holds about 90 percent of the time and if you are about 90 percent certain that your blind date is a Tau Alpha, then your assumption that your date will be attractive must be qualified by two factors of uncertainty. There is a 10 percent chance that your date is not a Tau Alpha, and even if she is, there is another 10 percent chance she is not one of the attractive ones. If you assert probabilities as though they were certainties, you are guilty of a reasoning error. It is better to use qualifiers that point out the uncertainty: "There is a *good chance* that my date will be attractive." If you point out the uncertainty in advance, you may not lose the audience's trust if your prediction does not come true.

Assumed causation is a common error that can creep into the reasoning of a speech. This fallacy starts with the assumption that if one thing comes before another in time, the first must be the cause of the second. In formal logic this type of error is known as the ***post hoc ergo propter hoc* fallacy** (after the event, therefore the effect of the event). This fallacy confuses association with causation. It is the basis of many superstitious beliefs. The same people who wear their lucky boots and shirts to ball games may also argue that we should have a tax cut because the last time we had one we avoided war, increased employment, and reduced crime. What a speaker must do is demonstrate that events are causally connected, not just make the assertion.

The final deductive error we shall discuss is the **fallacy of non sequitur** (it does not follow). A non sequitur error occurs when the minor premise is not related to the major premise or when the conclusion does not necessarily follow from the relationship between these premises. For example, if from the major premise "Kappa Taus are attractive" and the minor premise "John is attractive" one draws the conclusion "John is a Kappa Tau," the result is a non sequitur. (The minor premise is related to the wrong term in the major premise: not all attractive people are Kappa Taus!) If from the same faulty premises one drew the conclusion "therefore, we should go to a drive-in movie," this would be another non sequitur. Even if the premises were correct, they would not justify that particular conclusion.

Errors of Induction.

A common error in inductive reasoning is a **hasty generalization,** based on insufficient or nonrepresentative observations. Suppose you announced: "Eighty percent of our students are in favor of abolishing the foreign language requirement." To determine whether this claim is justified, we would have to consider the supporting evidence: how extensive it is and how it was obtained. If you questioned ten students on the way to class, we might well challenge the adequacy of your sample. If you surveyed only freshman business majors (who may not be required to take a foreign language), we would question the representativeness of your sample. Even when and where you collected your supporting data could create a problem. If you surveyed students outside the "drop" office on the last day for dropping and adding classes, your results could well differ from what you might obtain in the language department lounge early in the semester.

Another type of inductive error involves **contamination of the conclusion** by the inclusion of irrelevant or emotionally loaded words. For example, suppose you concluded, "Eighty percent of the *immature* students on campus favor abolishing the foreign language requirement." Do you mean that all students on the campus are immature? Does the claim cover all students or *only* the immature ones? Are you implying that "mature" students have a different opinion? Are you suggesting that being against the foreign language requirement is a sign of immaturity? The intrusion of just one ill-considered word can ruin an entire argument and waste the time you have put into your speech. Proof by mythos is especially susceptible to such abuse, for it can easily assume more importance in the conclusion of an inductive argument than it actually deserves. A conclusion such as "Be *patriotic!* Support the *American way of life!* Speak out against gun control!" might illustrate such abuse.

Defective Analogy.

A final flaw that can ruin an argument is a **faulty analogy,** which occurs when a speaker tries to draw a comparison between things that are dissimilar in some important ways. When the critical points of dissimilarity outweigh the similarities, the analogy is in trouble. Let us assume, for instance, that you have transferred from a college with 1,500 students to a university with 15,000 students. You plan a speech proposing a change in campus security measures. Should you argue by analogy that because such a plan worked well at the college, it could also solve the security problems of the university? The wisdom of that tactic depends on the essential points of similarity and dissimilarity between the two schools. Is the size difference important? Are the crime problems similar? Is one school located in an urban, the other in a rural, setting? Are the students from the same social and economic backgrounds? Dissimilarity of any or several of these factors could raise doubts about the analogy. You would have to overcome these doubts with proofs and evidence, point by point, to secure audience acceptance of the analogy.

Fallacies Related to Particular Designs

In addition to fallacies that contaminate evidence, proof, and argument, there are at least two major fallacies that affect the designs of persuasive speeches. The first of these, **either-or thinking,** occurs mainly in problem-solution speeches urging action. The fallacy occurs when the speaker informs listeners that they have only two options—one desirable, the other not. "Give me liberty or give me death!"—though a dramatic statement of American mythos—illustrates this kind of fallacy. In either-or thinking, the speaker blinds listeners to all other options, especially to compromise or creative alternatives not yet considered. Perhaps there *are* only two options for listeners, but as speaker you have a special obligation to investigate a problem thoroughly before you decide this. After all, you assume responsibility for the fate of listeners when you advise them how to behave.

The **straw man fallacy** is most often found in speeches of contention. This fallacy consists of understating, distorting, or otherwise misrepresenting the position of opponents for the sake of refutation. Extreme controversy seems to invite this kind of fallacy. In the abortion debate, cries of "women-haters" and "baby-killers" sometimes rise from the contending positions. Such rhetoric creates an atmosphere of unreality in which it is often impossible to consider opposing positions judiciously. As a persuasive speaker, you should represent an opposing position fairly and fully when you seek to refute it. Only then will intelligent members of the audience respect you and your arguments. The straw man fallacy is rightly regarded as an implicit admission of weakness and desperation and can only damage what may well be a legitimate case.

Persuasion is constantly threatened by flaws and deception. In a world of competing views, we often see human nature revealed in its petty as well as its finer moments. As you plan and present your arguments, be on guard against fallacies.

Persuasion relies on an integrated system of evidence, proof, and argument for its effectiveness.

Using Evidence Effectively. *Evidence* is supporting material used in persuasion. Facts and figures must justify positions as well as clarify points. Examples often must move listeners as well as illustrate the meaning of ideas. Narratives attempt to create identification as well as to arouse interest. Testimony calls upon witnesses to support a position and requires careful documentation. When you use evidence, strive for recent facts and figures, emphasize factual examples, engage listeners through narrative, and rely primarily on expert testimony.

Proving Your Points. *Proofs* are interpretations of evidence that provide listeners with compelling reasons for changing attitudes or behaviors. The forms of proof are logos, pathos, ethos, and mythos. *Logos* focuses on rational appeals such as facts and figures. *Pathos* stirs personal feelings through the use of examples. *Ethos* makes persuasion credible when the speaker makes a favorable impression and cites effective testimony. *Mythos* relates a subject to the culture and tradition of a group through its narratives. Proofs contain a statement, evidence to support the statement, and a conclusion drawn from the statement and evidence. Proofs are often stronger when used in combination in a particular speech.

Forming Arguments. An *argument* attempts to arrange proofs and evidence into a compelling case on one side of an undecided issue. Arguments may be based on deductive, inductive, and analogical patterns of reasoning. *Deductive argument* develops in the form of a *syllogism,* which includes a *major premise, minor premise,* and *conclusion.* Each of these elements may require supporting evidence and proof. *Inductive argument* begins with observations and draws a general conclusion from them. *Argument by analogy* draws conclusions based on critical points of comparison between similar situations. All three forms of argument are dependent on adequate definition of key terms for their effectiveness.

Avoiding Defective Persuasion. Mistakes and faults in persuasion are common. When they are unintentional, they can ruin the effectiveness of a speech and the credibility of a speaker. When they seem deliberate, they raise doubts about the speaker's ethics. Evidence can be defective when the speaker misuses facts, statistics, and testimony. Common errors include the confusion of fact with opinion; the *slippery slope fallacy,* which assumes that a single instance will establish a trend; and the *red herring,* the use of irrelevant material to divert attention. Statistical fallacies include the *myth of the mean,* in which averages create illusions that hide reality, and *incomparable percentages,* which attempt comparisons when the bases of the comparisons are unequal. Evidence can also be used inappropriately, featuring facts and figures when the situation calls for example, example when the audience needs facts and figures, testimony to hide the weakness of information, and narrative to justify unethical behavior.

Among all the problems that can plague proofs, those surrounding proof by ethos seem especially troubling. Proof by ethos is defective when it depends on a negative stereotype to discredit an opposing position. Likewise, *argument ad hominem,* or name calling, can divert attention from the issues to those who present them. In such cases disgusted audiences may decide not to trust *any* persuasive efforts in the situation.

Fallacies are common in all forms of argument. *Categorical imprecision* occurs in deductive reasoning when the wording of the major premise has not been carefully considered. Another error occurs when probability is passed off as certainty. Assumed causation, the *post hoc ergo propter hoc fallacy,* confuses association with causation. It can lead speakers to assert that one thing causes another when actually it only comes before it in time. The *fallacy of non sequitur* occurs when conclusions are drawn improperly from the premises that precede them. Inductive reasoning can suffer from a *hasty generalization,* drawn from insufficient or nonrepresentative observations. *Contamination of the conclusion* occurs when irrelevant and emotional language is used. Argument by analogy is defective when important dissimilarities outweigh similarities.

Either-or thinking can be a special problem in speeches calling for action. This fallacy reduces audience options to only two, one advocated by the speaker, the other undesirable. When speeches of contention understate, distort, or misrepresent an opposing position, they commit the *straw man fallacy.*

TERMS TO KNOW

evidence
proofs
argument
logos
pathos
ethos
mythos
counterargument
deductive argument
syllogism

major premise
minor premise
conclusion
inductive argument
argument by analogy
fallacy
slippery slope fallacy
red herring
myth of the mean
incomparable percentages
argument *ad hominem*
begging the question
categorical imprecision
confusion of probability and
   certainty
post hoc ergo propter hoc fallacy
fallacy of non sequitur
hasty generalization
contamination of the conclusion
faulty analogy
either-or thinking
straw man fallacy

DISCUSSION

1. Find examples of effective and ineffective uses of testimony in the student speeches in Appendix B. Are the sources carefully documented? Are expert, prestige, and lay forms of testimony used appropriately? How might these have been used more effectively?

2. Bring to class examples of advertisements that demonstrate the four basic types of persuasive proof: logos, pathos, ethos, and mythos. Discuss the ways in which these proofs are used and why you think they are or are not effective.

3. Look for examples of the misuse of evidence, proof, and argument in newspaper and magazine advertising. In your judgment, do these misuses reflect badly on the credibility of the product? Do the ads seem effective nonetheless?

4. Look for examples of defective persuasion in the letters-to-the-editor section of your local newspaper. Bring them to class for discussion.

APPLICATION

1. Find a news story that interests you. Taking the information provided, (1) show how you might use this information as evidence in a persuasive speech, (2) structure a proof that would make use of this evidence, and (3) design an argument in which this proof might be functional.

2. In *The Ethics of Rhetoric,* Richard Weaver observed that frequent arguments over the definitions of basic terms in the premises of syllogisms are a sign of division within a social group. Look for examples of public argument over the definition of one of the following terms:

   a. liberty
   b. national defense
   c. education
   d. abortion
   e. gun control
   f. prayer in the school
   g. peace

   Do the arguments reflect the kind of social division Weaver suggested?

NOTES

1. Karl R. Wallace, "The Substance of Rhetoric: Good Reasons," *Quarterly Journal of Speech* 49 (1963): 239–49; and Walter R. Fisher, "Toward a Logic of Good Reasons," *Quarterly Journal of Speech* 64 (1978): 376–84.
2. Representative of this scholarship is Ernest G. Bormann, "Fantasy and Rhetorical Vision: The Rhetorical Criticism of Social Reality," *Quarterly Journal of Speech* 58 (1972): 396–407; Walter R. Fisher, "Narration as a Human Communication Paradigm: The Case of Public Moral Argument," *Communication Monographs* 59 (1984): 1–22; Michael C. McGee, "In Search of 'The People': A Rhetorical Alternative," *QJS* 61 (1975): 235–49; Michael Osborn, "Rhetorical Depiction," in *Form, Genre, and the Study of Political Discourse,* ed. Herbert W. Simons and Aram A. Aghazarian (Columbia: University of South Carolina Press, 1986), pp. 79–107; and Janice Hocker Rushing, "The Rhetoric of the American Western Myth," *Communication Monographs* 50 (1983): 14–32.
3. "Nicaragua," *Weekly Compilation of Presidential Documents,* 24 Mar. 1986, p. 371.
4. Martha Solomon, "The 'Positive Woman's' Journey: A Mythic Analysis of the Rhetoric of STOP ERA," *Quarterly Journal of Speech* 65 (1979): 262–74.
5. Rushing, "The Rhetoric of the American Western Myth," 14–32.
6. Roderick P. Hart, *The Political Pulpit* (West Lafayette, Ind.: Purdue University Press, 1977).
7. John Fitzgerald Kennedy, "Acceptance Address, 1960," in *The Great Society: A Sourcebook of Speeches,* ed. Glenn R. Capp (Belmont, Calif.: Dickenson Publishing Company, Inc., 1969), p. 14.

8. *The Silent Scream,* comp. Donald S. Smith and ed. Don Tanner (Anaheim, Calif.: American Portrait Films Books, 1985), p. 16.
9. Smith and Tanner, p. 14.
10. Smith and Tanner, p. 13.
11. Public Broadcasting System, *The Abortion Battle,* 1985.
12. Lisa M. Ross, "Buckley Says Drug Attack Won't Work," *Commercial Appeal* (Memphis, Tenn.), 14 Sept. 1989, p. B-2.
13. Mortimer B. Zuckerman, "The Enemy Within," *U.S. News & World Report,* 11 Sept. 1989, p. 91.
14. "When Civil War Is Waged by Women," in *Feminism: The Essential Historic Writings,* ed. Miriam Schneir (New York: Random House, 1972), pp. 297–98.
15. Michael M. Osborn, "The Abuses of Argument," *Southern Speech Communication Journal* 49 (1983): 1–11.

[People] who celebrate . . . are fused with each other and fused with all things in nature.

— *ERNST CASSIRER*

15

CEREMONIAL SPEAKING

This Chapter Will Help You

◆ appreciate the importance of ceremonial speaking.

◆ use the techniques of identification and magnification in ceremonial speeches.

◆ understand the purposes and procedures for speeches of tribute, acceptance, introduction, and inspiration.

◆ prepare a toast or an after-dinner speech.

Your college has just reached a great moment in its history. An ambitious fund-raising campaign to create scholarships and attract outstanding teachers, researchers, artists, and lecturers has been successfully concluded. A big celebration banquet is planned. As the leader of student volunteers who spent many hours telephoning for contributions, you have been invited to be master of ceremonies. In this capacity you are likely to both give and hear many kinds of speeches: speeches of tribute, speeches accepting awards, speeches of introduction, speeches of inspiration, and after-dinner speeches. During the evening there will be times of seriousness and moments of hilarity. They are all part of what we call ceremonial speaking.

I t is easy to underestimate the importance of ceremonial speaking. After all, informative speaking shares knowledge, and persuasive speaking affects our attitudes and actions. In comparison, ceremonial speaking, with its occasional moments of humor or inspiration, may not seem that significant.

Only when we consider what is going on beneath the surface does the true importance of ceremonial speaking emerge. **Ceremonial speaking** stresses the sharing of identities and values that unites people into communities. The philosopher John Dewey observed that people "live in a community in virtue of the things which they have in common; and communication is the way in which they come to possess things in common. What they must have in common . . . are aims, beliefs, aspirations, knowledge — a common understanding. . . ."[1] It is ceremonial speaking that celebrates and reinforces our common aims, beliefs, and aspirations. In so doing, ceremonial speaking helps people gain an appreciation of themselves through awareness of their common heritage.

Ritual and ceremony are important to all groups because they draw people together.[2] Ceremonial speaking imprints the meaning of a community on its members by providing larger-than-life pictures of their identity and ideals.[3] It answers four basic questions: "Who are we?" "Why are we?" "What have we accomplished?" and "What can we become together?" As it answers these questions, ceremonial speaking provides people with a sense of purpose and helps create an "ordered, meaningful cultural world."[4]

There is also a very practical purpose served by ceremonial speaking. As our opening example indicates, ceremonies put the spotlight on the speaker. As you conduct the college's celebration of its fund-raising campaign as master of ceremonies, others will be looking at you and thinking, "Wouldn't she make a good student body president?" or "Wouldn't he be a fine candidate for city council?" From the time of Aristotle, scholars have recognized that ceremonial speaking puts leadership on display.

Ceremonial speeches also serve to establish standards for action or provide the ethical, moral basis for future arguments.[5] Because such speaking centers on the values, beliefs, and attitudes within the traditions of a community, it contributes to the integration phase of persuasion described in Chapter 13. In this chapter we discuss the techniques and major forms of ceremonial speaking.

TECHNIQUES OF CEREMONIAL SPEAKING

Many of the techniques of ceremonial speaking are simply variations on those we have already discussed. Two techniques, however, are basic to all forms of ceremonial speaking and deserve special attention: identification and magnification.

Identification

We have already defined *identification* as the creation of close feelings among the members of the audience and between the audience and the speaker. Because the function of ritual and ceremony is to draw people closer together, identification is the heart of ceremonial speaking. Without it, ceremonial speaking cannot achieve its desired effects. Speakers may promote identification through the use of narratives, through the recognition of heroes, or through a renewal of group commitment.

Use of Narrative.   Ceremonial speaking is the time for reliving shared golden moments. For example, if you were preparing a speech for the fundraising celebration, you could recall certain things that happened during those long evenings when student volunteers were making their calls. You might remember moments of discouragement, followed by other moments of triumph, when the contributions were especially large or meaningful. Your story would reflect the meaning of the celebration and would be a tribute both to donors and to the student volunteers who endured frustration and discouragement on their way to success.

Recognition of Heroes.   As you speak of the trials and triumphs of fund raising, you may want to single out those who made outstanding contributions, but be careful! If hard work was performed by many, you run the risk of leaving out someone who deserves recognition. This omission could create resentment, a divisive feeling that defeats identification. Therefore, *recognize specific individuals only when they have made truly unusual contributions or when they are representative.* You might say, for instance, "Let me tell you about one student, Mary Tyrer. She is just one of the many who for the last two months have spent night after night on these phones — talking, coaxing, winning friends for our school, and raising thousands of dollars in contributions. Mary, and all the others like you, we salute you!"

Renewal of Group Commitment.   Ceremonial speaking is a time both for celebrating accomplishments and for renewing commitment. Share with your listeners a vision of what the future can be like for your college if their commitment continues. Plead with them not to be satisfied with present accomplishments, great as they are. Renew their identity as an action group moving toward even greater goals. Now is *not* the time to present specific new programs and challenges — after all, there is a time for relaxation and celebration as well as a time for action. But you should at least leave listeners thinking about the brighter future they are shaping.

In his "First Inaugural Address," delivered on the eve of the Civil War, Abraham Lincoln used the technique of identification in an effort to reunite the nation.

> I am loth to close. We are not enemies, but friends. We must not be enemies. Though passion may have strained, it must not break our bonds of affection. The mystic chords of memory, stretching from every battle-field, and patriot grave, to every living heart and hearthstone, all over this broad land, will yet swell the chorus of the Union, when again touched, as surely they will be, by the better angels of our nature.[6]

Magnification

In the *Rhetoric* Aristotle noted that by selecting certain features of a person or event and dwelling on them, we can magnify them until they fill the minds of listeners and seem to characterize the subject. This technique is called **magnification,** and its effect is to emphasize certain values the selected features represent. For example, imagine that you are preparing a speech honoring Jesse Owens's incredible track and field accomplishments in the 1936 Olympic Games. In your research you come up with a variety of facts, such as:

- He had a headache the day he won the medal in the long jump.

- He had suffered from racism in America.

- He did not like the food served at the Olympic training camp.

- He won his four gold medals in front of Adolf Hitler, who was preaching the racial superiority of the Germans.

- Some friends did not want him to run for the United States.

- After his victories he returned to further discrimination in America.

If you used all this information, your speech might seem aimless. Which of these items should you magnify, and how should you proceed? To make your selection among the data you have collected, you need to know what themes are best to develop when you are magnifying the actions of a person. These themes include the following:

1. The person must seem to overcome great obstacles.

2. The accomplishment must be unusual.

3. The performance must be superior.

4. The person's motives must be pure, not selfish.

5. The accomplishment must benefit society.

As you consider these themes and your purpose, it becomes clear which of the items concerning Jesse Owens you should magnify and how you should go about it. To begin, you would stress that Owens *had to overcome obstacles* such as racism in America to make the Olympic team. Then you would point out that his *accomplishment was unusual,* that no one else had ever won four gold medals in Olympic track and field competition. Moreover, *the performance was superior,* resulting in world records that lasted many years. Because Owens received no material gain from his victories, *his motives were pure,* his performance driven solely by personal qualities such as courage, competitiveness, and determination. Finally, you would demonstrate that because his victories repudiated Hitler's racist ideology, causing the Nazi leader public humiliation, *Owens's accomplishments benefited our society.* The overall effect would be to magnify the meaning of Jesse Owens's great performances both for himself and for his nation.

In addition to these basic themes, magnification also uses certain tools of language to create dramatic word pictures. *Metaphor* and *simile* can magnify a subject through creative associations, such as, "He was a whirlwind, roaring down the track in search of world records." *Anaphora* can also help magnify a subject by repeating key words in a certain order, until these words become representative of the subject. If you were to say of Mother Theresa, "Whenever there was hurt, she was there. Whenever there was hunger, she was there. Whenever there was human need, she was there," you would be magnifying her dedication and selflessness. This technique should make those qualities seem to resonate in the minds of listeners.

Magnification often favors certain speech designs over others. Comparison and contrast designs promote magnification by making selected features stand out. For example, you might contrast the purity of Owens's motives with those of today's well-paid athletes. Historical designs enhance magnification by dramatizing certain events as stories unfold over time. The causation design serves magnification when the selected features are emphasized as the powerful causes of certain effects: Jesse Owens's victories, a speaker might say, *caused* Nazi propaganda to lose its appeal for many people.

Whatever designs ceremonial speeches use, it is important that *they build in effect until they conclude.* Speakers should save their best stories, their most telling points, until the end of the speech. Ceremonial speeches must never dwindle to a conclusion.

Types of Ceremonial Speeches

Ceremonial speeches include the speech of tribute (including the toast), acceptance speeches, the speech of introduction, the speech of inspiration, and the after-dinner speech.

The Speech of Tribute

If you had developed a speech honoring Jesse Owens's Olympic victories, you would have prepared a **speech of tribute.** The speech of tribute, which may center on a person or on events, recognizes and celebrates accomplishments. For example, you might be called on to honor a former teacher at a retirement ceremony.

Accomplishments and events are usually celebrated for two basic reasons. First, they are important in themselves: the influence of the teacher may have contributed to the success of many of her former students. Second, they are important as symbols. The planting of the American flag at Iwo Jima during some of the most intense fighting of World War II came to symbolize the fortitude of the entire American war effort; it represented commitment and was more important as a symbol than as an actual event. Sometimes the same event may be celebrated for both actual and symbolic reasons. A speech honoring the raising of $60 million for African famine relief would celebrate both aspects. This achievement was important in itself because it helped feed many starving people; it was also a symbol of global generosity. When you plan a speech of tribute, you should consider both the actual and the symbolic values that are represented.

Developing Speeches of Tribute.
As you prepare a speech of tribute, there are several guidelines that you should keep in mind. First, do not exaggerate the tribute so that it becomes unbelievable. If you are too lavish with your praise or use too many superlatives, you may embarrass the recipient. Second, focus on the honoree rather than yourself. Even if you know what effort the accomplishment required because you have done something similar, don't mention that at this time. It will just seem as though you are praising yourself when the focus should be on the honoree. Third, create vivid, concrete images of accomplishments. Speeches of tribute are occasions for illustrating what someone has accomplished, the values underlying those accomplishments, and their consequences. Tell stories that make those accomplishments come to life. Finally, be sincere. Speeches of tribute are a time for warmth, pride, and appreciation. Your manner should reflect these qualities as you present the tribute.

Speeches of Tribute: An Illustration.

Earlier we asked you to imagine yourself preparing a speech to honor Jesse Owens. Following his death in 1980, many such speeches were actually presented. The following comments by Congressman Thomas P. O'Neill, Jr., then Speaker of the House, illustrate some of the major techniques we have discussed:

O'Neill's opening highlights the themes of unusual and superior accomplishment. He begins with the actual value of Owens's victories, and then describes their symbolic value.

... I rise on the occasion of his passing to join my colleagues in tribute to the greatest American sports hero of this century, Jesse Owens.... His performances at the Berlin Olympics earned Jesse Owens the title of America's first superstar....

No other athlete symbolized the spirit and motto of the Olympics better than Jesse Owens. "Swifter, higher, stronger" was the credo by which Jesse Owens performed as an athlete and lived as an American. Of his performances in Hitler's Berlin in 1936, Jesse said: "I wasn't running against Hitler, I was running against the world." Owens' view of the Olympics was just that: He was competing against the best athletes in the world without regard to nationality, race, or political view....

Jesse Owens proved by his performances that he was the best among the finest the world had to offer, and in setting the world record in the 100-yard dash, he became the "fastest human" even before that epithet was fashionable....

These comments magnify the values represented by Owens's life and develop the theme of benefit to the community.

That Owens remained a patriotic American in the face of racism and indifference magnifies his character.

O'Neill's conclusion emphasizes the symbolic, spiritual values of Owens's life.

In life as well as on the athletic field Jesse Owens was first an American, and second, an internationalist. He loved his country; he loved the opportunity his country gave him to reach the pinnacle of athletic prowess. In his own quiet, unassuming, and modest way — by example, by inspiration, and by performance — he helped other young people to aim for the stars, to develop their God-given potential....

As the world's first superstar Jesse Owens was not initially overwhelmed by commercial interests and offered the opportunity to become a millionaire overnight. There was no White House reception waiting for him on his return from Berlin, and as Jesse Owens once observed: "I still had to ride in the back of the bus in my hometown in Alabama."

Can one individual make a difference? Clearly in the case of Jesse Owens the answer is a resounding affirmative, for his whole life was dedicated to the elimination of poverty, totalitarianism, and racial bigotry; and he did it in his own special and modest way, a spokesman for freedom, an American ambassador of good will to the athletes of the world, and an inspiration to young Americans.... Jesse Owens was a champion all the way in a life of dedication to the principles of the American and Olympic spirit.[7]

Making Toasts.

You may encounter many ceremonial occasions in which it is appropriate to offer a **toast,** which is a minispeech of tribute. You might be asked to present a toast to a co-worker who has been promoted, to a friend who has won an award, or to a couple at a wedding reception. The occasion may be formal or informal, but the message should always be eloquent. It won't do simply to mutter, "Here's to Tony, he's a great guy!" Such a feeble toast is "a gratuitous betrayal — of the occasion, its honoree, and the desire [of the audience] to clink glasses and murmur, 'Hear, hear' in appreciation of a compliment well fashioned."[8]

Whenever you think you might be called upon to offer a toast, plan your remarks in advance. Keep your toast brief. Select one characteristic or event that epitomizes your message, illustrate it with a short example, then conclude. You might toast the "coach of the year" in the following way:

> I always knew that Larry was destined for greatness from the time he led our junior high basketball team to the city championship. In one game in that tournament, Larry scored twenty-eight points, scrambled for eight rebounds, and dished off thirteen assists. And he was only five feet two inches tall! Here's to Larry, coach of the year!"

Because a toast is a speech of celebration, you should refrain from making negative remarks. For example, it would be inappropriate at a wedding reception to say, "Here's to John and Mary. I hope they don't end up in divorce court in a year as I did!" Although most public speeches are best presented extemporaneously, a toast should be memorized. Practice presenting your toast with glass in hand until it flows easily. If you have difficulty memorizing your toast, it is probably too long. Cut it.

The Speech of Acceptance

If you are receiving an award or honor, you may be expected to respond with a **speech of acceptance.** A speech of acceptance should express gratitude for the honor and acknowledge those who made the accomplishment possible. In addition, a speech of acceptance should focus on the values the award represents and be presented in language that matches the dignity of the occasion.

Consider a situation in which you are being awarded a scholarship by your hometown historical society. The award is being presented at a banquet, and

SPEAKER'S NOTES   *Making an Acceptance Speech*

1. Modestly express your gratitude for the honor.

2. Acknowledge those who made your accomplishment possible.

3. Highlight the values the award represents.

4. Make sure your language fits the formality of the occasion.

Acceptance speeches express gratitude and acknowledge those who made the accomplishment possible. At ceremonies announcing her appointment as secretary of labor, Elizabeth Dole made a speech of acceptance after being introduced by President Bush.

you must make a public acceptance. You would not go amiss if you began with, "Thank you. I appreciate the honor of this award." Let others praise; you should remain modest. When Elie Wiesel was awarded the 1986 Nobel Peace Prize, he began his acceptance speech with these remarks: "It is with a profound sense of humility that I accept the honor you have chosen to bestow upon me."[9] Follow his lead and accept an award with grace and modesty.

You should also give credit where credit is due. If the county historical society is awarding you a scholarship, it would be appropriate for you to mention some teachers who prepared you for this moment. You might say something like, "This award belongs as much to Mr. Del Rio as it does to me. He opened my eyes to the importance and relevance of history in our world today." When Martin Luther King, Jr., accepted his Nobel Peace Prize in 1964, he did so in these words: "I accept this prize on behalf of all men who love peace and brotherhood. . . . Most of these people will never make the headlines and their names will not appear in *Who's Who*. Yet when years have rolled past . . . men and women will know and children will be taught that we have a finer land, a better people, a more noble civilization — because these humble children of God were willing to suffer for righteousness' sake."[10]

As you accept your award, express your awareness of its deeper meaning. If you were accepting a history scholarship, you might wish to focus on the values of a liberal arts education and the contributions of history to our understanding of present-day problems. In their acceptance speeches, both Mr. Wiesel and Dr. King stressed the value of freedom and the importance of involvement — of overcoming hatred with loving concern.

Finally, your language should fit the situation. An acceptance speech is an occasion for dignity. Your remarks should be carefully planned and styled in appropriate language. Slang and jokes are usually out of place because they might suggest that you do not value the award or take the occasion seriously.

The stylistic techniques of magnification are especially useful in speeches of acceptance. Dr. King relied heavily on an extended movement metaphor in his acceptance speech. He spoke of the "tortuous road" from Montgomery, Alabama, to Oslo, Norway, a road on which, in his words, "millions of Negroes are traveling to find a new sense of dignity." In a similar manner Mr. Wiesel told the story of a "young Jewish boy discovering the kingdom of night" during the Holocaust. This personal, metaphorical narrative was introduced early in the speech and repeated in the conclusion when Mr. Wiesel remarked, "No one is as capable of gratitude as one who has emerged from the kingdom of night."

Although your rhetorical style may not be as eloquent as these Nobel Prize winners, you should make a presentation that befits the dignity of the occasion.

The Speech of Introduction

One of the more common types of ceremonial speeches is the **speech of introduction,** in which you introduce a featured speaker to the audience. The importance of this speech can vary, depending on how well the speaker and listeners know each other. At times the introduction can be very brief: "We are very pleased and honored today to have as guest speaker the president of our university, Dr. Sally Sorenson." At other times the introduction can be more elaborate as you work to accomplish three goals: first, to make the speaker feel welcome; second, to establish or strengthen the ethos of the speaker; and third, to tune the audience for the speech that will follow.

You make a speaker feel welcome by both what you say and how you say it. Let the speaker know that the audience wants to hear the message and feels honored by his or her presence. For example, you might open with, "We feel very fortunate to have Kelvin Andrews as our guest today. We know how busy he is, so it's a special treat and a real compliment to us that he should be here." When such words are delivered with honest warmth and sincerity, the speaker should feel truly welcome.

Once you have welcomed the speaker, you can begin to establish or strengthen the speaker's ethos. As soon as you know you will be introducing a speaker, find out as much about the person as you can. Often guest speakers will provide a résumé listing their experiences and accomplishments. If you can, talk with the speaker beforehand to see what he or she would like you to emphasize. If this is not possible, or if the speaker is noncommittal ("Oh, just say anything you want to"), there are still some good guidelines to follow that will help create respect for the speaker and lay the groundwork for speaker-audience identification:

- Create respect by magnifying the speaker's main accomplishments.

- Don't be too lavish with your praise. An overblown introduction can be embarrassing and make it difficult for speakers to get into their messages. One featured speaker was so overcome by an excessive introduction that he responded, "If you do not go to heaven for charity, you will certainly go somewhere else for exaggeration or downright prevarication."[11]

- Mention those achievements that are relevant to either the speaker's message, the occasion on which the speech is being presented, or the audience that has assembled.

- Be selective! If you try to present too many details and accomplishments, you may take up some of the speaker's time and make listeners weary. Introducers who drone on too long create real problems for the speakers who follow.

You can lay the groundwork for speaker-audience identification by mentioning aspects of the speaker's background that are familiar to the audience. The following introduction welcomes the speaker, establishes her ethos, and humanizes her by talking about her family and her connection to the community where the speech is being presented:

SPEAKER'S NOTES   *Introducing Main Speakers*

1. Be sure you know how to pronounce the speaker's name.

2. Ask the speaker what he or she would like you to emphasize.

3. Make the speaker feel welcome. Be warm and gracious.

4. Focus on parts of the speaker's background relevant to the topic, audience, and occasion.

5. Spotlight the title of the speech and tune the audience for it.

6. Be brief!

Not only is tonight's speaker the state's foremost expert on criminal liability, but Judge Polisky is also the mother of two children. She shares our concern for the rights of children. Her grandfather lived in Maryville, and she still remembers our delicious Maryville strawberries that she enjoyed as a child. Let's welcome back Judge Mary Polisky and share her thoughts on the topic "Law and Disorder."

The final function of an effective introduction is to tune the audience for the speech that will follow. In Chapter 4 we discussed how preliminary tuning can establish a mood predisposing an audience to respond positively or negatively to a speech. You can tune the audience as you introduce a speaker by arousing a sense of anticipation in listeners and making them want to listen. However, this does not mean that you should preview the speech in your introduction. Unless you have special knowledge of what the speaker is going to say, previewing can create problems. You might miss the point completely, in which case the speaker may have to begin with a disclaimer. Even if you have seen the speech ahead of time and are aware of its content, leave the presentation to the speaker. *Introduce the speaker; don't present the speech.*

The Speech of Inspiration

The **speech of inspiration** is directed at awakening or reawakening an audience to a goal, purpose, or set of values or beliefs. Speeches of inspiration can give listeners a push in the right direction and motivate them to take action. Therefore, these speeches serve the acceptance and integration functions we discussed in Chapter 13 in relation to persuasive speeches. Inspirational speeches may be commercial, political, or social. When a sales manager introduces a new product to marketing representatives, pointing up its competitive advantages and its glowing market potential, the speech is both inspirational and persuasive. The marketing reps should feel inspired to push that product with great zeal and enthusiasm. Speeches at political conventions that praise the principles of the party, such as keynote addresses, are inspirational in tone and intent. As different as these speech occasions may seem, they have important points in common.

First, speeches of inspiration are enthusiastic. Inspirational speakers accomplish their goals through their personal commitment and energy. Both the speaker and the speech must be active and forceful. Speakers must set an example for their audiences through their behavior both on and off the speaking platform. They must practice what they preach. Their ethos must be consistent with their advice.

Second, speeches of inspiration often draw upon past success to encourage future accomplishment. In the later years of his life, when his athletic prowess had faded, Jesse Owens became known as a great inspirational speaker. According to his obituary in the *New York Times,* "The Jesse Owens best remembered by many Americans was a public speaker with the ringing, inspirational delivery of an evangelist. . . . [His speeches] praised the virtues of patriotism, clean living and fair play."[12]

Third, whatever their specific purpose, speeches of inspiration seek to revive appreciation for underlying values or beliefs. In the Owens speech that follows, we shall see the ideals of brotherhood, tolerance, and fair competition set forth in an exciting story. The effect of such revitalized values can be to strengthen our sense of mythos, the distinctive code of values underlying our society. A strengthened mythos in turn creates a resource for persuasive proofs, such as we discussed in Chapter 14. For example, an audience that heard the Owens speech might listen more favorably to a speech extolling the values of economic competition in a capitalist society. Thus, speeches of inspiration can contribute to the effectiveness of other speeches that follow.

Speeches of Inspiration: An Illustration.   In his inspirational speeches to budding athletes, Jesse Owens frequently talked of his Olympic achievements. The following excerpts, taken from a statement protesting America's withdrawal from the 1980 Summer Olympic Games, illustrate his inspirational style. Jesse Owens was unable to deliver this message orally. It was prepared shortly before his death from cancer.

Owens's introduction suggests the larger meaning of his victories and sets the stage for identification.

Note the use of graphic detail to recapture the immediacy of the moment.

Owens's use of dialogue helps listeners feel they are sharing the experience.

This narrative leaves open the meaning of Owens's "inside" victory: perhaps it was over self-doubt or his own stereotype of Germans. Perhaps it was both.

This scene presents an inspirational model of

What the Berlin games proved . . . was that Hitler's "supermen" could be beaten.

Ironically, it was one of his blond, blue-eyed, Aryan athletes who helped do the beating.

I held the world record in the broad jump. Even more than the sprints, it was "my" event. Yet I was one jump from not even making the finals. I fouled on my first try, and playing it safe the second time, I had not jumped far enough.

The broad jump preliminaries came before the finals of my other three events and everything, it seemed then, depended on this jump. Fear swept over me and then panic. I walked off alone, trying to gather myself. I dropped to one knee, closed my eyes, and prayed. I felt a hand on my shoulder. I opened my eyes and there stood my arch enemy, Luz Long, the prize athlete Hitler had kept under wraps while he trained for one purpose only: to beat me. Long had broken the Olympic mark in his very first try in the preliminaries.

"I know about you," he said. "You are like me. You must do it all the way, or you cannot do it. The same that has happened to you today happened to me last year in Cologne. I will tell you what I did then." Luz told me to measure my steps, place my towel 6 inches on back of the takeoff board and jump from there. That way I could give it all I had and be certain not to foul.

As soon as I had qualified, Luz, smiling broadly, came to me and said, "Now we can make each other do our best in the finals."

And that's what we did in the finals. Luz jumped, and broke his Olympic record. Then I jumped just a bit further and broke Luz's new record. We each had three leaps in all. On his final jump, Luz went almost 26 feet, 5 inches, a mark that seemed impossible to beat. I went just a bit over that, and set an Olympic record that was to last for almost a quarter of a century.

I won that day, but I'm being straight when I say that even before I made that last jump, I knew I had won a victory of a far greater kind — over something inside myself, thanks to Luz.

The instant my record-breaking win was announced, Luz was there, throwing his arms around me and raising my arm to the sky. "Jazze Owenz!" he yelled as

international
cooperation.

Owens shows how in-
dividuals can rise
above ideologies, as
Long's final message
invites identification.

Owens ends with a
metaphor of the "road
to the Olympics."

loud as he could. More than 100,000 Germans in the stadium joined in. "Jazze Owenz, Jazze Owenz, Jazze Owenz!"

Hitler was there, too, but he was not chanting. He had lost that day. Luz Long was killed in World War II and, although I don't cry often, I wept when I received his last letter — I knew it was his last. In it he asked me to someday find his son, Karl, and to tell him "of how we fought well together, and of the good times, and that any two men can become brothers."

That is what the Olympics are all about. The road to the Olympics does not lead to Moscow. It leads to no city, no country. It goes far beyond Lake Placid or Moscow, Ancient Greece or Nazi Germany. The road to the Olympics leads, in the end, to the best within us.[13]

The After-Dinner Speech

Some occasions call for an **after-dinner speech.** Such occasions may mark the beginning or end of a process, such as the kickoff for a fund-raising campaign or the end of school year. They can also function as political rallies or award banquets.

The after-dinner speech is one of the great rituals of American public speaking and public life. In keeping with the nature of the occasion, after-dinner speeches should not be too difficult to digest. Speakers making these presentations usually do not introduce radical materials that require listeners to rethink their values or that ask for dramatic changes in belief or behavior. Nor are such occasions the time for anger or negativity. They are a time for people to savor who they are, what they have done, or what they wish to do. A good after-dinner speech, however, leaves a message that can act as a vision to guide and inspire future efforts.

The Role of Humor.   Humor is an essential ingredient in most after-dinner speeches. In the introduction humor can place both the speaker and audience at ease. It can also relieve tension. Enjoying lighter experiences can remind us that there is a human element in all situations and that we should not take ourselves too seriously. Humorous stories can create identification by building an "insider's" relationship between speaker and audience that draws them closer together. In sharing humor, the audience becomes a community of listeners.[14]

Humor may develop out of the immediate situation. Dick Jackman, the director of corporate communications at Sun Company, opened an after-dinner speech at a National Football Foundation awards dinner (the complete text appears at the end of this chapter) with a pointed reference to the seating arrangements, and then warned those in the expensive seats under the big chandelier that it "had been installed by the low bidder some time ago." His speech also contained lighthearted references to well-known members of the audience, including some who were there to receive an award. In her keynote address at the Democratic National Convention in 1988, Texas state treasurer Ann Richards used pointed humor as she took her party to task for not involving women more directly:

Appropriate humor can relax both speakers and audiences. Speakers who tell amusing stories about themselves often endear themselves to listeners. In sharing the pleasure of laughter, audience members identify more closely with each other as well as with the speaker.

> Twelve years ago Barbara Jordan, another Texas woman, ... made the keynote address to the convention, and two women in 160 years is about par for the course.
>
> But if you give us a chance, we can perform. After all, Ginger Rogers did everything that Fred Astaire did. She just did it backwards and in high heels.[15]

Humor requires thought, planning, and caution to be effective in a speech. If it is not handled well, it can be a disaster. For example, religious humor is usually dangerous, and racist humor is absolutely forbidden. The first runs the risk of offending some members of the audience and can make the speaker seem intolerant. The second reveals a devastating truth about the speaker's character and can create such negative reactions from the audience that the rest of the speech doesn't stand a chance. Nor can humor be forced on a speech. If you decide to begin with a joke simply because you think one should start a speech that way, the humor may seem contrived and flat. Rather, humor must be functional in a speech, useful to make a point.

Often the best kind of humor is that which centers on speakers themselves. Speakers who tell amusing stories about themselves usually endear themselves to their listeners. When this technique is successful, the stories that seem to put the speakers down are actually building their ethos. A rural politician once told the following story at a dinner on an urban college campus:

You know, I didn't have good schooling like all of you have. I had to work real hard to educate myself for public office. Along the way I just tried not to embarrass myself like another fellow from around here once did. This man wanted to run for Congress. So he came up here to your college to present himself to all the students and faculty. He worked real hard on a speech to show them all that he was a man of vision and high intellect.

As he came to the end of his speech, he intoned very solemnly, "If you elect me to the United States Congress, I'll be like that great American bird, the eagle. I'll soar high and see far! I won't be like that other bird that buries its head in the sand, the oyster!" There was a wonderful reaction from the audience to that. So he said it again — said he wasn't going to be no oyster.

Well, I've tried hard not to be an oyster as I represent you, even though I know there's some folks who'd say, "Well, you sure ain't no eagle, either!"[16]

This story, which led into a review of the politician's accomplishments, was warmly appreciated for both its humor and its modesty. It suggests that humor takes time to develop and must be rich in graphic detail to set up its punch line. The story would not have been nearly as effective had the speaker begun with, "Did you hear the one about the politician who didn't know an ostrich from an oyster?"

Developing an After-Dinner Speech.   After-dinner speeches are more difficult to develop than their lightness and short length might suggest. Like any other speech, they must be carefully planned and practiced. They must have an effective introduction that commands attention right away, especially since some audience members may be more interested in talking to table companions than in listening to the speaker. After-dinner speeches should be more than strings of anecdotes to amuse listeners. The stories told must either establish a mood, convey a message, or carry a theme forward. Such speeches should build to a satisfying conclusion that conveys the essence of the message.

Above all, perhaps, after-dinner speeches should be mercifully brief. Long-winded after-dinner speakers can leave the audience fiddling with coffee cups and drawing pictures on napkins. After being subjected to such a speech, Albert Einstein once commented: "I have just got a new theory of eternity."[17]

Ceremonial speeches serve important social functions. They reinforce the values that hold people together in a community and give listeners a sense of order and purpose in their lives. They also promote effective leadership.

Techniques of Ceremonial Speaking.   Two major techniques of ceremonial speaking are identification and *magnification*. The first creates close feeling, and the second selects and emphasizes those features of a subject that will convey the speaker's message. Themes worthy of magnification include overcoming obstacles, achieving unusual goals, performing in a superior manner, having pure motives, and benefiting the community.

Types of Ceremonial Speeches.   *Speeches of tribute* may recognize the achievements of individuals or groups or commemorate special events. Speeches of tribute should help us understand and appreciate the values these achievements represent. Accomplishments and events may be significant in themselves or in what they symbolize. *Toasts* are minispeeches of tribute that may be given on special occasions. *Speeches of acceptance* should begin with an expression of gratitude and an acknowledgment of others who deserve recognition. They should focus on the values that the honor represents. Acceptance speeches often call for more formal language than other speeches and for simple eloquence that suits the occasion.

Speeches of introduction should welcome the speaker, establish his or her ethos, and tune the audience for the message to follow. Introductions should focus on information about the speaker that is relevant to the speech topic and the occasion or that has special meaning for the audience. *Speeches of inspiration* help listeners appreciate values and make them want to pursue worthy goals. Such speeches often call on stories of past successes. *After-dinner speeches* should be lighthearted, serving up humor and insight at the same time. Humor should be functional in such speeches, illustrating a point or serving some larger purpose.

TERMS TO KNOW

ceremonial speaking	speech of acceptance
magnification	speech of introduction
speech of tribute	speech of inspiration
toast	after-dinner speech

DISCUSSION

1. The speeches in Appendix B by Bill Cosby, Elie Wiesel, and Ronald Reagan are ceremonial addresses. How do they relate to the basic questions of "Who are we?" "Why are we?" "What have we accomplished?" and "What can we become together?" What values do they celebrate? How do they achieve identification and magnification? Which tools of language do they use? Which speech designs do they follow?

2. Is there a speech of inspiration you heard some time ago that you still remember? Why do you feel it made such an impression on you?

3. List five heroes who are often mentioned in ceremonial speeches. Why do speakers refer to them so frequently? What does this tell us about the nature of these heroes, about contemporary audiences, and about the ceremonial speech situation? Be prepared to discuss this in class.

4. When someone has died, a speech of tribute often begins a process of "mythifying" the deceased, speaking in ideal rather than real terms about the person's life. Can this process of idealization be justified? Why or why not?

APPLICATION

1. Prepare a speech of introduction that you might give for the next speech of one of your classmates. Which features would you select for magnification? How would you go about promoting speaker-audience identification? How would you tune the audience for the speech?

2. Develop a speech of tribute in honor of a classmate, friend, or family member in which you celebrate the real and/or symbolic importance of some achievement. Remember to consider the five themes of magnification as you plan your tribute.

3. Prepare a toast for a classmate who you feel either (a) has made the most progress as a speaker this semester or (b) has given a speech you will likely remember long after the class is over. Strive for brevity and eloquence in your toast. Be ready to present your toast in class.

NOTES

1. John Dewey, *Democracy and Education* (New York: Macmillan, 1916), p. 4.
2. Bronislaw Malinowski, "The Problem of Meaning in Primitive Languages," in C. K. Ogden and I. A. Richards, *The Meaning of Meaning: A Study of the Influence of Language upon Thought and of the Science of Symbolism,* 8th ed. (New York: Harcourt, Brace & World, 1946), p. 315.
3. Michael Osborn, *Orientations to Rhetorical Style* (Chicago: Science Research Associates, 1976), p. 32.
4. James W. Carey, "A Cultural Approach to Communication," *Communication* 2 (1975): 6.
5. Christine Oravec, "Observation in Aristotle's Theory of Epideictic," *Philosophy and Rhetoric* 9 (1976): 162–74.
6. *American Speeches,* ed. Wayland Maxfield Parrish and Marie Hochmuth (New York: Longmans, Green, 1954), p. 43.
7. *Congressional Record,* 1 Apr. 1980, pp. 7459–60.
8. Owen Edwards, "What Every Man Should Know: How to Make a Toast," *Esquire,* Jan. 1984, p. 37.

9. Elie Wiesel, "Nobel Peace Prize Acceptance Speech," 10 Dec. 1986, reprinted in *New York Times,* 11 Dec. 1986, p. A-8.

10. Martin Luther King, Jr., "Nobel Peace Prize Acceptance Statement," reprinted in *The Cry for Freedom: The Struggle for Equality in America,* ed. Frank W. Hale, Jr. (New York: Barnes, 1969), pp. 374–77.

11. Cited in Morris K. Udall, *Too Funny to be President* (New York: Holt, 1988), p. 156.

12. *Congressional Record,* 1 Apr. 1980, p. 7249.

13. *Ibid.,* p. 7248.

14. For more on the social function of laughter, see Henri Bergson, *Laughter: An Essay on the Meaning of the Comic,* trans. Cloudsley Brereton and Fred Rothwell (London: Macmillan, 1911).

15. Ann Richards, "Keynote Address," delivered at the Democratic National Convention, Atlanta, Ga., 18 July 1988, in *Vital Speeches of the Day* 54 (15 Aug. 1988): 647–49.

16. Thanks for this story go to Professor Joseph Riggs, Slippery Rock University.

17. *Washington Post,* 12 Dec. 1978.

SAMPLE AFTER-DINNER SPEECH

Address at Awards Dinner of National Football Foundation

—— *Dick Jackman* ——

Jackman begins on a light note, using the seating arrangements as a source of humor. The impromptu nature of these remarks builds his ethos as a clever person.

Jackman moves into the major theme of his speech: leadership, teamwork, and optimism make a good football team and a good country. *O.K.* is not a transition we normally recommend.

Jackman narrows his theme to optimism and urges listeners to "export" optimism to others.

This humorous narrative illustrates the importance of optimism in daily affairs. Note how the use of dialogue helps the story move along.

Thank you. Sorry I'm so late getting up here. It's about a $2 cab ride from the back row. All of us back there in the cheap seats admire these young athletes, and some of us remarked that we have underwear older than they are.

I'm pleased to be here to share this moment. I look at the logistics here on the dais — Doug Flutie seated alongside Joe Greene. That's like parking a Volkswagen alongside a school bus. And for those of you sitting under the chandelier, you should be aware that it was installed by the low bidder some time ago.

O.K. A football team seems to do best when it produces a combination of leadership and teamwork, and America seems to do best when it produces that same combination. Teamwork being that special quality that helps us look at life not from the standpoint of what's in it for us but from the standpoint of what we can do to help, and leadership being that special quality that helps an awful lot of people in and out of this room stand up on their tiptoes and look over the horizon and lead people there.

You cannot possibly leave this hotel tonight without a great deal of optimism about the future of not only football but America, because there's so much of it in here, and optimism is not meant to be stored. It's meant to be exported. You export it to other people. You make them determined to do that something extra in life that brings a response from others.

Let me mention the finest illustration I've ever heard of doing something extra. We had a teenage neighbor back home, a nice fellow. One day he got home at midnight. His mother said, "Where have you been?" He said, "I was out with my girl." His mother said, "I ought to give you a whipping for staying out so late, but you're being honest with me. I admire your honesty. Have some cookies and go to bed." The next night the kid got home at 1:00 A.M. His mother said, "Where were you tonight?" He said, "Same place. Out with my girl." His mother said, "I ought to give you the whipping of your life, but since you're being honest with me, have some more cookies and go to bed." The next night, he came home at 2:00 A.M. His father was waiting up for him. The kid walked into the house. The father picked up a huge frying pan and turned to face him. The mother leaped to her feet and screamed, "Please don't hit him!" The father said, "Who's going to hit him? I'm going to fry him some eggs. He can't keep this up on

Presented at an awards dinner of the National Football Foundation and Hall of Fame. The dinner was held at the Waldorf-Astoria Hotel in New York City on December 4, 1984.

The story of the bumblebee and the other brief examples that follow function as evidence for the claim that people, through optimism, can overcome their limitations.

cookies." So good people, if you sometimes have difficulty keeping up the pace and the love and the concern for other people on cookies, then let me encourage you to fry some eggs.

By this time we've all learned that, aerodynamically, the bumblebee shouldn't be able to fly. The body is too large. The wings are too small. Every time it takes off it should plunge back to the earth. But fortunately, the bumblebee does not understand its engineering limitations. And it's a good thing it doesn't, or we'd be living in a world of plastic flowers and putting mustard on our pancakes. It's a good thing that Scott Hamilton, at 5'3" and 115 pounds, did not realize that he could not possibly become the world's greatest ice skater, and that Mary Lou Retton, at 4'10", and Doug Flutie, who is here with us tonight, about a foot taller than that, did not realize that they could not possibly become the best at what they do, and that Shakespeare, whose mother could not read or write, did not realize that he couldn't possibly become the world's most honored writer.

And perhaps it's a great thing that 208 years ago, Betsy Ross took out her needle and thread. She did not realize that she could not possibly be sewing together an emblem that would one day umbrella the greatest experiment in human opportunity ever tried on this planet.

Let us not look at our limitations tomorrow morning. Let us pursue our possibilities.

On our track team at the University of Iowa we had a cross-eyed javelin thrower. He didn't win any medals, but he certainly kept the crowd alert. Perhaps part of our mission tonight and all the nights and days to follow is to keep the crowd in our homes, in our schools, and in our country alert to their possibilities and not their limitations.

That's far enough. Have an exciting life. Good night.

Jackman finishes on a note that is both inspirational and humorous. The humor keeps his speech from ending on too serious a note.

A

GROUP COMMUNICATION

When we listen to a speaker present information on a vital issue or make recommendations concerning an important problem, what we hear is one person's perception and interpretation of a situation. That point of view may be distorted by bias or self-interest, or it simply could be wrong. How can we minimize the risk of listening to just one person on issues that are vital to us?

One answer is to empower a group of at least three people working together to investigate, analyze, and make recommendations about the problem. Group problem solving reduces the risk inherent in a single point of view and has other advantages as well. In effective problem-solving groups, people on all sides of an issue have an opportunity to discuss their differences in a controlled environment. Participants often discover some things they can agree on. These areas of agreement may be the foundation for a resolution of differences. Additionally, people are often more willing to examine their differences openly in small group meetings than in larger, more public confrontations. In small group settings they may feel free to explore compromises or new options. For these reasons, a group approach to problem solving is used often in social or business settings. In fact, it is estimated that executives normally spend from 500 to 700 hours each year in group meetings.[1]

Although group deliberations have many virtues, there are also some problems inherent in problem-solving groups. First, there is the possibility that one participant may dominate the group through the force of personality. When this happens, the group may simply endorse that individual's suggestions without seriously questioning them or investigating other options. This can result in **groupthink,** the development of a single, uncritical frame of mind that leads to ill-considered decisions.[2] Groupthink is especially dangerous because outsiders are apt to assume that the problem-solving group has deliberated carefully and responsibly. Another problem that arises in groups is that they can be aimless and unproductive, unless they are ably led. Ineffective leadership may be one reason why business executives complain that their meetings take too long and accomplish too little.[3]

How can you participate effectively in group deliberations? This appendix offers suggestions for group participants and leaders.

THE PROBLEM-SOLVING PROCESS

Group deliberations that are orderly, systematic, and thorough are most likely to result in high quality decisions reached through consensus.[4] There are a variety of methods that problem-solving groups can use.[5] The approach that we suggest is a modification of the reflective-thinking technique first advanced by John Dewey in 1910.[6] This systematic approach to solving problems proceeds in five steps. The amount of time devoted to each of these steps depends on the depth and complexity of the problem.

Step 1:
Defining the Problem

Groups often mistakenly assume that the "assigned" problem is the problem that really exists. Quite often, however, the assigned problem may be only a symptom of the real problem, or it may be just a part of that problem. So even though the problem you will consider may seem obvious, your group needs to define it carefully before considering possible solutions. The following questions may help the process of definition:

1. Precisely what is the nature of the problem? (*Define it as concretely and specifically as possible.*)

2. Why has the problem occurred?

3. What is its history?

4. Who is affected by the problem and to what degree?

5. What if the problem is solved? Would things automatically be better? Could they become worse?

6. Does the group have the information it needs to understand the problem completely? If not, how and where can it get this information? (*Do not proceed further until this information is in hand.*)

7. Has the problem been defined and stated so that everyone understands what the group will work on? (*Do not proceed further until you reach consensus on definition.*)

Step 2:
Generating Solution Options

Once your group has determined the nature and extent of the problem and gathered relevant information, members can begin generating options for solving the problem. **Brainstorming,** a group technique that encourages all members to contribute freely to the range of options, can stimulate the flow of ideas. Brainstorming aims at producing a large number of alternatives. At this stage in the problem-solving process, any attempt to evaluate the options or to settle on the right or best option is premature. The following rules of brainstorming may be used as a guide:

1. The leader asks each member in turn to contribute an idea. If members do not have an idea when it is their turn, they simply pass.

2. A recorder writes down all the ideas suggested by the members. These should be recorded on flip-chart sheets or a blackboard so that members can see the ideas as they accumulate.

3. Participants offer any ideas that come to mind, no matter how far-fetched they may seem. The objective at this stage is to generate as many ideas as possible. Once expressed, ideas can be elaborated on by others.

4. No criticism of ideas is permitted during the brainstorming process. The leader should tactfully discourage any critical comments by calling for other ideas.

5. Brainstorming continues until all members have passed. The leader should discourage any one person from dominating the discussion.

6. The list of ideas is reviewed for clarification. At this time participants may expand the list of options or combine related ideas into other alternatives.

7. Once the group is satisfied that all options have been exhausted, the final list of alternatives is posted for everyone to see.

Step 3:
Evaluating Solution Options

The options suggested in Step 2 should be discussed thoroughly in the order in which they were proposed. Each option should receive full and careful consideration. The seven questions that follow may be used as a guide to evaluating options:

1. How costly is the option?

2. How likely is the option to be successful?

3. How difficult will it be to enact the option?

4. How soon will the option take effect?

5. Will the solution solve the problem completely?

6. What additional benefits might the solution produce?

7. What additional problems might the solution create?

It is often helpful to use a flip-chart sheet for each option to summarize the answers to these questions. These can then be posted so that participants can refresh their memories and compare the various options.

As options are being evaluated, some of them will prove to be weak and will be dropped, while others will be improved and refined. The group also may combine options to generate new hybrid alternatives. For example, if the group is caught between Option A, which promises improved efficiency, and

Option B, which promises lower cost, it may be possible to generate hybrid Option C, which combines the best features of both. After each alternative has been thoroughly considered, participants should rank the options in terms of their acceptability. The option receiving the highest overall rank becomes the proposed solution.

During the evaluation step the group leader should keep the focus of the discussion on ideas and not on participants. It is not unusual for group members to become personally involved with the solutions they propose. Resist this impulse in yourself and be tactfully aware of it in others. Keep your evaluations focused as much as possible on the ideas, not on those who propose them. Sometimes discussing the strengths of an option before talking about its weaknesses can take some of the heat out of the process. Accept differences of opinion as a natural and necessary part of problem solving.

Step 4:
Planning for Action

Once the group has decided on a solution, the next step is to work out the sequence of steps needed to implement it. For example, to improve company morale, a group might recommend a three-step plan: (1) better in-house training programs to increase upward mobility of employees, (2) a pay structure that rewards success in the training programs, and (3) increased participation in decision making for the newly trained employees as they move into more responsible positions. As the group develops this plan, it should consider what might help or hinder it, the resources needed to enact it, and a timetable for completion.

If the group is unable to develop a sequential action plan for the solution, or if insurmountable obstacles appear, the group should return to Step 3 and reconsider its options.

Step 5:
Planning for Evaluation

Not only must a problem-solving group plan how to implement a solution, it must also determine how to evaluate its results. In essence, the group must answer three vital questions:

1. *What* will constitute success?

2. *When* can we expect results?

3. What will we do *if* the plan doesn't work as expected?

The first two questions require the group to specify the desired outcomes and indicate how they can be recognized when the solution goes into effect.

To monitor the ongoing success of a solution such as the three-part plan to improve company morale presented in Step 4, the group would have to decide on a reasonable set of expectations for each stage in the process. That way, the company could detect and correct problems as they occur, before they damage the plan as a whole. Having a scheduled sequence of expectations also provides a way to determine results while the plan is being enacted, rather than having to wait for the entire project to be completed. Positive results at interim points can encourage group members by showing them they are on the right track. The third question indicates the importance of contingency plans: what to do if things don't go as expected.

PARTICIPATING IN SMALL GROUPS

In addition to understanding the process of problem solving, you must also understand your responsibilities as a participant in group communication situations. Group members should prepare themselves by conducting research in advance of meetings. They should be open minded, willing to listen to other positions and to learn from other participants. They should be concerned with contributing to the overall effort rather than with dominating discussion. Although members should have a well-defined point of view they can express with conviction, they should not be afraid to concede a point when they are wrong. Nor should they become defensive when challenged.

Group members must be effective listeners as well as speakers. They should speak out when they can add information, summarize or synthesize what others have said, or ask for clarification. But they also should listen carefully to other participants, granting them the courtesy of completing their points without interruption. Effective listening can lead to intelligent questions that help clarify a confused situation.

In short, each participant should strive to make a positive contribution to group effectiveness. To become a more effective group communicator, you should start by analyzing your group communication skills. The self-analysis form (Figure A.1) can steer you toward more constructive group communication behaviors.

As you participate in groups you should also be conscious of the following questions:

1. What is happening now in the group?

2. What should be happening in the group?

3. What can I do to make this come about?[7]

If you notice a difference between what the group is doing and what it should be doing to reach its goals, you have the opportunity to assume group leadership.

Figure A.1

Group Communication Skills Self-Analysis Form

	Need to DO LESS	Doing FINE	Need to DO MORE
1. I make my points concisely.	___	___	___
2. I am forceful and definite rather than hesitant and apologetic.	___	___	___
3. I provide specific examples and details.	___	___	___
4. I synthesize and make explanations.	___	___	___
5. I let others know when I do not understand what they have said.	___	___	___
6. I let others know when I agree with them.	___	___	___
7. I let others know tactfully when I disagree with them.	___	___	___
8. I express my opinions.	___	___	___
9. I suggest solutions or courses of action.	___	___	___
10. I listen to understand rather than to prepare my next remarks.	___	___	___
11. I check to make sure I understand before agreeing or disagreeing.	___	___	___
12. I ask questions in ways that get more information than just "yes" or "no."	___	___	___
13. I ask others for their opinions rather than assuming I know them.	___	___	___
14. I check for group agreement as discussion proceeds.	___	___	___
15. I try to reduce tension and hostility.	___	___	___
16. I accept help from others.	___	___	___
17. I offer help to others.	___	___	___
18. I let others have their say.	___	___	___
19. I stand up for myself.	___	___	___
20. I urge others to participate.	___	___	___

LEADERSHIP IN SMALL GROUPS

For over thirty-five years, social scientists have been studying leadership by analyzing communication patterns in groups.[8] The research suggests that two basic types of leadership behaviors emerge in working groups: **task leadership behavior,** which directs the activity of the group toward a specified goal, and **social leadership behavior,** which concerns building and maintaining positive and productive relationships among group members.

Task leaders initiate goal-related communication, including both giving and seeking information, opinions, and suggestions. A task leader might say,

"We need more information on just how widespread grade inflation is on this campus. Let me tell you what Dean Johnson told me last Friday...." Or the task leader might say, "I know Gwen has some important information on this point. Tell us about it, Gwen." Social leaders initiate positive social communication behaviors, such as expressing argrement, helping the group release tension, or behaving in a generally friendly and supportive manner toward others. The social leader looks for chances to bestow compliments: "I think Gwen has made a very important point. You have really helped us by finding that out." The supportive effect of sincere compliments helps keep members from becoming defensive, and it helps keep the communication atmosphere constructive. In a healthy communication climate the two kinds of leadership behavior support each other and work to keep the group moving toward its goal in a positive way. When the same person combines both styles, that person is likely to be a highly effective leader.

Developing a Meeting Plan

The techniques of effective leadership also include knowing how to plan and run meetings. The following guidelines should help you plan more effective meetings:

1. *Have a specific objective and purpose for holding a meeting.* Unnecessary meetings give meetings a bad name. If your goal is simply to increase interaction, plan a social event rather than a meeting.

2. *Prepare an agenda for the meeting* and distribute it to participants at least twenty-four hours before the meeting. Having a list of topics to be covered gives members time to prepare for the meeting and to assemble whatever information or materials they might need to contribute effectively. Be sure to solicit agenda items from participants.

3. *Keep meetings short and to the point.* After about an hour groups can grow weary and tempers short under the strain of problem solving. Don't try to cover too much ground in any one meeting.

4. *Keep groups small.* You will get more participation and interaction in a smaller group. In larger groups people may be inhibited from asking questions or contributing ideas.

5. *Keep groups homogeneous.* In business settings, you may get better interaction if the group participants come from the same or near the same working level in the organization. This is especially true for problem-solving groups, in which the presence of an employee's direct supervisor may inhibit honest interaction.

6. *Plan the site of the meeting.* Try to arrange for privacy and freedom from interruptions. A circular table or seating arrangement contributes to mem-

ber participation because there is no power position in the arrangement. A rectangular table or a lectern and classroom arrangement may inhibit interaction.

7. *Prepare in advance for the meeting.* Have a short form of the agenda available for distribution at the meeting. Be certain that you have all of the supplies the group will need, such as chalk, flip chart, markers, note pads, and pencils. If you plan to use audio-visual equipment, check in advance to be sure it is in working order.

Conducting an Effective Meeting

Group leaders have more responsibilities than other members. Leaders must understand the problem-solving process the group will use so that deliberations can proceed in an orderly, constructive way. Leaders also should be well informed on the issues involved, so that they can answer questions and keep the group moving toward its objective. The following check list should be helpful in guiding your behavior as a group leader.

- Prepare and present any background information concisely and objectively.

- Encourage participants to express differences of opinions. Get conflict out in the open so that it can be dealt with directly.

- Urge all members to participate. If members are reticent, you may have to ask them directly to contribute.

- Keep the discussion on the main subject.

- Summarize what others have said so that all group members remain focused on the issues.

- At the close of a meeting, summarize what the group has accomplished. All members of the group should agree that your summary is objective and accurate.

As group leader, you may need to present the group's recommendations to the organization that appointed the group. *In this task, you function mainly as an informative speaker.* You should present the recommendations offered by the group, along with the major reasons for these recommendations. You should also mention any opposing reasons or reservations that may have surfaced during group deliberations. Your job in making this report is not to advocate, but to educate. Later, you may join in the discussion that follows your report with persuasive remarks that express your convictions on the subject.

GUIDELINES FOR FORMAL MEETINGS

The larger the group, the more it may need formal procedures to conduct a successful meeting. Also, if a meeting involves a subject that may generate a great deal of conflict or controversy, it is often wise to establish in advance a set of rules for conduct. Such guidelines help keep meetings from becoming chaotic and assure fair treatment of all participants. Many groups choose to operate by **parliamentary procedure.**[9]

Parliamentary procedure establishes an order of business for a meeting and defines the way the group initiates discussions and reaches decisions. Under parliamentary procedure a formal meeting proceeds as follows:

1. The chair calls the meeting to order.

2. The secretary reads the minutes of the previous meeting, which are corrected, if necessary, and approved.

3. Reports from group officers and committees are presented.

4. Unfinished business from the previous meeting is considered.

5. New business is introduced.

6. Announcements are made.

7. The meeting is formally adjourned.

All business in formal meetings goes forward by means of **motions,** which are proposals set before the group. Consider the following scenario. The chair of a group has asked: "Is there new business?" A member responds: "I *move* that we allot $100 to build a Homecoming float." This member has offered a **main motion,** which proposes to commit the group to some action. Before the motion can be discussed, it must be seconded. If no one volunteers a second, the chair may ask, "Is there a second?" Another member will typically respond, "I second the motion." The purpose of a **second** is to assure that more than one person wishes to see the motion considered. Once a main motion is made and seconded, it is open for discussion. It must be passed by majority vote, defeated, or otherwise resolved before the group can move on to other business. With the exception of a few technical motions (such as "I move we take a fifteen-minute recess" or "Point of personal privilege. Can we do anything about the heat in this room?"), the main motion remains at the center of group attention until resolved.

Let us assume that as the group discusses the main motion in our example, some members believe the amount of money proposed is insufficient. At this point, another member may say: "I move to amend the motion to provide $150 for the float." The **motion to amend** gives the group a chance to modify a main motion. It also must be seconded and, after discussion, must be resolved by majority vote before discussion goes forward. If the motion to amend passes, then the amended main motion must still be considered. How does a group come to the point of decision on a motion? There usually comes a point when discussion has pretty well played itself out. At this point the chair might say, "Do I hear a call for the question?" A motion **to call the question** ends the discussion, and requires a two-thirds vote for approval. Once the group votes to end discussion, it must then vote to accept or reject the motion.

At times, discussion of a motion may reveal that the group is deeply confused or sharply divided about an issue. At this point a member may move **to table the motion** or "to lay [the motion] on the table," as it is technically called. This can be a backdoor way to dispose of a troublesome or defective motion without the pain of further divisive or confused discussion. At other times, discussion may reveal that the group lacks vital information needed to come to an intelligent decision. At that point, we might hear from yet another member: "In light of our uncertainty on the cost issue, I move that we postpone further consideration of this motion until next week's meeting." The motion **to postpone consideration,** if approved, gives the chair a chance to appoint a committee to gather the information needed.

These are just some of the important motions and procedures that can help assure that formal group communication remains fair and constructive. For more information on formal group communication procedures, consult the authoritative **Robert's Rules of Order.**

NOTES

1. M. Kriesberg, "Executive Evaluative Administrative Conferences," *Advanced Management* 15 (1950): 15–17; and S. L. Tubbs, *A Systems Approach to Small Group Communication* (Reading, Mass.: Addison-Wesley, 1978), p. 5.

2. Irving L. Janis, *Groupthink: Psychological Studies of Policy Decisions and Fiascoes,* 2nd ed. (Boston: Houghton Mifflin, 1982), p. 9.

3. Gerald M. Goldhaber, *Organizational Communication* (Dubuque, Iowa: William C. Brown, 1983), p. 263.

4. Harold Guetzow and John Gyr, "An Analysis of Conflict in Decision-Making Groups," *Human Behavior* 7 (1954): 367–82; and Norman R. F. Maier and Richard A. Maier, "An Experimental Test of the Effects of 'Developmental' vs. 'Free' Discussion on the Quality of Group Decisions," *Journal of Applied Psychology* 41 (1957): 320–23.

5. For an overview of other methods, see Patricia Hayes Andrews and John E. Baird, Jr., *Communication for Business and the Professions* (Dubuque, Iowa: William C. Brown, 1989), pp. 256–64.

6. The problem-solving process described here is adapted from William C. Morris and Marshall Sashkin. "Phases of Integrated Problem Solving (PIPS)," *The 1978*

Annual Handbook for Group Facilitators, ed. J. William Pfeiffer and John E. Jones (La Jolla, Calif.: University Associates, Inc., 1978), pp. 109–16.

7. Adapted from David G. Smith, "D-I-D: A Three-Dimensional Model for Understanding Group Communication," *The 1977 Annual Handbook for Group Facilitators,* ed. John E. Jones and J. William Pfeiffer (La Jolla, Calif.: University Associates, Inc., 1977), p. 106.

8. Robert F. Bales, *Interaction Process Analysis: A Method for the Study of Small Groups* (Cambridge, Mass.: Addison-Wesley, 1950), and *Personality and Interpersonal Behavior* (New York: Holt, Rinehart & Winston, 1970).

9. This discussion is based on Henry M. Robert, *Robert's Rules of Order* (New York: The Berkley Publishing Group, 1983).

B

SPEECHES
— FOR —
ANALYSIS

FREE AT LAST

————— Rodney Nishikawa —————

Rod Nishikawa presented this sensitive and moving self-introductory speech in his public speaking class at the University of California–Davis. Although most of his class-mates were *aware* that there was prejudice in their world, Rod's personal narrative — about his first encounter with prejudice as a child — helped them *feel* the prob-lem. Delivered early in the term, Rod's willingness to open up to his classmates helped to turn the class into a positive, supportive, and sharing community of students.

When I sat down the other day to prepare this speech, I remembered the last time I had to make a formal speech. It was almost three years ago at my high school graduation: I made a speech as my class valedictorian.

Ironically, with Martin Luther King Jr.'s birthday observance this past weekend, I ended that speech by quoting Dr. King — shocking the audience by shouting, "Free at last, free at last, thank God Almighty, I'm free at last." At that time I was only expressing the happiness and joy I felt about graduating, but today, I realize those words have a deeper meaning for me and hopefully you will understand after my message. When I am finished, you should under-stand what "Free at last" means to me.

When I think back to the event in my life that had the greatest effect on me, I remember something that happened over twelve years ago. I was eight years old. I was a shy, naive, innocent little boy. I knew I was Japanese, but I didn't consider myself different from my friends, nor did I realize anyone else noticed or even cared. But at least one person did. The "bully" in our class made it a point to remind me by calling me a Jap, telling me I didn't belong in America, and that I should go back to Japan.

This upset me very much and it was hard for me to understand what he meant, because like my parents I was born here in this country. I didn't know what to do when I was taunted, and I honestly can't remember what I did at the time. What I do remember is going home after school and crying to my mom. I told my mom that I wished I wasn't Japanese, but that if I did have to be Japanese, why did I have to be born in this country?

Of course my mother knew exactly how I felt. She was about the age I was then when the Japanese attacked Pearl Harbor. She told me how she too had experienced prejudice at school, but that the prejudice she encountered was over a hundred times worse. When my father came home from work, my mom and I told him what had happened. Although my father was understanding, he said that I would never know the meaning of true prejudice because I did not grow up on the West Coast during World War II.

My encounter with the school bully taught me what I know about preju-dice — that it is a bad part of human nature that lies buried deep within all of us. It taught me that some people like to make themselves feel good by putting others down. The experience also helped teach me how to deal with such problems when they arise. It was the advice from my mother that helped me the most.

My mother explained to me the meaning of the Japanese word *gaman.* *Gaman* means to "bear within" or "bear the burden." It is similar to the American phrase "turn the other cheek," but it means more to "endure" than to "ignore." She told me that when I go back to school, I should practice *gaman* — that even if I am hurt, I should not react with anger or fear, that I should bear the burden within. She said that if I showed anger or fear it would only make things worse, but if I practiced *gaman* things would get better for me. She was right. When I went back to school, I remembered what she had said. I used *gaman.* I bore the burden within. It wasn't easy for an eight year old, but I did not show any anger. I did not show any fear to the bully, and eventually he stopped picking on me.

From my early encounter with prejudice and from learning about *gaman,* I feel I have acquired a lot more inner strength than most college students. Whereas Gary [another student in the class] said he is a "competitor," I believe I am a "survivor." I look around my environment, recognize my situation, and I cope with it. Because I have been practicing *gaman* in my daily life since I was eight years old, I rarely experience feelings of anger or fear — those negative emotions that can keep a person from really being "free."

Being freed from such negative feelings has also helped me to better understand and accept myself. When I first encountered prejudice, I was ashamed of who I was. I didn't like being different, being a Japanese-American. But as I've grown to maturity, I have realized that I'm really proud to be Japanese-American: Japanese by blood — with the rich culture and heritage of my ancestors behind me — and American by birth — which makes me equal to anyone in this room because we were all born in this country and we all share similar everyday lifestyles.

Although my Japanese ancestors might not have spoken out today in this manner as I have, I am basically an American, which makes me a little outspoken. And therefore, I am able to speak to you of such experiences, of what they have meant to me, and because of this, I can truly say that I am "free at last."

GOLF AND COLLEGE

—— David N. Smart ——

The range of possible topics for the self-introductory speech is as diverse as the students in the classroom. The following speech, presented by David Smart in his public speaking class at Indiana University, expounds on the lessons he learned from playing golf. This speech demonstrates that the topic for a self-introductory speech need not necessarily be "sensitive." If handled with imagination and sincerity, almost any topic can be the basis for an effective self-introductory speech. Incidentally, the day did come when college "finally fell into place" for David. He graduated in the honors program from Indiana University and is now a financial analyst with the Ford Motor Company in Cincinnati.

You might not think that playing golf has very much to do with being a college student, or would be very helpful unless it won you a scholarship, but you are mistaken. I want to share with you how even a "duffer" like me has learned something from the game of golf. The two aspects of college life that golf has taught me a lot about are frustration and determination.

Golf is very frustrating to me because I'm just not that good. I've played for years, but I have never really mastered the game. Even on those rare occasions when I do play well, golf can still be very frustrating. One of the worst times I've ever had on the golf course was a day last summer when my friends and I went out to play one night after work. We were happy to be finished work and enjoying the beautiful weather, even though the forecast had called for rain. After the fifth hole I was even par. I know that doesn't sound that great, but for me it was nothing short of spectacular.

As we approached the sixth tee, we noticed that clouds had started to move in from the west. I had never been in a cloudburst before, and I didn't think it could rain *that* hard, but believe me, it can! We decided to walk to the clubhouse and wait for the rain to stop because it had started to lightning. We weren't worried about getting hit by the lightning because we all had our one irons above our heads. As every golfer knows, you are safe in a lightning storm with your one iron over your head because even God can't hit a one iron.

Even though it was storming fiercely, I was still hoping we would be able to finish because I was playing so well that day. As we headed towards the clubhouse, we noticed that the pond in front of the ninth green had flooded and there was a river running down the fairway. We had to wade through this river to get to the clubhouse. The water was up to my knees. It was at that time that I finally accepted the fact that I wouldn't get to finish that day and have my chance to shoot par. Another day, perhaps, when the sun is shining and there isn't a deluge in the forecast. . . .

College life can also be frustrating. Superficially, it is frustrating to have to hassle with registration, drop-and-add, parking stickers, or trying to get anything accomplished through the campus bureaucracy. But college life is also frustrating for me on a deeper level because I am just not sure what I am doing here. I am in the pre-business program, but I haven't made up my mind on my career goals yet. This can be frustrating because I sometimes feel like I'm just wasting my time here.

My experiences with golf have taught me that frustrations are temporary, that there are some things you cannot control, and that it doesn't help matters to get in a snit about them. I know that sooner or later I'll make it through registration; sooner or later I'll get to the front of the line in drop-and-add; sooner or later I'll get a parking sticker; and sooner or later I'll decide what I want to do with my life, and that my basic classes will count toward graduation.

The patience you have to develop to deal with frustrations also contributes to the determination you need to get through college. It takes real determination for me to go out and play golf night after night, knowing it will be a rare occasion when I shoot par. But I do it because I love the game. In college it has taken determination for me to take this public speaking class, which is something I wanted to avoid. It takes determination for me to get up and go to class day after day after day — especially when it's cold or raining and I have to walk a mile from my dorm to the classroom. One accomplishment that I'm most proud of is that I haven't missed one class yet in four semesters of college.

My experiences playing golf have given me this attitude about college: I don't let the little frustrations bother me and I keep going no matter what happens. In golf even though you hit a bad shot, you still have to go and hit the next one. You have to shake off the frustration and be determined to hit a good shot. You can't walk off the course just because things aren't going your way. College life is the same way. If you have a bad day or do poorly on a test, you can't just give up and go home. You have to get up the next day and keep trying.

I know that someday my golf game will finally fall into place, and I will play consistently and do the things I want to do on a golf course. Just as I know that day will come, I know the day will come when college also finally falls into place, and I will start heading down the right road and have my career goals set. I just hope these days will come soon.

THE "MONUMENT" AT WOUNDED KNEE

——— *Cecile Larson* ———

Cecile Larson's classroom speech serves two informative functions. First, it shapes the perceptions of the audience because of the way it describes the "monument" and the perspective it takes on the situation — most of her classmates had had little or no contact with Native Americans, and this might have been their first exposure to this type of information. Second, the speech serves the agenda-setting function in that it creates an awareness of a problem and thus increases its importance in the minds of the audience. The speech follows a spatial design. Cecile's vivid use of imagery and the skillful contrasts she draws between this "monument" and our "official" monuments create mental pictures that should stay with her listeners long after the words of her speech have been forgotten.

We Americans are big on monuments. We build monuments in memory of our heroes. Washington, Jefferson, and Lincoln live on in our nation's capital. We erect monuments to honor our martyrs. The Minute Man still stands guard at Concord. The flag is ever raised over Iwo Jima. Sometimes we even construct monuments to commemorate victims. In Ashburn Park downtown there is a monument to those who died in the yellow fever epidemics. However, there are some things in our history that we don't memorialize. Perhaps we would just as soon forget what happened. Last summer I visited such a place — the massacre site at Wounded Knee.

In case you have forgotten what happened at Wounded Knee, let me refresh your memory. On December 29, 1890, shortly after Sitting Bull had been murdered by the authorities, about 400 half-frozen, starving, and frightened Indians who had fled the nearby reservation were attacked by the Seventh Cavalry. When the fighting ended, between 200 and 300 Sioux had died — two-thirds of them women and children. Their remains are buried in a common grave at the site of the massacre.

Wounded Knee is located in the Pine Ridge Reservation in southwestern South Dakota — about a three-hour drive from where Presidents Washington, Jefferson, Theodore Roosevelt, and Lincoln are enshrined in the granite face of Mount Rushmore. The reservation is directly south of the Badlands National Park, a magnificently desolate area of wind-eroded buttes and multi-colored spires.

We entered the reservation driving south from the Badlands Visitor's Center. The landscape of the Pine Ridge Reservation retains much of the desolation of the Badlands but lacks its magnificence. Flat, sun-baked fields and an occasional eroded gully stretch as far as the eye can see. There are no signs or highway markers to lead the curious tourist to Wounded Knee. Even the *Rand-McNally Atlas* doesn't help you find your way. We got lost three times and had to stop and ask directions.

When we finally arrived at Wounded Knee, there was no official historic marker to tell us what had happened there. Instead there was a large, hand-made wooden sign — crudely lettered in white on black. The sign first directed our attention to our left — to the gully where the massacre took place. The mass grave site was to our right — across the road and up a small hill.

Two red-brick columns topped with a wrought-iron arch and a small metal cross form the entrance to the grave site. The column to the right is in bad shape: cinder blocks from the base are missing; the brickwork near the top has deteriorated and tumbled to the ground; graffiti on the columns proclaim an attitude we found repeatedly expressed about the Bureau of Indian Affairs — "The BIA sucks!"

Crumbling concrete steps lead you up to the mass grave. The top of the grave is covered with gravel, punctuated by unruly patches of chickweed and crabgrass. These same weeds also grow along the base of the broken chain-link fence that surrounds the grave, the "monument," and a small cemetery.

The "monument" itself rests on a concrete slab to the right of the grave. It's a typical, large, old-fashioned granite cemetery marker, a pillar about six feet high topped with an urn — the kind of gravestone you might see in any cemetery with graves from the turn of the century. The inscription tells us that it was erected by the families of those who were killed at Wounded Knee. Weeds grow through the cracks in the concrete at its base.

There are no granite headstones in the adjacent cemetery, only simple white wooden crosses that tell a story of people who died young. There is no neatly manicured grass. There are no flowers. Only the unrelenting and unforgiving weeds.

Yes, Americans are big on monuments. We build them to memorialize our heroes, to honor our martyrs, and sometimes, even to commemorate victims. But only when it makes us feel good.

RAPE BY ANY OTHER NAME

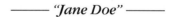

"Jane Doe"

The student who presented this courageous informative speech in a public speaking class at Memphis State University gave us permission to reprint the text using the pseudonym "Jane Doe." Although the topic is quite sensitive and personal, it deals with an important problem that many college students must face. "Jane" handled the subject in good taste with a matter-of-fact, unemotional presentation. Her introduction was especially effective. She used a telephone as a visual aid and presented the first part of the introduction with her hair pulled back and wearing dark glasses. To signal the change from male to female speaker in her introduction, "Jane" hung up the phone, removed the combs holding back her long hair, and took off the glasses. The use of dialogue and slang in the introduction added to its impact.

Yo, Kevin. Man, what's up? Did you go to that party Saturday night? You did? Man, did you see that girl in the blue dress? Yea, man, she was cool, the girl was wild! I had been lookin' at her all night, man, when a slow song came on and I asked her to dance. I knew she liked me by the way she kept smiling and looking at me. She told me her name was 'Jane' and so I said, 'Hey, Babe, why don't we go back to my room for a couple of drinks or something?' She said, 'Yeah,' man and I *knew* I was gonna make a move! Man, when we got back to my room, we sat on the bed and started kissin', then, man, when I started to lay her down on the bed, she started sayin' 'No.' I said, 'No? Hey babe if this isn't what you wanted then why'd you come up to the room?' Man, she started cryin' and stuff after. . . . You know girls don't want to seem too easy. But man, you could tell by the way she was lookin' in that dress *she wasn't no virgin*! . . . Hold on a minute, man." (Pause while the speaker clicks the phone over to call waiting.) "Hello? . . . Yes, this is he . . . Who? . . . Oh! . . . Jane . . . Hey, Baby. Yeah . . . You did *what*? *Pressing charges*? But . . . but . . . but . . . Hello . . . hello . . . hello. . . ."

"I met him at a party. He was really good-looking and had the nicest smile. I wanted to meet him, but I wasn't sure how. Then he came over and introduced himself to me. We danced and talked for a long time and found out that we had a lot in common. When he asked me to go to his dorm room for a drink, I didn't think anything of it, so I went. When we got there, the only place to sit was on his bed, so I did. He sat down next to me and after we'd talked a while, he kissed me. It wasn't bad, so I didn't stop him. But then, he pushed me down on the bed. I tried to get up and I told him to stop, but he wouldn't. He was so much bigger and stronger . . . I got scared and I started to cry. I froze and he raped me. When it was over, he kept asking me what was wrong . . . like what he did was okay . . . like what he did wasn't wrong! He drove me home and said he wanted to see me again. I'm afraid to see him again. I never thought anything like this would happen to me."

Date rape. What you've just heard was adapted from a brochure produced by the American College Health Association entitled *Acquaintance Rape*. Date rape — acquaintance rape — social rape — by any other name, it is still rape. We need to understand what it is, what causes it, and what its effects usually are. We need to know what we can personally do to keep date rape from happening, and what we should do if and when it does happen.

First, what is date rape and what causes it? Date rape is a forced or unwanted sexual relationship involving two people who know each other — who are friends or acquaintances. Most of the time the female victim is on a "date" with the rapist. She has voluntarily gone with him as opposed to having been forcefully abducted. And, although she knows the man involved and may consider him a friend, she does not want and she does not agree to a sexual relationship.

How can a social relationship, or a date, end up in a rape? What are some of the causes of date rape? Date rape typically occurs because of sex role stereotypes and poor communication between two people of opposite sexes. Many people firmly believe that men are competitive and aggressive and women are yielding and passive. When these stereotypes are treated as "just the way things are," then men may presume that men *should be* aggressive and forceful in relationships and that women *should be* passive and submitting. They turn a misinformed description into a prescription for behavior. There's also a potential for date rape when two people don't have a clear understanding of each other's sexual intentions and expectations. Date rape can happen because of mixed messages and learned violence. Mixed messages occur when a man, thinking a woman is playing hard to get, believes she really means "yes" when she says "no." Mixed messages may be communicated verbally such as through suggestive or flirtatious conversation — the verbal game-playing that goes on at parties. Mixed messages can also be communicated non-verbally through body language or in many cases by the way a woman dresses. On television and in the movies violence is often shown as a way to solve problems, so some men feel it's okay to use "a little force" to get what they want from a woman.

We've looked at what date rape is and some of the reasons why it happens, so now let's explore some of the effects of date rape. The female victim of a date rape may experience a loss of trust — particularly of men — and find it difficult to feel comfortable in close relationships. I can speak from my own experience in saying that date rape does have a devastating effect on future relationships. It's hard to be open and warm and friendly because you're always afraid it will happen again. The victim may feel guilty because she thinks maybe she did something to cause it or because she thinks she should have been able to prevent it. These negative feelings can cause some victims of date rape to experience depression or sexual adjustment problems that call for professional counseling. The man may also be considered a victim — in a way, like the guy in my opening example who didn't seem to realize that "no" means "no" — period. He may not be able to understand or accept that what he did was wrong. In that sense, he is a victim of his distorted beliefs. And if the female presses charges, he too may suffer from the consequences.

Date rape is real, and it is a problem, but it's a problem we can do a lot to keep from happening if both men and women learn how date rape can be avoided. One way to help prevent date rape is to always clearly express what *you* want before getting involved in a relationship with a person of the opposite sex. Know your limits. Beware of alcohol and drugs. It's hard to cope with a date rape situation. It's much harder to be in control if you're under the influence of these substances. Be aware of how much your date drinks, too. Avoid secluded places. *Don't* go to a beach, park, deserted bridge, or "make-out spot" with someone you've just met. Suggest meeting in public places like the mall or the movies when getting to know someone. Have your own transportation. Don't rely on your date for it (especially if you don't know him very well). Drive your own car, double date, or take the bus.

It's also important for each of us to know our individual rights and those of anyone we may be socially involved with. A woman may dress any way she pleases. If she is scantily clad and flirts, that doesn't necessarily mean, "Let's do it!" Even if she lets things advance to the point of having sex, she can change her mind at any time. It should not be assumed that if (1) "I paid for dinner!" or (2) we met at a beer party, or (3) we've had sex before, then it's okay to force someone into having sex.

Any instance of sexual assault, including date rape, should be reported to the authorities. Date rape is sometimes not seen as serious as "real rape" — or sexual assault by a stranger — BUT IT IS! Sometimes a woman thinks that she won't be believed if she reports the crime. She may be afraid that people will accuse her of "asking for it." But it is a crime, and it has to be reported. Next, the victim should go to a hospital immediately. *She should not shower, change clothes, douche, or even comb her hair*! Finally, the victim should get some type of emotional support, be it a friend, minister (whom I confided in about my situation), or if neither of these, there are rape crisis hotlines with compassionate counselors you can call.

Date rape, acquaintance rape, social rape, silent rape, or cocktail rape. By any name, date rape is and always will be considered a crime. So remember to be aware of what causes date rape so you will be alert to the danger signs. Know its effects before you let a dangerous situation go too far, and be aware that everyone plays a part in the control of date rape.

THE NATIONAL DRUG CONTROL STRATEGY

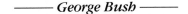

——— *George Bush* ———

Presented September 5, 1989, this was the first major televised speech to the people George Bush made as president. The speech was basically informative, but with an underlying, secondary persuasive purpose. First, President Bush wanted the public to be aware of the nature and extent of the drug problem in this country and his program for dealing with it. Second, he hoped to obtain public support that would give his program an edge when it came before Congress for funding. The speech is a model of careful structure and is well documented with expert testimony and information. The president used visual aids (where noted in the text) very effectively. The setting, the Oval Office at the White House, made the speech seem especially authoritative and important.

Good evening. This is the first time since taking the oath of office that I felt an issue was so important, so threatening, that it warranted talking directly with you, the American people. All of us agree that the gravest domestic threat facing our nation today is drugs. Drugs have strained our faith in our system of justice. Our courts, our prisons, our legal system are stretched to the breaking point. The social costs of drugs are mounting. In short, drugs are sapping our strength as a nation. Turn on the evening news, or pick up the morning paper and you'll see what some Americans know just by stepping out their front door: Our most serious problem today is cocaine and, in particular, crack.

Who's responsible? Let me tell you straight out: everyone who uses drugs, everyone who sells drugs, and everyone who looks the other way.

Tonight, I'll tell you how many Americans are using illegal drugs. I will present to you our national strategy to deal with every aspect of this threat. And I will ask you to get involved in what promises to be a very difficult fight.

From *Weekly Compilation of Presidential Documents,* 11 Sept. 1989, pp. 1304–8.

This is crack cocaine [the president shows a bag containing a white substance] seized a few days ago by Drug Enforcement agents in a park just across the street from the White House. It could easily have been heroin or PCP. It's as innocent looking as candy, but it's turning our cities into battle zones, and it's murdering our children. Let there be no mistake: This stuff is poison. Some used to call drugs harmless recreation. They're not. Drugs are a real and terribly dangerous threat to our neighborhoods, our friends, and our families.

No one among us is out of harm's way. When 4-year-olds play in playgrounds strewn with discarded hypodermic needles and crack vials, it breaks my heart. When cocaine, one of the most deadly and addictive illegal drugs, is available to school kids — school kids — it's an outrage. And when hundreds of thousands of babies are born each year to mothers who use drugs — premature babies born desperately sick — then even the most defenseless among us are at risk.

These are the tragedies behind the statistics, but the numbers also have quite a story to tell. Let me share with you the results of the recently completed Household Survey of the National Institute on Drug Abuse. It compares recent drug use to 3 years ago. It tells us some good news and some very bad news. First, the good.

As you can see in the chart, [chart comes up on the screen] in 1985 the Government estimated that 23 million Americans were using drugs on a "current" basis; that is, at least once in the preceding month. Last year that number fell by more than a third. That means almost 9 million fewer Americans are casual drug users. Good news.

Because we changed our national attitude toward drugs, casual drug use has declined. We have many to thank: our brave law enforcement officers, religious leaders, teachers, community activists, and leaders of business and labor. We should also thank the media for their exhaustive news and editorial coverage and for their air time and space for antidrug messages. And finally, I want to thank President and Mrs. Reagan for their leadership. All of these good people told the truth: that drug use is wrong and dangerous.

But as much comfort as we can draw from these dramatic reductions, there is also bad news, very bad news. Roughly 8 million people have used cocaine in the past year. Almost 1 million of them used it frequently — once a week or more. What this means is that, in spite of the fact that overall cocaine use is down, frequent use has almost doubled in the last few years. And that's why habitual cocaine users, especially crack users, are the most pressing, immediate drug problem.

What, then, is our plan? To begin with, I trust the lesson of experience: No single policy will cut it, no matter how glamorous or magical it may sound. To win the war against addictive drugs like crack will take more than just a Federal strategy: It will take a national strategy, one that reaches into every school, every workplace, involving every family.

Earlier today I sent this document, our first such national strategy, to the Congress. It was developed with the hard work of our nation's first Drug Policy Director, Bill Bennett. In preparing this plan, we talked with State, local, and community leaders, law enforcement officials, and experts in education, drug prevention, and rehabilitation. We talked with parents and kids. We took a long, hard look at all that the Federal Government has done about drugs in the past — what's worked and, let's be honest, what hasn't. Too often, people in government acted as if their part of the problem — whether fighting drug production or drug smuggling or drug demand — was the only problem. But turf battles won't win this war; teamwork will.

Tonight, I'm announcing a strategy that reflects the coordinated, cooperative commitment of all Federal agencies. In short, this plan is as comprehensive as the problem. With this strategy, we now finally have a plan that coordinates our resources, our programs, and the people who run them. Our weapons in this strategy are the law and criminal justice system, our foreign policy, our treatment systems, and our schools and drug prevention programs. So, the basic weapons we need are the ones we already have. What's been lacking is a strategy to effectively use them.

Let me address four of the major elements of our strategy. First, we are determined to enforce the law, to make our streets and neighborhoods safe. So, to start, I'm proposing that we more than double Federal assistance to State and local law enforcement. Americans have a right to safety in and around their homes. And we won't have safe neighborhoods unless we're tough on drug criminals — much tougher than we are now. Sometimes that means tougher penalties, but more often it just means punishment that is swift and certain. We've all heard stories about drug dealers who are caught and arrested again and again, but never punished. Well, here the rules have changed: If you sell drugs, you will be caught. And when you're caught, you will be prosecuted. And once you're convicted, you will do time. Caught. Prosecuted. Punished.

I'm also proposing that we enlarge our criminal justice system across the board — at the local, State and Federal levels alike. We need more prisons, more jails, more courts, more prosecutors. So, tonight I'm requesting — altogether — an almost $1.5 billion increase in drug-related Federal spending on law enforcement.

And while illegal drug use is found in every community, nowhere is it worse than in our public housing projects. You know, the poor have never had it easy in this world. But in the past, they weren't mugged on the way home from work by crack gangs. And their children didn't have to dodge bullets on the way to school. And that's why I'm targeting $50 million to fight crime in public housing projects — to help restore order and to kick out the dealers for good.

The second element of our strategy looks beyond our borders, where the cocaine and crack bought on America's streets is grown and processed. In Colombia alone, cocaine killers have gunned down a leading statesman, murdered almost 200 judges and 7 members of their Supreme Court. The besieged governments of the drug-producing countries are fighting back, fighting to break the international drug rings. But you and I agree with the courageous President of Colombia, Virgilio Barco, who said that if Americans use cocaine, then Americans are paying for murder. American cocaine users need to understand that our nation has zero tolerance for casual drug use. We have a responsibility not to leave our brave friends in Colombia to fight alone.

The $65 million emergency assistance announced 2 weeks ago was just our first step in assisting the Andean nations in their fight against the cocaine cartels. Colombia has already arrested suppliers, seized tons of cocaine and confiscated palatial homes of drug lords. But Colombia faces a long, uphill battle, so we must be ready to do more. Our strategy allocates more than a quarter of a billion dollars for next year in military and law enforcement assistance for the three Andean nations of Colombia, Bolivia and Peru. This will be the first part of a 5-year, $2 billion program to counter the producers, the traffickers, and the smugglers.

I spoke with President Barco just last week, and we hope to meet with the leaders of affected countries in an unprecedented drug summit, all to coordinate an inter-American strategy against the cartels. We will work with our allies and friends, especially our economic summit partners, to do more in the fight against drugs. I'm also asking the Senate to ratify the United Nations antidrug convention concluded last December.

To stop those drugs on the way to America, I propose that we spend more than a billion and a half dollars on interdiction. Greater interagency cooperation, combined with Defense Department technology can help stop drugs at our borders.

And our message to the drug cartels is this: The rules have changed. We will help any government that wants our help. When requested, we will for the first time make available the appropriate resources of America's Armed Forces. We will intensify our efforts against drug smugglers on the high seas, in international airspace, and at our borders. We will stop the flow of chemicals from the United States used to process drugs. We will pursue and enforce international agreements to track drug money to the front men and financiers. And then we will handcuff these money launderers and jail them, just like any street dealer. And for the drug kingpins — the death penalty.

The third part of our strategy concerns drug treatment. Experts believe that there are 2 million American drug users who may be able to get off drugs with proper treatment. But right now only 40 percent of them are actually getting help. This is simply not good enough. Many people who need treatment won't seek it on their own. And some who do seek it are put on a waiting list. Most programs were set up to deal with heroin addicts, but today the major problem is cocaine users. It's time we expand our treatment systems and do a better job of providing services to those who need them.

And so, tonight I'm proposing an increase of $321 million in Federal spending on drug treatment. With this strategy, we will do more. We will work with the States. We will encourage employers to establish employee assistance programs to cope with drug use. And because addiction is such a cruel inheritance, we will intensify our search for ways to help expectant mothers who use drugs.

Fourth, we must stop illegal drug use before it starts. Unfortunately, it begins early — for many kids, before their teens. But it doesn't start the way you might think, from a dealer or an addict hanging around a school playground. More often, our kids first get their drugs free, from friends or even from older brothers or sisters. Peer pressure spreads drug use. Peer pressure can help stop it. I am proposing a quarter-of-a-billion-dollar increase in Federal funds for school and community prevention programs that help young people and adults reject enticements to try drugs. And I'm proposing something else. Every school, college and university and every workplace must adopt tough but fair policies about drug use by students and employees. And those that will not adopt such policies will not get Federal funds. Period.

The private sector also has an important role to play. I spoke with a businessman named Jim Burke who said he was haunted by the thought — a nightmare really — that somewhere in America, at any given moment, there is a teenage girl who should be in school instead of giving birth to a child addicted to cocaine. So, Jim did something. He led an antidrug partnership, financed by private funds, to work with advertisers and media firms. Their partnership is now determined to work with our strategy by generating educational messages worth a million dollars a day every day for the next 3 years — a billion dollars worth of advertising, all to promote the antidrug message.

As President, one of my first missions is to keep the national focus on our offensive against drugs. And so, next week I will take the antidrug message to the classrooms of America in a special television address, one that I hope will reach every school, every young American. But drug education doesn't begin in class or on TV. It must begin at home and in the neighborhood. Parents and families must set the first example of a drug-free life. And when families are broken, caring friends and neighbors must step in.

These are the most important elements in our strategy to fight drugs. They are all designed to reinforce one another, to mesh into a powerful whole, to mount an aggressive attack on the problem from every angle. This is the first time in the history of our country that we truly have a comprehensive strategy.

As you can tell, such an approach will not come cheaply. Last February, I asked for a $700 million increase in the drug budget for the coming year. And now, over the past 6 months of careful study, we have found an immediate need for another billion and a half dollars. With this added $2.2 billion, our 1990 drug budget totals almost $8 billion, the largest increase in history. We need this program fully implemented — right away. The next fiscal year begins just 26 days from now. So, tonight I'm asking the Congress, which has helped us formulate this strategy, to help us move it forward immediately. We can pay for this fight against drugs without raising taxes or adding to the budget deficit. We have submitted our plan to Congress that shows just how to fund it within the limits of our bipartisan budget agreement.

Now, I know some will still say that we're not spending enough money. But those who judge our strategy only by its price tag simply don't understand the problem. Let's face it, we've all seen in the past that money alone won't solve our toughest problems. To be strong and efficient, our strategy needs these funds. But there is no match for a united America, a determined America, an angry America. Our outrage against drugs unites us, brings us together behind this one plan of action, an assault on every front.

This is the toughest domestic challenge we've faced in decades. And it's a challenge we must face not as Democrats or Republicans, liberals or conservatives, but as Americans. The key is a coordinated, united effort. We've responded faithfully to the request of the Congress to produce our nation's first national drug strategy. I'll be looking to the Democratic majority and our Republicans in Congress for leadership and bipartisan support. And our citizens deserve cooperation, not competition; a national effort, not a partisan bidding war. To start, Congress needs not only to act on this national drug strategy but also to act on our crime package announced last May, a package to toughen sentences, beef up law enforcement, and build new prison space for 24,000 inmates.

You and I both know the Federal Government can't do it alone. The States need to match tougher Federal laws with tougher laws of their own: stiffer bail, probation, parole, and sentencing. And we need your help. If people you know are users, help them get off drugs. If you're a parent, talk to your kids about drugs — tonight. Call your local drug prevention program. Be a Big Brother or Sister to a child in need. Pitch in with your local Neighborhood Watch program. Whether you give your time or talent, everyone counts: every employer who bans drugs from the workplace; every school that's tough on drug use; every neighborhood in which drugs are not welcome; and most important, every one of you who refuses to look the other way. Every one of you counts. Of course, victory will take hard work and time. But together we will win. Too many young lives are at stake.

Not long ago, I read a newspaper story about a little boy named Dooney, who, until recently, lived in a crack house in a suburb of Washington, DC. In Dooney's neighborhood, children don't flinch at the sound of gunfire. And when they play, they pretend to sell each other small white rocks they call crack. Life at home was so cruel that Dooney begged his teachers to let him sleep on the floor at school. And when asked about his future, 6-year-old Dooney answers: "I don't want to sell drugs, but I'll probably have to."

Well, Dooney does not have to sell drugs. No child in America should have to live like this. Together as a people we can save these kids. We've already transformed a national attitude of tolerance into one of condemnation. But the war on drugs will be hard won, neighborhood by neighborhood, block by block, child by child.

If we fight this war as a divided nation, then the war is lost. But, if we face this evil as a nation united, this [holds up package of crack] will be nothing but a handful of useless chemicals. Victory, victory over drugs is our cause, a just cause. And with your help, we are going to win.

Thank you, God bless you, and good night.

ADDRESS TO THE U.S. CONGRESS

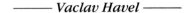

——— Vaclav Havel ———

Vaclav Havel was elected by Parliament as president of Czechoslovakia on December 29, 1989. Havel, an award-winning playwright and essayist, was frequently jailed as a dissident by the discredited communist regime in his country. His most recent arrest took place about two months before he assumed the presidency. His writing is reminiscent of the work of George Orwell (*Animal Farm, 1984*), for he parodies the governmental systems that "destroy human personality," and pays particular attention to the role of language in the dehumanization process. The following address was delivered in Czech, with a simultaneous translation in English. It was presented to a joint session of the U.S. Congress on February 21, 1990.

Dear Mr. Speaker, dear Mr. President, dear Senators, and Members of the House, ladies and gentlemen:

My advisers advised me to speak on this important occasion in Czech. I don't know why. Perhaps they wanted you to enjoy the sweet sounds of my mother tongue.

The last time they arrested me, on October 27, of last year, I didn't know whether it was for 2 days or 2 years.

Exactly 1 month later, when the rock musician Michael Kocab told me that I would probably be proposed as a Presidential candidate, I thought it was one of his usual jokes.

On the 10th of December 1989, when my actor friend Jiri Bartoska, in the name of the Civic Forum, nominated me as a candidate for the office of President of the Republic, I thought it was out of the question that the Parliament we had inherited from the previous regime would elect me.

Nineteen days later, when I was unanimously elected President of my country, I had no idea that in 2 months later I would be speaking in front of this famous and powerful assembly, and that what I say would be heard by millions of people who have never heard of me and that hundreds of politicians and political scientists would study every word I say.

When they arrested me on October 27, I was living in a country ruled by the most conservative Communist government in Europe, and our society slumbered beneath the pall of a totalitarian system. Today, less than 4 months later, I am speaking to you as the representative of a country that has set out on the road to democracy, a country where there is complete freedom of

From the *Congressional Record — House,* 21 Feb. 1990, pp. H392–95.

speech, which is getting ready for free elections, and which wants to create a prosperous market economy and its own foreign policy.

It is all very extraordinary.

But I have not come here to speak for myself or my feelings, or merely to talk about my own country. I have used this small example of something I know well, to illustrate something general and important.

We are living in very extraordinary times. The human face of the world is changing so rapidly that none of the familiar political speedometers are adequate.

We playwrights, who have to cram a whole human life or an entire historical era into a 2-hour play, can scarcely understand this rapidity ourselves. And if it gives us trouble, think of the trouble it must give to political scientists, who spend their whole lives studying the realm of the probable. And have even less experience with the realm of the improbable than us, the playwrights.

Let me try to explain why I think the velocity of the changes in my country, in Central and Eastern Europe, and of course in the Soviet Union itself, has made such a significant impression on the face of the world today, and why it concerns the fate of us all, including you Americans. I would like to look at this, first from the political point of view, and then from a point of view that we might call philosophical.

Twice in this century, the world has been threatened by a catastrophe; twice this catastrophe was born in Europe, and twice you Americans, along with others, were called upon to save Europe, the whole world and yourselves. The first rescue mission — among other things — provided significant help to us Czechs and Slovaks.

Thanks to the great support of your President Wilson, our first President, Tomas Garrigue Masaryk, could found our modern independent state. He founded it, as you know, on the same principles on which the United States of America had been founded, as Masaryk's manuscripts held by the Library of Congress testify.

In the meantime, the United States made enormous strides. It became the most powerful nation on Earth, and it understood the responsibility that flowed from this. Proof of this are the hundreds of thousands of your young citizens who gave their lives for the liberation of Europe, and the graves of American airmen and soldiers on Czechoslovak soil.

But something else was happening as well: the Soviet Union appeared, grew, and transformed the enormous sacrifices of its people suffering under a totalitarian rule, into a strength that, after World War II, made it the second most powerful nation in the world. It was a country that rightly gave people nightmares, because no one knew what would occur to its rulers next and what country they would decide to conquer and drag into their sphere of influence, as it is called in political language.

All of this taught us to see the world in bipolar terms, as two enormous forces, one a defender of freedom, the other a source of nightmares. Europe became the point of friction between these two powers, and thus it turned into a single enormous arsenal divided into two parts. In this process, one half of the arsenal became part of that nightmarish power, while the other — the free part — bordering on the ocean and having no wish to be driven into it, was compelled, together with you, to build a complicated security system, to which we probably owe the fact that we still exist.

So you may have contributed to the salvation of us Europeans, of the world and thus of yourselves for a third time: you have helped us to survive until today — without a hot war this time — but merely a cold one.

And now what is happening is happening: the totalitarian system in the Soviet Union and in most of its satellites is breaking down and our nations are looking for a way to democracy and independence. The first act in this remarkable drama began when Mr. Gorbachev and those around him, faced with the sad reality of their country, initiated their policy of "perestroika." Obviously they had no idea either what they were setting in motion or how rapidly events would unfold. We knew a lot about the enormous number of growing problems that slumbered beneath the honeyed, unchanging mask of socialism. But I don't think any of us knew how little it would take for these problems to manifest themselves in all their enormity, and for the longings of these nations to emerge in all their strength. The mask fell away so rapidly that, in the flood of work, we have literally no time even to be astonished.

What does all this mean for the world in the long run? Obviously a number of things. This is, I am firmly convinced, a historically irreversible process, and as a result Europe will begin again to seek its own identity without being compelled to be a divided armory any longer. Perhaps this will create the hope that sooner or later your boys will no longer have to stand on guard for freedom in Europe, or come to our rescue, because Europe will at last be able to stand guard over itself. But that is still not the most important thing: the main thing is, it seems to me, that these revolutionary changes will enable us to escape from the rather antiquated straitjacket of this bipolar view of the world, and to enter at last into an era of multipolarity. That is, into an era in which all of us — large and small — former slaves and former masters — will be able to create what your great President Lincoln called the family of man. Can you imagine what a relief this would be to that part of the world which for some reason is called the Third World, even though it is the largest.

I don't think it's appropriate simply to generalize, so let me be specific:

First, as you certainly know, most of the big wars and other conflagrations over the centuries have traditionally begun and ended on the territory of modern Czechoslovakia, or else they were somehow related to that area. Let the Second World War stand as the most recent example. This is understandable: whether we like it or not, we are located in the very heart of Europe, and thanks to this, we have no view of the sea, and no real navy. I mention this because political stability in our country has traditionally been important for the whole of Europe. This is still true today. Our government of national understanding, our present Federal Assembly, the other bodies of the state and I myself will personally guarantee this stability until we hold free elections, planned for June. We understand the terribly complex reasons, domestic political reasons above all, why the Soviet Union cannot withdraw its troops from our territory as quickly as they arrived in 1968. We understand that the arsenals built there over the past 20 years cannot be dismantled and removed overnight. Nevertheless, in our bilateral negotiations with the Soviet Union, we would like to have as many Soviet units as possible moved out of our country before the elections, in the interests of political stability. The more successful our negotiations, the more those who are elected in our places will be able to guarantee political stability in our country even after the elections.

Second, I often hear the question: How can the United States of America help us today? My reply is as paradoxical as the whole of my life has been: You can help us most of all if you help the Soviet Union on its irreversible but immensely complicated road to democracy. It is far more complicated than the road open to its former European satellites. You yourselves know best how to support, as rapidly as possible, the nonviolent evolution of this enormous, multinational body politic toward democracy and autonomy for all of its peoples. Therefore, it is not fitting for me to offer you any advice. I can only say that the sooner, the more quickly, and the more peacefully the Soviet Union begins to move along the road toward genuine political pluralism, respect for the rights of nations to their own integrity and to a working — that is, a market — economy, the better it will be, not just for Czechs and Slovaks, but for the whole world. And the sooner you yourselves will be able to reduce the burden of the military budget borne by the American people. To put it metaphorically: The millions you give to the East today will soon return to you in the form of billions in savings.

Third, it is not true that the Czech writer Vaclav Havel wishes to dissolve the Warsaw Pact tomorrow and then NATO the day after that, as some eager journalists have written. Vaclav Havel merely thinks what he has already said here, that for another hundred years, American soldiers shouldn't have to be separated from their mothers just because Europe is incapable of being a guarantor of world peace, which it ought to be, in order to make some amends, at least, for having given the world two world wars. Sooner or later Europe must recover and come into its own, and decide for itself how many of whose soldiers it needs so that its own security, and all the wider implications of that security, may radiate peace into the whole world. Vaclav Havel cannot make decisions about things that are not proper for him to decide. He is merely putting in a good word for genuine peace, and for achieving it quickly.

Fourth, Czechoslovakia thinks that the planned summit conference of countries participating in the Helsinki process should take place soon, and that in addition to what it wants to accomplish, it should aim to hold the so-called Helsinki II conference earlier than 1992, as originally planned. Above all, we feel it could be something far more significant than has so far seemed possible. We think that Helsinki II should become something equivalent to the European peace conference, which has not yet been held; one that would finally put a formal end to the Second World War and all its unhappy consequences. Such a conference would officially bring a future democratic Germany, in the process of unifying itself, into a new pan-European structure which could decide about its own security system. This system would naturally require some connection with that part of the globe we might label the "Helsinki" part, stretching westward from Vladivostok all the way to Alaska. The borders of the European states, which by the way should become gradually less important, should finally be legally guaranteed by a common, regular treaty. It should be more than obvious that the basis for such a treaty would have to be general respect for human rights, genuine political pluralism and genuinely free elections.

Fifth, naturally we welcome the initiative of President Bush, which was essentially accepted by Mr. Gorbachev as well, according to which the number of American and Soviet troops in Europe should be radically reduced. It is a magnificent shot in the arm for the Vienna disarmament talks and creates favorable conditions not only for our own efforts to achieve the quickest possible departure of Soviet troops from Czechoslovakia, but indirectly as well for our own intention to make considerable cuts in the Czechoslovak Army, which is disproportionately large in relation to our population. If Czechoslovakia were forced to defend itself against anyone, which we hope will not happen, then it will be capable of doing so with a considerably smaller army, because this time its defense would be — not only after decades but after even centuries — supported by the common and indivisible will of both its nations and its leadership. Our freedom, independence, and our newborn democracy have been purchased at great cost, and we shall not surrender them. For the sake of order, I should add that whatever steps we take are not intended to complicate the Vienna disarmament talks, but on the contrary, to facilitate them.

Sixth, Czechoslovakia is returning to Europe. In the general interest and in its own interest as well, it wants to coordinate this return — both politically and economically — with the other returnees, which means, above all, with its neighbors the Poles and the Hungarians. We are doing what we can to coordinate these returns. And at the same time, we are doing what we can so that Europe will be capable of really accepting us, its wayward children. Which means that it may open itself to us, and may begin to transform its structures — which are formally European but de facto Western European — in that direction, but in such a way that it will not be to its detriment, but rather to its advantage.

Seventh, I have already said this in our parliament, and I would like to repeat it here, in this Congress, which is architecturally far more attractive: for many years Czechoslovakia — as someone's meaningless satellite — has refused to face up honestly to its coresponsibility for the world. It has a lot to make up for. If I dwell on this and so many important things, it is only because I feel — along with my fellow citizens — a sense of culpability for our former reprehensible passivity, and a rather ordinary sense of indebtedness.

Eighth, we are of course delighted that your country is so readily lending its support to our fresh efforts to renew democracy. Both our peoples were deeply moved by the generous offers made a few days ago in Prague at the Charles University, one of the oldest in Europe, by your Secretary of State, Mr. James Baker. We are ready to sit down and talk about them.

Ladies and gentlemen. I've only been president for 2 months and I haven't attended any schools for presidents. My only school was life itself. Therefore I don't want to burden you any longer with my political thoughts, but instead I will move on to an area that is more familiar to me, to what I would call the philosophical aspect of those changes that still concern everyone, although they are taking place in our corner of the world.

As long as people are people, democracy in the full sense of the word will always be no more than an ideal; one may approach it as one would a horizon, in ways that may be better or worse, but it can never be fully attained. In this sense you too are merely approaching democracy. You have thousands of problems of all kinds, as other countries do. But you have one great advantage: You have been approaching democracy uninterruptedly for more than 200 years, and your journey toward the horizon has never been disrupted by a totalitarian system. Czechs and Slovaks, despite their humanistic traditions that go back to the first millennium, have approached democracy for a mere 20 years, between the two world wars, and now for the 3 1/2 months since the 17th of November of last year.

The advantage that you have over us is obvious at once.

The Communist type of totalitarian system has left both our nations, Czechs and Slovaks — as it has all the nations of the Soviet Union and the other countries the Soviet Union subjugated in its time — a legacy of countless dead, an infinite spectrum of human suffering, profound economic decline, and above all enormous human humiliation. It has brought us horrors that fortunately you have not known.

At the same time, however — unintentionally, of course — it has given us something positive: a special capacity to look, from time to time, somewhat further than someone who has not undergone this bitter experience. A person who cannot move and live a somewhat normal life because he is pinned under a boulder has more time to think about his hopes than someone who is not trapped that way.

What I'm trying to say is this: we must all learn many things from you, from how to educate our offspring, how to elect our representatives, all the way to how to organize our economic life so that it will lead to prosperity and not to poverty. But it doesn't have to be merely assistance from the well-educated, the powerful and wealthy to someone who has nothing and therefore has nothing to offer in return.

We too can offer something to you: our experience and the knowledge that has come from it.

This is a subject for books, many of which have already been written and many of which have yet to be written. I shall therefore limit myself to a single idea.

The specific experience I'm talking about has given me one great certainty: Consciousness precedes Being, and not the other way around, as the Marxists claim.

For this reason, the salvation of this human world lies nowhere else than in the human heart, in the human power to reflect, in human meekness and in human responsibility.

Without a global revolution in the sphere of human consciousness, nothing will change for the better in the sphere of our Being as humans, and the catastrophe toward which this world is headed, be it ecological, social, demographic or a general breakdown of civilization, will be unavoidable. If we are no longer threatened by world war, or by the danger that the absurd mountains of accumulated nuclear weapons might blow up the world, this does not mean that we have definitely won. We are in fact far from the final victory.

We are still a long way from that "family of man"; in fact, we seem to be receding from the ideal rather than drawing closer to it. Interests of all kinds: personal, selfish, state, national, group and, if you like, company interests still considerably outweigh genuinely common and global interests. We are still under the sway of the destructive and vain belief that man is the pinnacle of creation, and not just a part of it, and that therefore everything is permitted. There are still many who say they are concerned not for themselves, but for the cause, while they are demonstrably out for themselves and not for the cause at all. We are still destroying the planet that was entrusted to us, and its environment. We still close our eyes to the growing social, ethnic and cultural conflicts in the world. From time to time we say that the anonymous megamachinery we have created for ourselves no longer serves us, but rather has enslaved us, yet we still fail to do anything about it.

In other words, we still don't know how to put morality ahead of politics, science and economics. We are still incapable of understanding that the only genuine backbone of all our actions — if they are to be moral — is responsibility. Responsibility to something higher than my family, my country, my company, my success. Responsibility to the order of Being, where all our actions are indelibly recorded and where, and only where, they will be properly judged.

The interpreter or mediator between us and this higher authority is what is traditionally referred to as human conscience.

If I subordinate my political behavior to this imperative mediated to me by my conscience, I can't go far wrong. If on the contrary I were not guided by this voice, not even 10 presidential schools with 2,000 of the best political scientists in the world could help me.

This is why I ultimately decided — after resisting for a long time — to accept the burden of political responsibility.

I am not the first, nor will I be the last, intellectual to do this. On the contrary, my feeling is that there will be more and more of them all the time. If the hope of the world lies in human consciousness, then it is obvious that intellectuals cannot go on forever avoiding their share of responsibility for the world and hiding their distaste for politics under an alleged need to be independent.

It is easy to have independence in your program and then leave others to carry that program out. If everyone thought that way, pretty soon no one would be independent.

I think that you Americans should understand this way of thinking. Wasn't it the best minds of your country, people you could call intellectuals, who wrote your famous Declaration of Independence, your Bill of Human Rights and your Constitution and who — above all — took upon themselves the practical responsibility for putting them into practice? The worker from Branik in Prague that your President referred to in his State of the Union message this year is far from being the only person in Czechoslovakia, let alone in the world, to be inspired by those great documents. They inspire us all. They inspire us despite the fact that they are over 200 years old. They inspire us to be citizens.

When Thomas Jefferson wrote that, "Governments are instituted among Men deriving their just Powers from the Consent of the Governed," it was a simple and important act of the human spirit.

What gave meaning to that act, however, was the fact that the author backed it up with his life. It was not just his words, it was his deeds as well.

I will end where I began: history has accelerated. I believe that once again, it will be the human mind that will notice this acceleration, give it a name, and transform those words into deeds.

Thank you.

DRINKING AND DRIVING RESPONSIBLY

——— *Betty Nichols* ———

Betty Nichols had several problems to overcome when she presented this speech to her public speaking class at Memphis State University in 1987. First, since Betty was considerably older than most of her classmates, she had to be certain that her listeners did not look at her as if she were their mother talking to them. Second, although the problem of drinking and driving is important, most audiences are exposed to a barrage of messages that tell them, "If you drink, don't drive." To reach her audience, to attract and sustain their attention, she needed a fresh approach to the problem. Moreover, Betty needed to provide her audience with a plan of action or the knowledge of how to drink and drive responsibly.

During our lifetime half of us — I mean those of us in this room — will be involved in an alcohol-related car accident. Chances are good that one of us won't make it — or will be crippled for life. We will either be the drunk behind the wheel or the innocent victim.

Why don't we do something? Haven't we been warned, and warned repeatedly? I suspect that the reason we don't do something is that the old approach to drinking and driving simply does not work for most of us. We need to replace the old notion of "If you drive, don't drink" with a new idea of *responsible* drinking and driving. Today I would like to review with you the dimensions of this problem and suggest a new approach that just might work.

One reason why we may not have solved this problem is that riding in a car gives us a sense of false security — a security that should dissolve rapidly once you hear these numbers. Drunk driving causes 24,000 deaths per year and 65,000 serious injuries. Let's compare these numbers with the risk of being a homicide victim. We have a 1 in 150 chance of being murdered, but we have a 1 in 33 chance of being killed or crippled in an alcohol-related accident. But almost all of us take greater measures to protect ourselves from murder or bodily assault than we do to protect ourselves from drunks behind the wheel of a car. Why do we do this? Why does being inside a car make us feel safe? Do we believe that this machine made of steel and iron will protect us and make us invincible? It feels safer somehow to drive down a highway than to walk around the block at night. Yet the statistics I just shared with you clearly show the greater danger to be on the highways. Our car, which makes us feel so safe, so secure, so powerful, can become our assassin, our coffin.

The real villain, however, is irresponsible drinking. The cars and highways are merely the weapons and the scene of the crime. According to the Memphis DWI [Driving While Intoxicated] Squad, 7,200 people are arrested here each year. That's 600 each month. And these are only the ones who get caught.

A second reason why we may not have solved this problem is our "Prohibition mentality," which gave rise to the slogan "If you drive, don't drink." Alcohol has been around almost as long as man has. And I doubt it will ever go away. Attempts to regulate alcohol consumption date back to the sixth century, but nothing has ever totally stopped production or consumption. It is here to stay. It is a fact of life. Sure, we have rules and regulations governing the use of alcohol — you have to be 21 before you can buy it; you have to have a license to sell it — but rules and regulations are easy to get around, easy to bend.

Some people believe it is morally wrong to drink; some people believe it is morally wrong *not* to drink, that their civil rights have been violated if they can't have a drink when and where they want. Personally, I don't think drinking is morally wrong. I think you and I should have the freedom to choose whether we are going to drink or not. But if we demand the freedom to choose, then we have to accept the responsibility that goes with it. I don't think the old adage "If you drive, don't drink" presents us with the right challenge. I think the challenge must be aimed at our responsibility.

When someone offers you a drink, you also must accept certain obligations. You must be able to say, "No, I've had enough," or "No more, I'm driving tonight." If you can't do this, then you indeed ought not drink, for you may well become the drunk driver on the road tonight. Are you willing to take that risk to us and to yourself? Let's look at what happens if you are stopped for DWI.

Mr. Jack Haley is director of the DWI school here in Memphis. He states that the first-time offender is sentenced to 15 days in jail. If he is lucky, 13 days are suspended, but he still must serve two days in jail. It's not exactly heaven. He is placed on probation for 11 months and 29 days, and his driver's license is revoked for one year. He also has to attend DWI school one night a week for five weeks. The second time he is picked up for DWI, the offender gets 45 days in jail, his license is suspended for two years, and he must pay a minimum fine of $500. The third-time offender is fined from $1,000 to $5,000 and serves 120 days in jail. His license is revoked for three to ten years.

This is what happens if you are merely stopped for DWI and no accident or injuries are involved. If you injure or kill someone — some one of us, perhaps — that could well determine the course of the rest of your life. Stiffer sentences are being handed down every day by judges, and the emotional and financial costs in guilt and lost opportunities are overwhelming.

What does it take to be arrested for DWI? A blood alcohol level of .10. This is roughly two glasses of wine or two beers in an hour. Don't take this unnecessary risk. Don't be passive about this. Take an active responsibility for this freedom. It is easy to do, if you will follow these three steps toward responsible drinking and driving suggested by Anna Whalley, an alcohol and drug abuse counselor at the Berclair Mental Health Center.

First, recognize your tolerance for alcohol and how it affects you. This varies from person to person and depends on body size and weight, the amount of food you have eaten, how much you drink in a given period, your past experience with drinking, and even your mood.

Second, know what you are drinking. Many people mistakenly think that beer is less intoxicating than whiskey, but a 12-ounce beer, a 5-ounce glass of wine, and a mixed drink with 1½ ounces of hard liquor are approximately equal in alcohol content and have the same effect on your sobriety level.

Third, be aware of how much and how fast you are drinking. A good rule of thumb is to limit yourself to one drink per hour.

These are *easy* things to do. There are no risks involved in doing them. There is more risk in *not* doing them.

But what about protecting yourself from the drunk driver who is a friend? What about being a friend in need to a friend who's smashed? This is where we all too often cop out. Too much risk. "I'd be too embarrassed to tell her she is too drunk to drive," or "I couldn't tell him I won't ride home with him because he is too drunk." Instead, we take the gamble. We'd rather risk being killed or letting a drunk friend kill himself or innocent people than risk being embarrassed!

This dilemma, too, is easy to remedy. Talk with your friends about this problem and how together you would like to handle it. It's probably not a question of *if* it happens but more a question of *when* it happens. Talk about it beforehand. Agree to provide safe transportation for each other. It's something you would do anyway. There is not one of us here who would not go help a friend get home safely if he called and asked us to. So, put it in words. Make your mutual arrangement to help each other. Don't wait until it is too late — too late for you, too late for us.

Alcohol consumption is here to stay. To drink or not to drink is one choice. Some of us may choose not to drink at all, and that's fine. But for many of us, a better choice is to drink responsibly. To be aware of what our tolerance for alcohol is, to be aware of what we are drinking and how much we are drinking. If we have too much to drink and our judgment is impaired, or if we don't want to ride home with someone who is drunk, it would not only be *nice* to have a friend we could call, it could be *lifesaving*. It could be the difference between arriving dead or alive.

If we don't learn how to drink and drive responsibly, odds are that one of us will pay a large price for this problem. Look around you. And now look at yourself and at me. Who will it be?

ARE THE SKIES THAT FRIENDLY?

——— *Juli Pardell* ———

Juli Pardell developed this speech in her public speaking class at Indiana University. The speech is primarily persuasive in character. It exposes a problem situation to urge a change in the audience's attitude toward air travel. The speech makes good use of expert testimony and facts and figures as evidence. It develops in a categorical design.

With Spring Break less than a month away, many of us are daydreaming about our vacations to Florida, California, and other spring hot spots. But since the warm weather lies many hundred miles south, we won't be able to walk to our destinations. While some of us will be hitting the highways, others will opt for jet travel — after all, planes are the safe kind of travel, right?

Sorry about that. Despite the Federal Aviation Administration's promises that air travel is "safer than ever," airline safety leaves a lot to be desired. In this speech I want to explore why this is so. I will identify a number of problems that beg for improvement. You will see from the nature of these problems how many of them could be improved. You ought not climb aboard any jet thinking that everything is fine and dandy in the friendly skies.

So what are the problems? They include overworked and unqualified air traffic controllers, congested skies, inadequate airplane maintenance, and a shortage of inspectors. Let's consider each problem briefly, and sketch its dimensions.

The origin of the air controller problem goes back to 1981, when President Reagan fired the nation's 11,345 air traffic controllers after a strike for higher pay and better working conditions. 11,300 new controllers filled the empty positions, yet many of them lacked experience. And unfortunately, many of them still lack the skills necessary to maintain an acceptable level of air safety. For example, the Los Angeles airport, at which one-third of the air controllers are not fully trained, suffered a crash last September which killed 67 people. *Time* magazine of October 6, 1986, suggests that a shortage of controllers plagues our airports: "Besides working 6-day weeks without relief, controllers are under too much stress."

Not surprisingly, the controllers' lack of skills affects air safety. The National Air Traffic Controllers Association estimates that only 62% of today's controllers are fully qualified for their jobs. *U.S. News & World Report* of October 14, 1985, takes us back to August of that year, when a crash at the Dallas–Fort Worth airport killed 137 travellers: "The controllers didn't tell the plane's pilot about severe weather conditions that would later cause the crash." That tragedy is hardly isolated: during a six-month period during 1985, air traffic controllers were responsible for 54 near-misses in the skies.

Yet we can't level all the blame at air traffic controllers. Overcrowded skies also contribute to less than desirable airline safety. Private aircraft currently take up too much airspace, and *U.S. News & World Report* of September 15, 1986, points out a danger of this increased presence: "Too many people are flying for sport — people who don't know the rules." A private pilot needs only 35 logged hours of flight time in order to obtain a license, and such an obvious dearth of hands-on experience took its toll last October. A private pilot, unknowingly straying into restricted airspace, crashed into a DC-9 and killed 85 people. And for the professional pilots who log countless hours of flight time, their job has become more complicated. *Time* from September 1, 1985, notes that "it becomes suicidal for commercial pilots to ignore looking out their cockpits in search of maverick pilots."

In order to fully comprehend the problem of congested skies, we can focus on a specific airport's situation. The Los Angeles airport deserves special attention. The *Christian Science Monitor* of October 29, 1985, contends that it "exemplifies the growing congestion that decreases safety margins." Thirty other airports lie within a 90-mile radius of Los Angeles airport, creating a hubbub of planes in the sky. Within a 45-mile radius, 197 planes vie for space in the skies at any given moment. Overcongestion only enhances the chance for planes to crash, such as they did last October.

Finally, faulty airplane maintenance plays a significant role in the air safety problem. The airlines, for their part, have allowed maintenance to take a back seat to profits. "In an effort to cut costs," *U.S. News & World Report* of March

31, 1986, explains: "airlines have cut parts of the safety infrastructure, including spare parts and mechanics." Three years ago, an engine fell off a Boeing 727 in midair. The cause: an unrepaired drain valve.

Unfortunately, the very agency that should be preventing such accidents, the Federal Aviation Administration, is not doing its job. Among other problems, the FAA suffers from a shortage of inspectors. One implication of the shortage is that there are fewer inspectors to catch the unintentional safety mistakes of airlines. But *U.S. News & World Report* from October 14, 1985, claims that the shortage may also cause airlines to intentionally cut back on safety measures, knowing they won't be caught: "When there is a shortage of inspectors, airlines can pencilwhip the hell out of anything."

Well, after this bleak picture, the old skies don't seem quite so friendly, do they? Many of you dreaming of sunshine and warm Southern beaches may still hop aboard jets to get to them quickly, and with a little luck I may be among you. But I think we have every right to demand changes in this picture I have painted. After all, we're the ones taking the risks. Let's become part of the pressure towards constructive change in the airlines industry. Let's make it possible to paint those skies blue, not bloody.

THE GIFT OF LIFE

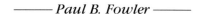

―――― *Paul B. Fowler* ――――

This classroom persuasive speech was presented by Paul B. Fowler in 1983 while he was a student at Alderson Broaddus College in Philippi, West Virginia. It illustrates the problem-solution design, and develops an effective combination of proofs, relying on the emotional power of examples and the rational power of statistical and expert evidence.

One morning in 1954, Richard Harrick woke up, stared in the mirror, and discovered that his eyes had become swollen and puffy. Alarmed, he went for a medical examination, and was told that he was suffering from nephritis, a fatal kidney disease. Richard, however, was going to dodge death. Doctors at a Boston hospital had been waiting on just such a case as his to embark towards a new medical frontier, human organ transplantation. Richard had a twin brother, Ronald, so there were closely related genes. This made the chance of a successful transplant more likely, and that's all the incentive the doctors needed. On December 23, 1954, Ronald Harrick gave his brother one of his kidneys, a Christmas gift of life.

In December, 1976, yet another operation would bring this new science of human organ transplantation to the center stage of world attention. In Cape-town, South Africa, Dr. Christiaan Barnard transplanted the first human heart, and the science of medicine would never be quite the same. While the patient in that case did not live long, the impact of the operation on the imagination of the world community was revolutionary and enduring. Life has been given wondrously anew to thousands of people through the miracle of organ transplants.

Yet all is not happy in this picture. People suffering from fatal diseases, whose only hope is an organ transplant, are placed now on waiting lists. Their status on these lists depends on the seriousness of their condition and on the availability of an organ with a proper tissue match. Often they languish there. Sometimes they die there, waiting for the gift of life.

According to the *Transplant Organ Procurement Foundation Manual,* more than 25,000 kidney transplants have been performed since 1963. Pittsburgh surgeons alone transplant over 100 kidneys per year. However, only 25 percent of kidney patients can receive a kidney from a living family member. Most must wait for several years for an organ from a donor. In the Pittsburgh area alone, over 120 patients are waiting right now for a phone call telling them a kidney has become available. Nationwide, over 5,000 people are waiting.

The Cardiac Transplant Program in the University of Pittsburgh's School of Medicine is one of only seven in the nation. This program performed fourteen heart transplants during its first four years of operation. Sadly, four patients died before a suitable donor-heart became available. These people are martyrs to a problem that again has national dimensions.

The nation's only major liver transplant program has been located in the University of Pittsburgh's Medical School since January, 1981. The alternative for those waiting for liver transplants is certain death within weeks or months. Twenty-six people received liver transplants in 1981. Sixteen died before a liver became available for them.

Gallup polls indicate that most of you, 80 percent nationwide, are willing to donate your organs, to offer the gift of life should you die. So where does the problem lie? Why do people die needlessly? The answer to this question involves two major problems which we must address if we are to stop the needless heartbreak and death. These problems are: first, inadequate funding, and second, inadequate communication.

The funding problem is itself complex. First, organ transplants are incredibly costly to those in need. Second, federal financial support for transplants is severely limited in scope. And third, federal support for making the new technologies accessible is also very limited. Consider the cost to the sufferer, let us say, to the degenerative kidney disease victim who, according to Simmons and Klien in their book, *Gift of Life,* is forced to pay upwards of $5,000 a year just for dialysis. This figure includes the maximum aid from the federal government and includes only routine dialysis. Most medical insurance plans do not cover transplant costs at all. If they do, it's only for kidney transplants, and such insurance is very expensive. Even if the insurance companies covered transplants, poor people could not afford the insurance. This fact becomes startling when you consider the cost of a kidney transplant, which according to William A. Nolan in his book, *Spare Parts for the Human Body,* costs $40,000. This fact becomes a death sentence for some people. Because kidney transplantation is the ultimate in life-giving operations, what these people lose is not just life, but a practically normal lifestyle.

The second dimension of the funding problem is that federal support is limited in scope. Only kidney transplants receive any kind of federal funding. Costs covered under the Chronic Kidney Disease Amendment to the Social Security Act of 1972 do not cover costs of liver, heart, or pancreatic transplants. This simply dumps the staggering financial burden directly on the backs of sufferers and their families. Many simply can't bear that burden and really have no alternative.

The third dimension of the funding problem limits access to the new technologies of organ transplantation. *Gift of Life* tells us that the monies needed to provide such access are simply not available. As a result, the centers offering such technology are often isolated, and some patients just don't receive the latest and best medical care.

So inadequate funding is a big part of the problem. But so is inadequate communication. And it too is a complex problem. One part of it is linking donors and recipients. As we said, many are willing to donate. But Simmons and Klien say that many hospitals have no communication link to transplant centers, and thus have no idea of what organs are needed. Lack of donor/recipient communication results in needless death.

The second part of the communication problem is that the circumstances of death often contribute to the lack of acceptable donors. The book, *Post Mortem Organ Procurement Protocol,* tells us that physicians of dying patients or on the scene of recently killed persons are often reluctant to approach grieving families as to the possibility of organ donation. Even though many families would give the gift of life to needy children or adults, they are often not aware of such opportunity.

The final dimension of the communication problem is the knowledge lag between new technologies and practicing physicians. *Gift of Life* claims that physicians often are not aware of these technologies and of new medical advances that might save their patients' lives. Therefore, physician ignorance, much of it resulting from inadequate communication, adds to the problem of needless death.

So what can we do about it? If the problem is so complex, what can ordinary people like ourselves do to unravel it? Well first of all, we need to become supporters of more and better financial support to those waiting on the lists. Let's let our legislators, congressmen, and senators know that we support funds to needy patients, a broader range of federal support for transplants, and an expansion of treatment centers. If each of us is willing to pay a few extra tax bucks each year, we can defeat the financial part of this problem. We can give the gift of life to others, and — who knows? — perhaps someday to ourselves and our loved ones.

How can we deal with the communication problem? We need to let our hospitals know that we expect them to establish adequate communication links to transplant centers so they can better match donors with recipients. In this day of instant computer communication, that should not be so difficult. How about our physicians? Refresher courses and workshops in the new transplant technologies should be made available for them, perhaps through the auspices of the expanded treatment centers. We have every right to expect our doctors to remain up-to-date. Ask your doctor if he or she would know how to help you, should you ever need an organ transplant. If you're not happy with the answer, get yourself a new doctor. Finally, all of us need to know more about the need to become a potential donor and how to donate. Communication on this problem could be helped a great deal by public education programs conducted through newspapers, television, and radio. The public needs to know that any person 18 years or older can sign a "Uniform Organ Donor Card." Families can agree to sign the necessary forms for each other, if such a card is not available. Some states, including West Virginia, will print the words "Organ Donor" on a driver's license, if requested to do so. As more people become aware of the need, more organs will become available and more people will receive the gift of life.

The problem I have described is indeed complex, but all of us can help in our small way to reduce it.

In the July issue of the *Association of Operating Nurses Journal,* Mrs. Lee Kimball tells her own personal story of grief and hope. Her 17-year-old son, Donald, committed suicide in March, 1980. When she learned that her son had died, someone suggested organ donation and she agreed. Mrs. Kimball tells her story this way: "Three hours after my son, Donald, died, a mother and three children waited anxiously at another hospital. Their husband and father lay dying. All eyes looked up as the physician entered the waiting area. As he spoke, new hope flooded the room. The man would live. He had just received a healthy, loving heart from a 17-year-old boy. It had been the 'gift of life.'"

I challenge you today: Become a part of the solution. Support better funding, demand better communication, and make your own personal commitment by signing the donor's card. Help give the most precious gift, the Gift of Life.

NOBEL PEACE PRIZE ACCEPTANCE SPEECH

——— *Elie Wiesel* ———

Elie Wiesel delivered the following speech in Oslo, Norway, on December 10, 1986, as he accepted the Nobel Peace Prize. The award recognized his lifelong work for human rights, especially his role as "spiritual archivist of the Holocaust." Wiesel's poetic, intensely personal style as a writer carries over into this ceremonial speech of acceptance. He uses narrative very effectively as he flashes back to what he calls the "kingdom of night" and then flashes forward again into the present. The speech's purpose is to spell out and share the values and concerns of a life committed to the rights of oppressed peoples, in which, as he puts it so memorably, "every moment is a moment of grace, every hour an offering."

It is with a profound sense of humility that I accept the honor you have chosen to bestow upon me. I know: your choice transcends me. This both frightens and pleases me.

It frightens me because I wonder: do I have the right to represent the multitudes who have perished? Do I have the right to accept this great honor on their behalf? I do not. That would be presumptuous. No one may speak for the dead, no one may interpret their mutilated dreams and visions.

It pleases me because I may say that this honor belongs to all the survivors and their children, and through us, to the Jewish people with whose destiny I have always been identified.

I remember: it happened yesterday or eternities ago. A young Jewish boy discovering the kingdom of night. I remember his bewilderment, I remember his anguish. It all happened so fast. The ghetto. The deportation. The sealed cattle car. The fiery altar upon which the history of our people and the future of mankind were meant to be sacrificed.

I remember: he asked his father: "Can this be true? This is the 20th century, not the Middle Ages. Who would allow such crimes to be committed? How could the world remain silent?"

And now the boy is turning to me: "Tell me," he asks. "What have you done with your life?"

And I tell him that I have tried. That I have tried to keep memory alive, that I have tried to fight those who would forget. Because if we forget, we are guilty, we are accomplices.

And then I explained to him how naive we were, that the world did know and remain silent. And that is why I swore never to be silent whenever and wherever human beings endure suffering and humiliation. We must always take sides. Neutrality helps the oppressor, never the victim. Silence encourages the tormentor, never the tormented.

Sometimes we must interfere. When human lives are endangered, when human dignity is in jeopardy, national borders and sensitivities become irrelevant. Wherever men or women are persecuted because of their race, religion or political views, that place must — at that moment — become the center of our universe.

Of course, since I am a Jew profoundly rooted in my people's memory and tradition, my first response is to Jewish fears, Jewish needs, Jewish crises. For I belong to a traumatized generation, one that experienced the abandonment and solitude of our people. It would be unnatural for me not to make Jewish priorities my own: Israel, Soviet Jewry, Jews in Arab lands.

But there are others as important to me. Apartheid is, in my view, as abhorrent as anti-Semitism. To me, Andrei Sakharov's isolation is as much a disgrace as Iosif Begun's imprisonment. As is the denial of Solidarity and its leader Lech Walesa's right to dissent. And Nelson Mandela's interminable imprisonment.

There is so much injustice and suffering crying out for our attention: victims of hunger, or racism and political persecution, writers and poets, prisoners in so many lands governed by the left and by the right. Human rights are being violated on every continent. More people are oppressed than free.

And then, too, there are the Palestinians to whose plight I am sensitive but whose methods I deplore. Violence and terrorism are not the answer. Something must be done about their suffering, and soon. I trust Israel, for I have faith in the Jewish people. Let Israel be given a chance, let hatred and danger be removed from her horizons, and there will be peace in and around the Holy Land.

Yes, I have faith. Faith in God and even in His creation. Without it no action would be possible. And action is the only remedy to indifference: the most insidious danger of all. Isn't this the meaning of Alfred Nobel's legacy? Wasn't his fear of war a shield against war?

There is much to be done, there is much that can be done. One person — a Raoul Wallenberg, an Albert Schweitzer, one person of integrity, can make a difference, a difference of life and death. As long as one dissident is in prison, our freedom will not be true. As long as one child is hungry, our lives will be filled with anguish and shame.

What all these victims need above all is to know that they are not alone: that we are not forgetting them, that when their voices are stifled we shall lend them ours, that while their freedom depends on ours, the quality of our freedom depends on theirs.

This is what I say to the young Jewish boy wondering what I have done with his years. It is in his name that I speak to you and that I express to you my deepest gratitude. No one is as capable of gratitude as one who has emerged from the kingdom of night.

We know that every moment is a moment of grace, every hour an offering; not to share them would mean to betray them. Our lives no longer belong to us alone; they belong to all those who need us desperately.

Thank you Chairman Aarvik. Thank you members of the Nobel Committee. Thank you people of Norway, for declaring on this singular occasion that our survival has meaning for mankind.

UNIVERSITY OF SOUTH CAROLINA COMMENCEMENT ADDRESS

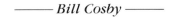

—— Bill Cosby ——

Bill Cosby, one of the beloved entertainers of our time, delivered the speech that follows as a commencement address at the University of South Carolina on May 17, 1986. The speech sparkles with Cosby humor, humor that makes fun of the typical graduation address that invites graduates to "go forth . . . to change the world."

Instead, Cosby's good-natured laughter brings a gentle realism to the graduation occasion. The "real world," he tells graduates, loves "fresh blood." Graduates now need to seek "maturity, that ability to read other human beings, that maturity to make a decision based on what is needed as opposed to what you want...." He invites them to "find out where 'forth' is," and to seek an occupation in which they will be doing something they enjoy.

For all of the grads, obviously, this is supposedly your moment. However, for the first time in your lives, you carry other people with you. Specifically, Mom and Dad paved the way, whether all of it, some of it, half of it. It was a road that needed to be paved. The job you've done, studying; their job — taking care of tuition, fees, incidentals, "ask-a-dentals." This day that you'll receive your paper is a great day.

All across the United States of America, people are graduating. And they are hearing so many guest speakers tell them that they are going forth. As a parent I am concerned as to whether or not you know where "forth" is. Let me put it to you this way. We have paved a road — the one to the house was already paved. "Forth" is not back home.

Yes, we love you, and we are proud of you, and we are not tired of you, but you can make us tired. Nothing is worse than a daughter or son with a college degree still at home. "Forth" could be next door to us, with you paying the rent.

All of these years of college you've spent second-guessing, third-guessing great politicians, great doctors, great lawyers, great anybody — the way you would have done it. Now your chance is supposed to be here, but it isn't. And I'm speaking specifically to those who've graduated for the first time. I'm speaking to all of you who have your diploma and now are being told you're going forth, that you have an opportunity to change the world. My question is with what?

What noises are you going to make to get someone's attention? Those of us who graduated long before you have comfortable places and uncomfortable places, and if you think that your little diploma is going to take away what we've worked so hard to get, you're out of your mind. You can come out here if you want to, waving your little diploma — we didn't ask for it, your parents told you to get one.

So, I'm saying to you, those people who are giving speeches across this nation — "Yes, you can make change and you can do this" — you can't do anything yet. You don't know how to do it. You don't know how to play the game out there. There are some old ones waiting for you.

Every person with a college diploma is not necessarily an overachiever. Don't you believe it! I've met some great underachievers — graduated from college — went on to graduate school. Some great underachievers — lawyers, some great underachievers — doctors, some great underachievers — engineers. You look at them and wonder how the hell they got a degree.

These are the people you're going to have to usurp. These are the people you're going to have to move out of the way so that you can do better, if you can do better. When you get your diploma today and you throw your hat in the air — some of you may be sitting out there with your cap and gown and nothing on underneath, passing a bottle of champagne around, and you are ready because you have a four-year degree. You have nothing. You have nothing.

You've made your parents very, very happy. Make them happier. Find out where "forth" is. However, the "real world" is waiting for you, and many thousands and thousands of people have been out here a long time and know how to play the game. We're waiting for you. We love fresh blood. We love nice clean-cut looking people. We'll run you around for about four years doing nothing. You say, "Well, I think I'm. . . ." "No, not yet, just keep following me. I'm going to show you something else." Then you begin to wonder, you begin to doubt yourselves. I just want you to know the truth.

It's a happy, happy time today. Turn to your family; that's where love is. Those of you with younger sisters and brothers, you show them what you've done. As a parent I know that four years of college brings nothing more than a learned person in terms of books, tests, notes; but that maturity, that ability to read other human beings, that maturity to make a decision based on what is needed as opposed to what you want — there's no degree for that and there's no time specification.

Yes, the world needs leaders. But if any of you sitting there think that upon your walking out of this building with that paper and your parents smiling and you get into the car and you're going to have a party at so-and-so's house, and shaking of the hands — that does not give you a credit card into the big-spending world. It's a happy time for you. It's a time to get it together, collect your family, collect the love, and then collect yourselves because now comes the maturity of self, the decisions to be made. And it's a wonderful world out here. You look at these old faces back here — leaders — but look at what it's done to them.

As a parent, I get a great, great feeling about this because as a parent I realize how difficult it is to say "college" to a child. You can say it. And more and more as a parent, the old saying — I don't know how old it is but when you become a parent and the longer you remain a parent, the more old sayings keep coming — you don't know who said it, you just know it's old — "[You can] lead a horse to water, but you can't make him drink." That's one of my favorites so far.

Ladies and gentlemen, young ladies and gentlemen, this is not your world yet. You have to make it.

I had my own television show three times and failed. Yet, they remember this one, and they act like this is the only one I ever had. I had one show that lasted seven weeks. I was number 67 out of 63 shows for seven weeks when they unmercifully pulled the plug. I asked them to pull the plug at the end of the second week, but they wanted to punish me.

And so now through timing, hard work is not hard work when you're successful. Power is not felt when you're busy doing what you enjoy doing.

Do you hear me? Do you all hear me, these people here? Do you hear me? I just want to give you this message, because we don't have time to deal with words like that.

You're doing what you enjoy doing. We all know somewhere in these number of years you worked you did something where you just couldn't wait to get up. As a matter of fact, you didn't even go to sleep, you just couldn't wait. Whatever the project was, you didn't care what you put into it; you didn't care about the extra step you took because you weren't tired. You enjoyed it.

It isn't hard work, especially when you're enjoying it. You don't have time to think about power when you enjoy what you're doing. And so, if there is a message — which I think I've already given — [there is] the fun of knowing that "forth" is not back at your parents' home, the fun of knowing that now your work is cut out for you to mature and get on with whatever it is you think you want to do.

There are many people out there who graduated twenty, thirty-five, two years ago. You can take their place. But every year graduates someone who can take your place if you're not enjoying what you're doing.

I want to congratulate all of the parents who understand exactly what I'm saying. And on this particular day let me say to any parent, "If you want to come up here with your child and get that diploma, let it be today."

TRIBUTE TO THE CREW OF THE SPACE SHUTTLE *CHALLENGER*

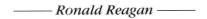

———— Ronald Reagan ————

President Ronald Reagan presented this eulogy for the crew of the space shuttle *Challenger* at a memorial service held at the Johnson Space Center in Houston, Texas, on January 31, 1986. The eulogy, a form of ceremonial speaking, has two basic purposes: to comfort the living and to honor the dead. Such speaking can also affirm values and virtues that the deceased exemplified in their lives, and can renew a sense of purpose among the living.

Reagan opened his speech with words of solace by using the technique of identification. The audience is depicted as united in grief, but through the sharing of sorrow able to find strength to continue. In paying tribute to the courage, character, and fortitude of the individual *Challenger* crew members, Reagan demonstrated how they exemplified American values. By using the "frontier" and "pioneer" culturetypes, the President created a narrative that tied the present to the past, relating these modern pioneers to those who often suffered and died on the Oregon Trail. The narrative carries a note of optimism: just as past disasters were only temporary setbacks in an overall success story, this disaster will not stop the ultimate conquest of space.

We come together today to mourn the loss of seven brave Americans, to share the grief that we all feel, and perhaps in that sharing, to find the strength to bear our sorrow and the courage to look for the seeds of hope.

Our nation's loss is first a profound personal loss to the family and the friends and the loved ones of our shuttle astronauts. To those they left behind — the mothers, the fathers, the husbands and wives, brothers and sisters, yes, and especially the children — all of America stands beside you in your time of sorrow.

What we say today is only an inadequate expression of what we carry in our hearts. Words pale in the shadow of grief; they seem insufficient even to measure the brave sacrifice of those you loved and we so admired. Their truest testimony will not be in the words we speak, but in the way they led their lives and in the way they lost their lives — with dedication, honor, and an unquenchable desire to explore this mysterious and beautiful universe.

The best we can do is remember our seven astronauts, our *Challenger* Seven, remember them as they lived, bringing life and love and joy to those who knew them and pride to a nation.

They came from all parts of this great country — from South Carolina to Washington State; Ohio to Mohawk, New York; Hawaii to North Carolina to Concord, New Hampshire. They were so different; yet in their mission, their quest, they held so much in common.

We remember Dick Scobee, the commander who spoke the last words we heard from the space shuttle *Challenger.* He served as a fighter pilot in Vietnam earning many medals for bravery and later as a test pilot of advanced aircraft before joining the space program. Danger was a familiar companion to Commander Scobee.

We remember Michael Smith, who earned enough medals as a combat pilot to cover his chest, including the Navy Distinguished Flying Cross, three Air Medals, and the Vietnamese Cross of Gallantry with Silver Star in gratitude from a nation he fought to keep free.

We remember Judith Resnik, known as J.R. to her friends, always smiling, always eager to make a contribution, finding beauty in the music she played on her piano in her off-hours.

We remember Ellison Onizuka, who as a child running barefoot through the coffee fields and macadamia groves of Hawaii dreamed of someday traveling to the Moon. Being an Eagle Scout, he said, had helped him soar to the impressive achievements of his career.

We remember Ronald McNair, who said that he learned perseverance in the cottonfields of South Carolina. His dream was to live aboard the space station, performing experiments and playing his saxophone in the weightlessness of space. Well, Ron, we will miss your saxophone; and we *will* build your space station.

We remember Gregory Jarvis. On that ill-fated flight he was carrying with him a flag of his university in Buffalo, New York — a small token, he said, to the people who unlocked his future.

We remember Christa McAuliffe, who captured the imagination of the entire nation; inspiring us with her pluck, her restless spirit of discovery; a teacher, not just to her students, but to an entire people, instilling us all with the excitement of this journey we ride into the future.

We will always remember them, these skilled professionals, scientists, and adventurers, these artists and teachers and family men and women; and we will cherish each of their stories, stories of triumph and bravery, stories of true American heroes.

On the day of the disaster, our nation held a vigil by our television sets. In one cruel moment our exhilaration turned to horror; we waited and watched and tried to make sense of what we had seen. That night I listened to a call-in program on the radio; people of every age spoke of their sadness and the pride they felt in our astronauts. Across America we are reaching out, holding hands, and finding comfort in one another.

The sacrifice of your loved ones has stirred the soul of our nation and through the pain our hearts have been opened to a profound truth: The future is not free; the story of all human progress is one of a struggle against all odds. We learned again that this America, which Abraham Lincoln called the last, best hope of man on Earth, was built on heroism and noble sacrifice. It was built by men and women like our seven star voyagers, who answered a call beyond duty, who gave more than was expected or required, and who gave little thought to worldly reward.

We think back to the pioneers of an earlier century, the sturdy souls who took their families and their belongings and set out into the frontier of the American West. Often they met with terrible hardship. Along the Oregon Trail, you could still see the gravemarkers of those who fell on the way. But grief only steeled them to the journey ahead.

Today the frontier is space and the boundaries of human knowledge. Sometimes when we reach for the stars, we fall short. But we must pick ourselves up again and press on despite the pain. Our nation is indeed fortunate that we can still draw on immense reservoirs of courage, character, and fortitude; that we're still blessed with heroes like those of the space shuttle *Challenger*.

Dick Scobee knew that every launching of a space shuttle is a technological miracle. And he said, "If something ever does go wrong, I hope that doesn't mean the end to the space shuttle program." Every family member I talked to asked specifically that we continue the program, that that is what their departed loved one would want above all else. We will not disappoint them.

Today we promise Dick Scobee and his crew that their dream lives on, that the future they worked so hard to build will become reality. The dedicated men and women of NASA have lost seven members of their family. Still, they, too, must forge ahead with a space program that is effective, safe, and efficient, but bold and committed.

Man will continue his conquest of space. To reach out for new goals and ever greater achievements — that is the way we shall commemorate our seven *Challenger* heroes.

Dick, Mike, Judy, El, Ron, Greg, and Christa — your families and your country mourn your passing. We bid you goodbye; we will never forget you. For those who knew you well and loved you, the pain will be deep and enduring. A nation, too, will long feel the loss of her seven sons and daughters, her seven good friends. We can find consolation only in faith, for we know in our hearts that you who flew so high and so proud now make your home beyond the stars, safe in God's promise of eternal life.

May God bless you all and give you comfort in this difficult time.

GLOSSARY

after-dinner speech　A brief, often humorous, ceremonial speech presented after a meal that offers a message without asking for radical changes in attitude or action. (15)

alliteration　The repetition of initial consonant sounds in closely connected words. (10)

amplification　The art of developing ideas by strategic repetition in a speech. (10)

analogous color　Colors adjacent on the color wheel; used in a visual aid to suggest both differences and close relationships among the components represented. (9)

analogy　A connection established between two otherwise dissimilar ideas or things. (12)

analogy design　A pattern for a persuasive speech whose body consists of an extended comparison supporting the speaker's proposal. (13)

anaphora　The use of the same initial wording in a sequence of phrases or sentences. (10)

antithesis　A language technique that combines opposing elements in the same sentence or adjoining sentences. (10)

archetypal metaphor　Using metaphors that draw upon human experience that is common, intense, and enduring to arouse group feeling. (10)

argument　A combination of evidence and proofs designed to produce a strong case for one side of an issue. (14)

argument *ad hominem*　An attempt to discredit a position by attacking the people who favor it. (14)

argument by analogy　Creating a strategic perspective on a subject by relating it to something about which the audience has strong positive or negative feelings. (14)

articulation　The manner in which individual speech sounds are produced. (11)

assimilation　The tendency of listeners to interpret the positions of a speaker with whom they agree as closer to their own views than they actually are. (3)

attitudes　Pre-existing complexes of feelings, beliefs, and inclinations to action that we have toward people, places, events, or ideas. (4)

audience dynamics　The motivations, attitudes, beliefs, and values that influence the behavior of listeners. (4)

bar graph　A kind of graph that shows comparisons and contrasts between two or more items or groups. (9)

begging the question　Assuming that an argument has been proved without actually presenting the evidence. (14)

beliefs　Things accepted as true about a subject. (4)

bias　Prejudice or lack of objectivity, resulting from self-interest in an issue. (1)

body　The middle part of a speech, used to develop the main ideas. (2)

body language　Communication achieved using facial expressions, eye contact, and movements and gestures. (11)

boomerang effect　An audience's hostile reaction to a speech advocating too much or too radical change. (13)

brief example　A specific instance illustrating a more general idea. (6)

categorical design   The use of natural or traditional divisions within a subject as a way of structuring an informative speech. (12)

categorical imprecision   Vague or careless wording of an argument's major premise. (14)

causation design   A pattern for an informative speech that shows how one condition generates, or is generated by, another. (12)

ceremonial speech   A group of speech types that emphasizes the importance of shared values. Includes the speech of tribute, the speech of acceptance, the speech of introduction, and the after-dinner speech. (1, 15)

co-active approach   A way of approaching reluctant audiences in which the speaker attempts to establish good will, emphasizes shared values, and sets modest goals for persuasion. (13).

cognitive restructuring   The process of replacing negative thoughts with positive, constructive ones. (2)

communication apprehension   Concern or nervousness experienced before or during speaking in public. (2)

communication environment   The overall conditions in which communication occurs. (1)

comparison and contrast design   A pattern for an informative speech that relates an unfamiliar subject to something the audience already knows or understands. (12)

complementary color   Colors opposite one another on the color wheel; used in a visual aid to suggest tension and opposition among various elements. (9)

concluding remarks   The speaker's final reflections on the meaning of the speech. (2)

conclusion   The last part of a speech, which should include a summary statement and concluding remarks (2); the proposition that follows the major and minor premises of a syllogism and directs the audience toward the speaker's point of view. (14)

conferred power   A perceived strength arising from a speaker's position or status. (2)

confusion of probability and certainty   A fallacy in an argument in which something likely is passed off as something definite. (14)

connotative meaning   The emotional or attitudinal reactions evoked by certain words. (3)

consciousness-raising function   The result of a presentation that has made an audience more sensitive to an issue and more receptive to future persuasion. (13)

contamination of the conclusion   A kind of inductive error involving the use of irrelevant or emotionally loaded words. (14)

contrast effect   A tendency by listeners to distort the positions of a speaker with whom they disagree and to interpret those positions as even more distant from their own opinions than they actually are. (3)

coordination   The requirement that statements equal in importance be placed on the same level in an outline. (8)

counterargument   A method of weakening or refuting an argument. (14)

critical listening   A learned skill that involves hearing, comprehending, analyzing, remembering, and responding to a message. (3)

critical thinking   An integrated way of assessing information, ideas, and proposals that calls not for accepting them at face value, but for exploring the grounds for these views, checking them against previous experience, and discussing them with knowledgeable others. (3)

critique   An evaluation of a speech. (3)

culturetype   A term expressing the values and goals of a group's culture. (10)

deductive argument   A kind of proof that begins with a generally accepted truth, connects an issue with that truth, and draws a conclusion based on the connection. (14)

deliberation   Allowing all sides to express their opinions before a decision is made. (13)

demographic audience analysis   A systematic study of such factors as the audience members' age, gender, educational level, group memberships, race, and social class. (4)

denotative meaning   The literal, dictionary definition of a word. (3)

descriptive statistics   Numbers demonstrating the size and distribution of an object or occurrence. (6)

dialect   A speech pattern associated with an area of the country or with a cultural or ethnic background. (11)

dialogue Conversation that is reproduced exactly, rather than paraphrased. (6)

either-or thinking A fallacy that occurs when the speaker informs listeners that they have only two options, only one of which is desirable. (14)

enunciation The manner in which individual words are articulated and pronounced in context. (11)

ethos Those characteristics that make a speaker appear honest, credible, and appealing (1); a kind of proof created by a speaker's own favorable impression and by association with credible testimony. (14)

evidence Supporting materials used in persuasive speeches, including facts and figures, examples, narratives, and testimony. (14)

example A verbal illustration for an oral message. (6)

expert testimony Information derived from authorities within a field. (6)

extemporaneous presentation A form of presentation in which a speech, although carefully prepared and practiced, is not written out or memorized. (1, 11)

extended example A detailed illustration that allows a speaker to build impressions. (6)

fact Verifiable unit of information. (6)

factual example An illustration based on something that actually happened or that really exists. (6)

fallacy An error in persuasion. (14)

fallacy of non sequitur A deductive error occurring when conclusions are drawn improperly from the premises that preceded them. (14)

faulty analogy A comparison drawn between things that are dissimilar in some important way. (14)

feedback The audience's immediate response to a speaker. (1)

figurative analogy A comparison made between things that belong to different fields. (12)

filtering Listening to only part of a message, the part the listener wants to hear. (3)

flow chart A visual method of representing power and responsibility relationships. (9)

formal outline The final outline in a process leading from the first rough ideas for a speech to the finished product. (8)

general purpose A speech's overall function. (5)

good form A primary principle of structure, based on simplicity, symmetry, and orderliness. (7)

great expectation fallacy The mistaken idea that major change can be accomplished by a single persuasive effort. (13)

habitual pitch The level at which people speak most frequently. (11)

hasty generalization An error of inductive reasoning in which a claim is based on insufficient or nonrepresentative information. (14)

historical design A structure for an informative speech, using a chronological narrative of the subject's background. (12)

hyperbole A technique of language that employs exaggeration to make points and arouse feeling. (10)

hypothetical example A representation of reality, usually a synthesis of actual people, situations, or events. (6)

idea A complex of thoughts and feelings concerning a subject. (1)

identification The close involvement of subject, speaker, and listener. (1, 15)

ideograph A word conveying a group's basic political faith or system of beliefs. (10)

image A mental picture created by the use of vivid examples. (10)

impromptu speaking A talk delivered with minimal or no preparation. (11)

incomparable percentages Comparisons offered as evidence even though the bases of comparison are unequal. (14)

inductive argument The use of specific instances to build general conclusions. (14)

inferential statistics Numbers employed to make predictions, show trends, and demonstrate relationships. (6)

information card A record of facts and ideas obtained from an article or book used in research. (5)

informative speech Speech aimed at extending understanding. (1)

internal summary   Reminding listeners of major points already presented in a speech before new ideas are introduced. (7)

introduction   The first part of a speech, intended to gain the audience's attention and prepare it for the rest of the presentation. (2)

inversion   Changing the normal word order to make statements memorable and emphatic. (10)

key-word outline   An abbreviated version of a formal outline, used in presenting a speech. (8)

lay testimony   Information that is derived from the firsthand experience of ordinary citizens. (6)

line graph   A visual representation of changes across time; especially useful for indicating trends of growth or decline. (9)

listening log   A record of listening lapses kept by students to improve their attention spans. (3)

literal analogy   A comparison made between subjects within the same field. (12)

logos   A form of proof that makes rational appeals based on facts and figures and expert testimony. (14)

magnification   A speaker's selecting and emphasizing certain qualities about a subject in order to stress the values that they represent. (15)

major premise   A general truth that is part of a syllogism. (14)

malapropism   A language error that occurs when a word is confused with another word that sounds like it. (10)

manuscript presentation   A speech read from a manuscript. (11)

maxim   A brief and particularly apt saying. (10)

medium   The channel that transmits the speaker's message, usually the air through which the sound travels. (1)

memorized text presentation   A speech that is committed to memory and delivered word for word. (11)

message   The fabric of words, illustrations, voice, and body language that conveys the idea of the speech. (1)

metaphor   A figure of speech in which anticipated words are replaced by new, surprising language in order to create a new perspective. (10)

metonymy   A language technique that evokes an idea by employing a term that is associated with it. (10)

minor premise   The claim made in a syllogism that an important idea is related to a generally accepted truth (or major premise). (14)

mirror question   A question that includes part of a previous response to encourage further discussion. (5)

monochromatic color   Variations in one color; used in visual aids to suggest changes in a subject. (9)

motivated sequence design   A persuasive speech design that proceeds by arousing attention, demontrating a need, satisfying the need, visualizing results, and calling for action. (13).

motivation   Internal forces that impel action and direct human behavior toward specific goals. (4)

multisided presentation   A speech in which the speaker's position is compared favorably to other positions. (13)

myth of the mean   The deceptive use of statistical averages in speeches. (14)

mythos   A form of proof that connects a subject to the culture and tradition of a group through the use of narratives. (14)

narrative   A story used to illustrate some important truth about a speaker's topic. (6)

natural power   A favorable impression created by a speaker's competence, integrity, decisiveness, and confidence. (2)

onomatopoeia   The use of words that sound like the objects they signify. (10)

optimal pitch   The level at which people can produce their strongest voice with minimal effort and that allows variation up and down the musical scale. (11)

orderliness   A consistent pattern used to develop a speech. (7)

parallel construction   Wording an outline's main points in the same way in order to emphasize their importance and to help the audience remember them. (8)

paraphrase   A summary of something said or written. (6)

pathos   Proof relying on appeals to personal motives and emotions. (14)

personification   A figure of speech in which non-human or abstract subjects are given human qualities. (10)

perspective by incongruity   A language technique used to shock audiences into new ways of understanding; usually relies on extreme metaphors. (10)

persuasive speech   Speech intended to influence the attitudes or actions of listeners. (1)

pictograph   On a chart, a visual image symbolizing the information it represents. (9)

pie graph   A circle graph that shows the size of a subject's parts in relation to each other and to the whole. (9)

pitch   The position of a human voice on the musical scale. (11)

plagiarism   Presenting the ideas and words of others without crediting them as sources. (1)

post hoc ergo propter hoc **fallacy**   A deductive error in which one event is assumed to be the cause of another simply because the first preceded the second. (14)

precision   Using information that is closely and carefully related to the specific purpose; particularly important when a topic varies widely from place to place. (5)

preliminary tuning effect   The effect of previous speeches or other situational factors in predisposing an audience to respond positively or negatively to a speech. (4)

preparation outline   A tentative plan showing the pattern of a speech's major parts, their relative importance, and the way they fit together. (8)

presentation   Utterance of a speech to an audience, integrating the skills of nonverbal communication, especially body language, with the speech content. (11)

prestige testimony   Information coming from a person who is highly regarded but not necessarily an expert on a topic. (6)

principle of closure   The need for a satisfactory end or conclusion to a speech. (7)

principle of proximity   The idea that things occurring together in time or space should be presented in the order in which they normally happen. (7)

principle of similarity   The principle that like things should be grouped together. (7)

probe   A question that asks an expert to elaborate on a response. (5)

problem-solution design   A persuasive speech pattern in which listeners are first persuaded that they have a problem, and then are shown how to solve it. (13)

pronunciation   The use of correct sounds and of proper stress or accent on syllables in saying words. (11)

proof   An interpretation of evidence that provides reasons for listeners to change their attitudes or behaviors. (14)

proxemics   The study of how human beings use space during communication. (11)

purpose   The goal that a speech attempts to accomplish. (5)

rate   The speed at which words are uttered. (11)

receiver   The audience that processes the message. (1)

recentness   Ensuring that the information in a speech is the latest that can be provided. (5)

red herring   The use of irrelevant material to divert attention. (14)

refutative design   A persuasive speech design in which the speaker tries to raise doubts about, damage, or destroy an opposing position. (13)

reinforcer   A comment or action that encourages further communication from someone being interviewed. (5)

reliability   The trustworthiness of information critical to the credibility of a speech. (5)

research overview   A listing of the main sources of information used in a speech and of the major ideas from each source. (7)

response   The audience's reaction, both immediate and delayed, to a speech. (1)

responsible knowledge   An understanding of the major features, issues, experts, latest developments, and local applications relevant to a topic. (5)

rhetorical question   A question that has a self-evident answer, or that provokes curiosity that the speech then proceeds to satisfy. (7)

rhetorical style   The unique way a speaker chooses and arranges words in a presentation. (10)

self-awareness inventory A series of questions that a speaker can ask to develop an approach to a speech of introduction. (2)

sequence chart Visual illustrations of the different stages of a process. (9)

sequential design A pattern for an informative speech that presents the steps involved in the process being demonstrated. (12)

setting the agenda Employing information to create a sense of what is important. (12)

sexist language The use of masculine nouns and pronouns when the intended reference is to both sexes, or the use of derogatory emotional trigger words when referring to women. (4)

sexual stereotyping Generalizations based on oversimplified or outmoded assumptions about gender and gender roles. (4)

shock-and-startle technique A method of gaining attention and arousing the audience's curiosity about a topic. (7)

simile A language tool that clarifies something abstract by comparing it with something concrete; usually introduced by *as* or *like*. (10)

simplicity A desirable quality of speech structure. Suggests that a speech have a limited number of main points and that they be short and direct (7)

sleeper effect A delayed reaction to persuasion. (13)

slippery slope fallacy The assumption that once something happens, an inevitable trend is established that will lead to disastrous results. (14)

source The person who begins the communication process with intent to express an idea. (1)

source card A record kept of the author, title, place and date of publication, and page references for each research source. (5)

spatial design A pattern for an informative speech that orders the main points as they occur in physical space. (12)

specific purpose The speaker's particular goal or the response that the speaker wishes to evoke. (5)

speech of acceptance A ceremonial speech expressing gratitude for an honor and acknowledging those who made the accomplishment possible. (15)

speech addressing attitudes Persuasive speech that attempts to form, reform, or reinforce audience attitudes. (13)

speech of contention Persuasive speech that confronts the opposition by systematically refuting its claims. (13)

speech of demonstration An informative speech aimed at showing the audience how to do something or how something works. (12)

speech of description An informative speech that creates word pictures to help the audience understand a subject. (12)

speech of explanation A speech that is intended to inform the audience about abstract and complex subjects, such as concepts or programs. (12)

speech of inspiration A ceremonial speech directed at awakening or reawakening an audience to a goal, purpose, or set of values. (15)

speech of introduction A ceremonial speech in which a featured speaker is introduced to the audience. (15)

speech of tribute A ceremonial speech that recognizes the achievements of individuals or groups or commemorates special events. (15)

speech urging action Persuasive speech that urges the audience to take action, either as individuals or as a group. (13)

statistics Facts numerically expressed. (6)

straw man fallacy Understating, distorting, or otherwise misrepresenting the position of opponents for the sake of refutation. (14)

stream chart A way of depicting how several forces can converge over the course of time. (9)

subordination The requirement that material in an outline descend in importance from main points to subpoints to sub-subpoints. (8)

subpoints The major divisions within a speech's main points. (8)

substance A quality possessed by a speech when it has an important message, a careful plan of development, and adequate facts, examples, and testimony. (1)

sub-subpoints Divisions of subpoints within a speech. (8)

summary statement The speaker's reinterpretation of the speech's main idea at the end of a presentation. (2)

supporting materials The facts and figures, testimony, examples, and narratives that constitute the building blocks of successful speeches. (6)

syllogism The basic structure of deductive reasoning, consisting of a major premise, a minor premise, and a conclusion. (14)

symmetry   Achieving a balance among the major parts of a presentation. (7)

synecdoche   A language technique in which part of a subject is used to represent the whole of it. (10)

target audience   That person or persons who are capable of making the speaker's words effective. (4)

testimony   The employment of the observations, opinions, or conclusions of other people or institutions to enhance the credibility of a presentation. (6)

textual graphics   Visual presentation of key words in a speech using a chalkboard, poster board, flip chart, transparency, slide, or handout. (9)

thematic statement   The speech's central idea. (2, 5)

thoroughness   Providing complete and accurate information about a topic. (5)

toast   A short speech of tribute, usually offered at celebration dinners or meetings. (15)

transitions   Connecting elements used in speeches. (7)

tree chart   A chart that demonstrates how a few things can grow into many over the course of time. (9)

trigger word   A term or word inspiring positive or negative emotions in listeners. (3)

values   Standards of desirable or ideal behavior. (4)

verbatim   Using the exact words of a source. (6)

verifier   A statement by an interviewer confirming the meaning of what has just been said by the person being interviewed. (5)

visual aids   Supplemental materials used to enhance the effectiveness and clarity of a presentation. (9)

INDEX

Text Credits

Page 26: "Credo for Free and Responsible Communication in a Democratic Society." Reprinted by permission of the Speech Communication Association.

Page 112: "I Keep Six Honest Serving Men . . . ," from *Just So Stories* by Rudyard Kipling. Copyright © 1921. Used by permission.

Page 138: "So You Think It's A Man's World: Men — An Endangered Species," by Charles F. Hampton, from *Vital Speeches of the Day* 50 (15 Mar. 1984). Copyright © 1984. Used by permission.

Page 141: "Health Care in the '80s: Changes, Consequences and Choices," by William L. Kissick, M.D., from *Vital Speeches of the Day* 52 (15 Jan. 1986). Copyright © 1984. Used by permission.

Page 145: "Acceptance Speech," by Geraldine Ferraro, from *Vital Speeches of the Day* 50 (15 Aug. 1984). Copyright © 1984. Used by permission.

Pages 153–54: "Keynote Address," by Mario Cuomo, from *Vital Speeches of the Day* 50 (15 Aug. 1984). Copyright © 1984. Used by permission.

Page 244: "The Whiskey Speech," by N. S. Sweat, Jr., from William Raspberry, "Any Candidate Will Drink to That," *Austin American Statesman* 11 (May 1984). Reprinted with permission of N. S. Sweat, Jr.

Page 246: Reprinted from Claire Perkins, "The Many Symbolic Faces of Fred Smith: Charismatic Leadership in the Bureaucracy," *The Journal of the Tennessee Speech Communication Association* 11 (1985). Used by permission.

Page 265: "Malapropisms Live," collected by William J. Crocker, from *Spectra,* May 1986. Used by permission.

Pages 286–87: "mehitabel and her kittens," by Don Marquis, from *the lives and times of archy and mehitabel.* Copyright 1927 by Doubleday & Company, Inc. Reprinted by permission of the publisher.

Pages 403–4: Speech prepared by Jesse Owens. Reprinted by permission of United Features Syndicate, Inc.

Page 406: Thanks for this story go to Professor Joseph Riggs, Slippery Rock University. Used by permission.

Pages 410–11: Speech by Dick Jackman. Copyright © 1985 by *Harper's Magazine.* All rights reserved. Reprinted from the March 1985 issue by special permission.

Pages 414–18: Adaptation of J. William Pfeiffer and John E. Jones, eds., *The 1978 Annual Handbook for Group Facilitators.* San Diego, Calif.: University Associates, Inc., 1978. Used by permission.

Pages 456–58: "Nobel Peace Prize Acceptance Speech," by Elie Wiesel. Copyright © The Nobel Foundation 1986. Used by permission.

Pages 458–61: "University of South Carolina Commencement Address," May 1986, by Bill Cosby. Used by permission.

Photo Credits

Chapter 1: **Page 4 (Opener),** J. B. Diederich/Contact Press Images; **9,** Bob Daemmrich/The Image Works, Inc.; **18,** Bob Daemmrich/The Image Works, Inc.

Chapter 2: **Page 28 (Opener),** Terry McKoy/The Picture Cube, Inc.,; **33,** Bob Daemmrich/Stock Boston; **36,** Annie Griffiths/Woodfin Camp & Associates.

Chapter 3: **Page 54 (Opener),** Arthur Grace/Stock Boston; **58,** Paul Fusco/Magnum Photos, Inc.; **68,** John Coletti/TSW/Click-Chicago, Ltd.

Chapter 4: **Page 78 (Opener),** Medford Taylor/Black Star; **83,** Paula Lerner; **99,** John Ficara/Woodfin Camp & Associates.

Chapter 5: **Page 106 (Opener),** Charles Feil/Stock Boston; **121,** Seth Resnick/